A volume in the series

Cornell Studies in Security Affairs

edited by Robert J. Art, Robert Jervis, *and* Stephen M. Walt

A full list of titles in the series appears at the end of the book.

Japan Prepares for Total War

THE SEARCH FOR ECONOMIC SECURITY, 1919–1941

MICHAEL A. BARNHART

Cornell University Press

ITHACA AND LONDON

First published 1987 by Cornell University Press
First printing, Cornell Paperbacks, 1988

Printed in the United States of America

Library of Congress Cataloging-in-Publication Data
Barnhart, Michael A., 1951–
    Japan prepares for total war.

    (Cornell Studies in security affairs)
    Bibliography: p.
    Includes index.
    1. Japan—Economic conditions—1918–1945. 2. Japan
—Economic policy. 3. Japan—National security.
4. Japan—History—1912–1945. I. Title. II. Series.
HC462.B36 1987   952.03'3   86-16821
ISBN 0-8014-1915-8 (cloth: alk. paper)
ISBN 0-8014-9529-6 (pbk.: alk. paper)

Cornell University Press strives to use environmentally responsible suppliers and materials to the fullest extent possible in the publishing of its books. Such materials include vegetable-based, low-VOC inks and acid-free papers that are recycled, totally chlorine-free, or partly composed of nonwood fibers. For further information, visit our website at www.cornellpress.cornell.edu.

Paperback printing   10 9 8 7 6 5

Contents

Preface

Of all the lessons that countries learned from the collapse of Germany in 1918, Japan's may have been the most significant for its long-term effects. War hereafter would be protracted, according to Asian observers of the European conflict, and nations had to be able to supply themselves during wartime with adequate quantities of raw materials and manufactured goods. Reliance on other countries for the materiel of war was a sure path to defeat. Through the efforts of a "total war" cadre of officers, abetted by bureaucrats intent on political change, the empire began to reorganize itself in a search for self-sufficiency.

The coalition of officers for autarky and bureaucrats for reform appeared potent within the Japan of the twenties and thirties, but on the empire's frontiers it came into conflict with other visions of the world. The United States was what Japan aimed to be—rich in resources, internally strong, and dependent on no one. American ideals in trade and governance (and American treaty rights in China) flatly contradicted those of Japan. From that contradiction stemmed a complicated and gradually more belligerent relationship. It would culminate in the attack on Pearl Harbor.

This book is about interwar Japan's search for economic security and the gradual molding of that quest into the attempt to acquire a resource-rich zone in mainland Asia. The need for security became, slowly, an impulse for empire, and it led directly to the Pacific War. But though the causes of the war have provoked the writing of what now amounts to a substantial library, no previous book has exploited archives on both sides of the Pacific to illuminate the Japanese quest for economic security. It is in the details of that developing quest, and the long debates it provoked in Tokyo and with Washington, that I hope to contribute something new to understandings of the coming of war.

Throughout this book, Japanese proper names are given in Japanese order: family name first followed by given name. For given names, it is not uncommon for Japanese ideograms to carry more than one pronunciation, which in a phonetic language such as English yields more than one possible spelling. In these cases I use the pronunciation as specified by *furigana* in Nihon Kindai Shiryō Kenkyūkai, ed., *Nihon Riku-Kaigun no seido, soshiki, jinji* (Tokyo: Tokyo Daigaku Shuppankai, 1971), a directory of army and navy personnel and organization. When most other scholarly works use a different spelling, I provide that alternative in a footnote and give a cross-reference in the index. Whenever possible, Chinese names and places are rendered by the Wade-Giles, not the Pinyin, system.

Unless otherwise specified, translations from the Japanese are mine.

My first and, in many respects, deepest debt is to Richard W. Leopold, who instilled in me a love of the study of history and the desire and background to pursue that study. He was, and remains, the model of what a mentor should be. Ernest May was always a stimulating graduate adviser who did much to broaden my view of international relations. Without his support, I would not have attempted this book. He was ably assisted by Edwin Reischauer, whose comments on my Japanese chapters immeasurably improved them, and Peter Stanley, who did much to make occasionally onerous course and research work bearable. Special mention should also be reserved for Oda Yori and Kuno Susumu, without whom I would probably still be mired in a language lab.

Many other scholars, in America and Japan, contributed to this book. Akira Iriye provided encouragement and advice for years. Dorothy Borg enabled me to converse with other young students of American–East Asian relations, forming friendships that have endured. Stephen Pelz, Jonathan Utley, Roger Dingman, and my colleague Richard Kuisel all examined the manuscript in painstaking detail at various stages of its evolution. The result is much the better for their efforts. In Japan, Nakamura Takafusa and Hara Akira were unsparing in their help. Hosoya Chihiro cannot go unmentioned in this regard, either. Asada Sadao acted as faculty sponsor during my stay in Japan.

Without librarians and archivists, the craft of history would be impossible. Special thanks are due the staffs of Houghton and Widener libraries at Harvard University, the Sterling Memorial Library of Yale University, the Hoover Institution of Revolution, War, and Peace collection at Stanford University, the Herbert Hoover and Franklin D. Roosevelt presidential libraries, and the National Diet Library in Tokyo. Archivists at the National Archives, in Washington and at the Suitland annex, were most helpful, as were their counterparts at the Library of Congress, especially Key Kobayashi of the Orientalia Division, who permitted me to explore his holdings of crumbly South Manchurian Railway studies at leisure and to my content. Although not archivists in the true sense, the many compilers of the 100-volume-plus official Bōeichō history and the spectacular *Gendaishi shiryō* series merit thanks for their bringing literally thousands of documents to light in an easily accessible form. Most valuable in this respect for my particular purposes was the tireless work of Ishigawa Junkichi, whose collection of mobilization documents was truly indispensable.

More than thanks should go to Janet, my wife, who endured more than a fair share of missed days together and distractions from her own academic and other research work, but this is all I can offer—on these pages, anyway!

Words are even less appropriate to express my feelings for Yamane Shin. Shin, one of Asada's graduate students, befriended me from my first day in Japan. He was utterly selfless and a wonderful human being, whether in deciphering difficult Japanese phrases or in ensuring that an American stranger spent many enjoyable days and nights in his country. He was also a first-class student of history, dedicated to writing a study of Japanese influence in Southeast Asia in the immediate aftermath of World War II. His sudden death in Taipei, while conducting research, renders our profession, and my life, much the poorer.

MICHAEL A. BARNHART

Stony Brook, New York

Abbreviations

In writing this book I have used several collections of documents, published and unpublished. References in notes to these books are made by abbreviation. For works of more than one volume, such as the GDS titles, only one abbreviation is provided. Full citations are given in the bibliography.

DBFP   Butler, *Documents on British Foreign Policy*
DF   United States, National Archives, State Department Decimal File
DR   Bōeichō, *Daihon'ei rikugunbu*
FES   *Far Eastern Survey*
FRUS   United States, Department of State, *Foreign Relations of the United States*
FRUSJ   United States, Department of State, *Foreign Relations of the United States: Japan, 1931–1941*
GDS   *Gendaishi shiryō*
IKS   Tsunoda, *Ishiwara Kanji shiryō*
KG   Bōeichō, *Kaigun gunsembi*
PHA   United States, Congress, *Pearl Harbor Attack*
RGD   Bōeichō, *Rikugun gunju dōin*
SWT   Yomiuri, *Shōwashi no tennō*
TSM   Nihon Kokusai, *Taiheiyō sensō e no michi*

Japan Prepares
for Total War

Map 1. East Asia before World War II

Introduction

From the commencement of the Meiji Restoration to the conclusion of the Pacific War, Japan pursued the status of a great power through expansion abroad and reform at home. The requisites of that status, however, changed over the decades. This book traces one such change.

Japanese statesmen of the Restoration looked first to restore the elemental aspects of national sovereignty. They worked toward the abolition of Western rights of extraterritoriality and the restoration of Japan's tariff autonomy. Such achievements were not to be had simply for the asking. Japan had to construct domestic laws and institutions that would satisfy foreign concerns.

Even as Japan achieved full recognition of its status as a nation, however, it found itself engaged in a struggle for territorial security. In 1894 came war with China, over strategically vital Korea. Victory yielded both territory and an indemnity sizable enough to enlarge the Imperial Army and Navy. These new forces were bloodied a decade later during the Russo-Japanese War, a product of Tokyo's desire to consolidate its position on the Korean peninsula. By the close of that conflict the Japanese Empire had established dominance over southern Manchuria as well.

In the years that followed this success, Japanese leaders endured transient war scares with America, the overthrow of an ancient dynasty in China, and the outbreak of a colossal conflict in Europe. None of these threatened Japan's security. Indeed, two of them enhanced it, by weakening the capacity of Tokyo's Asian neighbor and its European rivals to resist further Japanese expansion.

[17]

But Japan's status as a great power was shaken by Germany's collapse in 1918. Superficially this collapse strengthened Japan's position in the world arena. Tokyo had been allied with the winning side, acquired the German concessions in Shantung, and was recognized as a ranking power at the Paris peace conference. More deeply, however, the German collapse caused certain officers in the Imperial Army to have second thoughts about the future safety of their country. To be sure, the government had approved substantial increases in the size of the army and navy during the European war. Yet Germany, though it had far more formidable forces, had been vanquished.

These officers concluded that, for their Asian empire, the lessons of the European conflict were ominous. Future wars would be fought not only with guns but with the entire resources of nations, from engineers to doctors, from cotton to iron ore. Without these requisites of *economic* security, the mightiest army would be paralyzed. And without a modern industrial base that could be mobilized in time of need, even these requisites would prove useless. A nation that could not supply all of its own needs in wartime, a nation that was vulnerable to economic pressure from other nations, would be neither truly secure nor truly sovereign.

At first, these concerns were muted, for the 1920s were the decade of military retrenchment, international cooperation, and "Taishō Democracy" in Japan. Still, men dedicated to achieving economic security for their country were not idle. They laid the foundations for a program combining expansion abroad and reform at home which would accomplish their objective.

By the mid-thirties these "total war officers" had repulsed challenges to their plans, challenges both from within the services and from without. Japan had assumed direct control of Manchuria and was making impressive strides toward the economic absorption of the rich provinces of northern China. A special session of the Diet had been called for July 1937, and it would consider a colossal plan to expand the productive capacity of Japan's heavy industries.

That same month, however, shooting near the Marco Polo Bridge erupted into a full-scale clash between China and Japan. Those Japanese leaders committed to economic security vigorously opposed the decision to escalate from the initial skirmishing, certain that war would jeopardize their plans for industrial expansion and perhaps even the territories already won. They were overruled.

For the next four years, the Japanese Empire labored to win the war in China and become self-reliant. The task was impossible. Fighting on the mainland made Tokyo more, not less, dependent on outside

[18]

powers (particularly the United States) for the means with which to make war. To escape this dilemma, Japan's leaders elected to ally themselves with Hitler's Germany and strike to the south, where the rich European colonies of Indochina and the East Indies held out the promise that Tokyo might yet achieve the goal of self-sufficiency. Success, however, proved short-lived.

The principal foreign obstacle to Japan's attempt to achieve economic security was a United States committed to a world of fewer barriers to international trade and political liberalism. Americans often considered open trade a prerequisite to political freedom. As Cordell Hull reasoned,

> if we could get a freer flow of trade—freer in the sense of fewer discriminations and obstructions—so that one country would not be deadly jealous of another and the living standards of all countries might rise, thereby eliminating the economic dissatisfaction that breeds war, we might have a reasonable chance for lasting peace.[1]

In the years after World War I these words acquired a double edge. As commercial connections increased, forming a road to world peace, nations that violated the peace by aggression were to be punished by being deprived of all economic intercourse. A ban on trade with and loans to states that refused to obey accepted canons of international behavior was a novel idea. Nevertheless, the notion was enshrined in Article 16 of the Covenant of the League of Nations. The United States did not join the league, but its rejection of the institution by no means entailed rejection of the principle. Woodrow Wilson first applied it in July 1919 against the new Bolshevik regime, declaring, "For any Government to permit them to increase their power through commercial intercourse with its nationals would be to encourage a movement which is frankly directed against all Governments and would certainly invite the condemnation of all peoples desirous of restoring peace and social order."[2] Succeeding Republican administrations may have emphasized restrictions on the export of arms and foreign loans, but overall their policies were not far different.[3]

The Great Depression ended Republican rule, as it also weakened the international economic community. One after another, nations

1. Cordell Hull, *Memoirs*, 2 vols. (New York: Macmillan, 1954), 1:81.
2. Quoted in N. Gordon Levin, *Woodrow Wilson and World Politics* (New York: Oxford University Press, 1968), 232.
3. See, for example, Herbert Feis, *The Diplomacy of the Dollar* (Baltimore: Johns Hopkins University Press, 1950).

rejected multilateral solutions to their woes and sought solutions within their own borders. Franklin Roosevelt's America was no exception.

Some thoughtful diplomats began to suspect that at least two countries, Germany and Japan, had determined to see this trend through to its logical conclusion: complete autarky. Both countries seemed at the same time to embrace political totalitarianism at home and territorial aggression abroad. The combination of aggression, totalitarianism, and autarky posed a threat that the liberal world could not ignore.

At first, officials in the State Department charged with analyzing Japanese foreign policy refused to believe in the sincerity of Tokyo's attempt to attain self-sufficiency. Japan's paucity of all strategic resources made the attempt appear wildly impractical. Ironically, it was the outbreak of war between China and Japan in 1937, the war that ended the dreams of the total war officers in Japan, which convinced American observers that Tokyo was indeed aiming for autarky.

For the next two years, the American administration groped for a response to this growing threat to global peace and stability. For nearly another year, it engaged in a program of cautious pressure against Tokyo. Finally, in increasing frustration, it commenced eighteen months of economic "cold war" ended only by the Imperial Navy's attack at Pearl Harbor.[4]

Throughout this time Roosevelt's lieutenants variously advocated and opposed a wide array of options that America should adopt toward Tokyo. The debate first raged in the State Department. Some diplomats supported U.S. participation in multilateral economic pressure against Japan for its violations of international law and American rights in East Asia. Others preferred a more cautious approach, one that would divorce U.S. initiatives from those of other countries. Within a short time new parties joined these discussions. Representatives of the War and Treasury departments had ideas of their own, ideas often pressed on the president without State's approval. Meanwhile Japanese acts in China led to outrage among American citizens, outrage that spurred congressional resolutions and the development of lobbying organizations. With the coming of a second European war and the first halting steps toward rearmament in the United States, officials in charge of the preparedness effort became engaged, almost

4. The phrase "cold war" is from Akira Iriye, *Power and Culture: The Japanese-American War, 1941–1945* (Cambridge: Harvard University Press, 1981), 1.

unwittingly, in the discussions of policy toward Japan. These are discussions that bear close examination.

There is a certain irony inherent in the courses that the United States and Japan pursued in the years before Pearl Harbor. In Tokyo leaders committed their resource-poor empire to an attempt to achieve self-sufficiency, so that Japan might be secure in any future conflict. They were instrumental in plunging Japan into a war that made first self-sufficiency and then national security itself impossible. In Washington, at the same time, defenders of a vision of all nations trading freely and in peace resorted to the harshest of commercial pressures, in order to seal off trade between their country and Japan. The result eventually was war—a war that neither nation desired, but one that neither could avoid.

[1]

The Rise of Autarky in Japanese Strategic Planning

The Japan that Commodore Matthew Perry found had no means to support modern warfare. Conflict was waged with swords, shields, and bows and arrows, which skilled artisans manufactured one at a time.

The Meiji Restoration changed all this. Its slogan "Rich country; strong army" illustrates the commitment of Japan's new leaders to create factories that could produce modern weapons. The Yokohama Iron Works began constructing warships in 1865. Six years later the Imperial Army acquired its own arms factories and by 1880 was producing the first rifle of Japanese design. Both services directed the growth of a military industry that, by the close of the Russo-Japanese War, was capable of maintaining an army over a million strong and a navy that had decisively defeated the tsar's finest fleet. In the process, of course Japan's demand for iron, steel, and the other essentials of modern conflict soared.[1]

Throughout these years little thought was given to the problem of acquiring these essentials. In every war waged since 1815 neutral powers had supplied the belligerents with the necessary financing and materials. Because conflicts in Asia, as in Europe, were invariably short, the Japanese military concentrated on drafting plans that would ensure the fastest possible mobilization of money, guns, and horses. They did not prepare to muster the full power of the Japanese economy for a protracted contest.[2]

1. Ushisaburo Kobayashi, *Military Industries of Japan* (New York: Oxford University Press, 1922), 3–4, 21, 30, 42, 220.
2. *RGD1*, 1–8.

This pattern was abruptly altered in the summer of 1915, when the fury of World War I's initial autumn offensives gave way to grinding trench warfare. Japanese staff officers in Europe submitted reports that revolutionized thinking about the nature of modern warfare. There were no neutrals; war was sure to last more than a year, perhaps far longer; belligerents who were not self-reliant were lost. As Colonel Ugaki Kazunari, chief of the important Military Affairs Section in the Army Ministry, observed in Tokyo, it was no longer enough that Japan was able to construct its own warships and artillery pieces. The nation now needed secure access to iron ore and other necessary items.[3]

The Army Ministry charged Colonel Koiso Kuniaki, a close associate of Ugaki's, to analyze Japan's security problem in light of these new developments. Koiso toured Japan and northern and central China, and he eagerly translated a study of German attempts to achieve wartime autarky. His findings, which received much attention in high civilian and military circles, urged a two-pronged program for Japan. Neither the home islands nor the empire in Formosa, Korea, and south Sakhalin could provide resources sufficient for waging modern war. The control of richer territories, such as China, was imperative.

Establishing the necessary control would take time, but Japan could adopt the second aspect of Koiso's program at once. Without a well-ordered domestic economy, one that could mobilize rapidly and efficiently for war, more resources would be of no value. What was needed, Koiso resolved, was a comprehensive plan for mobilization.[4]

This recommendation received immediate support from the Army Ministry, which had dispatched Major Suzumura Kōichi to Europe expressly to study the industrial mobilization of the belligerents. In late 1917 Suzumura began drafting a central plan for Japan.[5]

The first result of these efforts was the Munitions Mobilization Law (Gunju dōin-hō). The army's bill proposed a central organ for mobilization, one that would directly control those industries which produced items deemed necessary for military use in time of war or "incidents." The organ would be staffed and operated by the Imperial Army and Navy, although it would fall under the administrative jurisdiction of the prime minister.

In normal times there would have been little hope for cabinet,

3. Ugaki is also known as Ugaki Kazushige. *RGD1*, 15–16; Tsunoda Jun, ed., *Ugaki Kazunari Nikki*, 3 vols. (Tokyo: Misuzu Shobō, 1968–71), 1:103–4; and *DR1*, 246.

4. *SWT*, 16:141, 133–38, and *RGD1*, 34–42.

5. *RGD1*, 44–48.

much less Diet, approval of the idea. But the winter of 1917–18 was hardly normal, for in Russia a full-scale revolution was in progress. The Imperial Army was certain that Japan had an opportunity to drive Russian power out of northeastern Asia. Its General Staff planned a thrust into Siberia using twelve divisions—an operation that would require partial mobilization of the Japanese economy.

The cabinet limited the proposed force to two divisions but found refusal of the mobilization measure difficult, particularly because it was committed to provide substantial material aid to anti-Bolshevik Russians. The Diet passed the bill in March 1918, but not without amendment. The key powers of the mobilization organ were to be exercised only during full-scale wars, not incidents, insuring that they could not be invoked during the Siberian expedition.[6]

To administer the new law, a small munitions bureau (Gunjukyoku) was established in June. Its first task was to survey Japan's economic capacity for war, with a view to developing plans to mobilize that capacity. In reality the bureau could do little else. It might suggest guidelines regarding war finance to the Finance Ministry, for example, but it had no power to enforce them. Unless war came, it could only advise.

This arrangement served to retard actual planning, and so the military pressed for more authority for the bureau. It succeeded in May 1920 with the organization of the National Strength Evaluation Board (Kokusei-in) and the promulgation of an imperial command, the "Order Related to Munitions Research" of August, which compelled all cabinet ministers to cooperate with the prime minister in planning for mobilization.[7]

The military's victories proved short-lived, however, as the board was abolished in November 1922. No evidence sheds light on the precise causes, but lecturers at Japan's Military Academy later blamed the board's interference in the traditional administrative spheres of other ministries. Army planners were dismayed, terming the abolition the greatest setback yet to control of the empire's resources. They were equally mortified to find that the duties remaining in mobilization planning fell to the Ministry of Agriculture and Commerce.[8]

Planning languished until Ugaki, now a major general, became army minister in early 1924. His interest in preparing a peacetime Japanese economy for war had grown over the years, and so had his

6. James W. Morley, *The Japanese Thrust into Siberia, 1918* (New York: Columbia University Press, 1957), 269–77, app. B, and RGD1, 53–62.
7. RGD1, 68–69, 143–49.
8. RGD1, 151–52.

political sophistication. He directed the attention of instructors at the Military Academy to the importance of mobilization. He recreated the defunct Munitions Bureau and established a new Equipment Bureau (Seibikyoku), this time within the Army Ministry. And he appointed young officers to posts within these agencies, placing the brilliant Lieutenant Colonel Nagata Tetsuzan at the head of the ministry's Mobilization Section.[9]

Ugaki's interest in these concerns extended beyond his own ministry. He joined the opposition to Prime Minister Katō Takaaki's retrenchment program, which promised to reduce the national budget by over 15 percent and the army's by an unheard-of thirty million yen. Ugaki secured less drastic cuts, which nevertheless resulted in the dissolution of four divisions—a loss that poisoned his reputation in the service for years. But in exchange he secured two key concessions. Part of the funds saved would be returned to the army, to allow the formation of modern, mechanized units. Far more important, the army minister obtained Diet approval to establish a full-fledged central mobilization agency.[10]

Ugaki wasted no time, and by May 1927 the Cabinet Resources Bureau had been established. Under Major General Matsuki Naosuke,[11] the bureau completed a study of the scope and nature of national mobilization. It differed radically from past proposals. Rather than concentrate on the mustering of materials for direct military use only, Matsuki's plan encompassed all of Japan's economic activity. Every individual, from train conductors to dentists, was to be accounted for; labor actions and management profits were to be strictly controlled; and direct military supervision would no longer be confined to those factories producing only munitions and other implements of war.[12]

The Resources Bureau required further legal authority to complete actual plans of such vast scope. To secure that authority, it drafted a resources research law, which the Diet approved in April 1929. By June the bureau had obtained cabinet sanction for research guidelines and regulations compelling every ministry, civilian and military alike, to draw up detailed estimates of its needs for two years of a war so total that, in the phrasing of the instructions, it "gambles the fate of the nation." In preparing these figures, each ministry was to calculate

9. *RGD1*, 241–44, and *SWT*, 16:151.

10. Jun, *Ugaki*, 1:115, 460, 523; Peter Duus, *Party Rivalry and Political Change in Taisho Japan* (Cambridge: Harvard University Press, 1968), 196; and *RGD1*, 228–39.

11. Matsuki had been chief of the Equipment Bureau, another of Ugaki's creations.

12. *RGD1*, 255–58.

[25]

the very smallest amount of each resource it would require for its functioning as well as the amount needed to keep the Japanese civilian population at a minimum standard of living.[13] The Resources Bureau would coordinate these estimates and draw up an overall plan. It could adjust a ministry's calculations or negotiate with the ministry to secure revisions, but whichever course it chose, it could at last begin serious mobilization planning.[14]

Members of the Resources Bureau realized that the process could not be completed rapidly. Nor did they want to complete it only to discover insurmountable practical difficulties. In February 1929, accordingly, the bureau developed a trial plan for the Kansai (Osaka-Kyoto) area.

The exercise operated over a ten-day period in the early summer. Nearly all of the government's ministries sent observers, though the army and navy officers greatly outnumbered the civilians. The exercise started when the Resources Bureau declared a state of total mobilization. The populace was duly told of the first forays of Imperial air forces over enemy territory and of retaliatory strikes against northern Kyushu, which included the use of poison gas. During this mock activity, military officers assumed real control over civilian factories and directed their rapid conversion to war production. The actual output of materials for the military, from aspirin to fuel oil, was measured carefully, and these figures were then compared with the trial plan's goals in an effort to determine Japan's actual capabilities for mobilization. The services purchased all the goods made during the exercise; factory owners reaped handsome profits; and the people generally experienced something of the likely nature of the next war.[15]

On the national scale planning proceeded apace. At the first mobilization conference, in April 1930, members of the Resources Bureau briefed representatives of the ministries about the precise information they needed. That conference also resolved thorny questions of ultimate jurisdictions (sometimes with amusing results: the Ministry of

13. Each ministry would also examine the availability of certain resources in the Japanese Empire.

14. *RGD1*, 262–71; Ishigawa Junkichi, comp., *Kokka sōdōin-shi: Shiryō-hen*, 6 vols. (Tokyo: Kiyomizu Insatsujo, 1975–76), 1:9ff.; and *RGD1*, 273–74. Ishigawa's compilations include reproductions of the actual documents used by Japan's economic mobilization agencies.

15. O. Tanin and E. Yohan, *When Japan Goes to War* (New York: Vanguard, 1936), 132, and Captain Yamamoto, "Shōwa 4-nendo sōdōin enshū ni tsuite," *Kaikosha kiji* no. 661 (October 1929), 6–7, 9–10, 15–16. A precise breakdown of operational results versus the planners' goals can be found in Yamamoto, 28–32.

Commerce and Industry was to oversee analysis of Japan's alcohol reserves, but the Home Ministry managed to secure for itself the study of the commodity "for medicinal purposes"). After the conference separate interministerial bodies, *bukai*, were formed to do the actual work for each large category of resources such as "fuel" or "factories." This approach greatly eased manpower problems for the researchers, because the military agreed to provide the bulk of the staff for each bukai.

One year later the bukai had collected preliminary data, and in late April 1931 a second conference met. Civilian and military planners resolved to complete an outline plan by the following March. Upon receipt of cabinet approval they would then provide Japan with its first comprehensive mobilization plan for total war. They aimed to have it ready by September 1932.

At first the bukai stayed on schedule. By June 1931 they had submitted estimates of wartime supply and demand for essential materials to the Resources Bureau. The bureau proceeded with refinement and synthesis of the data through the summer, but on 18 September 1931 events near Mukden ensured that the planners would not meet their spring deadline.[16]

Japan could not confine its attempt to achieve self-sufficiency to preparing the domestic economy for total mobilization. As Koiso's initial studies had indicated, the economy lacked adequate quantities of nearly all the materials needed for modern warfare—and this realization added an economic dimension to the already considerable strategic attractiveness of controlling nearby territories in China. The logical starting point was Manchuria.

Manchuria had been the setting for the principal battles of the Russo-Japanese War. Tokyo had waged that conflict primarily to secure the empire's claims to Korea, but the result had been the welcome establishment of a sphere of influence throughout southern Manchuria. Crucial were the rail lines running from inland Mukden to the port of Dairen.

The railroad's value was initially perceived as solely strategic: in any rematch with Russia, Japan would be able to transport troops rapidly northward to the border. But by the 1920s the railroad was yielding increasingly valuable economic results as well. In mid-1906 Tokyo had formed the quasi-public South Manchurian Railway Com-

---

16. Ishigawa, 51ff., and *RGD1*, 315–16, 337, 348–50. Charts showing the predominantly military composition of these bodies are in *RGD1*, 353–55; Ishigawa, 39ff.; and *RGD1*, 385–411.

pany from the rail and mining properties won from Russia. The company began intensive and successful development of the Dairen port facilities and the Fushun coal mines. Its central laboratory pioneered work on a wide range of industrial enterprises, from ceramics to steel. Its geological institute located large iron ore deposits at Anshan, in 1909. Unable to secure a concession from Chinese authorities in Manchuria, the Tokyo government deemed the find so vital that it included rights to develop it in the "Twenty-one Demands" of 1915—Japan's most vigorous attempt to secure dominance over China while war distracted the west. The Chinese yielded, and Japanese geologists explored the coal and iron deposits of the region. A decade later, technological problems involved in smelting the iron ore having been solved, pig iron production commenced.[17]

The Imperial military maintained a deep interest in these developments. Army circles saw the expanding Japanese presence in Manchuria as a natural—and necessary—complement to the mobilization program at home. Naval officers had a narrower but equally serious concern in the region, for the railway works at Fushun had produced Japan's first synthetic petroleum.[18]

For the Imperial Navy, self-sufficiency for security meant self-sufficiency in oil. By 1920 oil had supplanted coal as the fuel for first-line warships, and the navy's studies of the state of Japan's oil resources were not encouraging. Even in the near future Japan would be unable to supply the oil needed for wartime naval operations. Over the long term the prospects for supplying a modern fleet, particularly after the completion of Japan's huge wartime building program, grew even dimmer. Obviously the navy had to locate other sources of petroleum.[19]

One answer was to stockpile imported oil. By the end of 1926 the navy had stored over 1.5 million tons, principally from the United States and Borneo. But this solution was only temporary. Overseas shipments could be curtailed in crisis, and the storage tanks themselves were vulnerable to enemy attack.[20]

Another was to acquire oil-producing land directly. Drillings in Taiwan, part of the empire since 1895, proved disappointing, but naval subsidies begun in 1919 to get Japanese oil companies to ex-

---

17. Kungtu C. Sun, *The Economic Development of Manchuria* (Cambridge: Harvard University Press, 1969), 63–64, 66, 70–71.
18. Ibid., 73–74.
19. *KG1*, 685.
20. *KG1*, 689–91, and *RGD1*, 375.

plore in northern Sakhalin showed results. The region, however, though occupied by Imperial forces as part of the Siberian expedition, remained officially part of the new Soviet Union. To make matters worse, the Soviets had granted an American firm, Sinclair, survey and development rights to the area in question. In early 1923 a determined Imperial Navy secured a formal cabinet decision to deny Sinclair access. Two years later Japan's occupation of northern Sakhalin ended in return for confirmation of its rights to half of the area's oil production. By 1930 the navy was drawing over 100,000 tons of petroleum per year from these concessions.[21]

This amount, though substantial, was far short of the navy's requirements. But in the 1920s, rather than look further afield for territories rich in oil, it embarked upon an ambitious and expensive program to produce synthetic petroleum. The navy's chief partner was the South Manchurian Railway, which commenced production of oil from Manchurian oil shale at Fushun in 1926. In another project, established a year later, the navy and railroad began attempts to liquefy oil from coal.[22]

Both branches of Japan's military thus had significant economic interests in Manchuria; but the army's was the deeper. It was particularly manifest in an association of middle-ranking officers called the Issekikai. Founded in late 1928 by Major Suzuki Teiichi, a young associate of Nagata's who would play a vital role in Japan's attempt to achieve self-sufficiency, the Issekikai devoted itself to national policy issues. Its first meetings considered Manchuria.[23]

Japan's substantial presence in the area, built up since 1906, relied on a system of concessions and sphere of influence subjected to ever greater criticism from Western liberals and, more disturbingly, Chinese nationalists. The Chinese vehemently opposed Japan's retention of the German concessions in Shantung after 1918. Japanese businesses in China proper became targets for Chinese strikes and boycotts. At first these expressions brought few results because of China's deep political disunity, but Tokyo saw this factiousness ending in the late 1920s as the Kuomintang under Chiang Kai-shek rose

21. Hosoya Chihiro, "Washinton taisei no tokushitsu to hen-yō," in Hosoya Chihiro and Saitō Makoto, eds., *Washinton taisei to Nichi-Bei kankei* (Tokyo: Tokyo Daigaku Shuppansha, 1978), 7–8; Tōyō Keizai Shinbunsha, ed., *Shōwa Sangyōshi*, 3 vols. (Tokyo, 1950), 1:55, 76–77; and *RGD1*, 380.

22. *RGD1*, 375, 381–84.

23. Leonard A. Humphreys, "The Imperial Japanese Army, 1918–1929" (Ph.D. diss., Stanford University, 1974), 235.

to prominence. By May 1927 Chiang's forces had entered the Peking-Tientsin area in north China. To protect its interests, Japan responded with an armed expedition to Tsinan.[24]

As Imperial troops marched, the Eastern Conference convened in Tokyo. Japanese civil and military leaders agreed that, though Sino-Japanese amity was important—to facilitate the development of continental resources—all measures necessary for the protection of Japanese rights and interests should be undertaken. Younger army officers present, Suzuki among them, took this to mean that Manchuria should be removed from the administrative sphere of China proper and the Kuomintang.[25]

At Issekikai meetings debate raged as to how this might be accomplished. With China's revolution in 1911, Peking's control over the Manchurian provinces had vanished, and Japan had come to play an intricate game of power politics with the dominant warlord there, Chang Tso-lin. Chang's grip was challenged often enough in the early years to make him a tractable associate. By the time of the Eastern Conference, however, he was showing signs of independence.[26]

By that time, too, the Soviet Union had recovered from its own shattering internal upheavals and was rebuilding its forces in the Far East. Indeed, in late 1925 the Imperial Army's General Staff had decided to construct five new rail lines into northern Manchuria. These would be used for reinforcement and supply of Japanese forces if war broke out.[27]

But the lines could not be built without Chang's permission, so the two top officials of the South Manchurian Railway, Yamamoto Jōtarō and Matsuoka Yōsuke, met with the warlord in October 1927. They soon concluded an agreement that allowed the construction of all five lines. The arrangement was upset one month later, when the Kuomintang announced that it would not recognize any accords to which it was not a party. Forced to make a choice, Chang elected to turn away from his erstwhile partners in Tokyo and Dairen. His relations with Japan reached their nadir in May 1928, when Prime Minister Tanaka Gi'ichi ordered the Kwantung Army into Mukden to disarm Chang. A month later Kōmoto Daisaku, an army officer close to mem-

24. Akira Iriye, *After Imperialism* (Cambridge: Harvard University Press, 1965), 58–60, 71–72, 147–49, 154–55, and Bamba Nobuya, *Japanese Diplomacy in a Dilemma* (Vancouver: University of British Columbia Press, 1972), 288–89, 293.

25. Iriye, *After*, 151–52, 154–55, and *TSM*, 1:290.

26. Sadako N. Ogata, *Defiance in Manchuria* (Berkeley: University of California Press, 1964), 12–13.

27. *DR1*, 293, 288, 278.

bers of the Issekikai, took the more direct step of assassinating Chang himself.[28]

Kōmoto's act ended any chance of an "independent" regime in Manchuria friendly to Japan. Chang Hsueh-liang, the murdered warlord's son and successor, rapidly formed ties with the Kuomintang. By 1929 he had not only refused to allow the Japanese to build any railroads in Manchuria but also commenced construction of rival lines of his own. Army planners and railway officials feared that their entire interest and investment in Manchuria was in jeopardy.[29]

Officers of the Issekikai saw the Manchurian problem as only one aspect, albeit a vital one, of the empire's wider security problems. Developments inside and outside Japan threatened to unhinge Tokyo's world position. One member, Major Kawabe Torashirō, recalled,

> We were concerned not only over the Manchuria-Mongolia problem but also over domestic reform. Due to the First World War, Japanese capitalism had progressed rapidly, but so had its evils, especially for farmers and the smaller entrepreneurs. Hamaguchi's end of the gold embargo created great uneasiness. With the depression in America in 1929, these entrepreneurs were hurt more badly, and unemployment skyrocketed. Added to all this was hostility among the public and politicians against the military. We were fed up.[30]

Lieutenant Colonel Ishiwara Kanji, assigned to the Kwantung Army in late 1928, sketched a solution strikingly similar to Koiso's studies of the impact of the Great War in Europe. Deepening world depression and the inability of the Chinese to develop the region fruitfully proved the bankruptcy of the Western doctrine of the Open Door. Only Japan had the interest and the capability to modernize Manchuria, which promised resources to solve Tokyo's pressing population and food problems. In mid-1930 Ishiwara developed his theme more fully. Because economic modernization could not be accomplished under Chang's—or any other Chinese leader's—civil control, Manchuria had to be made into a new state. Once this was done, reforms within Japan and the development of Manchuria could in time give the empire the economic capacity to meet even the

---

28. *DR1*, 278, 285.
29. Ogata, 16–18, and F. C. Jones, *Manchuria since 1931* (New York: Oxford University Press, 1949), 17.
30. *DR1*, 304–5.

United States on equal terms while promoting the economic betterment of all Asians.[31]

The Manchurian problem blocked the realization of this bold vision. Ishiwara was joined in his planning by Colonel Itagaki Seishirō, appointed to the Kwantung Army's General Staff in May 1929. Both had the enthusiastic support of the South Manchurian Railway, which had produced many books and pamphlets stressing the value of Manchuria to the empire.[32]

By February 1931 Itagaki was making direct appeals for action to his superiors in Tokyo. Nagata, now a colonel in charge of the Army Ministry's Military Affairs Section, was sympathetic but cautious. In the summer he was made a member of the ministry's policy committee on Manchurian matters; Nagata did persuade the group to recommend action, but not action of the sort Itagaki had in mind. Chiang Kai-shek was to be approached and perhaps won over to Japanese views on Manchuria's future. If this failed, force would be used, but only after the committee had "familiarized" other ministries in Tokyo with the situation and obtained cabinet approval. To prevent diplomatic, or stronger, opposition, the committee believed, the Japanese public needed to be educated and foreign powers acquainted with Japan's resolve. Decisive action was to be deferred for a year, until the spring of 1932—coincidentally, after the completion of Japan's first comprehensive mobilization plan.[33]

Nagata meant just to delay, not to cancel, action. He wanted continental expansion, but not at the cost of embroiling Japan with other powers and jeopardizing its progress toward self-sufficiency. By early September his staff had readied a plan for resolving the Manchurian issue in 1932 and presented it to Major General Tatekawa Yoshitsugu, chief of the General Staff's Operations Division—a key player because he controlled actual troop movements. Tatekawa had long been a proponent of "Japan-Manchuria self-sufficiency." Unlike Nagata, however, he favored immediate action and so passed a warning to Ishiwara and Itagaki. These two and their partners in conspiracy, other junior officers in the Kwantung Army, brought forward to September 18 the date of their pretext to occupy Manchuria. On that day

31. *TSM*, 8:74–82, 183ff., and *TSM*, 1:365, 360–62, 267.
32. *TSM*, 1:365–66, 381; *TSM*, 8:89–90; Mantetsu, sōmubu, chōsaka, *Man-Mō yori nani o subekika* (Dairen: Mantetsu, 1924), passim; and Yamada Gōichi, *Mantetsu Chōsabu* (Tokyo: Nihon Keizai Shinbunsha, 1977), 89–94.
33. *TSM*, 1:378; Ogata, 53–56; GDS7, 165–67; and DR1, 306.

a small explosion occurred near a line of the South Manchurian Railway, and the Mukden Incident became history.[34]

In Tokyo top officials in the General Staff, and especially in the Army Ministry, reacted with dismay and determination. Their main concern was not the action itself but its timing. They particularly feared Soviet intervention, and that fear led to a cabinet resolution on 23 September ordering the Kwantung Army to stay out of northern Manchuria. But as October and November passed, the Russian bear showed little sign of waking. By late November, Japanese forces were entering Chichihar, far north of Mukden, and one month later the operation was completed, a total success.[35] By January 1932 the Kwantung Army and top echelons of the South Manchurian Railway were cooperating closely to draw up development plans for the new state. In March, Manchukuo was born.[36]

Three months later Count Uchida Nobuya, who had been the railroad's president during the takeover, was named foreign minister in Tokyo. One of his first tasks was the negotiation of military and economic agreements with Manchukuo which granted mining and related concessions to Japanese businesses in the name of imperial defense and under the supervision of the Kwantung Army. Existing rights and interests were guaranteed in perpetuity.[37]

The seizure of Manchuria was a great stride in the territorial aspect of the drive for self-sufficiency, but, as Nagata had feared, it badly disrupted domestic efforts to the same end. By September 1931 the interministerial bukai had submitted to the Resources Bureau their initial proposals for acquiring and allocating resources in wartime. Before the bureau could draft Japan's first comprehensive mobilization plan, however, the growing scope of the Mukden Incident diverted the predominantly uniformed staffers in bukai and bureau alike to

34. Mark R. Peattie, *Ishiwara Kanji and Japan's Confrontation with the West* (Princeton: Princeton University Press, 1975), 114; Iriye, *After*, 294–95, 297–98; Ogata, 56–57; *DR1*, 305; and Shinobu Seizaburō, "From Party Politics to Military Dictatorship," *Developing Economies* 5 (December 1967), 674.

35. *DR1*, 317, 319.

36. Jones, 19; Ogata, 80; Yamada, 100–101, 105; Harada Kumao, "The Saionji-Harada Memoirs," mimeo., International Legal Studies Library, Harvard Law School, entry of 24 October 1931; and *TSM*, 8:177–78, 172–73. The railway and the army cooperated closely. Indeed, some company employees received army decorations for their role in the acquisition of Manchuria.

37. Japan, Gaimushō, *Nihon gaikō nenpyō narabini shuyō bunsho*, 2 vols. (Tokyo: Gaimushō, 1955), 2:221–23, and *GDS7*, 503–5. Thirty-nine sites were granted in these first agreements. Six were for oil, another six for oil shale.

[33]

supervision and supply for the Kwantung Army. Work on the mobilization plan stopped. By the time military operations had been concluded, it was clear that the plan could not be completed before early 1933.[38]

Other obstacles had arisen. Lieutenant General Araki Sadao had become army minister with the cabinet change of December 1931. Although Araki also believed in pushing forward with a total mobilization plan, he was certain that the Soviet Union was actively preparing for war with Japan. To counter, in the spring of 1933 he approved negotiation of the Tangku Truce between the Kwantung Army and northern Chinese authorities, lest the Soviets strike at Japan's new northern flank. More important, he adopted an emergency policy for increasing Japan's national strength over a two-year period.

Araki's emergency policy had two principal components. Within the military he ordered a radical restructuring of the Resource Bureau's plan for comprehensive mobilization. No longer a means to marshal Japan's economic power over the long term, the plan was to become a crash program to prepare the empire for war with Russia by 1936. The bureau immediately commenced work on this emergency mobilization plan, on the basis of data it had already gathered.[39]

Araki also convened a meeting of key army officers in June 1933. All agreed that the Soviet Union was the chief threat to Japan's security, but discord erupted over how best to deal with it. Araki proposed a program of higher Japanese force levels, border fortifications, extension of railroads into northern Manchuria, and, of course, the mustering of Japan's economic strength in the emergency mobilization plan.

Nagata led the dissent. How, he asked, could Japan consider what was sure to be a long, draining war with the Soviet Union? Without an economic base that Japan had not yet constructed and without access to the rich resources of China, any war against Moscow seemed fanciful. Araki's program, Nagata argued, perverted mobilization planning and impeded Japan's drive to autarky.[40]

Nagata lost the debate and, soon after, his position in central headquarters. By August he was commanding an infantry regiment—a marked demotion. His two principal allies, Colonel Umezu Yoshijirō and Major General Tōjō Hideki, likewise were forced from high positions.[41]

---

38. *RGD1*, 413, 416.

39. *DR1*, 361; Harada, entries of 5 and 10 November 1932; and *RGD1*, 413, 416.

40. *DR1*, 345–47.

41. James B. Crowley, "Japanese Army Factionalism in the Early 1930s," *Journal of Asian Studies* 21 (May 1962), 315–16.

One month later, in September 1933, a confident Araki placed his program before the cabinet for adoption as imperial policy. He opened with the flat assertion that Japan would face an international crisis by 1936. To meet this challenge, the nation would have to consolidate its external and internal position. Externally, Japan should strengthen Manchukuo's defenses in the way that Araki had outlined in the June debates within the army. The Soviets would have to be stripped of allies; China in particular would have to be compelled to assume a friendly attitude. But if war did break out against the Russians, Japan was to protect its flank by creating a buffer state in north China.

Internally, the government had to adopt ideological and educational reforms to strengthen popular morale. Price supports would provide aid to farming villages and ensure ample supplies of domestically grown food. A crash program, especially in fuels, would enable the empire to wage a conflict of two years' duration by 1936. Rearmament was to be commenced at once. Araki held nothing back: he also asked that plans be drawn up for wartime control of the nation's finances.[42]

The army's program quickly drew criticism from Finance Minister Takahashi Korekiyo, Foreign Minister Hirota Kōki, and the navy. Takahashi favored agricultural relief but believed that Araki proposed financial burdens that were excessive. Implementation could disrupt Japan's recovery from the debilitating effects of the international depression. Hirota acknowledged that China had to be made friendly, but he wished to assure this outcome by diplomatic means alone.[43]

The navy's position was more complex. Only three years earlier that service had been rent by bitter struggle over ratification of the London Naval Treaty. Although the treaty appeared to allow Japan 70 percent of the forces of the United States or Britain, its provisions actually restricted the Imperial Navy to 60 percent, a ratio many admirals considered inadequate. The treaty had been ratified, but for its

---

42. *Gendaishi shiryō 8: Nitchū sensō 1* (Tokyo: Misuzu Shobō, 1964), 11–13, and Tsunoda, *Ugaki,* 1:121, 301. In asking for educational reform, Araki was following in Ugaki's footsteps. Ugaki had cited de Tocqueville's adage that "democracies are not suited for war." It should be noted that Araki was not a primitive, bayonets-against-tanks officer as he is often portrayed. Araki was just as interested in mobilization as Ugaki or Nagata, but he stressed ideology and education (such as military training in all upper schools) more than hardware—for two reasons. First, he doubted that Japan could ever hope truly to equal a great-power antagonist in material effort. Second, Araki had grave reservations about the army's intrusions—such as interference in the civilian economy—fearing that in turn nonmilitary persons would encroach upon military matters.

43. Shimada Toshihiko, introduction to *GDS8,* xxvi–xxvii.

Japanese supporters the victory was Pyrrhic. One by one they were removed from positions of influence and replaced by proponents of unrestricted naval construction, led by Navy Minister Ōsumi Mineo.

The navy therefore had its own interest in rearmament. But it could not embark upon rearmament until the hated naval treaty was abrogated, a step that required cabinet approval. Ōsumi was inclined to accept Araki's premise of a crisis in 1936, therefore, if the army provided support for abrogation of the treaties and funds for naval construction. He was even willing to agree that, in the interests of continental defense, north China should be separated from Nanking's political control. But Ōsumi was wary of the army's stress on conflict with Russia, because any diversion of funds and materials to the army would jeopardize his service's replenishment program. The navy minister also implied that, should Britain and America elect to intervene on Russia's behalf in an army-sponsored war, a budget-starved fleet might not be able to fulfill its duty to the emperor.[44]

Araki met Ōsumi's price. The result in late 1933 was a cabinet decision and interservice consensus on imperial policy. The decision reflected Hirota's concern that diplomacy, not force, be used to adjust Japan's relations with the powers and China, though it also endorsed the services' need for strength sufficient to meet any potential menace. Both services recognized that a crisis would occur in 1936—the navy at the bargaining table in London, where the treaties were due for renewal or cancellation, the army at the Soviet border with Manchukuo. The fleet replenishment program would receive funding, and so would the army's plans for internal reforms and expansion. The military's share of the overall budget would rise from 36 to 45 percent. The only loser in these accords seemed to be Takahashi, because only a continued reliance on deficit financing could make the package possible.[45]

But others objected just as loudly. In the van stood Nagata and his fellow total war officers. Araki, they charged, had made three key errors during his tenure as army minister. First, he had distorted the purpose of Japan's mobilization effort. In "The Needs in Domestic Policy for National Defense," the Military Affairs Section—within Araki's own ministry—asserted that to consider only the enemy's

44. Stephen E. Pelz, *Race to Pearl Harbor: The Failure of the Second London Conference and the Onset of World War II* (Cambridge: Harvard University Press, 1974), 19, 45–49; DR1, 353; GDS8, 9–10.

45. James B. Crowley, *Japan's Quest for Autonomy* (Princeton: Princeton University Press, 1966), 191–95, and Pelz, 19.

forces and how to meet them in battle was shortsighted. The twin questions of internal economic reform and acquisition of strategic resources abroad also needed attention. Without reform or acquisition, Japan would prove unable to fight even one great power. Heavy industry needed further aid, but little had been done under Araki; no plans yet existed for centralized control over the entire economy in time of war; nor was there any provision, if war should come, for securing resources from Japan's likely sphere of influence—a sphere to include China, northern Sakhalin and, it was hoped, the South Seas.[46]

Second, Araki had diverted the military's funds to the wrong programs. The army's and navy's rearmament drives were certain to make a substantial base of heavy industry in Japan far more difficult to achieve. Better to produce more steel mills now for more bullets later than to squander the empire's resources on short-term, stop-gap efforts. Nagata in particular proved to be a bitter foe of the navy's steel-hungry warship construction plans.[47]

Araki might nevertheless have retained his position as army minister but for a third failing. He had been appointed in the hope that the regional cliques of the Imperial Army, so prevalent since the days of Meiji, might be eliminated. This hope was realized, but the cost was the creation of a clique of his own. His wholesale dismissals of senior officers in the General Staff and Army Ministry made so many enemies that Araki found himself forced to resign in January 1934.[48]

The three years that followed were the heyday of the total war officers. Under the new army minister, Hayashi Senjurō, Nagata returned to central headquarters, this time as chief of the Military Affairs Bureau, a post that ensured him of the maximum possible exposure to elites outside the military. Inside, Hayashi directed Nagata to assemble an appropriate staff and plan for the development of the Manchurian region and control of the entire Japanese economy along the lines suggested in the study by the Military Affairs Section.[49]

Nagata first had to repair Araki's damage to planning for total mobilization. It was too late to alter the nature of the emergency plan significantly, and Nagata saw it completed in May 1934. Among its fifty-four thick volumes were studies of discovered and potential oil

---

46. *GDS8*, 15.

47. *GDS8*, 11–13.

48. Crowley, "Factions," 315–16, and Malcolm D. Kennedy, *The Estrangement of Great Britain and Japan, 1917–1935* (Berkeley: University of California Press, 1969), 289–90. Kennedy gives a good picture of factions in the Army Ministry in late 1933.

49. Crowley, *Quest*, 206–8.

reserves in Japan's Akita Prefecture, northern Sakhalin, and in oil shale near Fushun, with programs to expand production if emergencies or war made more oil necessary. Similar examinations of other crucial resources were included.

Nagata's labors had only begun. The emergency plan was meant only for use in 1934 and 1935 (actually in fiscal years, running from April 1934 to March 1936). After that time changing conditions abroad and altered industrial and import capabilities within Japan would render it outdated. Accordingly, in June 1934 the Resources Bureau began work on a second Term mobilization plan for 1936 and 1937.[50]

Like the emergency plan, this second term plan employed both private and official Japanese civilians. These men were not chosen only for their expertise. Like Ugaki before him, Nagata was sensitive to the need throughout elite circles for wide support for mobilization planning, and so he carefully cultivated influential political and financial figures. His efforts paid off in October, when the Army Ministry released its pamphlet "Basic Principles of National Defense and Proposals for Its Strengthening." Several high political figures publicly endorsed it.[51]

Nagata's successes were not repeated with the Imperial Navy and his own service's General Staff. Again the difficulty stemmed from Araki, this time from his consent while army minister to abrogation of the London naval treaties and resumption of substantial ship building plans in exchange for the admirals' agreement to the army's policy aims and increases in its budgets. Formal notice of abrogation was to be given to the United States and Britain at the end of the year.

Nagata was forced to fight on two fronts. Araki's departure had not diminished the enthusiasm of some army officers, particularly on the General Staff, for enlarging the forces at their disposal. These men, in fact, proposed a ten-year plan for a force of fifty divisions and two hundred air groups, a vast increase over previous levels (thirty divisions and fifty-four groups). Like Araki before them, they were willing to strike a deal with the navy to secure mutual force increases.

In vain did Nagata argue that Japan could not afford such increases. He was able to reduce the plan to a more modest target, 41 divisions and 142 air groups, but the General Staff would go no lower.[52] Even so, Nagata warned, if the London treaties were done

50. *RGD1*, 432, 435, 437, 487–89.

51. Gordon M. Berger, *Parties out of Power in Japan, 1931–1941* (Princeton: Princeton University Press, 1977), 89.

52. Nagata had the assistance of the Intendance Bureau of the Army Ministry for these reductions.

away with and the staff was to realize its force buildup, some new agreement would have to be concluded.[53]

The Army General Staff greeted this argument with apathy, the Imperial Navy with scorn. The navy's commitment to abrogation and fleet expansion was dramatically illustrated to one of Nagata's lieutenants, Colonel Suzuki Teiichi, when he visited Admiral Suetsugu Nobumasa during the summer of 1934. Suzuki asked whether the navy was seriously considering war with the United States; Suetsugu replied, "Certainly, even that is acceptable if it will get us a budget."[54]

Nagata was forced to relent. His superior, Hayashi, asked only for assurances that the ending of the naval treaty would not worsen the international situation nor cause significantly increased naval expenditures. He also requested renewed support for possible increases in the army's budget. Having received these assurances, the minister consented to abrogation at a five minister conference on 24 July 1934. In December the Foreign Ministry relayed its nation's intent to Washington and London.[55]

In the second aspect of the drive for autarky, territorial expansion, Nagata and the total war officers faced less formidable obstacles. This time their target was north China. Like Manchuria three years earlier, north China offered something to all groups in the Imperial Army. The General Staff and the Kwantung Army stressed its strategic significance. A secure north China meant a secure southern flank in any clash with the Soviets. Nagata's Military Affairs Bureau and Sakata Yoshirō, on the scene with Japan's Tientsin garrison, had emphasized the resources of the area, particularly coal and iron ore, both in quantities greater than Manchukuo's.[56] In December 1934 a conference of section chiefs in the Army, Navy, and Foreign ministries agreed that Kuomintang authority had to be excluded from the region.[57] This meant not an independent north China under Japanese tutelage but an autonomous political unit, still technically Chinese. Japan would create a corporation, not a government, to control north China's economic development, concentrating on increased production in iron ore, cotton, and other strategic goods.[58]

53. *DR1*, 380; *RGD1*, 546; Harada, entry of 6 March 1936; Crowley, *Quest*, 206–8; Pelz, 48–49; and *Gendaishi shiryō 12, Nitchū sensō 4* (Tokyo: Misuzu Shobō, 1966), 4, 16–18, 30, 33–34.

54. Nihon Kindai Shiryō Kenkyūkai, *Suzuki Teiichi danwa sokkiroku*, 2 vols. (Tokyo, 1971), 1:67.

55. Pelz, 56–57, and Harada, entry of 31 July 1934.

56. *DR1*, 361, and *GDS8*, 60–67.

57. *GDS8*, 22–24.

58. Shimada, xxxiv–xxxv.

The first chance to implement this policy came in May 1935, when several anti-Japanese demonstrations broke out in Tientsin and Peking. Two colonels visited local Chinese authorities in Peking to demand, presumably on their own authority, the complete removal of all Kuomintang advisers from the north and the creation of an autonomous political organ in the two-city area, a démarche that had not been anticipated by Hayashi and Nagata in Tokyo. The Imperial Navy raised objections. The two services' leaders and officials of the Foreign Ministry met, stressed the need to settle Sino-Japanese differences amicably, but approved the demands of the two officers. Days later the Umezu-Ho and Doihara-Ching agreements were concluded to expel the Kuomintang from Hopei and Chahar provinces.[59]

These two agreements were not simply political instruments, for both endorsed Sino-Japanese economic cooperation in north China. Immediately after they had been concluded, Major General Doihara Kenji met with the Kwantung Army's General Staff, urging that it approach the South Manchurian Railway for help in forming an extended economic bloc. In early July the railroad, which had created its own economic research group for north China in October 1934, dispatched a study mission to Tientsin. Its conclusions must have been encouraging. The railway's new president, Matsuoka Yōsuke, soon asked Tokyo to charter a company to develop coal in Shansi, iron ore in Chahar, oil in Shensi, and cotton throughout north China. By summer's end staffers from the Kwantung Army and the railway's Economic Research Association (Keizai Chōsakai) and Industrial Division (Sangyōbu) had completed detailed drafts of public finance policies for eastern Hopei in particular and north China as a whole. The group also welcomed formation of the Hopei Economic Association in August. Led by Wu Ting-chang and Chou Tso-min, both Japanese-trained financiers, the association declared itself ready to use Japanese technicians and equipment to develop and modernize China.[60]

Nagata's Military Affairs Bureau and his total war officers were pleased by these inroads, but even they wished to avoid undue friction with the Kuomintang. The Foreign Ministry and navy agreed, favoring some understanding with Chiang in order to bring long-term political stability to East Asia.[61] On 4 October the cabinet re-

---

59. Crowley, *Quest*, 214–17, 220–22, 277.

60. *FES*, 18 December 1935; Mantetsu, chōsabu, *Kita Shina tsuka kin'yu hōsaku* (Dairen: Mantetsu, 1937), passim; *FES*, 1 January 1936; and T. K. Koo, "Some Economic Documents Relating to the Genesis of the Japanese-Sponsored Regime in North China," *Far Eastern Quarterly* 6 (November 1946), 69.

61. *GDS8*, 102–8.

affirmed its commitment to encouraging the gradual emergence of autonomous regimes in the region. But it also endorsed an attempt to normalize Sino-Japanese relations known as Hirota's Three Principles. Hirota proposed that, first, Chinese movements directed against Japan be ended; second, Chiang accord diplomatic recognition to Manchukuo; third, Chiang conclude an agreement for joint efforts to combat communism in Inner Mongolia.[62]

Chiang offered two responses. In November he announced his willingness, should no change occur in the north, to negotiate on the basis of the principles. At the same time, however, with Britain's unwitting assistance, he began a radical challenge to Japan's position, political and economic, in the northern provinces.

Sir Frederick Leith-Ross, the British government's top financial adviser, came to China in early autumn. Prime Minister Neville Chamberlain hoped that Japan and Britain could join forces to promote a Sino-Japanese political détente and so restore stability. Then long-standing British economic interests in China could flourish once more.[63]

The hope was false. China and Japan had deep differences, and neither favored a settlement likely to benefit the British. But Chiang saw opportunity in the Leith-Ross mission. He had been under much pressure from Chinese bankers to rescue the yuan, upset greatly by America's silver purchasing policy, and he knew that Britain was willing to extend a loan to stabilize China's silver-backed currency. Accordingly, on 4 November the Kuomintang regime decreed the nationalization of all silver and ordered its exchange for bank notes issued by three central Kuomintang banks.[64]

Besides being an ingenious solution to a domestic problem, silver nationalization was a body blow to Japan in north China. The South Manchurian Railway and the Kwantung Army General Staff quickly concluded that because the Kuomintang banks were all in central and southern China, compliance by northern banks would make the entire financial system of the region entirely dependent on Nanking's will. Could the consolidation of the Kuomintang's political influence—and the ouster of the Japanese—be far behind?[65]

62. Ibid.; *DR1*, 360; and Crowley, *Quest*, 230–31.

63. Ann Trotter, *Britain and East Asia, 1933–1937* (Cambridge: Cambridge University Press, 1975), 148–51, and Stephen L. Endicott, *Diplomacy and Enterprise: British China Policy, 1933–1937* (Vancouver: University of British Columbia Press, 1975), 98–110.

64. Endicott, 113–17, and Dorothy Borg, *The United States and the Far Eastern Crisis of 1933–1938* (Cambridge: Harvard University Press, 1964), chap. 4.

65. Mantetsu, sōmubu, shiryōka, *Hokushi jichi undō gaikan* (Dairen: Mantetsu, 11 January 1936), 1, and *GDS8*, 116–19, 125–27.

Japan was saved by the unwillingness of north Chinese bankers to cooperate and by the quick action of field officers. On 6 November, Doihara met with Major General Tada Hayao of the Tientsin garrison, and together they planned for a new regime for three provinces of north China, Hopei, Chahar, and Shantung. One week later banks in these provinces announced their refusal to send any silver to the south. Demonstrations for local autonomy followed.

It was Chiang's turn to be alarmed. Determined to prevent a full-fledged autonomous regime, he dispatched General Ho Ying-ching to Peking and reiterated his willingness to discuss arrangements with Japan based on Hirota's principles. Ho arrived too late to stop the establishment of the East Hopei Anti-Communist Autonomous Committee, but he was able to strike a bargain with Doihara to preserve the semblance of Kuomintang authority in the rest of the region. The Hopei-Chahar Political Council was created in early December to work with Japan in combating the communists and in furthering economic development projects. Nanking's financial plans for both provinces were to be modified accordingly.[66]

These achievements actually reaffirmed Tokyo's intent to stabilize north China. The Foreign Ministry and navy remained opposed to further adventurism. Within the army, Nagata was gone, slain in August by Lieutenant Aizawa Saburō, a supporter of the out-of-power Araki wing of the army whose members Nagata had passed over in making key staff appointments. But Nagata was survived by his willingness to restrain field officers on the continent in the interests of consensus at home and the gradual pursuit of autarky. Literally days before his death Nagata had seen to it that several fellow-thinkers were given posts in the Operations Division of the General Staff. The most important of these, Colonel Ishiwara Kanji, became head of its Operations Section.[67]

If anything, Ishiwara was even more anxious than Nagata to curb Japanese activities in north China. His new duties included the drafting of operations plans for the army for 1936. Shock was the result. The Soviet force had grown from four rifle divisions in the Far East in 1932 to fourteen, with nearly a thousand tanks and as many warplanes in support; against them the Kwantung Army could field only three divisions with obsolete equipment. A fracas with Nanking, Ishi-

---

66. Mantetsu, *Hokushi*, 6–7, 9–10, 12, 17ff. The Kuomintang, albeit with Japanese approval, could appoint advisers to the political council.
67. *DR1*, 358, and Peattie, 198.

wara reasoned, would involve Japan with the wrong enemy at the wrong time.[68]

Ishiwara alone might have accomplished little. The abortive coup d'état of February 1936 led to the disgrace of top army officers, however, especially those associated with Araki, and their replacement with men sympathetic to Ishiwara's views on northern China and the need for long-term, large-scale economic planning for the Japanese Empire. Terauchi Hisa'ichi succeeded Kuwashima Kazuo as army minister. Army general Isogai Rensuke left his old post as military attaché to China to become chief of the vital Military Affairs Bureau; he had a long record of opposition to political and military activities in the northern provinces. Colonel Machijiri Kazumoto, Ishiwara's old friend and a powerful advocate of economic preparedness, assumed the leadership of that bureau's Military Affairs Section.[69]

This new group of officers in central headquarters moved rapidly to end the impetuous Kwantung Army's jurisdiction over the Tientsin garrison, and hence over affairs in north China, by creating a new North China Army under their direct control. Tada and Doihara were transferred out of China. In their places came men more in line with Ishiwara's views on the need to establish a self-sufficient economic bloc in East Asia with China as a relatively willing, if junior, partner. The Army Ministry created a special committee on the current situation in May. With representatives from the Navy and Foreign ministries, the committee supervised policy toward north China. It could not turn back the clock, of course; existing political organs continued to function, and the army retained administrative control over the area's economic development. But the army did pledge that no future incidents would arise.[70]

These were important steps, but they did little to address the immediate Soviet threat and the longer-term need to achieve self-sufficiency. As Ishiwara had remarked shortly after assuming his position in the General Staff, "in our army and navy we do have operations plans, but not really war plans." The services could draft schemes to

---

68. *DR1*, 371.

69. *DR1*, 375, 381. The February 1936 coup, best studied by Ben-Ami Shillony, *Revolt in Japan: The Young Officers and the February 26, 1936, Incident* (Princeton: Princeton University Press, 1973), was the result of some junior officers' belief that only radical action—the overthrow of the cabinet form of government, abolition of political parties, banishment of economic (capitalist) elites, and establishment of a pure regime of the emperor supported by a military purged of collaborators with the establishment (such as Nagata had been)—could save Japan. The effort failed quickly and decisively.

70. Crowley, *Quest*, 291–93, and *GDS8*, 372–73.

attack the Soviets or the Americans, but neither had integrated Japan's overall economic capacity into its strategic thinking.[71]

In 1936, as if to illustrate this observation, the navy had initiated discussions to form a new consensus on Japan's fundamental defense policy. Unsurprisingly, it claimed that the most ominous threat was American and the best hope for self-reliance the development of the South Seas. In the navy's "Outline of National Policy," submitted to the Five Minister Conference in April by Navy Minister Nagano Osami, the admirals endorsed the economic exploitation of Inner Mongolia and the five provinces of north China but insisted that the southwestern Pacific had become the region most vital to the empire's defense, economic and otherwise.[72]

The total war officers vigorously objected to the navy's outline. Ishiwara personally visited his counterpart, Captain Fukudome Shigeru, chief of the Operations Section of the Naval General Staff, to protest. How, he asked, could Japan realistically be expected to deal with the Soviet Union and the United States simultaneously? Why prepare for a two-front war that could not possibly be won?

Fukudome would not yield, and the interservice negotiations that followed produced only an accord in early June which endorsed both requests for further force increases. All that Ishiwara gained was one lone concession: because "the thing to be most feared is that future wars will be prolonged," Japan was to make necessary preparations. Overall, however, interservice politics had once again overwhelmed a coherent imperial strategy of autarky.[73]

The cabinet-level discussions of the summer of 1936 did little to address Ishiwara's concern. Their result, "The Fundamental Principles of National Policy," was a vague set of directives promising all things to all parties. Japan would lead the development of both Manchukuo and the South Seas, making both part of the empire's economic defense program. Because friendship with Germany would check Soviet ambitions in the north and lead to a better relationship with Holland and its East Indian colonies in the south, Tokyo would seek closer ties with Berlin. Japan would encourage eventual political autonomy for all five provinces of northern China and develop that region's national defense resources.[74] A separate interministerial decision, "Second Policy for North China," listed the resources targeted

71. *DR1*, 377.
72. *DR1*, 392; *GDS8*, 351–53, 354–55; and Crowley, *Quest*, 285–98.
73. *DR1*, 380; Shimada, lii; and *GDS8*, 356.
74. The principles did favor developing north China with the assistance of private, even American, capital.

[44]

for specific attention—iron ore, coking coal, and industrial salt among them—and noted promising sites. At the same time the Foreign Ministry was to woo the Kuomintang to an anti-Soviet, pro-Japanese posture. Tokyo could then send resource survey teams to remote Chinese provinces such as Kansu, Tsinghai, Szechwan, and Sinkiang, in order to find additional opportunities for Sino-Japanese codevelopment.[75]

The army's defense planners wondered how these fine-sounding goals were to be realized. Unable to challenge the "fundamental principles" directly, Ishiwara created a new office, the War Leadership Section (Sensō shidōka) under the Operations Division of the General Staff, to develop ways to prepare Japan for protracted war, particularly against the army's likeliest enemy, the Soviet Union. The section's first study, completed that summer, asserted that good relations with the United States were indispensable to meeting this threat. But Japan still had to increase productive capacity substantially to make expansion of the armed forces feasible; even with good U.S. relations, the nation needed peace for at least five years.[76]

Ishiwara's group was not alone in its concern over the imperfections in the fundamental principles. The empire's second term mobilization plan was due to be completed in mid-1936, and the plan's authors saw that the interservice and cabinet-level decisions of the summer placed a fantastic burden upon them. Neither military branch wanted the term plan to deprive it of materials and missions that it saw as vital to its own expansion programs, of course, and so the plan had to assume that the army would fight the Soviet Union even as the navy fought the United States. As the army's chief mobilization planner, Major Okada Kikusaburō, readily admitted, this premise went well beyond his nation's resources and industrial capabilities.[77]

So the second term plan was riddled with paradox. As the imperial fleet was sinking American warships, Japan would be importing cotton from American growers, spinning and weaving it, and selling the finished products to a principally American market. The United States was to supply the special steels and alloys, especially manganese and molybdenum, necessary for the Japanese war effort. America too was the primary source of the machine tools and other sophisticated equipment that Tokyo required to mobilize. The ob-

75. GDS8, 361–62, 363–65, 366–67, 374–75, and Crowley, *Quest*, 293–96.
76. GDS8, 357–58.
77. RGD1, 524–25.

vious conclusion, at least to men such as Okada, was that war with America was unthinkable and the navy's Third Replenishment Program self-defeating.[78]

The only long-term solution to Japan's security quandary was the rapid expansion of Japan's productive capacity. By August 1936 Ishiwara was preparing for it.

Nearly a year earlier Ishiwara had directed his War Leadership Section and an old friend from the South Manchurian Railway, Miyazaki Masayoshi, to plan for war with the Soviet Union by 1941. The plan was to stress development of heavy industry in order to wage protracted hostilities, and planners were to assume that northern China's resources could be exploited without obstacle. Japan was to remain at peace with the United States and, it was hoped, the Kuomintang regime.[79]

By August 1936 the task had been completed, and on the seventeenth Miyazaki explained his team's work to the General Staff and appropriate members of the Army Ministry. Separate studies examined a wide range of topics, including the latest research on liquid fuels, recent government controls over expenditures in France and the United States, and a comprehensive report on foreign exchange and financial control policies.[80]

Miyazaki's plan itself was breathtaking in scope. It proposed drastic increases in Japan's war-making potential. Iron and steel production was to more than double over the plan's five years; machine tool production would nearly quadruple; and oil output, much of it syn-

---

78. *RGD1*, 505–8, 514–16, 522–23. Okada equally lamented the utter lack of interservice guidelines for cooperative use of resources and factory facilities. As matters stood, the army, if it went to war against the Soviets, could not employ naval plants to increase production of, say, armor or artillery. Nor would the navy be able to call on army facilities to build or repair ships in the event of a naval war. Determined to change this, Okada drew up an army-navy accord on shared materials. Even his colleagues in the War Preparations Section opposed it. Only after Okada circumvented the regular lines of authority, including his counterpart in the navy's Military Affairs Bureau, did he find a receptive navy man in that bureau, Yagi Hideoka, who had done mobilization work earlier with Okada in the Resources Bureau. By November the two men engineered an agreement to share military aircraft factories. If Japan were involved in operations against the Soviets, the army would receive 65 percent of total plane production; if against a maritime foe, the navy. Simultaneous wars would see each service receive half. Other accords followed, none easily. After hard bargaining the army obtained part-time use of the 10,000 ton hydraulic press at the steel-processing plant in Muroran. Elsewhere, by mid-1937 each service was still relying principally on its own plants and denied use of them to its counterpart. See *RGD1*, 533–37, 540–41.

79. Peattie, 208; *RGD1*, 588–90; and *GDS8*, 677–78, 682.

80. *GDS8*, 695–702.

thetic, was to rise fifteenfold. The plan would require the expenditure of over seven billion yen.

The plan had still more sweeping provisions. Every major industry was to be "rationalized" for more efficient administration of the plan and, later, of the war effort. Even the old cabinet system would have to go. In its place a national affairs board, with a prime minister and four ministers of state, would supervise the country and its economy.[81]

Ishiwara strongly supported the plan, but reactions within the Army Ministry were mixed. Staffers in the Equipment Bureau, who were closest to these concerns, readily conceded the need for industrial expansion and strongly supported the creation of a central mobilization organ. But they were shocked by the immensity of Miyazaki's proposal and dismayed by its political radicalism.[82]

Their suspicions were confirmed in late December, as the Diet session opened. Many representatives were uneasy about immense military budgets and rumors of a central control agency. Even before the session began, Ikeda Seihin, influential leader of the Mitsui combine, expressed reservations to Baron Harada Kumao, *genrō* Prince Saionji Kimmochi's personal secretary. On 21 January 1937 Hamada Kumitaro of the Seiyūkai party attacked Army Minister Terauchi openly, accusing him, his service, and reformist bureaucrats of subverting parliamentary government. The episode led to Terauchi's resignation and the fall of the Hirota cabinet.[83]

To Ishiwara's delight, General Hayashi Senjurō became the next premier. Hayashi had shown strong sympathy for economic mobilization three years earlier, when he had returned Nagata to central headquarters. And he assumed his new post only after acceding to two General Staff demands: the increases in army force levels, agreed to in August, would be kept intact, and the empire would commit itself to an attempt to become fully self-sufficient by 1941.

Ishiwara's delight was soon tempered, however. Hayashi's cabinet could not secure ministers from business circles until the premier removed Ishiwara's representative, Sogō Shinji—a director of the South Manchurian Railway—from his committee to select cabinet

81. For the cost of the plan, see Nakamura Takafusa, *Senzen-ki Nihon keizai seichō no bunseki* (Tokyo: Iwanami Shoten, 1971), 240; Peattie, 208; *RGD1*, 588–90; and *IKS*, 2:153–68.

82. *RGD1*, 589, 565, 566ff.

83. The *genrō* (literally, "elder statesmen") were the Founding Fathers of modern Japan during the Meiji Restoration of 1868. Berger, 112–13; Harada, entries of 30 September, 14 October, and 4 December 1936; and Crowley, *Quest*, 311–13.

appointees. In other moves to placate Japan's economic and financial elites, Hayashi made Yūki Toyotarō finance minister, with Kaya Okinori as vice-minister—both were respected in the financial community—and awarded Satō Naotake, former ambassador to Great Britain and a strong advocate of friendly ties with that country and the United States, the Foreign Ministry portfolio.[84]

These developments, though initially distasteful to the total war officers, proved to be a blessing in disguise, because they commenced a period of close cooperation between moderates in the Army Ministry and businessmen and financial bureaucrats. In April 1937 Ikeda, who had become president of the Bank of Japan, asked Izumiyama Sanroku, a member of Mitsui Bank's Research Division, to act as his delegate to Miyazaki and the Army Ministry's economic planners. Izumiyama and the economic planners began to modify Miyazaki's original proposal. By mid-May their work was finished.

A good deal of the original proposal remained intact. The Cabinet Investigative Bureau would be expanded into a planning office (Kikaku-chō) to oversee the plan's passage through the Diet and its subsequent execution—though the office was not to be a supreme organ of control. Most of Miyazaki's specific goals, including the increase in steel production from five to thirteen million tons per year by 1941, were revised downward, but only slightly.[85]

The fate of Miyazaki's plan was unresolved when the Hayashi cabinet resigned at the end of May 1937. It became a central issue in the formation of Prince Konoe Fumimaro's first cabinet.

Konoe had closely followed the negotiations between Izumiyama, Miyazaki, and the army economic planners, and he supported their result. This stance required that the new minister of finance approve Miyazaki's amended plan. One contender for the portfolio, a former governor of the Yokohama Specie Bank, Kodama Kenji, had a long talk with Major General Ushiroku Jun, chief of the Military Affairs Bureau, and his judgment that the expansion plan would be too costly put him out of the running. Another possibility was Baba

84. Nakamura, 238–39; Berger, 115–17; Crowley, *Quest,* 317; Ishiwata Sōtaro Denki Hensankai, ed., *Ishiwata Sōtaro* (Tokyo, 1954), 207; and Peattie, 110n.

85. In the case of steel to a "mere" ten million tons. *GDS43*, 201ff., and *IKS*, 2:148–50. Izumiyama agreed to these provisions, but not without complaint. In his reports to Ikeda he noted that the plan still paid little attention to nonmaterial factors. Japan's skilled workers, especially machinists, were in short supply. Its foreign exchange reserves, posited for growth in the plan, would more likely decline, because of sharply increased imports and resulting inflation. Moreover, Izumiyama warned, there was virtually no consideration of attaining adequate raw resources. See Nakamura, 239–40, 251–52, and Nakamura Takafusa and Hara Akira, Introduction to *GDS43*, xix.

Eiichi. As finance minister under Hirota, Baba had supported the huge military budgets of early 1937 before the Diet, support that the Ikeda group, which expected a finance minister to act as a brake on the military, found intolerable. Konoe gave Baba the Home portfolio, which made keeping Yūki impossible, so Yūki's vice-minister, Kaya Okinori, succeeded his old chief.[86]

Kaya was disposed to support the expansion plan, but he had conditions. Yoshino Shinji was to be made minister of commerce and industry, the other key post in the execution of the plan. After the first meeting of the new cabinet, Kaya and Yoshino publicly announced three principles basic to Japan's future economic policy, serving notice that, though both ministers approved of expanding Japan's productive power, they did so only as long as that expansion caused no undue deficits in the empire's international balance-of-payments position or otherwise endangered a sound economy.[87]

Their approval paved the way for formal Diet consideration of the five-year plan to expand production, the domestic keystone of the drive for autarky. The cabinet resolved to call a special Diet session to begin on 23 July. In preparation, explanatory materials and guidelines for polishing and then implementing the plan—after it passed—were sent to the various ministries on 24 June.[88]

In nearly two decades since the end of World War I, officers committed to total war planning had made impressive strides toward a self-sufficient Japanese Empire. Manchuria had been absorbed completely. The rich provinces of northern China were becoming increasingly available for Japan's economic security. In the home islands the Diet was about to sanction a colossal plan that would provide the large industrial base necessary to use the newly opened resources on the continent.

Yet there were contradictions in Japan's drive for self-sufficiency, contradictions that threatened all these gains. To build an industrial base required five years of absolute peace. Japan's encroachments in north China were leading to growing friction with the Kuomintang regime. At the same time they were creating deep suspicion and mistrust in the United States—the one country that, until Japan achieved autarky, could devastate the imperial economy without firing a shot.

86. Berger, 118–22, and *SWT*, 16:13–14. Ushiroku's meeting with Kodama upset the navy, which suspected an army attempt to undercut its own force expansion plans. See Harada, entry of 9 June 1937.

87. *SWT*, 16:14–15, and Berger, 122–24.

88. Berger, 124–27, 139; Crowley, *Quest*, 320; *DR1*, 429; and *GDS8*, 695–702.

[2]

International Law
and Stove-Pipe Hats

The United States was what Japan sought to be. Interwar America was self-sufficient in every major respect, from food and energy to coal and iron. Indeed, the United States was a principal and often the world's leading exporter of such strategic goods as petroleum, rare metals, and sophisticated machinery. America boasted an immense industrial base unmatched by any other great power. As a result, the American War Department could assume in its industrial mobilization plans that even if the United States were denied all imports for two years of hostilities, substantial shortages would occur only in manganese, chromium, and rubber.[1]

America had attained autarky, moreover, without conscious effort. The United States had acquired vast, rich territories during its first century and a half, but it did not take these lands in the name of national economic security. Even the expansion of the 1890s, when the rhetoric of economic crisis filled the air, focused concern on obtaining foreign markets for surplus American production, not on seizing resources abroad to keep American factories running.

American views about the essentials of national security, therefore, were strikingly different from those of the Japanese. These differences increased after 1918. Japanese leaders strove to render their empire immune to the fate that had befallen Germany. American statesmen, meanwhile, decided that their nation's safety depended upon the reestablishment of global order based on international law.

---

1. Brooks Emeny, *The Strategy of Raw Materials: A Study of America in Peace and War* (New York: Macmillan, 1934), 23, 39, 174.

That order would be founded upon the rights of each nation to enjoy political independence and free, equal opportunity to trade with the rest of the world.

It was to uphold such an order that the victors of World War I formed the League of Nations. The new league's chief weapons for maintaining global peace and free trade were the application of economic pressure and, in extreme cases, military force against violators. The American president, Woodrow Wilson, did not see the irony, reasoning that any law-breaking nation had forfeited its right to enjoy the benefits of economic intercourse. The United States never joined the league, but its foreign policy under Wilson's Republican successors remained committed to the construction of a world based on peace, prosperity, and stability.[2]

In the decade following the war, few Americans considered Japan a menace to such a world. The Washington Conference of 1921 22 appeared to eliminate the two chief sources of friction between Tokyo and Washington, the race in naval armaments and conflicting ambitions in East Asia. Observers were convinced that a new era of cooperation had begun. Even Japan's dispatch of troops to the Shantung Peninsula in early 1928 failed to shake this belief. Indeed, American diplomats in China viewed the action as an unsurprising, even a welcome step to restore order, not as a new Japanese encroachment. Officials at home neither condemned nor approved the move but remained convinced that no likelihood existed of serious American-Japanese conflict.[3]

Not all American policy makers shared this outlook. Junior admirals and captains in the navy maintained that the era of tranquil relations with Tokyo ushered in by the Washington treaties limiting naval armaments was a dangerous illusion. They saw Japan as an expanding power with interests contrary to those of the United States. And they balked when their seniors refused to raise the Japanese issue, as politically inexpedient, in a period of declining budgets.[4]

2. David H. Miller, *The Drafting of the Covenant*, 2 vols. (New York: Putnam, 1928), 1:15–16, and Melvyn P. Leffler, "Political Isolationism, Economic Expansionism, or Diplomatic Realism: American Policy toward Western Europe, 1921–1933," *Perspectives in American History* 8 (1974), 419.

3. Eleanor Tupper and George McReynolds, *Japan in American Public Opinion* (New York: Macmillan, 1937), 166, and Akira Iriye, *After Imperialism* (Cambridge: Harvard University Press, 1965), 218–19, 221–22.

4. John A. Ordway, Jr., "America at Peace: The United States Navy Adjusts to the Washington Treaties of 1921–1922" (B.A. thesis, Harvard University, 1979), 96–98, 101–2, 107–8, 114–22.

These officers were in no position to influence American foreign policy. But a fellow-thinker, Stanley Hornbeck, was. Hornbeck, an academic who had taught in China and the United States, joined the army in 1917 and became a government expert on East Asia. Unlike many of his generation, he believed that resoluteness and power, not treaties outlawing war and limiting arms, were central to the maintenance of international peace. In the Far East, Hornbeck was convinced, the chief threat to that peace came from a Japan dedicated to establishing regional dominance. During the Paris Peace Conference he had labored to have America oppose Tokyo's acquisition of German rights in Shantung, certain that Japan would interpret any other stance as approval for further encroachments. During the 1920s Hornbeck served a stint in the State Department's Office of the Economic Adviser, an experience that encouraged him to follow Japan's economic programs closely. In one study sent to the army's War Plans Division in 1927, reservist Hornbeck observed that if the new Kuomintang movement in China blocked foreign investment and slowed growth, it would compel Japan to force economic development on the continent, even at the price of political disruption in China and severe policy differences with the United States. Japan's security depended on it.[5]

Hornbeck not only monitored Japan's expansion, he also paid attention to the other aspect of Japan's search for self-sufficiency. In July 1931, three years after becoming chief of the State Department's Far East Division, Hornbeck noted the Resources Bureau's preparations for industrial mobilization. Sure that Japan would produce a detailed and effective program, Hornbeck doubted that Tokyo could overcome its deficiencies in resources—a belief on which American policy toward Japan would be founded for nearly a decade to come.[6]

With the Mukden Incident of September 1931, however, neither

5. Kenneth G. McCarty, "Stanley K. Hornbeck and the Far East, 1931–1941" (Ph.D. diss., Duke University, 1970), 265–66, 20–23, and Hornbeck to assistant chief of staff, War Plans Division, "Study on Strategic Estimate Orange-Blue," January 1927, Orange File 2843, Records Section, Operations Division, War Department General Staff, National Archives. While in the Economic Affairs Division at State, considering American applications for oil concessions in the Persian Gulf area, Hornbeck remarked, "from a practical standpoint, first-comers must enjoy preference over subsequent applicants. It cannot be expected that equal commercial opportunity can be extended throughout an indefinite period of time." This was not a position calculated to increase sympathy for Japan, regardless of the logic Hornbeck saw in their steps. See Michael J. Hogan, *Informal Entente: The Private Structure of Cooperation in Anglo-American Economic Diplomacy, 1918–1928* (Columbia: University of Missouri Press, 1977), 182.

6. Stanley Hornbeck, "Japan: Combat Estimate," 31 July 1931, Box 228, Stanley Hornbeck Papers.

Hornbeck nor his superior, Secretary of State Henry Stimson, thought in terms of a concerted, well-considered drive to achieve self-sufficiency. Both attributed the incident to an irrational band of young Japanese officers. Stimson's initial reaction was to avoid condemnation. He feared arousing Japanese chauvinists against such moderates as Foreign Minister Shidehara Kijurō, who stood for cooperation with the West. With luck, these men could control the army hotheads and bring the affair to a rapid close.[7]

Stimson's optimism faded in early October, when Ishiwara Kanji led a Japanese air raid against the city of Chinchow. The raid suggested that the Japanese had designs on much more than a restored security along the South Manchurian Railway, and it indicated that Tokyo moderates were unable to exercise control. Also, the attack was in blatant disregard of the principles of international law.

Stimson had a deep respect for that law (without it, he believed, little lay between the world and ruinous anarchy), and he was inclined to accept an invitation from the Council of the League of Nations to participate in deliberations that China had urgently requested. Stimson knew that any move which implied direct collaboration with the league was certain to bring a storm of protest from the many isolationist Americans. He assured his countrymen that Prentiss Gilbert, the American consul at Geneva, would attend meetings of the council only under the terms of the Kellogg-Briand antiwar pact, which the United States had signed. In private Stimson went further, telling Gilbert explicitly that he was on no account to involve the United States in any pressure against Japan. Indeed, when the consul's attendance encouraged European partisans of the league to speak indiscreetly of putting teeth into the peace provisions of the covenant, Stimson quickly moved to recall Gilbert from the meetings. But at Britain's urging, the consul remained until after the council had resolved that Japan was to withdraw its troops from areas beyond the railway zone and commence negotiations with China. The council then adjourned.[8]

When the resolution proved useless, Stimson faced a dilemma. Japanese troops, far from withdrawing, were now advancing on Chinchow, evidently intending to absorb Manchuria by force. Neither the power of "world public opinion," in which he had placed faith, nor the abilities of the Japanese moderates had been able to

---

7. *FRUS, 1931* (Washington, 1946), 3:26, and Christopher Thorne, *The Limits of Foreign Policy: The West, the League, and the Far Eastern Crisis of 1931–1933* (New York: Capricorn, 1973), 136.

8. *FRUS, 1931*, 3:179, 190–91, 248–55, 299, and *DBFP*, 2d ser., 8:797–800.

reverse events. His policy of circumspection had failed. The league held the power, perhaps the obligation, to take concrete steps against Tokyo, most likely in the form of economic sanctions, yet the league powers were reluctant to do so, particularly if the United States opposed sanctions or refused to participate in them. America was sure to be accused of tacit acquiescence in Japan's violation of international law. But if, on the other hand, America joined in sanctions, it risked being drawn into an escalating conflict in the Far East.

Stimson elected to take a middle course. While reserving complete freedom of action for American policy, he indicated to league members that the United States would neither participate in nor interfere with economic measures. At the same time, aware of Japan's grave economic vulnerability—the same vulnerability that had inspired the total war officers in their quest for autarky—he sounded out first his advisers in the Department of State and then President Herbert Hoover about the possibility of applying pressure.

At first, officials favored moral sanctions alone. Hornbeck concluded that no action by the league or the United States could cause Japan to relinquish Manchuria. The United States should uphold its position only by refusing to recognize an illegal conquest. Hoover weighed the withdrawal of the American ambassador from Tokyo, but he too agreed that nonrecognition had merit.[9]

When the Kwantung Army resumed its march on Chinchow in late November, however, Stimson resolved that something more had to be done. Assurances from the Japanese Foreign Ministry had proven false. Despite Western patience, it seemed to the State Department, Japan had not restrained its irrational elements. In early December, Stimson polled his advisers again, stating his willingness to discuss economic pressure. Both Assistant Secretary James Rogers and special assistant Allen Klots—who had earlier favored working closely with the league—supported their chief. Undersecretary William Castle, who held views closer to Hoover's, opposed any embargo against Japan. The very canons of international law which Stimson meant to uphold, Castle argued, meant that an embargo would entail recognition of a state of war between China and Japan. Tokyo was sure to react by blockading all Chinese ports, in legitimate exercise of its belligerent rights. Then the United States would be forced to choose:

9. *DBFP*, 2d ser., 8:883, 923; Thorne, 152; *FRUS, 1931*, 3:477, 488–97; Henry L. Stimson, diary entries of 7, 9, and 19 November 1931, Henry L. Stimson Diary and Letters; and Hornbeck Papers, Box 453, memo of 21 November 1931.

abandon China and the principles of the Open Door, or go to war itself to contest the blockade.[10]

Hornbeck disagreed. Without encouragement, the league would do nothing. If the United States remained passive, it would be blamed for failing to uphold the international machinery for peace. Japan would be tempted by more aggression in the future. Denouncing Japan as a law-breaker and refusing to recognize the fruits of Japanese aggression would not change these facts. The West, in short, had to "put up or shut up."

The time had come, Hornbeck continued, to examine the advantages of economic pressure on Japan. He dismissed objections on humanitarian grounds to economic sanctions. An embargo was a weapon of defense, and Japan could protest it no more than it could protest American tariffs or coastal fortifications. An embargo now, moreover, was preferable to increased arms expenditures in the future.

Hornbeck next addressed the effectiveness of an embargo. Armed with detailed charts and statistics, he argued that Japan had doubtless studied the issue thoroughly. Tokyo had begun its defiance of international law in the belief that sanctions would never be employed—obviously, because Japan was far from self-reliant. So great was its dependence on the West, particularly America, that Japan would become reasonable the instant the powers announced their intent to commence an embargo. Actual enforcement might be superfluous. If not, Hornbeck asserted, a sustained embargo "would impose on Japan the necessity of attempting to reorganize her economic life on a self-supporting basis. The immediate cost and the ultimate futility of such an effort would be evident to Japan's statesmen from the beginning." He was confident that an embargo would cripple Japan within three months.[11]

Still, Hornbeck agreed that the initiative for sanctions had to be taken by the league. A few days later, on 10 December, its council voted to send an investigative commission to the Orient; at the same time Hoover repeated his opposition to any economic pressure. Stimson withdrew and on 7 January 1932 gave formal notice to Japan that the United States would recognize no "treaties, understandings, or

10. Stimson Diary, entries of 27 November and 6 December 1931, and Thorne, 156.

11. Hornbeck Papers, Box 453, memos of 5 and 6 December 1931. Tokyo's reaction, had an embargo been imposed in December 1931, is difficult to guess. But Hornbeck was certainly correct in arguing that the Japanese were unprepared for Western economic pressure, which would have been devastating—if applied comprehensively.

situations" in East Asia that infringed on any American treaty rights, or the Open Door of equal opportunity to trade, or the territorial or administrative integrity of China, or that were achieved by means contrary to the Kellogg-Briand pact.[12]

This nonrecognition doctrine and the league's dispatch of the Lytton Commission appeared to lay the Far Eastern Crisis to rest. The crisis was abruptly revived, however, when Chinese workers on the outskirts of Shanghai assaulted five Japanese subjects. Japan's consul general demanded a formal apology from the city's mayor, and the local commander of the Imperial Navy's forces upgraded his demand to an ultimatum, to expire on 28 January. Although the Chinese met its terms on time, he landed Japanese troops to protect the emperor's subjects; civilians then joined their guardians to clear an area around the Japanese concession in the city; and this composite force soon encountered Wang Ching-wei's Nineteenth Route Army. Heavy fighting erupted.[13]

Stimson saw this new crisis as an extension of the earlier one. Again Japan, doubtless buoyed by the West's weak reply to aggression in Manchuria, had employed illegal force. This time Stimson received vocal public support for strong measures. Japanese naval and naval air units had bombed the densely populated suburb of Chapei. To a public not yet inured to the killing of civilians in combat, these bombings seemed satanic. All across the United States, Americans read lurid accounts of Japanese atrocities under such headlines as "Babies Riddled with Bullets in Shanghai Stations." They responded by deluging the Japanese ambassador, Debuchi Katsuji, and the American government with angry letters, many asking why the United States sold Japan aircraft, bombs, and gasoline to be put to such obscene use. Public figures from Jane Addams and Corliss Lamont to William Loeb, Jr., and Thomas Dewey joined in the call for a boycott of Japanese goods. University presidents, such as Harvard's A. Lawrence Lowell, gave well-publicized radio addresses on the subject. The clamor spurred some congressmen into action: one bill before the House Foreign Affairs Committee proposed a formal arms embargo against Japan.[14]

12. *FRUSJ*, 1:60–62, and *FRUS, 1932*, 3:8–9.
13. Thorne, 206–9.
14. Tupper and McReynolds, 327–38; Stimson Diary, entry of 13 February 1932; and *Chicago Daily Tribune*, 29 January 1932, 1. The *San Francisco Chronicle* of the same day ran a story that began, "Men, women and babies cried helplessly, fear and agony distorting their pinched faces, it was a frightful scene of human misery. . . . The Japanese seem to enjoy the engagement and exhibited their military skill like children with new toys."

The outcry caught Stimson between his desire to align the United States with the cause of international morality and his responsibility as secretary of state to avoid needless friction with Japan. Responsibility won. Stimson discouraged the arms embargo bill, claiming that it ran counter to the equal opportunity provisions of the Treaty of Commerce and Navigation between Japan and the United States. Stimson also discouraged citizen supporters of a boycott. When one of them circulated reports in Europe that at one cabinet meeting only Hoover had opposed a boycott, Stimson angrily labeled the man "a damned liar."[15]

Stimson may have worked publicly for restraint, but privately his misgivings about Japanese policy were growing. Japan appeared to be under the control of elements attempting to create an economic bloc, with protected markets for products and sources of raw materials. The attempt ran contrary to the deepest strains of U.S. East Asian policy, from the opening of China and Japan to the Open Door notes and the Nine Power Treaty. America was dedicated to a world of political self-determination and unfettered international economic intercourse. Japan meant to subjugate its neighbors and reserve their goods for itself. In March, in his diary, Stimson gloomily prophesied that conflict seemed only too likely between such opposite values. As he had written six months earlier, "The peace machinery which western nations have hammered out does not fit these three [Asian] governments much better than a stovepipe hat fits a naked African savage."[16]

Stimson's unease continued through the summer. By mid-July, after two months of Sino-Japanese negotiations, Imperial troops had left Shanghai. But the Kwantung Army remained in Manchuria to establish the puppet state of Manchukuo. The moral sanction of public condemnation had failed to thwart this conquest; nonrecognition hardly affected it; and the purposeful application of economic measures had been ruled out. The idea that Japan had some legitimate

15. Stimson Diary, entries of 13 and 18 February 1932, and Stimson record of telephone call to Hugh Wilson, February 26, 1932, Decimal File 793.94/4458 1/2, Record Group 59.

16. The Open Door notes of 1899 and 1900 articulated and the Nine Power Treaty of 1922 codified (at least the American reading of that treaty codified) the Open Door principles of equal commercial opportunity for all nations in China and guarantees of the territorial integrity of China. Stimson Diary, entry of 9 March 1932, and Stimson to Fred R. Coudert, 9 September 1931, quoted in Michael D. Reagan, "The Far Eastern Crisis of 1931–1932: Stimson, Hoover, and the Armed Services," in *American Civil-Military Decisions*, ed. Harold Stein (Birmingham: University of Alabama Press, 1963), 29.

right, in the name of national economic security, to the region never occurred to Stimson. What steps, then, could he take to render Japan's aggression fruitless?

By the end of 1932 American statesmen were increasingly certain that "natural economic forces" would do what human protests had not. From Tokyo, the outgoing American ambassador W. Cameron Forbes wired that, though any pressure from outside would have unfavorable consequences, a policy of restraint would reveal a Japanese military embarrassed by the high cost of operations and the chimera of long-term economic benefits; Japanese leaders friendlier to the West would resume power. His replacement, Joseph Grew, likewise believed that Japan had two principal schools of thought. One, composed chiefly of older, experienced diplomats and leaders in politics, business, and finance, was realistic. These men understood that Japan could never hope to achieve autarky. The other, represented by the young idealists of the army, demanded that the Japanese Empire obtain the resources and markets necessary for its security regardless of the short-term cost. But the financial strain of developing Manchuria would discredit these chauvinistic influences behind Japanese aggression. There were signs of economic stress already, Grew wrote. Japan had left the gold standard in December 1931. During 1932 the yen had declined sharply in value, a decline that would badly harm Japan's international credit and force the country to adopt a defensive, not a provocative, stance before other nations. These pressures, Grew argued, would act on an economically frail Japan to produce the desired diplomatic results more effectively than sanctions ever could.[17]

Stimson agreed that Japan had no economic stamina. He too pointed to the sharp rise in its national debt and predicted that Japan would soon seek to confer with the powers on the question of Manchuria's future, perhaps using the Lytton Report as a basis for discussion. But Stimson was not content to see economics force Tokyo to disgorge Manchuria. He wanted some censure by the United States. Japan's very frailty, in his eyes and the eyes of all American hardliners in the decade to come, was reason to apply that censure. Frustrated throughout 1932 in his attempts to bluff Japan by threatening economic sanctions, Stimson turned to the threat of an embargo on arms shipments to Japan as an attractive way to symbolize the American position. In mid-December he suggested that Hoover ask Con-

17. *FRUS, 1932*, 3:364–65, 552–53, 664–66; *FRUS, 1932*, 4:143–48, 323, 344, 372–73; and Grew to Stimson, 13 August and 3 December 1932, Joseph C. Grew Papers, vol. 57.

gress to embargo such shipments to any nation engaged in aggression as determined by the president.[18]

Hornbeck too believed in Japan's fundamental economic vulnerability, but he cautioned against underestimating the militarists' political will. Japan might prove unable to develop Manchuria, but economic strain would not compel Tokyo to abandon its continental aspirations for a long time. Even the four months required for the Lytton Commission to complete its report would afford Japan a chance to put down deep roots throughout Manchuria. Once financial pressures had done their work, moreover, Hornbeck doubted the ability of the moderate Japanese to resume control. Worse, even if Japan were economically ruined in the process, the Kwantung Army could in time make itself self-supporting in Manchuria. The prospect was nightmarish: an army unto itself, a virtual state within a state in East Asia.[19]

Hornbeck understood that drastic steps, such as a boycott, were not possible for the United States. Throughout the early winter he discussed possible pressures with the office of Herbert Feis, the State Department's economic adviser, and officials of the Commerce and Treasury departments—men who would form the core of support for strong economic measures against Tokyo through 1941. All agreed that no sanctions of any sort would be legal unless the navigation treaty were abrogated. In the meantime the government could only impose a sharp increase in the ad valorem tariff on silk, crabmeat, and other articles imported mainly from Japan. Hornbeck strongly approved.[20]

In the end the Hoover administration did nothing. But its inaction was a result more of congressional opposition than of faith in Grew's natural economic forces. In January 1933 the outgoing president proposed embargo when the United States could obtain the cooperation of other arms-producing nations. Stimson sent a letter of support to the Hill for this tepid measure. Even so, not a few members of Congress, led by Hamilton Fish, charged that the administration actually wanted the power to stop arms shipments to Japan. Fish also claimed that Stimson wanted the power to embargo in order to make America a backdoor member of the League of Nations. Opposition forced Hoover and his secretary of state to accept an amendment limiting

18. *FRUS, 1932,* 4:349, and Robert A. Divine, *The Illusion of Neutrality* (Chicago: University of Chicago Press, 1962), 32.

19. Hornbeck Papers, Box 453, memo of 12 July 1932.

20. Hornbeck Papers, Box 369, memos of 27 September, 14 October, 10 November, and undated (October–November) 1932; ibid., Box 453, memo of 29 November 1932.

embargo power to the Western Hemisphere. Even this concession failed to appease Fish and his allies, who proclaimed their suspicions confirmed when Britain imposed an arms embargo over the Far East in late February. As Franklin Roosevelt was being sworn in as president on 4 March 1933, Stimson was obliged to admit defeat.[21]

Franklin Roosevelt shared many of Stimson's predispositions on the Far East. He too believed that Japan was weak and would retreat in the face of American firmness. Though he was not prepared during the American economic crisis of 1933 to adopt stronger measures, Roosevelt and his secretary of state, Cordell Hull, renewed the effort for an arms embargo. Indeed, Roosevelt had declared his support for an embargo of arms shipments to aggressors (and had met privately with Stimson to discuss the Far East) nearly two months before taking office. This stance pleased most officials in the State Department, particularly Joseph Green, who would administer any embargo. Green held that the international community in general, and Japan in particular, would construe an end to the attempt to secure congressional approval as tacit American assent for Japan's illegal acts.

Only Hornbeck dissented, and he nearly succeeded in sabotaging the effort to obtain the embargo. Never a believer in token, symbolic steps, Hornbeck pointed out that Japan already produced all the arms it needed. If Tokyo really was engaged in aggression contrary to vital American interests, measures designed to cripple—not to irritate— were in order. In mid-March, Hornbeck persuaded Undersecretary of State William Phillips that a cooperative arms embargo was unwise, and Phillips withdrew his department's letter of support from Congress, to the joy of Hamilton Fish and his allies. This turnaround was itself reversed in April, when Hull strongly endorsed the embargo resolution. His support was instrumental in April in securing House approval for a bill that included the president's power to apply an export ban against only the aggressor nation.

This power did not survive the bill's passage through the Senate. Despite Hull's reassurances that an embargo would not be applied against Japan, many senators still connected sanctions with Geneva. Roosevelt, anxious to distance himself from the league and to avoid a fracas that might imperil his domestic programs, approved a Senate amendment requiring that embargo be applied impartially to all belligerent parties, not just the aggressor. Hull, who had not been informed of this switch beforehand, was predictably upset, and he persuaded Roosevelt to drop the whole matter for the 1933 session of

21. Divine, 33–35, 37–39, 40.

Congress. In January 1934, when the next session convened, Green, now joined by Norman Davis, the president's "roving ambassador," again argued for a bill with discriminatory power. Roosevelt and the Congress would have none of it, and only an impartial embargo passed.[22]

The question now was whether Grew's "natural economic forces" would oust the Japanese militarists from Manchuria and restore the moderates to power in Tokyo. To assist those forces, the State Department preempted any official American quotation of Manchukuo's currency, a step that effectively denied the puppet state access to American credit markets. Hull meanwhile kept in touch with his officers in France, as Stimson had before him, to discover whether that nation's banks were lending money to the authorities of Manchukuo.[23]

It was not until late 1934 that the impact of economic forces on Japan was again assessed. The occasion was Tokyo's decision to abrogate the naval arms limitation treaties. These required any signatory power to give two years' notice before it could consider itself rid of its treaty obligations; in September, Foreign Minister Hirota Kōki gave such notice to Grew. On the first day of 1937 the Imperial Navy would be free to build as it pleased—but could it do so?[24]

Grew thought the distinction was academic. Japan's concern over the issue of parity with the United States was, he thought, symbolic, not substantial: Tokyo wanted to end an agreement that placed Japan in an openly inferior position. The Japanese would not try to win some future naval race with the United States because they recognized that they could not. It was even possible, Grew maintained, that the empire's admirals would come to the new naval conference with concessions to ensure successful negotiation of a revised set of treaties. At worst, a race would commence. Even so, Grew reasoned,

22. Edgar B. Nixon, *Franklin D. Roosevelt and Foreign Affairs,* 3 vols. (Cambridge: Harvard University Press, 1969), 1:28n.; Divine, 43–47, 53–54, 58–60; *FRUS, 1933,* 1:365–67, 369–78; and Frank B. Freidel, *FDR, Launching the New Deal* (Boston: Little, Brown, 1973), 367–68.

23. *FRUS, 1933,* 3:407–8, 438–39. The U.S. government did not ban American businesses from Manchuria. In April, Grew had asked Hull for instructions concerning an American steel contractor who wanted assistance in obtaining orders for machinery for the steel works at Anshan. Grew was told to take no special action on the contractor's behalf, but he was to watch for evidence of discrimination against American business. Grew Papers, vol. 65, entry of 25 April 1933.

24. *FRUS, 1934,* 1:303–4, and *FRUSJ,* 1:253–54.

if the United States maintained the old treaty ratios by additional building, Japan would have to ask for surcease.[25]

Hornbeck took a darker view. Observers had doubted Japan since 1904, when many had predicted that its economy would not permit war with tsarist Russia on equal terms. But the Japanese people were prepared to make sacrifices greater than most Westerners expected. Japan might not be able to engage in a naval race with the United States forever, Hornbeck conceded, but it certainly could for the foreseeable future. There was no hoping that economic collapse would compel Japan to come to terms. Indeed, Japan had violated Chinese territory and Western interests already, and notice of abrogation was a sign that it was preparing to expand the imperial fleet for wider action.[26]

This conviction led Hornbeck to approach the coming naval conference with suspicion. "Undertakings between human beings who are in the category of the 'haves' and those . . . of the 'have nots,' if and when made," he warned, "rest on unsound and insecure bases." It would be better to have no new treaty at all than to concede Japan an even greater preponderance in the western Pacific. Then no limits would impede construction of a mighty American fleet, the best guarantor of Japanese good conduct.[27]

Hornbeck got his wish; the conference never met. Only the British, eager for some negotiated limit on costly naval construction, favored new talks. Convinced that the Japanese would accept no ratios, London proposed limits on ship sizes but not on total numbers or tonnage for any power. Hull sent the American reply, a firm negative that effectively ended any chance for a conference.

Hull's decision stemmed from a mixture of hope and conviction. The secretary did not share Hornbeck's enthusiasm for a greatly enlarged U.S. Navy, but he did strongly believe that any naval treaty had to recognize the principles of international law, specifically the Nine Power Treaty that was to have safeguarded China's territorial and administrative integrity. Hull linked Japan's aggressive conduct

---

25. *FRUS, 1934,* 3:667–71; *FRUS, 1934,* 1:217–20; and *FRUS, 1935,* 3:821–29.

26. Herbert Feis supported Hornbeck's judgment. Feis predicted that Japan could build warships at an accelerated rate for two to five years. The national debt would rise rapidly, but the effort was economically possible.

27. DF 894.51/456, Feis to Hornbeck, 27 November 1934; *FRUS, 1934,* 3:189–93; Hornbeck Papers, Box 454, memo of 16 November 1934; and *FRUS, 1935,* 3:829–37. Hornbeck singled out James Harvey Rogers's letter to Secretary of the Treasury Henry Morgenthau of 27 October 1934 for particular criticism. Rogers had argued that Japan was too frail to consider sustained competition in naval arms with America. See DF 894.51/452, Hornbeck memo of 7 November 1934.

in Asia and increased arms expenditures with its demand for recognized naval parity. Although he hoped that Grew was right, that Japan soon would return to the conference table, he was determined not to compromise American principles. Roosevelt agreed. Nothing had shaken his belief that Japan was economically frail and could sustain no ambitious programs, neither territorial nor naval. Rather than sign an agreement in 1934 that domestic political opponents might label a failure, Roosevelt postponed any new naval accord.[28]

These views were typical of American misconceptions about the fundamentals of Japanese foreign policy. The Japanese fully realized that they could not win a naval race with the United States, particularly after hostilities commenced. Their admirals therefore maintained that, for security's sake, a large fleet was essential before hostilities began. Americans, apart from Hornbeck, thought that Japan, because it could not win a race against the richest nation on earth, would not make the attempt. More important, Japan had seized Manchuria by force when leading army officers became convinced that the region's economic value was too great to relinquish to the uncertainties of Chinese control. The American government was certain that Manchuria's seizure had been perpetrated by irrational men and that its absorption was sure to ruin Japanese finances.

In brief, Japanese economic staffers and their superiors in Tokyo labored to make Japan autarkic and thus secure from the threat of economic disruption by other nations. Americans, living in a country made self-sufficient by history, viewed with skepticism these Japanese efforts to march against "natural economic forces." No sane country, in Washington's view, would seriously pursue autarky against such odds and with such high stakes. Japan, by these Western lights, was an insane nation. Meanwhile America, in the eyes of the Japanese, had affronted their country as they attempted to secure its very survival, and it had done so over trivial matters of (Western) international law and (Western) standards of morality. It was not a relationship to foster mutual understanding.

28. Dorothy Borg, *The United States and the Far Eastern Crisis of 1933–1938* (Cambridge: Harvard University Press, 1964), 109–10; McCarty, 75–76; and Cordell Hull, *The Memoirs of Cordell Hull*, 2 vols. (New York: Macmillan, 1948), 1:281–89. For Roosevelt's belief that Japan could not compete in a naval race, see his letter to Norman Davis, 9 November 1934, Norman Davis Papers, Box 51.

[3]

Merging the Drives for Autarky and Reform

Plans for the total mobilization of Japan's economy for war could not ignore that economy in peace. In the 1930s the economy, like those of other powers, was wracked by the Great Depression. Although the skillful guidance of Finance Minister Takahashi Korekiyo mitigated the worst effects for much of Japan's industry, conditions throughout the decade in the farming and fishing villages far from Tokyo, Osaka, and Hiroshima were miserable. In 1934, for example, northeastern Honshū experienced genuine social panic. Suicide rates skyrocketed, and some peasants resorted to a traditional practice for relieving economic pressure by selling their daughters.[1]

At first observers tended to link this social distress to the rise in Japan of radical reform movements—usually on the Right. They pointed especially to the abortive coup d'état of 26 February 1936 as only the most conspicuous of efforts by young officers in the army, most of whom came from small agricultural communities, to effect social and political revolution in the island empire. In recent decades this view has fallen from favor; historians now eschew interpretations that stress such direct connections. Still, they concede that the coup was at least representative of a hostility toward liberalism and capitalism which pervaded the decade before Pearl Harbor.[2]

This hostility was real. It formed the basis in interwar Japan for an alliance between army officers and civilian bureaucrats. But the of-

1. *SWT*, 17:8.
2. See Ronald Dore, *Land Reform in Japan* (London: Oxford University Press, 1959), 116–25, and Ben-Ami Shillony, "Myth and Reality in Japan of the 1930s," in *Modern Japan*, ed. W. G. Beasley (Berkeley: University of California Press, 1975), 81–88.

ficers who forged the alliance held the ranks of lieutenant colonel and higher; they were hardly junior. And the bureaucrats with whom they allied often came from the Left, not the Right. The officers, in their drive to achieve autarky for Japan, and the bureaucrats, in their drive to reform Japan, found common cause.

If the military and bureaucrats were agents of this alliance, the Depression was its catalyst. Ruin provoked the belief that party government and traditional policies were unable to cope with immense new problems. This belief was hardly weakened by the ill-starred cabinets of Hamaguchi Yūkō and, after Hamaguchi's assassination, Wakatsuki Reijirō.[3] Hamaguchi and his finance minister, Inoue Junnosuke, had come to power in June 1929, and one of their first acts was to return Japan to the gold standard in early 1930—just as the Depression struck east Asia. As a result, gold and silver specie fled the country at a record rate. By the end of 1931 the Bank of Japan, the country's sole note-issuing body, had lost 60 percent of its entire specie reserves. The deflationary effects were enormous because, by the Convertible Bank Note Act of 1884, the amount of currency in circulation was directly proportional to reserves. Hit particularly hard were the prices of silk, cotton, and rice—all agricultural staples.[4]

Inoue, who retained his ministry when Wakatsuki formed his cabinet in late 1930, attempted to meet the situation with a policy of retrenchment. He hoped that reduced government expenditures, particularly by the army and navy, would restore confidence and an atmosphere conducive to recovery. He also intended to expand Japan's foreign trade (the prices of Japanese exports fell, of course, as a natural consequence of domestic deflation). But London's decision to leave the gold standard dealt Inoue's policy a sharp blow. Now British export prices declined rapidly, and renewed competition in shipping and textiles became intense. Under pressure, Wakatsuki proposed a cabinet shakeup, one that surely would have overthrown Inoue's financial policies. The finance minister refused to accept the idea, and the cabinet fell in December 1931, a victim more of the Depression than of its inability to come to terms with the army's operations in Manchuria. Inukai Tsuyoshi became premier and Takahashi Korekiyo the new finance minister.[5]

Takahashi's alternatives were relatively restricted. Right-wing pol-

---

3. Hamaguchi was shot in late 1930 and died in August 1931.

4. Laurence P. Dowd, "Japanese Foreign Exchange Policy, 1930–1940" (Ph.D. diss., University of Michigan, 1954), 28, 31–33, 35.

5. Dowd, 35–36, and Gordon M. Berger, *Parties out of Power in Japan, 1931–1941* (Princeton: Princeton University Press, 1977), 41.

iticians and military leaders alike opposed loans from the West to bolster the yen and reduce deflation. Nor was it likely that Western financiers would extend such loans, because Japan's excellent record in repaying past obligations was more than offset by the unsettled international situation after the occupation of Manchuria. Takahashi elected to continue recovery efforts by boosting exports, but unlike Inoue, he relied more on direct action by government than on allowing deflation to run its course.

Takahashi first acted to restrict the ruinous outflow of specie. The Capital Flight Prevention Law, put into effect in July 1932, ended most currency exchange transactions except by special permission of the Finance Ministry. The next spring brought an even stricter foreign exchange control law, which empowered the Bank of Japan, as the ministry's agent, to handle all foreign exchange affairs.

Takahashi also moved to increase exports. In March 1934 he secured the revision of the Industrial Association Law. Associations had been formed in 1931 to rationalize Japan's major industries in order to increase efficiency that would aid recovery and expansion. Now his revision allowed industry groups to regulate prices of goods to be exported and allocate export quotas on a per-factory basis. Markets were assigned, and an export duty, levied by the appropriate association, helped subsidize costly imports of raw materials.

The government also supported the mining of specie to provide direct relief for Japan's currency and balance-of-payments difficulties. Subsidies began in March 1932, and direct public aid to the mining companies soon followed. Two years later passage of the Gold Purchase Law gave the Finance Ministry absolute control over specie holdings in Japan. Silver smuggled from northern China to Japan and then to the United States also provided some assistance.[6]

Predictably, the results of these measures and others like them were mixed. Japan's heavy industries and mining firms, aided by governmental subsidies and increased military orders, increased production levels and profits, and their workers' wages rose rapidly as more skilled laborers were trained. But for Japan's older light industries, such as silk and cotton, even increased exports could bring no help to the small growers, spinners, and weavers. Indeed, a relative decline in wages was necessary to keep Japanese textile goods competitive on world markets. Worse, the export boom under Takahashi

6. Dowd, 38–39, 49, 63–65, 257–59. The silver purchase policy of America, doubtless to the amusement of some Kwantung Army officers, had not only encouraged the creation of the Hopei-Chahar Political Council but also helped finance Japan's continental activities.

led to friction with Chinese and Western producers. By the middle of the decade Japanese products faced many restrictions, both formal and informal. For the great majority of the islands' agricultural communities, Takahashi's programs brought scant relief.[7]

Those programs did, however, represent a new departure in the way the government approached social problems. Never before, save in wartime, had central control over Japan's economy been so strong. To men attempting to achieve autarky and reform, this was a trend to be encouraged.

The first major success came with the creation of the Cabinet Investigative Bureau (Chōsakyoku). By 1934, when Okada Keisuke formed his cabinet, conditions in the countryside, especially in northern Honshū, were appalling. The need for a new approach was evident. Although the Seiyūkai party controlled the Diet, the genrō Prince Saionji nevertheless felt that the times demanded a national unity, nonparty cabinet. Most Seiyūkai leaders flatly refused to cooperate with Okada's new government. But Okada greatly desired some Seiyūkai participation as he confronted the social crisis.

One way to obtain this participation was to create a new planning organ for an all-nation policy separate from the cabinet. There, in an atmosphere uncluttered by partisanship, new domestic policies could be considered. Dissident Seiyūkai politicians such as Tokonami Takejirō and Machida Chūji were indicating support for this step as early as September 1934. Members of the Okada cabinet, among them Foreign Minister Hirota Kōki and particularly Takahashi, also favored creating a council to "deliberate on the general mobilization of national resources" to combat the Depression. The research needed to weigh all possible alternatives required that a subordinate, investigative agency be established. By the following May these currents had combined to create the Cabinet Deliberative Council (Naikaku Shingikai) and its duty arm, the Cabinet Investigative Bureau.[8]

The Deliberative Council drew together leaders of the political and

---

7. Dowd, 301–3, 358–59; George C. Allen, *A Short Economic History of Modern Japan, 1867–1937*, new ed. (London: Allen & Unwin, 1972), 136–38, 150; and FES, 21 September 1934.

8. Berger, 55ff.; SWT, 17:6, 10; Harada Kumao, "The Saionji-Harada Memoirs," mimeo., International Legal Studies Library, Harvard Law School, entries of 30 December 1934, 3 May 1935, and 16 June 1935; and Ishiwata Sōtarō Denki Hensankai, ed., *Ishiwata Sōtarō* (Tokyo, 1954), 189. It is conceivable that Takahashi hoped to use the new agency as an instrument of budgetary control. He certainly wanted it, misguidedly, as a way to ensure that most of the Seiyūkai participated in the budget-making process, in order to commit that party to the result and, incidentally, silence its cries for increased military spending.

business worlds. Its charter members included former premier Saitō Makoto and Mitsui magnate Ikeda Seihin, as well as peers and career officials such as Aoki Nobumitsu and Izawa Takio. These men first had to choose a chairman for their Investigative Bureau. Takahashi suggested Baba Eiichi, one of his subordinates in the Finance Ministry and a man with strong views about the virtues of centralized economic planning. But Baba had obtained a seat on the council itself, and he declined. The position went to Yoshida Shigeru, a close friend of Okada's and the premier's top political aide.[9]

Just as the Deliberative Council was to weld the elites of Japan into a cohesive unit, so Yoshida's Investigative Bureau was to act as an instrument of interministerial cooperation at the lower, bureaucratic level. To do so, the bureau gathered representatives from every major civilian ministry and both military services. It was organized into five divisions: general, finance, industry, communications, and culture, each with an imposing agenda of problems to consider. These ranged from administrative reform to financial policy, from commercial and industrial problems to relief of the villages.

The last of these matters most concerned Yoshida. One of his first acts was to lure Matsui Haruo from his duties in the Resources Bureau to chair the bureau's General Affairs Division. Matsui had been working on the problems of price policy in (wartime) emergencies, but at the Investigative Bureau he spent most of his time creating the Northeast Development Bureau, an agricultural relief agency established in May 1936.[10]

This relief effort is a microcosm of the growing ties between economic reform and national security. To work with Matsui, Yoshida gathered men such as Minami Iwao, who had traveled to Germany in 1934 to study the Nazis' labor relief policies, and another recent college graduate named Sata, who had worked with staffers of the Army General Staff examining the Soviet Union's five-year plans. He had concentrated on the transition of an economy from light to heavy industry with a minimum of dislocation and disturbance.[11]

When these men considered the problem of long-term relief for Japan's northeast, they quickly concluded that the region's difficulties stemmed from its overreliance on agriculture. They had to encourage diversification and industrialization actively. To this end, Matsui's group proposed a wide variety of operations—all of them with obvious implications for national defense.

9. *SWT*, 17:10–12. Yoshida should not be confused with his namesake who served in the Foreign Ministry and became a well-known postwar prime minister.
10. *SWT*, 17:82–85, 99–100, 14, 18, 132.
11. *SWT*, 17:43.

The first step was the creation in May 1936, by special law, of the Northeast Development Bureau. This holding company had capital authorized at thirty million yen and the power to finance smaller operations as it saw fit. These operations would soon include a plant to extract magnesium from seawater in Yamagata Prefecture and, in conjunction with Japanese firms in Manchuria such as the Shōwa Electric Works (firms that were themselves often sponsored by the Kwantung Army), electric-powered factories to manufacture aluminum in Fukushima. Matsui's division inside the Investigative Bureau, with the enthusiastic support of its military members, also favored enterprises to produce gas from the northeast's lignite and iron from its iron sand. Another project, with less apparent but quite real applications to Japan's economic security, was the conversion of the region's large potato crop into alcohol.[12]

A bureau group under Ishiwata Sōtarō had observed that an admixture of alcohol with gasoline could dramatically reduce Japan's dependence on imported petroleum and provide welcome domestic employment at the same time. France and Germany had already implemented similar programs, with gratifying results. At a conference on the use of alcohol as fuel in early June 1936, Ishiwata presented his bureau's findings and proposals to representatives from the Resources Bureau, the ministries of Finance, Overseas Affairs, Agriculture and Forestry, and Commerce and Industry, and both military services. As Ishiwata stressed, the potatoes of the northeast were one possibility, but the chief source of alcohol was likely to be sugar-cane production in Taiwan. That island's production of 150,000 *seki* of sugar (one seki equals 0.18 kiloliters) per year could, with some difficulty, be doubled to yield greatly increased quantities of alcohol for fuel.[13]

---

12. SWT, 17:133–34, 137–39.

13. SWT, 17:169. The group also surveyed the possibility of electric cars, but adequate battery capacity was a problem, particularly for large vehicles such as busses and naval submarines: the navy had much interest in the work of the Investigative Bureau as well.

Debate immediately erupted over the alcohol-as-fuel proposals. The chief of Commerce and Industry's Fuel Section complained that any admixture plans should be integrated with his ministry's overall direction of fuel policy. Agriculture and Forestry pointed out that at present gasoline was cheaper to buy than alcohol would be to make; Ishiwata's plan would need subsidies. Overseas Affairs, with jurisdiction over Taiwan, demanded that these subsidies go toward encouraging the cultivation of cane. Agriculture and Forestry insisted that the northeastern potato-growing regions ought to receive the money. Others proposed as a way out of the dilemma that the government purchase sugar at a supported price instead of subsidizing production directly. But unauthorized imports of sugar to take advantage of such a price would relieve neither Japan's dependence on foreign fuel nor unemployment. The entire discussion dis-

It was through mobilization-oriented personnel from the Resources Bureau, such as Matsui, and through direct involvement in the Investigative Bureau and its projects, such as the alcohol-as-fuel program, that the army scored its first successes in integrating the drives for autarky and reform. These were soon followed by more. No man was more responsible for this successful merger than Colonel Suzuki Teiichi.

In the army Suzuki had a reputation as a bookworm. He had followed the ideas of one of Japan's foremost Marxist scholars, Kawakami Hajime, during and after World War I, and this interest led Suzuki to study economics, a study capped by a year's service in the Finance Ministry in 1919. Suzuki's concern with economic and social reform had not waned as his career in the army progressed. Throughout the twenties he was a leading figure in efforts to renovate the army, and he worked closely with Nagata Tetsuzan in the Issekikai and other reform societies. Later, in October 1934, when the Army Ministry under Hayashi and Nagata had issued the pamphlet on fundamental principles of national defense, Suzuki headed the ministry's Newspaper Group. He had ensured that the pamphlet included ideals popular with Araki's wing of the army, such as popular fitness, as well as Nagata's emphasis on developments in technology and weaponry.

By the mid-thirties Suzuki was one of the very few middle-echelon officers who could move with ease both in Araki's and Obata's circles—including the "young officers" who followed Araki—and in those of Nagata and his total war associates. In fact it was Nagata, a close friend of Yoshida Shigeru before being murdered in August 1935, who had engineered Suzuki's appointment to the Investigative Bureau as the army's first and leading representative.[14]

Before his death Nagata had given Suzuki three tasks for the Inves-

---

pleased the Imperial Navy. The real problem, it argued, was proper allocation of the limited funds available for actual research and development of the various alternatives for an overall fuel policy. Why should alcohol admixture necessarily receive priority over, for example, coal liquefaction, which yielded something a warship could burn? The army's delegate, Lieutenant Colonel Kagesa Sadaaki, was not worried about priorities. The goals of the Investigative Bureau's proposal deserved support; if the bureau's means brought relief to Japanese farmers, so much the better. But the objective was to render Japan self-sufficient in fuel. In the end the ministries agreed on a plan to encourage both potato and cane cultivation, providing subsidies and price adjustments as needed. See *SWT*, 17:167–68, 170–73, 181, 186–87.

14. *SWT*, 17:54–57, 60; Nihon Kindai Shiryō Kenkyūkai, ed., *Nihon Riku-Kaigun no seido, soshiki, jinji* (Tokyo: Tokyo Daigaku Shuppankai, 1971), 40; and Nihon Kindai Shiryō Kenkyūkai, ed., *Suzuki Teiichi-shi danwa sokkiroku*, 2 vols. (Tokyo, 1971), 1:55.

tigative Bureau. The first was to push for a national ministry of health.[15]

The army had long been interested in health issues, and events of the 1930s heightened its concern. Severe unemployment in Japan had led to a rapid increase in applications to the Imperial Army, but many prospective recruits failed their physical examinations. In time of need the army would need to draw on a large pool of manpower, and these men had to be healthy and robust. Nearly as unsettling were figures from the Manchurian Incident: two divisions had been dispatched to the continent and, although both had been rated first-line, illness rendered nearly five hundred men unfit for combat within weeks.[16]

Within the Japanese government only the lowly Hygiene Bureau of the Home Ministry supervised health policies. Suzuki and his service found this arrangement grossly inadequate. Using his post in the Investigative Bureau to make himself a liaison between ministries, Suzuki proposed that the government make full payments of medical expenses for Japanese subjects and centralize and nationalize the administration of all hospitals. Soon after, in the autumn of 1936, and with the strong endorsement of Koizumi Chikahiko, chief of the Army Ministry's Medical Affairs Bureau, Suzuki laid before the Investigative Bureau a comprehensive plan for a health ministry. Predictably, the Hygiene Bureau and its Home Ministry raised strong objections.

At first Suzuki encountered rough going. Prime Minister Hirota Kōki had gotten wind of his plans in late June and, already defending other controversial measures before the Diet, was in no mood to add to his legislative burden. Koizumi responded by negotiating directly and at length with his chief opponents in the Home Ministry. A satisfactory solution was reached by May 1937, but the Hayashi cabinet fell before it could consider the revised proposal.[17]

The new Konoe cabinent favored Suzuki's project, a stance that was hardly surprising—its slogan was *Fukushi Kokka*, which can be roughly rendered as "welfare state." The army pressed Konoe for rapid approval, and after some wrangling over the new body's name, the cabinet established the Kōsei-shō, Welfare Ministry, by resolution on 9 July 1937. The Diet sanctioned the move the next January. By that time the war with China was in full swing and the military tone

---

15. *Suzuki*, 1:82, and *SWT*, 17:60.
16. *SWT*, 17:213.
17. *SWT*, 17:216–17; *Suzuki*, 1:82–83.

of the new ministry more pronounced. As Hirose Kushimoto, a Home Ministry staffer transferred to Welfare, pointed out, "immediately after the China Incident, the ministry became absorbed in military-related work. Aid to the military, military hospitals, other health and labor problems—all our work ended up being based on the [National General] Mobilization Law." Suzuki had performed his first task well.[18]

His second, to nationalize Japan's electric power industry, proved more difficult. Suzuki maintained that nationalization, like a health ministry, could serve relief and mobilization at the same time. Something along the lines of America's Tennessee Valley Authority, he argued, could provide cheap electric power to Japan's depressed areas. Public control would ensure that, in time of war or emergency, the appropriate military industries could get power in ample amounts.[19]

This reasoning won the enthusiastic support of members of the Investigative Bureau, who had already worked on drafts of an electric power policy for the nation. The key man was Okumura Kiwao, who had been employed in Japan's infant electric industry during the twenties. After the establishment of Manchukuo in 1932 he had served as an adviser on communications policy to the Kwantung Army. In the spring of 1935 he returned to Japan, to join the Investigative Bureau.

Convinced that state control of electric power had worked well in Manchukuo, Okumura sought to repeat the pattern in Japan. By the end of 1935 he had completed a plan to form a single, national electric company under public control. Okumura took care to enlist the support of the minister of communications Tanomogi Keikichi, Deliberative Councillor Baba Eiichi, political leader Taki Masao, and, of course, Suzuki, who joined Okumura in preparing the plan's final version.

Suzuki's collaboration was ill advised. Tanomogi, who visited many political figures prior to the opening of the Seventieth Diet in December 1936, lobbied for the proposal as in the interests of Japan's defense. It was on exactly these grounds, however, that most Dietmen opposed it. Many believed that public control meant military control, and without attacking the merits of the proposal itself, they objected to the growing role of the army in traditionally civilian affairs. Okumura's and Suzuki's use of Article 27 of the Meiji Constitu-

18. *SWT*, 17:233–36, 238.
19. Hashikawa Bunzō, "Kakushin Kanryō," in *Kenryoku no shisō*, ed. Kamishima Jirō (Tokyo: Chikuma Shobō, 1965), 257–58.

tion confirmed their suspicions, for they were applying its provisions for abridging private ownership rights if the "public benefit" warranted in an alarmingly novel way. The Diet adjourned, and the Hirota cabinet fell without any favorable action.

The incoming Hayashi cabinet was too short-lived to submit any program of its own to the Diet, but Okumura continued work on his proposal. This time he found help from Nagai Ryūtarō, the new minister of communications in Konoe's first cabinet, and Suzuki remained discreetly in the background. The revised Okumura-Nagai draft offered some concessions to the private companies. These steps, combined with the outbreak of war with China in mid-1937, ensured the plan's approval by the Seventy-third Diet in the spring of 1938.[20]

Suzuki's third task brought him close to another of Nagata's total war "godsons," Ishiwara Kanji. By the summer of 1935, as Suzuki was joining the Investigative Bureau, Ishiwara had commenced work on a colossal plan to expand production. He was certain that the mammoth increases envisioned in the plan would make an unprecedented degree of central planning necessary to implement it. The Investigative Bureau was a natural choice to lead in the effort, and the civilian members of that bureau found much common ground with the mobilization planners of the army regarding an expansion of the powers of their agency.

From its very creation, the Investigative Bureau sought to take charge of every major national policy. Many of its members, such as Minami Iwao, who advocated a uniquely Japanese "family fascism," and Wada Hiroo, a disciple of "agriculturism," were convinced that only far-reaching reforms could save their country. The present governing system was incapable of embracing these reforms; fundamental administrative reform was in order.[21]

To this end, on 25 August 1936 the Investigative Bureau completed work on an ambitious set of proposals. As a first step, the less important cabinet ministers were to be demoted to departmental chiefs and stripped of cabinet rank. The Investigative Bureau would coordinate all cabinet policy, including ministry budgets to be sent to the Diet for approval. The expanded bureau then could proceed toward "Strengthening Control of Industry," as a long section of its August proposal was titled, its goal to achieve self-sufficiency in the production of liquid fuel, iron, steel, aircraft, and ships.[22]

20. Ibid., 258–59, 261–62, 266.
21. *SWT*, 17:79–80, 157–58, 187–88, 199–205.
22. Takahashi Kamekichi, "The Fiscal Policy of Finance Minister Dr. Baba," *Contemporary Japan* 5 (June 1936), 25–34, and *SWT*, 17:266–67.

[73]

The Investigative Bureau's proposals had a distinctly martial ring to them. During the spring and summer of 1936 the bureau greatly increased its ties with the strongly military Resources Bureau, which had direct charge of Japan's mobilization program. The Resources Bureau had submitted a proposal of its own, "Measures Particularly Needed in Order to Establish a Basis for Mobilization," to the cabinet in July.

These measures listed mobilization goals and the means to reach them in fields such as industry, commerce, electric power, propaganda, even food policy. One common theme appeared in every field. "We must establish," the proposal read, "a powerful central organ to form and execute a policy of promoting natural and synthetic fuel production." And "there is a need for a Science Research Bureau to devise means to correct deficiencies of natural resources" by coordinating all research, private and public, in Japan. "We must plan for a stronger unity of administration in all trade matters." Naturally, the controlling organs would themselves be coordinated, by a whole-nation policy body. It was unclear whether this body was to be an expanded resources bureau, a greater investigative bureau, or an amalgamation of the two.[23]

Ishiwara, leader of the army's drive for autarky, and Yoshida Shigeru, head of the Investigative Bureau, strongly endorsed these twin proposals. But the ideas engendered even more misgivings among cabinet ministers than the huge production expansion plan had done. Prime Minister Hirota in effect tabled the production and administrative reform plans by creating ad hoc committees of ministers to study them. And before these studies were complete, Hirota had been replaced by Hayashi Senjurō.[24]

In the end the link between production expansion and administrative reform led to reform's success. Under the new premier, the production expansion plan received the cabinet's blessing. But it still had to go before the Diet. The ministers agreed to establish a new, cabinet-level body to polish and present the plan. As a result, on 14 May 1937, the Investigative Bureau became the Cabinet Planning Office.

From the outset, the Planning Office enjoyed more power than its predecessor. The establishing directive ordered the office to research

23. Ishigawa Junkichi, comp., *Kokka sōdōin-shi: Shiryōhen*, 6 vols. (Tokyo: Kiyomizu Insatsujo, 1975–76), 1:61ff.

24. *SWT*, 17:266–67; Baba Tsunego, "Hirota's 'Renovation' Plans," *Contemporary Japan* 5 (September 1936), 166–77; and Saionji-Harada Memoirs, entry of 14 October 1936. Harada spoke with Hirota on 2 October.

and draft programs of wide-ranging national policy, beginning with the five-year plan to expand production. The office was also to review the important policy proposals that each ministry presented at cabinet meetings, attaching comments from the standpoint of overall national priorities. The Planning Office's first president underscored this latter power; he was Yūki Toyotarō, who concurrently held the finance portfolio.[25]

The influence of the Cabinet Planning Office increased further under the first cabinet of Prince Konoe Fumimaro, who came to power in June 1937. Konoe had already indicated his approval for a strong agency to unify national policy, perhaps one with true, formal executive powers. But who should lead it? Army Minister Sugiyama Gen and his service pushed vigorously for Baba Eiichi, who as finance minister under Hirota had favored rapid increases in military-related spending, as chief of the Planning Office and the Finance Ministry. But Baba had also moved to raise taxes and impose drastic restrictions on foreign exchange transactions to support those increases. He was unacceptable to finance bureaucrats Kaya Okinori and Yoshino Shinji.

Appointments to the Planning Office were far from a defeat for Sugiyama, however. Many of the new men, such as Wada Kōsaku, came from advisory positions in Manchukuo or had worked directly for the South Manchurian Railway Company. They concentrated on the final details of the production expansion plan and on integrating that plan with a similar five-year program already under way in Manchukuo. The plan would be presented to a special session of the Diet, to meet in late July 1937.[26]

The merged drives for autarky and reform had come a long way by mid-1937. Mid-level officers and civilian renovationist bureaucrats had forged powerful new controls over the peacetime Japanese economy. They had commenced relief programs that produced materials useful to defense. They had created and staffed an agency to oversee all national policies and saw it elevated to cabinet status. Moreover, they were to present Ishiwara's much-desired production expansion plan—a plan to make Japan truly self-sufficient—to the Diet for final approval. This coalition of officers for autarky and bureaucrats for reform had proved strong enough to set Japan on a course for true self-sufficiency in the long run. But in the short run the coalition

25. *SWT*, 17:275–76, and Takahashi, 25–34.
26. *SWT*, 17:313–14, 334; Saionji-Harada Memoirs, entries of 4 December 1935 and 9 June 1937; and Ishiwata Sōtarō, 215–16.

proved utterly unable to meet the challenges of the China Incident in July, challenges that would fatally cripple the drive to autarky of Ishiwara and the true total war officers. The incident provoked a perverted search for self-sufficiency which would lead ultimately to war with the West and ruin for Japan.

[4]

The Road to Ruin:
Japan Begins the China Incident

The total war officers, led by Ishiwara in the General Staff and Suzuki in the Cabinet Investigative Bureau, were gratified by their success in forging a coalition at home. But they realized that a second success—peace abroad—was equally important for achieving self-sufficiency. Peace had been jeopardized in late 1935 by the dramatic increase in friction with China. Hopes raised by Chiang Kai-shek's favorable response to Hirota's Three Principles had subsequently been dashed by the silver crisis and the creation of Japanese-dominated autonomous units in north China. Ishiwara and his fellow-advocates of autarky had employed their growing influence within the Imperial Army to calm the situation. They had created a new North China Army to ensure that the Kwantung Army would not even retain operational control over units south of the Great Wall. And they had transferred the two officers most closely identified with a forward policy, Tada and Doihara, out of China—men closer to Ishiwara's views on the need for peace replaced them.[1]

In Tokyo, Ishiwara's own War Leadership Section reinforced this caution in a fundamental reexamination of Japan's China policy completed by early September 1936. The study singled out northern China as an area where Japanese plots and intrigues had to stop. If Japan was to create a self-defense sphere in East Asia, the peoples of that region had to be enticed, not coerced, into cooperation.[2] Nor had Ishiwara and his Operations Division, engaged in the annual routine

---

1. GDS8, 372–73, and Shimada Toshihiko, Introduction to GDS8, liv.
2. DR1, 422.

[77]

of drafting an operations plan for China, forgotten the growth of Soviet power in northeast Asia. It would be vital to occupy the five provinces of north China if hostilities arose,[3] but the new operations plan explicitly stated that under no circumstances would the geographical scope of any conflict be enlarged.[4] Ideally, China would be persuaded not to intervene at all in any clash with Moscow.

Ironically the first challenge to the China policy of the total war officers came from the Imperial Navy. Chinese violence against Japanese subjects had smoldered through the mid-decade. Assaults on the empire's dignity were generally handled by local Chinese and Japanese authorities and settled quickly. But when they spread to the coastal city of Pakhoi, on 3 September 1936, the navy elected to use the provocation to further its demands for a southward advance of Japanese influence and an expanded role (and budget) for the fleet. Six days after the incident started, the Naval General Staff resolved that armed force was necessary in south China absolutely, in north and central China if conditions warranted. The navy proposed to seize Hainan as a base of operations. In a series of four ministers' conferences to consider the situation, Navy Minister Nagano Osami proposed an equally bold step: issuing an ultimatum to Chiang to demand far-reaching concessions.

Army leaders were horrified at the thought. The General Staff and Vice Army Minister Umezu Yoshijirō played for time, Umezu by arguing that his service could consent to no interministry policies before his minister, Terauchi Hisaichi, returned from a tour of military installations in Hokkaidō. Ishiwara himself visited the chief of the First Section of the Naval General Staff to convey the army's opposition to any war with China. Hawkish navy officers backed down, but not without securing the army's pledge of troops in the event of further disturbances in areas of central China where the navy had responsibility for maintaining order. The promise would return to plague Ishiwara and his total war officers within a few months.[5]

3. Shanghai also would be occupied.
4. *DR1*, 412.
5. *DR1*, 417–20; *GDS8*, 216; and Shimada, xlvi. Admiral Suetsugu Nobumasa was particularly eager to provoke a crisis. Aware that any clash with China would antagonize Britain and the United States, Suetsugu proposed to "blitz" China and prepare instantly for strikes against those Western powers. One draft composed during the incident even included the numbers and types of shells and other ordnance for operations against China and the Anglo-American navies, as well as a detailed study of precisely what the phrase "war preparations" against them meant. See *GDS8*, 223–24. Information concerning Chiang's November invitation to the British to occupy Hainan can be found in Stephen L. Endicott, *Diplomacy and Enterprise* (Vancouver: University of

The next challenge to Ishiwara's quiet policy came from inside his own service. In September 1935 the Kwantung Army had begun training Mongolian forces in Manchuria to "liberate" Inner Mongolia, specifically Suiyuan Province. When the shakeups of early 1936 prevented activities toward the south, it had turned its attention westward. In October, supported by Kwantung Army aircraft, secret funds, and hurriedly raised irregular units, the Mongolian prince Teh led fifteen thousand troops into Suiyuan.

Ishiwara, tipped off by the assistant military attaché in Peking, went to Dairen to spike the action himself but arrived a few days too late to do so. Infuriated, he raged at the Kwantung Army's leaders. To make matters worse, the Chinese defeated Teh decisively at Pailingmiao. Nationalistic fervor surged throughout China, nor was it confined to the ordinary Chinese. Chiang, who had anxiously resumed talks with Japan in the wake of the Pakhoi crisis, at once ended them. Soon after came the Sian Incident.[6]

The Sian Incident was a product of forces that had been gathering momentum since the spring of 1936. General Chang Hsueh-liang, victim of the Kwantung Army during the Manchurian Incident, and his army had been transferred to China's northwest at virtually the same time that the Chinese Communists were ending their Long March in northern Shensi. There Chang became increasingly receptive to the Communists' United Front movement; he met Chou En-lai in Yenan in May 1936. Alarmed by signs that Chiang Kai-shek was listening to stern Japanese terms after the Pakhoi affair and disturbed by the Mongols' acceptance of Japanese aid and advisers,[7] Chang asked Chiang to allow him to use his own Tungpei Army, based in Sian, against the Japanese in Suiyuan. The request angered the generalissimo, who journeyed to Sian to set matters aright. There Chiang reprimanded Chang and the other northern leaders, even threatening their authority by issuing instructions to their subordinates. Chang responded by arresting the Nationalist leader and demanding that the generalissimo's anticommunist campaign be abandoned in favor

---

British Columbia Press, 1975), 138–39. Details on the army-navy accord after Pakhoi appear in James W. Morley, ed., *The China Quagmire* (New York: Columbia University Press, 1983), 453–54n.

6. Morley, *Quagmire*, 212–24; James B. Crowley, *Japan's Quest for Autonomy* (Princeton: Princeton University Press, 1966), 304, 306–8; and Mark R. Peattie, *Ishiwara Kanji and Japan's Confrontation with the West* (Princeton: Princeton University Press, 1975), 278–79.

7. Shimada Toshihiko, "Designs on North China, 1933–1937," in Morley, *Quagmire*, makes clear the great degree of responsibility of Chinese leaders for Mongol disaffection. See 214–17.

[79]

of joint operations with the Soviet Union against Japan. A series of talks assured Chang that Chiang was sincerely anti-Japanese and would act on these concerns. Released on Christmas Day 1936, Chiang returned to Nanking.[8]

Ishiwara and his disciples in the War Leadership Section of the Army General Staff had followed these developments closely. In a series of memoranda in early January 1937, section officers argued that Sian had strengthened Chinese unity and probably put an end to the Chinese civil war. They even held the daring position that Chinese unity was to be welcomed as a step on the road to a true East Asian union—daring because Japan would have to give up its attempts to render north China autonomous. Ishiwara's officers also encouraged closer links between Manchukuo and north China in agriculture and mining operations, as a natural consequence of any new Sino-Japanese relationship.[9]

These ideas found a warm reception in the General Staff's Operations Division. The division was increasingly preoccupied with a growing Soviet presence along Manchukuo's borders. Indeed, at the end of January it forwarded to the Army Ministry a memo recommending a cessation of efforts for north Chinese independence and renewed attempts to further Sino-Japanese economic cooperation.[10]

Wider developments within Japan also favored a reassessment of policy toward China. In March, General Hayashi Senjurō—the man who had returned Nagata, dean of the total war officers, to central headquarters three years earlier—became the new premier. His foreign minister, Satō Naotake, made relations with China a top priority in his opening address to the Diet. Satō pointedly criticized the nation's China policy as a major source of friction with the West. Tokyo, he said, had to treat Nanking fairly and observe the principles of the Open Door in north China—a stance that implied the end of the autonomy movement.[11]

Satō's speech undoubtedly pleased Ishiwara and his allies. But as had happened with the mammoth five-year plan to expand production, their ideas had moved too far and too fast for many other influential Japanese elites. In particular, few outside Ishiwara's circle were

8. Wu Tien-wei, *The Sian Incident* (Ann Arbor: University of Michigan, Center for Chinese Studies, 1976), 195–201, 205–6, and Crowley, *Quest*, 308. Upon his return to the capital Chiang declared Chang under arrest. Still, the Kuomintang-communist civil war was effectively suspended.

9. *GDS8*, 378–83.

10. *GDS8*, 384.

11. Crowley, *Quest*, 317–18.

willing to relinquish Japan's already considerable position in north China, even if they could have retained the economic ties.

One source of opposition remained the Imperial Navy. Ever mindful of the need to embellish the fleet's roles and missions in order to justify sharp increases in size, and fearing that the decisions of August 1936 might be discarded if Ishiwara's ascent continued, the navy complained that new forces were leading China into a dangerously close liaison with the West or the Soviet Union. China could not be abandoned to the enemies of Japan; anti-Japanese activities had to cease. Japanese advisers ought to be posted throughout the country, and the navy also wanted regional resource surveys in Shantung, Shansi, and Suiyuan—with an eye to eventual economic concessions.

But the navy lacked support again. Satō's Foreign Ministry study of 20 February maintained that Japanese political efforts in the north had led to complications in Sino-Japanese relations, even though it agreed that a firmly anticommunist, pro-Japanese zone in the northern China provinces was necessary, and the economic value of the area could not be ignored. The navy decided to back down once more on 25 February, at a conference of bureau, section, and division leaders of the Navy Ministry and Naval General Staff. The political operations envisioned in the August 1936 decisions had to be discontinued, it decided, the autonomy movement stopped.[12]

Still, these decisions, which received official sanction at a four ministers' conference on 16 April,[13] were hardly an unalloyed triumph for the views of Ishiwara and his War Leadership Section. To be sure, their central demand, an end to the autonomy movement, was realized. But it would be a mistake to see the mid-April decisions as evidence of genuine retrenchment. The existing East Hopei and Hopei-Chahar political bodies were not dissolved, and they would guarantee that the region would choose (at worst) benevolent neu-

---

12. *GDS8*, 385–87, 391, 394–96, 397–99. The navy's nightmare, that the August decisions authorizing increased force levels (and therefore naval construction) would be overturned, did not come to pass.

13. *GDS8*, 400–401. Specifically, Japan would take an impartial attitude toward the Chinese unification movement led by Chiang Kai-shek. But it would strive to compel China to renounce its policy of reliance on the West and to control propaganda directed against Japan. Tokyo would stress cultural and economic enterprises to avoid additional aggravations. But these enterprises would include China's employment of Japanese advisers, an air route between Shanghai and Fukuoka, and a reduction in Chinese tariffs. A separate decision affirmed that north China was to be kept as a pro-Japanese, anti-Red zone and its resources exploited to prepare for the communist menace. Japanese political intriguing there would be stopped, but economic projects would receive increased support.

trality in the event of a Soviet-Japanese war. More to the point, the grand program of the advocates of autarky itself demanded secure Japanese access to the resources of north China. The line between economic access and political dominance was never a very clear one, particularly to Chinese eyes. Indeed, Japanese pressure on local authorities to allow a rail line from Tientsin to Shihchiachuang, an attractive prospecting area, would be one ingredient in the Marco Polo Bridge Incident.[14]

Nevertheless, in the spring of 1937 there were high hopes in Tokyo for a new era in Sino-Japanese relations. On 20 March, Kodama Kenji, head of the Japan-China Trade Association, had departed for China, leading an economic mission. In large part his mission was the result of pressure from Army Minister Terauchi, who wanted something further to be done to assure access to Chinese resources and materials for the Japanese defense effort. As such, it was well within the guidelines of the imminent April decisions. The Chinese did express interest in some of Kodama's projects. But they had an imposing list of prerequisites, including an end to (Japanese-encouraged) smuggling out of eastern Hopei and the cessation of efforts to isolate the northern provinces from the central government. On 17 April, upon his return to Tokyo, Kodama relayed these demands formally to staffers in the Navy Ministry. He also noted the disturbing rise of pro-Western groups in China, buoyed by Chiang's preparations for military action—this time against the Japanese.[15]

Equally bad news reached the army. In early May its General Staff summoned key officers stationed on the mainland to Tokyo. They reported that the Chinese leader was actively arming and, in doing so, increasing his dependence on the West. There was even the grim possibility that he was readying to join the Soviets against Japan. In all likelihood, they judged, Chiang would continue his anti-Japanese stance until Manchukuo itself was returned.[16] June brought new information confirming China's stridency. Colonel Nagatsu Sahishige, chief of the China Section of the General Staff's Intelligence Division, returned to Tokyo on 8 June to report that the Kuomintang's New Life Movement was evolving; it was becoming a means to mobilize China totally as a militaristic state ready for action. Colonel Shibayama Kaneshirō, head of the Military Affairs Section in the Army

---

14. *GDS8*, 368–71.

15. Shimada, lviii; *GDS8*, 421–22; and Morley, *Quagmire*, 229. Before the Sian Incident, Chiang directed his military excursions against the Chinese Communists, his chief domestic rivals.

16. *DR1*, 425–26.

Ministry, noted the next day that Chiang had skillfully used anti-Japanism to advance Chinese national unity.

By early summer, then, the need to reassess Japan's relations with China once more, particularly in the northern provinces, seemed clear. The mid-April decisions, which had endorsed the maintenance of Japan's position in the north but through economic not political devices, had only strengthened China's will to challenge that position. Japn now had two alternatives. It could attempt to come to terms with the newly assertive Chinese by accepting the conditions that they had given to Kodama, which might include the dismantling of the collaborator regimes in the north. Or it might elect to cling to those regimes and the influence they represented, paying the price in greater tensions with Nanking.

A developing crisis in the area around Peking forced Tokyo to choose. Rumors that Japan's North China Army was planning some sort of punitive action prompted Ishiwara to send Shibayama, Colonel Okamoto Kiyotomi, and a Captain Imoto to the mainland. They were to admonish the North China Army's commanders against any rash moves and to investigate the situation.[17]

Okamoto found no plot, but his team did experience the explosive atmosphere in north China at first hand. Imoto, who observed Chinese forces personally, was nearly arrested while with compatriot Major Sakurai close to the Marco Polo Bridge. (The incident was especially embarrassing because Sakurai was military adviser to Chinese general Sung Che-yuan, chairman of the Hopei-Chahar Political Council.) Shibayama, for his part, learned that though Sung and other top leaders in his Twenty-ninth Army "understood" Japan, most middle- and lower-ranking officers were of a decidedly different disposition. These men were convinced that the reinforcement of Japan's Tientsin garrison and its upgrading to the North China Army—although Tokyo intended the moves to restrain the Kwantung Army's adventures south of the Great Wall—meant that a second Mukden lay around the corner. But the recent Chinese victory in Suiyuan had instilled a belief in Sung's officers that this time they could fight and win. Sung himself had been under much pressure from Japan to allow construction of a Tientsin-Shihchiachuang railway. He had avoided the issue by cloistering himself in western Shantung since May; but he also allowed the Hopei-Chahar Political

17. Inoue Shinzō, "The North China Incident through the Lens of the Bureaucratic Politics Model," *Shakai Kagaku Janeru* no. 13 (1975), 140–41; *Gendaishi shiryō 12: Nitchū sensō 4* (Tokyo: Misuzu Shobō, 1966), 412; *SWT*, 16:60–61; and Peattie, 294, 294n.

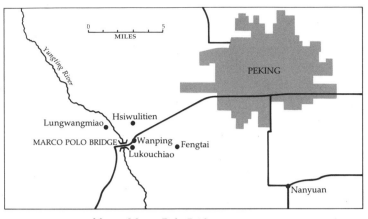

Map 2. Marco Polo Bridge area, 1937

Council, on 3 July, to demand that the North China Army henceforth give notice before performing maneuvers. The strings of collaboration were loosening.[18]

In Tokyo these developments were viewed with deepening apprehension. It appeared that the Chinese—if not Chiang himself, then at least substantial elements of Sung's forces—were embarking upon a serious initiative to reduce Japan's freedom of action in a highly sensitive region. The cabinet, now under Prime Minister Prince Konoe Fumimaro, met on 6 July to formulate a response. All agreed that the Chinese were up to something; Foreign Minister Hirota in particular was glum, forecasting little progress toward Sino-Japanese understanding. But the meeting did not reassess the ambivalent decisions of mid-April. Instead, Japan's leaders persisted in believing that they could maintain the country's position on the mainland—a position that Ishiwara and the total war officers held was essential to the realization of their national defense plans for Japan. They believed, moreover, that they could do so at no great cost—a belief that had disastrous consequences after Japanese and Chinese forces near the Marco Polo Bridge exchanged shots on 7 July 1937.[19]

Army headquarters greeted news of the skirmish with both suspicion and scorn. Colonel Mutō Akira, head of the Operations Section of the General Staff's Operations Division, wondered whether the incident was the opening round of an all-out offensive directed from

18. Inoue, 140–42, and *GDS8*, addendum.
19. *SWT*, 16:64, and *DR1*, 429.

[84]

Nanking. Would the Soviets enter the conflict later, to challenge Japan's entire position on the continent? In any event, the colonel held, it was imperative to nip the grand design in the bud by dispatching three divisions plus substantial air support to the Peking-Tientsin area. Mutō, who had been a section chief in the Kwantung Army before coming to Operations in Tokyo in March 1937, argued further: because both north China and Inner Mongolia had to be dealt with before anyone could consider operations against the Soviets, the present provided a good opportunity to resolve at last the nettlesome north China problem. Colonel Nagatsu of the China Section was optimistic that that problem could be solved easily. "If Japan mobilizes," he boasted, "we won't even have to debark [our troops] onto the continent."[20]

Army Minister Sugiyama Gen knew that a formal cabinet decision was required before any troops could be mobilized, much less dispatched to Peking. But he agreed with Mutō that, whether troops had to be landed or not, mobilization of three divisions was a wise step, one he duly proposed as the cabinet convened on 9 July. Navy Minister Yonai Mitsumasa was the first to object. He feared escalation and a consequent diversion of resources and material to the army. Hirota and Konoe agreed, anticipating international protests. The five ministers' conference that followed endorsed nonexpansion but wanted proper measures to be taken if the Chinese did not respond appropriately to Japanese restraint.[21]

The Chinese did not respond appropriately. General Ch'in Te-ch'un, commander of the Twenty-ninth Army in Sung's absence, agreed to withdraw his troops from the bridge. But Chiang exhorted Sung to hold his ground, declaring that he himself would send six divisions to the troubled area. The Kuomintang leader also insisted that he should review any local agreement, thereby ensuring that any settlement would have to address the delicate question of the future status of Hopei and Chahar provinces.[22]

On 10 July the Imperial Army's General Staff learned that elements of Chiang's Nationalist Army were marching toward Peking, apparently ready to violate the Umezu-Ho agreement that excluded them from northern China. Mutō and his allies, among them Colonel Tanaka Shin'ichi, chief of the Army Ministry's Military Duties Section (Gunjika), and personnel in the General Staff's own Intelligence Bu-

20. *DR1*, 429–30, 436.
21. Inoue, 150, 152–53, and *DR1*, 433.
22. Inoue, 154, and Crowley, *Quest*, 329.

reau, were certain that the Chinese meant to undo Japan's position on the continent. Mutō demanded that reinforcements from the Kwantung Army and the Korean Army be directed to Peking at once. If Chiang refused to restrain himself, three divisions and accompanying air support would have to be sent from Japan to cow—or to crush— the Nationalist challenge.[23]

These developments put Ishiwara and his total war officers in an awkward spot. Their five-year plan to expand production, the keystone of the attempt to achieve autarky, assumed full access to the resources of north China. Yet the completion of the plan also demanded five years of peace. Conflict over the northern provinces was certain to delay it.

This was a nice dilemma, one recognized most explicitly by Colonel Horiba Kazuo of Ishiwara's War Leadership Section. Mutō and his associates, Horiba maintained, had not faced up to the true character of the problem. If Japan intended to contest the Chinese initiative by force of arms, it had to take up Chiang's gauntlet properly: it meant war with Nanking, not just with Sung's local forces. Three divisions would not be enough. Horiba drafted a war leadership plan that put these assumptions into concrete form, calling not for a simple expedition to Peking but for conflict against the Nationalists which would last six months. At least fifteen divisions—one half of the Imperial Army's active strength—would be necessary. The campaign would cost 5.5 billion yen.[24]

Ishiwara recognized the cogency of Horiba's position, but as chief of the Operations Division, he was responsible for the safety of Japan's North China Army. Stung by Mutō's indignant "Aren't you taking a Japanese army for a Chinese one?" and under the impression that Chiang was indeed moving troops northward, Ishiwara advised Sugiyama to mobilize five divisions in Japan. Sugiyama contacted Konoe, who quickly agreed both to the move and to a meeting of the cabinet to approve it. Because troops were to be mobilized, the prime minister believed that a call for public support was also advisable.

Barely fourteen hours after approving mobilization, however, Ishiwara changed his mind. Now certain that the crisis could still be localized, he contacted Konoe directly—hardly standard procedure—

---

23. *DR1*, 434–35.

24. Inoue, 156, Hata Ikuhiko comments that Ishiwara at first believed that thirty divisions ought to be mobilized: six to be sent to China, five to held as a reserve in Japan, and nineteen for defense against the Soviets—a clear indication of his priorities that summer. See Hata's study in Morley, *Quagmire*, 454–55n.

and asked the premier to block mobilization by withholding consent at the five ministers' conference that was about to open. Ishiwara's cohorts in the Military Affairs Section, the Army Ministry's body in charge of developing the production expansion plan, appealed to their mid-level associates in the Foreign Ministry to have Hirota reject mobilization by the same maneuver. Most in the Foreign Ministry appeared sympathetic.[25]

But Ishiwara's superior was not. At the conference Sugiyama proposed that five divisions be mobilized in Japan and that the North China Army receive immediate reinforcements from Kwantung and Korea. Hirota said nothing; Konoe did not dissent. Yonai's objections were soon quashed when Sugiyama insisted that no action would jeopardize Japanese troops and civilians in north China and assured the other ministers that conflict would be confined to that area. The meeting ended with Finance Minister Kaya Okinori, relieved that Horiba's figures were not on the table, agreeing to help draft a supplemental budget. The full cabinet met and immediately ratified Sugiyama's plan, and Konoe then made a formal announcement calling for public support. Charging Sung's army with repeated, deliberate attacks on Japanese forces, he observed that Sung still was "reinforcing the front" and that Chiang's main forces were on the march.[26]

Hardly had Konoe finished speaking when word came that a local agreement had been reached in northern China. Ishiwara promptly suspended the mobilization order, although as chief of the Operations Division he did authorize the Kwantung and Korean armies to send assistance to Hashimoto's North China Army. Another five ministers' conference met, opening two hours before midnight on 11

25. Peattie, 297–98; Crowley, *Quest*, 330; and Inoue, 156–59. Mutō was certain that only 300 million, not 5.5 billion, yen would be required. Inoue writes that it was the Military Affairs Bureau (Gunmukyoku) that lobbied on Ishiwara's behalf, but it appears much more likely that it was the Military Affairs Section (Gunmuka), under Colonel Shibayama Kaneshirō. The section was assigned those officers chosen to work not only on the five-year production plan but also on other economic plans of interest to the Army Ministry and the Cabinet Investigative Bureau. It thus enjoyed a high concentration of total war officers.

26. Inoue, 159–61, and *DR1*, 437–39. Inoue speculates that Yonai might have been speaking for Konoe at the five ministers' conference. This is possible, but I lay greater stress on the navy's position itself. Yonai was concerned throughout the July debates with ensuring that if disturbances broke out in central and south China as a result of the army's actions in the north, then the army could and would provide land support in those areas—as it had promised to do in the wake of the Pakhoi Incident (see note 5; see also Hata's comments in Morley, *Quagmire*, 261).

July. There Sugiyama agreed that mobilization could be cancelled if the Chinese consented in writing to Japan's terms.[27]

Ishiwara and his total war officers hoped that these developments meant an end to the crisis. Their hope was ill-founded. The dispatch of additional troops to Peking from Manchuria and Korea scarcely reassured the Chinese, nor had Ishiwara's views won support in Tokyo. Many officers in the Army Ministry, including Sugiyama himself, now doubted the reliability of Sung and that of the Hopei-Chahar Political Council. The North China Army was ordered to deploy quietly for action—in case negotiations for a written accord broke down—by no later than the twentieth. In the meantime the General Staff's Intelligence Division continued to highlight news of continued skirmishings (some instigated by Sung's discontented juniors, others mere rumors, barren of truth) and the movement of Kuomintang forces to the north.[28]

Mutō and his allies used these reports and suspicions to bring pressure to bear on Ishiwara. Ishiwara reluctantly agreed to mobilization, but only if negotiations with the Chinese proved unsuccessful. Sugiyama then insisted on a deadline for those talks, preferably the nineteenth. Ishiwara stalled, hoping for favorable word from north China, but on the morning of the sixteenth he gave in. A five ministers' conference began several hours later. Sugiyama demanded that Sung apologize and sign the accord reached on the eleventh. The offending Chinese troops were to leave the area at once, and the irritating commander of the Thirty-seventh Division was to be removed. If the nineteenth came without compliance, Japan should break off talks and commence mobilization. Hirota, arguing that such measures might well lead to an unwelcome collision with Chiang's troops in the north, won Sugiyama's consent to a direct diplomatic approach to Nanking. But the conference, and the cabinet, approved the deadline and the demands.[29]

Ishiwara knew that time was short, but he was if anything more

27. Inoue, 161–62, and James B. Crowley, "A Reconsideration of the Marco Polo Bridge Incident," *Journal of Asian Studies* 22 (May 1963), 284.

28. Inoue Shinzō, "The North China Incident through the Lens of the Bureaucratic Politics Model," pt. 2, *Shakai Kagaku Janeru* no. 14 (1976), 95–98, 111n–12n. The Intelligence Division claimed that 400,000 troops were on the march. This number was plausible if one included all of Chiang's reasonably reliable units as well as quite a few others. But the intelligence estimate was wildly wrong for both the numbers in and the direction of the march.

29. Crowley, "Incident," 285; *DR1*, 445, 447–48; and Inoue, pt. 2, 101–2. There is some disagreement about the precise dating of these events. I have elected to follow the Boeichō's history and the Tokyo war crimes trial records instead of Inoue's account.

convinced than ever that a hard line invited disaster. "It will be what Spain was for Napoleon," he warned, "an endless bog." When he presented his draft of an operations plan to Sugiyama, Ishiwara observed that the force levels authorized by the decisions of the summer of 1936 did not yet exist. The Imperial Army could still field only thirty regular divisions. Of these, nineteen were committed to defending Manchukuo from the Soviets, and six more were needed for Japan's strategic reserve.[30] But fifteen would be required to defeat Chiang. Ishiwara at last came to grips with the dilemma of his drive for autarky: he declared himself ready to withdraw all Japanese forces to Shanhaikuan and north of the Great Wall. It would be better to develop Japan's economy in peace without sure access to the resources of north China, he argued, than to risk all in an immediate confrontation.[31]

Events on the continent unknown to Ishiwara, however, promised a quick end to the crisis. On the seventeenth Sung had attended the funeral of the former commander of the North China Army, General Tashiro Kan'ichirō. He had also ordered his forces to pull back, in near-open defiance of Chiang's demands that he prepare those troops for action. Sung apologized to the Japanese the next day. Hashimoto withheld news of the deadline, believing an end might soon be found to the affair. He was wrong. Chiang had made a bellicose address in Kuling, promising swift and stern action, and the speech was released on the nineteenth. Hashimoto was forced to make his deadline known to Sung with only two hours still left. Faced with an unhappy choice between Tokyo's and Nanking's displeasure, representatives of the hapless Sung signed Hashimoto's terms with an hour to spare. By the next day news of the formal signing reached Tokyo, and so did Hashimoto's arguments that the North China Army needed no reinforcement. On the basis of this new information Ishiwara once again stopped the mobilization.[32]

Other wheels continued to turn. Acting commander Hashimoto was relieved in due course by Katsuki Kiyoshi, depriving the forces of reconciliation of a powerful voice at the scene. Katsuki's first order sent the troops of his North China Army to jump-off points for operations around Wanping, as Mutō and Sugiyama had envisioned. On the other side General Hsiung Pin, vice-chief of the Chinese Central Army and Chiang's representative, arrived in Peking on the twenty-

30. Hata's figures are slightly different; see note 24.

31. *DR1*, 452, and Bōeichō, bōei kenshūjo, senshishitsu, *Shina Jihen rikugun sakusen 1: Shōwa 13-nen 1-gatsu made* (Tokyo: Asagumo Shinbunsha, 1975), 202.

32. Crowley, "Incident," 286–87, and Inoue, pt. 2, 107, 110.

second. Three days later fighting resumed. Soon after, officers of the Twenty-ninth Army declared themselves independent of Sung and denounced him as a collaborator.[33]

These events staggered Ishiwara. Apparently Sugiyama had been right about the unreliability of Sung and his army. At one o'clock in the morning on the twenty-sixth Ishiwara contacted Tanaka's Operations Section and, for the third time, authorized the immediate mobilization of three divisions. The cabinet met and sanctioned a polished operations plan. But it was Tanaka's plan that was sanctioned, not Ishiwara's, and it called for the use of three divisions in north China for only three months, at a cost of only 100 million yen. The army secured over 450,000 tons of civilian shipping on 28 July to support the expedition. So large a requisition promised to strain Japan's shipping capacity badly, jeopardizing the goals of the production expansion plan. Japan, with Premier Konoe Fumimaro in the van, thus decided to mortgage its empire's economic future to secure the rapid settlement of the Chinese crisis. The decision would doom both the plan and Japan's chances of achieving self-sufficiency without war against the West.[34]

33. Crowley, "Incident," 288, and *DR1*, 455–56.
34. Peattie, 303–4, and *DR1*, 457–58.

[5]

Bitter Mortgage: The Economic
Consequences of the China Incident

The Imperial Army commenced the China Incident in July 1937 with plans assuming that three divisions, three months, and 100 million yen would be sufficient to conclude the affair. Its troops would clear the Peking-Tientsin area, destroying the enemy's main force in the process, and then occupy key surrounding areas while Tokyo awaited for Chiang to sue for terms.[1] By the spring of 1938, however, though his capital of Nanking far to the south had been seized, the Chinese leader was still fighting. The Japanese General Staff found itself preparing new orders, readying the entire army for indefinite action. Twenty new divisions were to be raised on an emergency basis; over 2.5 billion yen had been appropriated for long-term hostilities, with the promise of more levies to come.

The China Incident had an equally serious impact on Japan's economy. In the early and middle thirties Japan had been nearly unique among the great powers in experiencing a strong recovery in its foreign, particularly its export, trade. By the spring of 1938, as a consequence of the China Incident, Japan's export industries were paralyzed. The nation's ability to import needed materials plummeted even as its real dependence on the West for war supplies increased. This economic deterioration powerfully affected Imperial foreign and defense policies. Even the army itself was forced to cancel offensives in China, because of material shortages. How had this occurred?

The first sign of trouble came from Shanghai. Since the end of 1936 the Kuomintang had been progressively infringing on truce terms

1. DR1, 462–63.

negotiated after the Shanghai Incident, by stationing ever larger numbers of troops inside the demilitarized zone established under the truce. The Japanese had remained circumspect until Lieutenant (j.g.) Ōyama Toshio was killed in Shanghai on 9 August. Third Fleet commander Vice-Admiral Hasegawa Kiyoshi promptly demanded that the Nationalists pull out of the truce zone. Back in Tokyo, Ishiwara Kanji, chief of the Army General Staff's Operations Division, who in July had opposed sending troops even to north China, considered the dispatch of forces to Shanghai to be out of the question. If the navy could not shoulder its responsibility and maintain order there, he held, it would be best to pull every Japanese national out of the city.[2]

Army Minister Sugiyama Gen ignored Ishiwara's advice once more. During the July debates Navy Minister Yonai Mitsumasa had asked repeatedly for assurances that the army would help if trouble spread beyond north China, specifically to Shanghai. Sugiyama had given no specific pledge, doubting that the occasion would arise—after all, the intelligence officers of the General Staff had been sure that Chiang's forces were heading north. But Sugiyama had no intention of allowing the navy to charge that his service was now shirking its responsibility. At a cabinet meeting on the tenth he agreed to begin preparations for an expedition should conditions continue to worsen.[3]

They did. By the fourteenth full-scale fighting was under way with the Chinese, in far greater numbers than anticipated. Hasegawa appealed for three army regiments to restore order, a request that the Naval General Staff raised to three divisions. At a hastily called cabinet meeting Sugiyama expressed doubts that such forces, virtually double the troop levels that his service had envisioned only weeks earlier, were necessary. But he deferred to his colleagues, Prime Minister Konoe Fumimaro, Foreign Minister Hirota Kōki, and Finance Minister Kaya Okinori, who united with navy representative Yonai in urging that troops be sent. On 15 August, as elements of the Third and Eleventh divisions prepared to sail for Shanghai, warships of the Imperial Navy shelled Nanking and other Chinese river and ocean ports. Chiang ordered all Nationalist units to mobilize and created a formal command structure. Escalation had begun.[4]

Many in Tokyo saw these developments as a blessing in disguise. An incautious navy, ever reluctant to see its rival service gain pub-

2. *DR1*, 464–65.
3. *DR1*, 465.
4. *DR1*, 465–67; James B. Crowley, *Japan's Quest for Autonomy* (Princeton: Princeton University Press, 1966), 344; and *RGD2*, 34.

licity, prestige, and funding, used the growing incident to justify an accelerated pace for its immense Third Replenishment Plan (sanctioned by the cabinet in August 1936 and commenced the following spring). The navy argued that the crisis not only demanded the speedier construction of new ships, but also warranted sharp increases in modernization programs and a significant enlargement of its air branch.[5]

The army was even more ambitious. Although Sugiyama did not believe Ishiwara's warning about an "endless bog," he was concerned about the possibility of Soviet intervention on China's behalf and, in any event, about the substantial increase in Soviet eastern forces since 1931. As insurance, the army decided to begin organizing twenty new "emergency" divisions. It gathered cadres of commissioned and noncommissioned officers for future expansion, an expansion already authorized—at least in part—by the force-level decisions of August 1936.[6]

As the total war officers feared, this increased effort threatened long-range plans for production expansion and autarky. Major Okada Kikusaburō, the key staffer in the Army Ministry's War Preparations Section (under the Equipment Bureau), was the first to spot the difficulty. Okada, who had served on the Resources Bureau, initially believed that the economic consequences of the China Incident could be minimized. As a result he assumed that materiel requirements would be far below those envisioned in existing army operations plans for war, which had assumed war with the Soviets. The problem, therefore, was straightforward: how to acquire what was needed for a sharp but short conflict.

The Shanghai expedition changed all this. In mid-August, Sugiyama directed the Equipment Bureau to establish materiel requirements for fifteen divisions in the field for a period of six months.[7] The army minister also asked if *gunju dōin*—a form of economic mobilization limited to factories producing goods for direct military use—was

5. Donald S. Detwiler and Charles B. Burdick, eds., *War in Asia and the Pacific, 1937–1945*, 15 vols. (New York: Garland, 1980), 2:31–32.

6. *RGD1*, 614.

7. By contrast, in July the army had directed the Resources Bureau to commence study of the requirements for the total mobilization of the empire's armed forces, principally in case the Soviets entered the fray unexpectedly. Specifically, the General Staff's operations planners wanted the bureau to estimate the amounts of various resources needed by a force of three divisions for six months. The study was to cover a wide range of materials, from steel to chromium, molybdenum, and other exotic alloy metals to iron scrap and machine tools, and the shipping to transport these materials and finished hardware. *RGD1*, 614, and *RGD2*, 27.

necessary. To this end Okada's section was to study whether the 1918 Munitions Industry Mobilization Law, which the Diet had amended specifically to exclude incidents, could be used to justify direct military control over the relevant plants. Okada was also to prepare proposals based on the drafts of legislation found in the Second Term Mobilization Plan for several new laws that would control the disposition of resources.[8]

It took Okada no time at all to conclude that gunju dōin was imperative. The material needs for fifteen-division effort demanded vastly increased output of all types of ordnance and related products. By 21 August, Sugiyama had approved Okada's recommendation for partial mobilization and his drafts of initial material requirements. The army minister turned to securing cabinet and Diet approval for these steps, and particularly for the new enabling legislation.[9]

He found little opposition in the cabinet. At a meeting held on the tenth, Navy Minister Yonai had consented to gunju dōin in exchange for army reinforcements for Shanghai. Konoe, who had become premier determined to forge consensus within his cabinet, calculated that the call for mobilization would ensure relatively easy passage through the Diet of the army's program for self-sufficiency and the renovationists' for reform.[10]

Indeed, for Konoe the timing could hardly have been better. In early June his cabinet had called for a special Diet session, to start on 23 July, to approve the spate of economic bills that made up the reform program. Events near the Marco Polo Bridge had done nothing to encourage postponement. From 23 July to 8 August the Seventy-first (Emergency) Diet met. It approved a supplemental budget totaling nearly 100 million yen and, far more important, a barrage of bills covering virtually every major sector of the Japanese economy. The Synthetic Oil Industry Law and Imperial Fuel Industry Corporation Law looked to create a "national policy company" that would help render Japan self-reliant in this vital resource. The Gold Industry Law was designed

8. *RGD2*, 33–35.

9. *RGD1*, 619, and *RGD2*, 38.

10. Gordon M. Berger, *Parties out of Power in Japan, 1931–1941* (Princeton: Princeton University Press, 1977), 121–22, and Yabe Teiji, *Konoe Fumimaro* (1952; Tokyo: Yomiuri Shinbunsha, 1976), 262–63. The navy had its own motives in consenting to gunju dōin. In addition to its urgings for immediate increases in ship construction, discussed earlier, it formed in mid-August a war preparations research committee to draft plans for protracted conflict, including any intervention by a third (maritime) power. From these plans came proposals over the next four years for further sharp increases in naval spending. What the army could do by raising the Soviet specter, the navy was determined to repeat in its own way for its own increases in allocations. Detwiler, 2:31–32.

to increase production of specie, which would earn the extra foreign exchange necessary to secure the imports required by the efforts to expand production. The Iron and Steel Industry Law—highly controversial during Hayashi's cabinet—was passed, providing for increased governmental regulation and, if need be, control over that key industry. A step toward direct control of foreign trade (as distinct from the control through exchange policy already adopted as a Depression recovery measure) was taken in the Trade and Related Industries Regulation Law. The Commerce Union Law allowed the government to supervise in each industry the cartels charged with organizing materials and markets. It also enabled the government to require companies to create and participate in such cartels. Existing cartels were to be scrutinized under the Industrial Combination Reform Law.[11]

Even so, these measures were not enough. The mid-August decision to send substantial reinforcements to Shanghai and Okada's recommendation for gunju dōin showed that Japan's mobilization needs would increase inescapably and astronomically. The expansionary economic policies begun in 1936, largely caused by increased military spending, had led to price inflation and a concomitant drop in Japanese exports and weakness in the yen. Moreover, it was apparent that, until the self-sufficiency program was completed, the overwhelming bulk of needed materials would have to be imported. But Japan, in no small part because of quiet pressure originating in Washington, could not borrow overseas.[12] The government would have to generate additional funds domestically, probably by floating large bond issues. To meet this need, the Seventy-second (Emergency) Diet met from 4 to 9 September, authorizing a supplemental expenditure of over two billion yen (three-quarters of it for the army). Combined with supplements passed earlier in the year, over 2.5 billion yen had been appropriated, even though the entire Japanese budget for fiscal year 1937–38 had initially been only 2.77 billion.[13]

Konoe and the military had reason to be pleased in other respects as well. The Diet allowed them to apply the 1918 Munitions Mobilization Law to the China Incident. An emergency export-import control law empowered the Ministry of Commerce and Industry rigidly to

11. *RGD2*, 29–30; Berger, 140–41; *RGD1*, 615; and Jerome B. Cohen, *Japan's Economy in War and Reconstruction* (Minneapolis: University of Minnesota Press, 1949), 14.

12. For an example of American discouragement of Japanese borrowing overseas, see Thomas W. Lamont to S. Sonoda, Yokohama Specie Bank, 10 March 1932, Lamont Papers.

13. *RGD1*, 621, and Berger, 140–41.

regulate precisely which goods could be imported (and exported); those destined for immediate military use received top priority. Imports of leading peacetime raw materials for industry, such as cotton, wool, wood, rubber and leather, were severely curtailed.[14] The Diet also enacted a capital control law to make certain that Japan's capital funds would be invested in war industries. Export industries, by contrast, were explicitly forbidden to expand plant capacity by investing new capital.[15]

It was a calculated gamble but an immense one. Japan meant to divert all of its resources to deal a decisive blow to China even as it commenced the huge five-year self-sufficiency program. In order to do so, its leaders had elected to starve not just the civilian consumer sector but also the export industries that were essential in order to earn the foreign exchange needed over the long run to finance that program. If they could end the fighting in China quickly and successfully, all would be well: exports could be resumed and the five-year plan supported. If not, however, Japan would find the payments on Konoe's mortgage bitter indeed.

The two emergency Diets had given the cabinet the tools necessary to enforce economic priorities. It remained to establish the governmental structure that would set those priorities.

This initiative was the army's. On 18 July, Sugiyama forwarded to the cabinet a proposal for a north China incident industrial mobilization committee, to be chaired by one of the Resources Bureau's top men. An informal working group held its first meeting on 4 August. All of the cabinet's vice-ministers attended; so did service chiefs and Matsui Haruo of the Resources Bureau.

To the dismay of the army, however, Matsui and Commander Toyoda Soemu of the navy's Military Affairs Bureau opposed both mobilization and the creation of a superagency to oversee it. Matsui prophetically argued that such a step would jeopardize progress on the five-year plan. Toyoda and his chief feared a diversion of re-

14. Further, the export of essential military articles, ranging from coal, fluorite, and steel alloys to cotton waste and rabbit fur was prohibited. And imports of such useful military-related items as nonferrous metals were closely monitored to ensure that the services got what they wanted. Nonessential foodstuffs and manufactured goods were banned altogether.

15. Cohen, 12–14; Yabe, 284–85; *RGD1*, 619–22; and Laurance P. Dowd, "Japanese Foreign Exchange Policy, 1930–1940" (Ph.D. diss., University of Michigan, 1953), 83–84, 93–94. Dowd exemplifies the Western misperception that Japan was attempting to gird itself for a long war with China in the autumn of 1937. He correctly narrates the exchange crisis that Japan's gamble on a short war led to, but his interpretation of the implications and causes is off the mark.

sources away from naval construction programs; their objections proved short-lived, however, because only a week later, after fighting broke out around Shanghai, the navy yielded. The China Incident Total Mobilization Committee was formed, reluctant Matsui at its head.[16]

The army was not satisfied, for it wanted something that would endure long after the bothersome, and brief, China Incident was over. Army section chiefs and their staffers took up residence in cabinet conference waiting rooms and harassed Kazami Akira, Konoe's chief secretary, urging him to put the matter of a permanent mobilization organ on the cabinet's agenda. Major General Yokoyama Isami, head of the Resources Bureau's Planning Division, visited Matsui to lobby for the creation of a total mobilization office.

These efforts paid off. On 18 September the cabinet consented to reform the Planning Office, which had been created only in May from the old Cabinet Investigative Bureau. Eleven days later Kazami asked for Matsui's advice on the change. Matsui, sympathetic to the long-range goal, agreed not to block creation of any new body. But, still steadfastly opposed to the China war, he vowed to resign in protest of the decision to use the agency to help prosecute hostilities. Soon after the cabinet resolved to merge the Planning Office and the Resources Bureau to form the Planning Board (Kikaku-in), which commenced operations on 25 October. Matsui resigned. Taki Masao, Konoe's Legislative Bureau chief and former professor of law at Kyoto University, became the board's first president.[17]

Taki's new agency had two pressing tasks. It had to draft capstone legislation that would control the Japanese economy and establish its future course.[18] The most important element in this effort promised to be Diet passage of the deferred five-year plan for production expansion and the National General Mobilization Law. Just as important was the need for the Planning Board rapidly to devise practical means by which to secure the economic requisites of military campaigns in China while building up Japan's longer-term industrial capacity.

In the summer and autumn of 1937 the task seemed easy. The board's antecedent committees and the military services themselves were all certain that the fighting in China would not last long. Indeed, the army's mobilization efforts in late 1937 were geared more to the

16. *RGD1*, 630, and *SWT*, 17:334.

17. *RGD1*, 630–31; *SWT*, 17:335–36; *RGD2*, 126; Berger, 155; and Chalmers Johnson, *MITI and the Japanese Miracle* (Stanford: Stanford University Press, 1982), 137.

18. Taki was chosen, presumably, because he had experience in drafting legislation.

long-haul effort to prepare against the Soviet Union than to combat Chiang Kai-shek. Constructing aircraft and armored and other ground vehicles, and obtaining fuel for those machines, were emphasized. As the army's own "Materials Mobilization Outline" of late August bluntly stated, "along with supplying operations in north China, it is our objective to be able to address the possibility of the Soviet Union entering the war." Other directives reveal that fighting on the mainland was not to touch Japan's oil stockpiles. Only local supplies, those on hand in the Shanghai and Hong Kong areas, would be used. For the balance of its short-term needs, Japan would temporarily increase imports of crude oil and aviation gasoline from the United States. Clearly this was not the planning of a military that envisaged prolonged war with China.[19]

For more general and longer-range requirements, the Planning Board began work on the 1938 materials mobilization plan. This document promised nothing less than the estimation of needs and the control of nearly a hundred key commodities. It would calculate the amounts of each good that the military and civilian sectors required for that year's consumption and for investment toward the goals of the five-year plan. Board planners would then decide how much Japan needed to import of each commodity. Once this was done, they could approximate import costs and attempt to square the figures with Japan's overall capacity to raise foreign exchange. Finally, the board could decide when necessary on substitutes or conservation. Aided by representatives from the services and the civilian ministries, on 24 December the board completed Japan's first report on the state of materials mobilization.[20]

By that time, however, the premises of that mobilization had changed radically. In late August, even after fighting had commenced around Shanghai, the Imperial Army had been certain that the incident would be over quickly. Once north China was forcefully pacified, Chiang would ask for terms, just as he had after the Manchurian Incident. The Shanghai clashes would be settled even more quickly than the month required in 1932.

These estimates were wrong for both regions. In the north the Kwantung Army at last escaped the chafing restrictions imposed in 1936. Its leaders and those of the North China Army, which had completed operations in the Peking-Tientsin area by the end of August, soon were calling for more troops; they wanted to push forward

---

19. *RGD2*, 39–43.

20. *RGD2*, 134–35, and Tanaka Shin'ichi, *Nihon sensō keizai hishi* (Tokyo: Conputa Eijisha, 1975), 21–22.

to Kalgan and on into Suiyuan Province, finally securing Man-
chukuo's southern flank. Ishiwara Kanji's Operations Division in
Tokyo stubbornly opposed this proposed escalation, ordering the
North China Army alone to prepare a minor probe southward in early
September. But that army objected, and the Kwantung Army (led,
ironically, by Ishiwara's old comrade-in-arms of 1931, Lieutenant
General Itagaki Seishirō and his Fifth Division) attacked westward
into Shansi. By late September the fighting was hard.

In Shanghai initial estimates were belied by Chiang's stubbornness.
The Nationalist leader committed his best, German-trained troops to
the struggle. This step, coupled with the acute shortage of ordnance,
particularly artillery, of the Japanese forces forced their commander
to appeal for reinforcement.[21] Ishiwara stoutly resisted, sure that this
newest escalation would doom his five-year plan and Japan's hopes
for self-sufficiency. His reward was prompt removal from the General
Staff. His successor, Major General Shimomura Sadamu,[22] quickly
agreed to divert three divisions from the north (two from north
China, one from Manchuria) and also to commit one of the newly-
formed "emergency" divisions from Japan. By the end of October
there were more Japanese troops around Shanghai than in north
China. On 4 November the Imperial Army landed forces at Hang-
chow Bay, and three days later it created the Central China Army to
seek out and destroy the core of Chiang's forces. Within a week the
Chinese leader was issuing orders to retreat.[23]

On 20 November both services and Konoe agreed to establish a
supreme command headquarters (Daihon'ei) to coordinate
operations.[24] The first order of business was to decide whether to
advance on Chiang's capital city of Nanking. There was little debate.

21. The commander was General Matsui Iwane.

22. Mark Peattie names Hashimoto Gun as Ishiwara's immediate successor. This is
incorrect. Hashimoto followed Shimomura, after the latter's illness, in January 1938,
not September 1937. Crowley, who puts Ishiwara's retirement in November 1937, is
wrong too. See Nihon Kindai Shiryō Kenkyūkai, ed., *Nihon Riku-Kaigun no seido, soshiki,
jinji* (Tokyo: Daigaku Shuppansha, 1971), 38, 57–58.

23. *DR1*, 489, 492–93, 500; Frank Dorn, *The Sino-Japanese War, 1937–1941* (New York:
Macmillan, 1974), 75–77; and Detwiler, 13:65–68.

24. The navy, wary that this was simply the latest bid to divert influence and materials to its rival, initially objected. But after receiving assurances that the headquarters
would not consider any matters outside the narrowly military "right of supreme command" (*tōsuiken*) and that each service would have its separate and coequal division in
that body, it relented. Konoe, displeased by the appearance that civilian cabinet members did not take part in war policy decisions, gave his blessing in exchange for the
simultaneous creation of a liaison body between top civilian ministers and the military.
Harada Kumao, "The Saionji-Harada Memoirs," mimeo., International Legal Studies

Ishiwara, who would have opposed this latest expansion of the war, was gone, and his brainchild, the War Leadership Section in the General Staff, had been abolished in late October. His replacement strongly believed in a Nanking expedition. The longer Japan waited, Shimomura argued, the more likely Soviet intervention became. Already too many troops had been diverted from Manchuria.[25]

Few other options presented themselves. In early November, Foreign Minister Hirota Kōki had indicated Japan's initial conditions for peace. Those terms reflected Japanese ambitions of long standing. They demanded the establishment of an autonomous regime in Inner Mongolia, a demilitarized zone in north China south of Peking and Tientsin, a larger (and more carefully observed) such zone around Shanghai, an end to Chinese anti-Japanism, and a guarantee of political and economic rights for Japanese subjects in China. Chiang replied by demanding a return to the status quo ante, which very few in Tokyo found acceptable. Nor did Konoe, riding high politically, reveal any desire to end his nation's military successes.[26]

There were other triumphs, too. By the close of 1937 Japan's North China Army had consolidated control over much of the five northern provinces. By mid-December, as Nanking fell, the provisional Chinese People's Federated Government was proclaimed. It had the active support of hardliner Colonel Tanaka Shin'ichi of the Japanese Army Ministry. In time, its sponsors hoped, the new regime might supplant Chiang's entirely.[27]

But well before then Japan would start to reap the economic rewards of the mainland. As early as 16 October the first plan to exploit the wealth of north China had been completed. Although a three-way struggle among the Kwantung Army, the South Manchuria Railway, and the North China Army lasted until February 1938, the final outcome mirrored the October study: a holding firm, based on the existing China Development Company, was to supervise various projects in the region.[28] By year's end the Planning Board had begun to incorporate north Chinese resources into its economic planning.[29]

These developments did not augur well for peace with Chiang. Nor

---

Library, Harvard Law School, entry of 18 November 1937; DR1, 495; and Kazami Akira, *Konoe naikaku* (Tokyo: Nihon Shuppan Kyōdō kabushiki kaisha, 1951), 51–53, 62–63.

25. *RGD2*, 135, 148, and *DR1*, 504–5.

26. *DR1*, 516–17, and Crowley, 355, 358.

27. *DR1*, 513–14, and George E. Taylor, *The Struggle for North China* (New York: Institute of Pacific Relations, 1940), 20–22.

28. Its first president, Ōtani Son'yū, left his post as Konoe's overseas affairs minister to operate it.

29. John H. Boyle, *China and Japan at War, 1937–1945: The Politics of Collaboration*

did Japan's last proposal of 1937, approved by the cabinet on 21 December. As well as making a wide array of substantial economic concessions to Japanese interests throughout China,[30] Chiang was to recognize Manchukuo and a regime in Inner Mongolia under Prince Teh. North China would be under nominal Chinese sovereignty, but actions there would be subject to a special economic organ cooperating closely with Japan and Manchukuo.[31]

In Tokyo, as 1938 began, Japan's future appeared promising. The Nanking expedition had been an unbounded military success, and steps were well under way to incorporate the riches of the mainland. Nevertheless, doubts had begun to surface, from no less a figure than Lieutenant General Tada Hayao, the army's vice-chief of staff. Economic officers inside and outside the army, less prominently but in the long run more decisively, also began to sound notes of alarm. All was not well.

Tada's concerns were strategic. In November he and a small group of officers who had consistently aligned themselves with the departed Ishiwara had opposed the Nanking campaign.[32] Already more than half of the army's available manpower was in China—a dangerous diversion from the chief threat to the north. Anyway, Tada argued, even Nanking's fall would probably not bring Chiang's surrender. Tada urged a negotiated solution, and he even cabled Ōshima Hiroshi, Japan's military attaché in Berlin, to propose German mediation.[33]

Equally alarming news came from economic planners within the army. Japan was unable to manufacture more than a fraction of the materiel and fuel it needed to continue the war against China. The nation was, in short, becoming more reliant on imports than ever before. Colonel Kawabe Torashirō warned that stores of ordnance in China were exhausted. Even the stocks in Japan furnished barely

---

(Stanford: Stanford University Press, 1972), 63–64, and George E. Taylor, *Japanese Sponsored Regimes in North China* (1939; New York: Garland, 1980), 105.

30. Japanese businesses in China were to receive substantial reductions in many Chinese levies—a significant commercial advantage, particularly for Japanese light industries moving in greater numbers to north China. The Chinese tariff was to be reduced for Japan's benefit. Air communications would be opened between the two nations and run by Tokyo's fiat. Japanese resource acquisition teams could roam the Chinese hinterland with first crack at any promising finds.

31. Crowley, 366, and *DR1*, 517–18.

32. These officers included Colonel Shibayama Kaneshirō, leader of the Army Ministry's Military Affairs Section, and Major General Hashimoto Gun, who succeeded the ailing Shimomura as Operations Division chief in January 1938.

33. *DR1*, 506–8, 528–31; Crowley, 357–58; Detwiler, 8: "Chinese Army Operations Record, July 1937–November 1941," 15; and Mark R. Peattie, *Ishiwara Kanji and Japan's Confrontation with the West* (Princeton: Princeton University Press, 1975), 305.

sufficient materiel for existing operations, and expanded efforts were impossible. If the Soviets entered the fray, the situation would quickly become critical. Kawabe held little hope for quick relief. Gunju dōin was proceeding slowly: thousands of workers would still have to be trained for positions in munitions and other military plants—even after those plants had been constructed. Until then a heavy reliance on foreign purchase of the finished products necessary to wage war was unpleasant and inevitable.[34]

Local fuel supplies in China had also been exhausted well before the end of 1937. The navy earmarked a substantial part of funds proffered by both emergency Diets to pay for pure 100 octane aviation gasoline, most of which came from America.[35] The total exceeded half of all Japanese imports of refined petroleum products in 1936, and demand seemed certain to grow.[36]

The army was in worse shape. It had only just begun its storage program in the autumn of 1936. One year later, as these stocks dried up with no end to the China fighting in sight, it was clear that the halting of imports of foreign oil would fatally cripple Japan.[37] Led by the army's economic staff officers, by the end of September the ministries of the Army, Commerce and Industry, and Finance had established a special company (with virtually compulsory private backing) devoted solely to importing and storing 800,000 metric tons of crude and fuel oil and smaller amounts of lighter distillates. By April 1938 the company had largely accomplished its goals, with no sign of American resistance to the large quantities involved (see Table 5.1). But the oil purchase, and an equally ambitious (and, again because of American tolerance, equally successful) program to import machine tools in vast quantities,[38] had a cost for Japan's dwindling reserves of foreign exchange that can only be described as horrific.[39]

34. *DR1*, 528–29.

35. Specifically, over a thousand kiloliters from the United States, three times the amount imported from refineries in the Netherlands East Indies.

36. *KG*, 699, and *RGD2*, 166. The army's 1936 storage plans called for a reserve of only 40,000 kiloliters, an amount judged adequate for several years. By the end of 1937 the army alone imported 150,000 kiloliters of aviation fuel from the United States for a single year. Detwiler, 3:27.

37. In this case it was clear to Colonel Hori Mitsuya, chief of the interministerial Fuel Bureau.

38. The dire shortage of machine tools, essential even for the limited step of gunju dōin, merited another crash program with an emergency mission to the United States led by Colonel Imamura Teiji, allotted 2.4 million yen. Japan produced 20 million yen worth of machine tools in 1936 and imported another 20 million yen worth that same year. Imamura's purchases alone exceeded 10 percent of the value of all machine tools produced in Japan during all of 1936. *RGD2*, 80.

39. *RGD2*, 80, and *KG*, 707–8. Hori reasoned that a corporation's orders for such

Table 5.1. Objectives and April 1938 results of Hori's crash import program of petroleum products (in metric tons)

Product	Import Objective	Actual imports
Aviation gasoline	20,000	0
Crude oil refinable to aviation gasoline	223,000	283,881
Crude oil refinable to regular gasoline	371,000	427,922

SOURCE: Bōeichō, bōei kenshūjo, senshishitsu, *Kaigun gunsembi* (Tokyo: Asagumo Shinbunsha, 1969), 708.

The impact of these large, ad hoc purchases and of the summer's decision drastically to curtail imports of nonessential, nonmilitary goods was felt first in the Planning Board's materials mobilization plan for 1938, completed on 24 December 1937. The findings were not encouraging. The board estimated that Japan's total import needs for 1938 would cost 4.1 billion yen. It projected only 2.6 billion yen of foreign exchange as available.[40] A range of measures was imperative to bridge the gap. Discarded goods would have to be recycled; existing stockpiles, at least in the civilian sector, could be depleted; and the people had to be spurred to produce more as they consumed less. If these steps were taken, and if exports yielding exchange could be increased, it might be possible to limit imports to 3 billion yen and to pay for them.

Neither attempt promised to be painless. Konoe's summer gamble—ending the incident with one immediate blow and paying for the effort later—had failed. Japan's import requirements had skyrocketed as the war dragged on, just as the gamble was strangling its export industries, which earned the foreign exchange necessary to carry the imports. In an implicit indictment of Konoe's policy the Planning Board proposed measures to encourage exports. These included the

---

huge amounts, if parceled out properly, would create less suspicion among foreign governments than direct military purchases. To the same end he forbade all publication of its purchases.

40. There was a good deal of squabbling over just how much exchange would be available for purchasing imports. In early January the Finance Ministry observed that the board's figure of 3,040 million yen was optimistic. The Bank of Tokyo agreed, putting available foreign exchange at 2,906 million; the Yokohama Specie Bank put the number even lower. Finance also complained that the board's draft included no plans to obtain investment capital to develop north and central China, a key long-range goal of the continental war—but one the board itself thought optimistic (see subsequent discussion in the text). The Planning Board can be accused, if of anything, of excessive optimism concerning Japan's economic position going into 1938. Ishigawa, 1:160–64.

usual subsidy programs but added much more, for example a formal link between exports and imports of raw materials. Purchases of raw cotton fiber from abroad would be allowed, for example, so long as they led to exports of cloth.[41] Even so, severe consumption economies were necessary. Members of the board were most concerned about shortages of steel. There overall usage would have to be reduced by nearly one-third; even the vital railroad industry had to absorb a 25 percent reduction in steel use, shipbuilding a 15 percent cut.[42] Nor was relief in sight for the longer term. Increases in domestic production were unlikely. The Planning Board doubted that north and central China, whose resources were incorporated into the mobilization plan, could be successfully developed for Japan's purposes in the foreseeable future. Indeed, it[43] concluded that even if Japan occupied all China and Southeast Asia, it would still find itself unable to wage a long war without relying on Anglo-American resources.[44]

Mounting evidence of the economic consequences of the first half-year of the China Incident should have led to renewed interest in terminating conflict. At the very least, Vice-Chief of Staff Tada might have used Japan's increasing inability to counter a growing Soviet presence in Northeast Asia in his struggle to do so. More fundamentally, the board's clear indications that Japan was growing more dependent on the West even as its actions against China increased friction with the West might have led to a basic reconsideration of Japanese foreign policy.

Neither happened. After Nanking fell, Tada again moved to stop the plunge toward a long war. This time Home Minister Suetsugu Nobumasa, a recent addition to the Konoe cabinet, led the counterattack. At a liaison conference of 10 January 1938 Suetsugu maintained that Chiang had shown no sincerity in negotiations since the incident began. In any event he was now reduced to the status of a local warlord, and his regime might collapse altogether. Other cabinet members agreed that chances for a diplomatic solution were slim. But Tada, still concentrating on the Soviet threat, insisted upon an imperial conference to confirm that negotiations were not to be discarded altogether. After the chief of the Naval General Staff, Admiral Prince

41. Ishigawa Junkichi, comp., *Kokka sōdōin-shi*, 6 vols. (Tokyo: Kiyomizu Insatsujo, 1975), 1:158–59, 159–60.
42. Tanaka, 23–25.
43. Actually, the board's Second Committee.
44. Ishigawa, 1:165–66, and Yamamura Katsurō, "The Role of the Finance Ministry," in *Pearl Harbor as History*, ed. Dorothy Borg and Shumpei Okamoto (New York: Columbia University Press, 1973), 297.

Fushimi Hiroyasu, agreed that a conference was necessary, Tada's opponents granted it to him.[45]

Konoe quickly rendered Tada's success nugatory. He advised court officials that because the cabinet (to which Tada did not belong) had decided its China policy, it would be best if the emperor ventured no awkward inquiries. So the Imperial Conference, the first since the Russo-Japanese War, was brief. Even the army chief of staff, General Prince Kan'in—Tada's immediate (if somewhat symbolic) superior—indicated that he concurred with cabinet policy. The emperor remained mute throughout, and Konoe's policy was reaffirmed.[46]

Tada did not give up at once, but his effort was futile. Navy Minister Yonai suggested that, if Tada could not agree with cabinet policy as sanctioned by the emperor, his resignation was in order. Tada even had Prince Kan'in ask for a direct meeting with the monarch, but this came to nothing as well.[47] Finally, after a stormy liaison conference on 15 January 1938, Tada relented and gave the General Staff's consent to a forward policy. One day later Konoe, in his famous *aite ni sezu* address, proclaimed that henceforth his government would deal with Chiang only on the battlefield and at the surrender table.[48]

This electrifying declaration was as much an instrument to obtain approval for sweeping reform legislation—as much a continuation of Konoe's gamble—as it was an indication of the end of patience with Chiang Kai-shek. When the Seventy-third Diet opened on 26 December 1937, the Konoe cabinet had readied eighty-six bills and a huge budget to make the Japanese Empire self-sustaining and reformed—as though the worrisome predictions of the Planning Board did not exist. The linchpin of this program was the national mobilization bill.

In late August, Konoe had considered setting such a bill before the emergency Seventy-second Diet. A modicum of political caution, and the reorganization of the Resources Bureau into the Planning Office, had delayed the move. In spirit the bill was far older, harking back to the Munitions Mobilization Law of 1918 and the work of the Resources Bureau since its creation in 1927. Its terms were breathtaking. All Japanese subjects would register their professional and technical

45. *DR1*, 506–8; Crowley, 367–69; and Yabe, 303–5.
46. Crowley, 370–72.
47. Crowley holds that the courtiers blocked Kan'in from ever seeing the emperor. Boyle, 79, writes that Tada himself was uncertain of the wisdom, constitutional and otherwise, of this attempt and that Kan'in had little stomach for it anyway.
48. Crowley, 374–75; Boyle, 80–81; and *DR1*, 526–27.

capabilities. The government could compel individuals to train, whether as electrical engineers or as boilermakers, in preparation for wartime needs. It could switch labor among or within industries to increase the production of desired materials. All industries, even if not military-related, were to form cartels to implement the government's economic plans. Furthermore, the regime could seize buildings and land at will for wartime production purposes, and it could order factories to expand facilities or ban expansion.[49]

Many Dietmen were willing to wage war and punish Chiang, but they saw little need for a bill of such scope. During the first days of February, when the bill was considered in the Diet's lower house, opposition built up quickly. Konoe did move to strike some particularly objectionable constitutional restrictions from the bill;[50] he also indicated that the bill's stiffer terms would not be invoked until the China Incident had been concluded. He then continued to push for its adoption.

The moves nearly backfired. The promise of deferment revealed that Konoe meant to use the patriotic fervor of the moment in order to obtain the enabling powers that would forward the long-term reform of Japan and autarky of the empire. One Dietman asked why, for the present conflict, the bill was needed at all. Others fed rumors of a new Ugaki-Ikeda cabinet that would pursue less unorthodox economic and foreign policies. Konoe reminded nobles at court that the army still found Ugaki unacceptable for the premiership. He reassured the Diet by offering to create a mobilization council, composed principally of Dietmen, to oversee the new law. Konoe also revived the threat of a national unity party that would put the others out of business, holding a "secret" cabinet meeting on 5 March to set tongues wagging. On 1 April the bill became the National General Mobilization Law.[51] Soon after a companion bill passed the Diet nationalizing control of electric power—the legacy of Okumura Kiwao and Suzuki Teiichi's cooperation in the Cabinet Investigative Bureau, two years earlier.[52]

The mobilization law had its difficulties, but in contrast the colossal budget for fiscal year 1938 (April 1938 to March 1939) sailed through

49. *RGD1*, 636; Berger, 149–51; *RGD2*, 150–57; and Yabe, 310–11.

50. These restrictions pertained to public assembly and media freedoms.

51. Yabe, 311–14; Berger, 151–57; *RGD2*, 145, 148; and Elizabeth B. Schumpeter, ed., *The Industrialization of Japan and Manchukuo, 1930–1940* (New York: Macmillan, 1940), 818–24. Berger is right in suspecting that Konoe conceded the noninvocation point quite early in the Diet's debates.

52. Berger, 158–60, and Yabe, 314–16.

the legislature. The previous year's allocation of 2.77 billion yen, even when supplemented by the 2.5 billion provided by the two emergency Diets, was dwarfed by a new proposal for 8.36 billion. Of this total, approximately 3.5 billion went to general budget expenses, leaving 4.86 billion for, in essence, military expenditures.[53] Over two billion went to the operational maintenance of troops in (or soon to be in) the field. Total revenues would not exceed three billion yen, and so public bonds were to finance the bulk of military expenditures and two-sevenths of the general budget. Despite the qualms that this plan created in high financial circles, the Diet passed the budget with few revisions.[54]

The plan also created qualms among true devotees of the pursuit of autarky. True, the Seventy-third Diet had enacted laws that Nagata, Ishiwara, and Suzuki had long sought. And the huge new budget included ample provisions for getting the production expansion plan under way. Still, they had much cause for doubt and disappointment.

Central were the debilitating effects of the ever-expanding China Incident. The total war officers—despite the label—had long realized that hostilities, particularly the lengthening ones with China, jeopardized their drive for self-sufficiency. War diverted huge amounts of resources for immediate consumption while causing friction with the West, and Western commodities were indispensable to the achievement of self-sufficiency. Time and again in mid-decade these officers had stood against adventurism on the continent. But by early 1938 their stand had resulted in the assassination of Nagata, the banishment of Ishiwara, and the departure of Suzuki from the inner circles of the General Staff. Other officers, such as Vice-Chief of Staff Tada, were less far-sighted but equally concerned about the drain of resources, because they saw the Soviet Union as the main threat to Japan. Tada too had failed to restrain by negotiation the expansion of the China Incident.

Even after his January defeat, however, Tada was determined to use his office's power to limit operations in China and to strengthen defenses in Manchuria. Near the end of the month the General Staff's Operations Section under Colonel Kawabe Torashirō drafted "War Leadership Plan, 1938." The document emphasized the need to prepare for war by 1941 at the latest against the Soviet Union. It was essential that Japan engage only in limited operations to pacify China, establish a new Chinese government to replace Chiang, bolster the

---

53. In addition to the standard budgets in general expenses.
54. *DR1*, 545.

defenses of Manchuria and Inner Mongolia, and maintain good relations with the United States.[55]

At first all went well. Tada transferred several divisions and independent units from central and north China to Manchuria. Other forces left the Yangtze Valley for Japan. The reduced commands that remained in central China were amalgamated into a Central China Army and ordered to stabilize areas already seized. In early March the North China Army received the same command.[56]

But the same constellation of forces that had blocked Tada's bid for negotiations with Chiang now thwarted his endeavor to limit the scope of hostilities. The Imperial Navy urged an attack up the Yangtze River to Anking. The Army Ministry, including Sugiyama, agreed, as did the army's field commanders. Within the General Staff, proponents of caution lost a key supporter when, as part of the regular March reshufflings of personnel, Kawabe was replaced by Lieutenant Colonel Inada Masazumi. Inada agreed that the China Incident was draining Japan's strength, but he wanted to end the fighting by eliminating Chiang's regime.[57]

Even the Chinese proved uncooperative. As part of its pacification effort the Imperial Army had decided to seize Suchow, to link the areas controlled by the North and the Central China armies and to consolidate its hold on Shantung Province. In the process, the army hoped, large elements of Chiang's forces could be cut off in eastern Shantung and northeast Kiangsu and defeated piecemeal. But the Chinese turned the tables, and as the leading elements[58] of the North China Army reached the walls of Taierhchwang in late March, they were isolated by Chinese forces. By 8 April the emperor's forces had fought their way out of the trap, but at high cost to the men and material of the North China Army and the prestige of Japan.[59]

Senior officers on the General Staff moved quickly to prevent further escalation. After Suchow was taken on 20 May, Major General Hashimoto Gun, who had become chief of the Operations Division in January, sent some of his staff officers to the mainland to make certain that local commanders did not slake their thirst for revenge with unauthorized probes. But the sense of outrage at the reversal at

---

55. *DR1*, 532–33. Kawabe's plan demanded friendly relations with the United States throughout the 1938–41 period so that Japan might be able to produce materials needed by the military and for the production expansion plan.

56. *DR1*, 530–31.

57. *DR1*, 534–35, 537–38.

58. A full division.

59. *DR1*, 539–42, and Dorn, 146–52, 157.

Taierhchwang, and the alliance of the Navy and Army ministries with Konoe to demand stern measures, ensured that a major new campaign, this time to seize Hankow, would get under way in the summer. The army's new reinforcements would be marching up the valley of the Yangtze, not across Manchuria.[60]

Japan's inability to restrict the flow of materials to the war, its willingness, in fact, to countenance substantial new military efforts, created severe difficulties for national finances as well as for the economy. Finances had not been robust even at the start of hostilities. In April 1937 Japan's worsening trade imbalance had forced Finance Minister Yūki Toyotarō to restrain imports of luxury goods. And to correct the depreciation of the currency, the ministry revalued the gold-yen ratio (from 750 milligrams of gold per yen to 290 milligrams), realizing a book profit that it used as initial capital for an exchange stabilization fund.[61] The opening of war with China dramatically worsened the trend. By the end of 1937 Japan had been forced to ship abroad nearly half of its gold reserves.[62] Terms of trade continued to deteriorate: exports over the same year rose in value by 18 percent, but imports were costing 37 percent more. The Foreign Trade Control Law passed by the Seventy-second Diet in September had severely curtailed imports of the raw materials for Japan's export industries—cotton, wool, jute, wood, hides, and leather among others—just as it was supposed to. It had also banned the export of exchange-earning goods, such as cotton waste and coal, once these materials were designated as for military use. The results, as the *Oriental Economist* complained, further injured Japan's competitive position in world markets and the nation's ability to import goods.[63]

So significant was the impact that, by the time of the Taierhchwang debacle and the decision to commence the Hankow campaign, it forced the government to take notice. The Japan-Manchuria Finance and Economic Research Association, organized in 1935 by Ishiwara and Miyazaki to draft the original plan to expand production, still had close contacts with the Planning Board in the spring of 1938. Its estimate of the nation's economic power, released in May, was an exercise in bluntness.

The estimate put the good news first. Japan was not dependent on foreign nations for war finances; no foreign loans were required. But the remainder of the report made for unsettling reading. Japan had

60. *DR1*, 539–42, 544.
61. *FES*, 4 August 1937.
62. Not including, however, the Bank of Japan's currency reserves.
63. *FES*, 15 June 1938, and Dowd, 84–86, 93–94.

run an import surplus of 112 million yen in the first four months of 1938. Japan's exports were declining at an alarming pace and were certain to continue falling as the war made increased demands. Import controls bred higher costs for goods produced for export. The huge shipping requisitions for the China Incident deprived Japan of much exchange earned by the shipping sector in the past. Indeed, the balance-of-payments deficit for early 1938 actually exceeded the import surplus, a most ominous sign for a nation that had always run a surplus in invisibles. Unless a radical restructuring of the economy could realize startling improvements in efficiency or peace be effected with China, the 1938 materials mobilization plan could not be executed. Substantial shortages were inevitable.[64]

Predictably the Planning Board concurred. Even under existing conditions, the import and supply targets of the materials plan would not be realized, and the plan did not allow for the immense effort that a Hankow campaign would require. The army's chief economic officer, Lieutenant Colonel Okada Kikusaburō,[65] estimated that for operations against Hankow, the army alone would need over three billion yen worth of military equipment—a sum exceeding the Japanese Empire's capacity to import for all of 1938—in addition to actual operating expenses.[66]

Changes were imperative. On 23 June 1938 the president of the Planning Board briefed cabinet members on a revised 1938 materials mobilization plan. The original had estimated that Japan could and would import materials worth three billion yen, but the new plan estimated a capability to purchase only 2.42 billion. The civilian sector would bear the brunt of reductions. Even in steel, where the Planning Board limited cuts by imposing more Draconian reductions on other commodities, the civilian allotment would fall over 30 percent, from five million tons to 3.45 million. The original quota for imports of fuels, 566 million yen, fell to 510 million in the revised plan, which would drastically curtail storage and use of oil, especially in civilian industries. Factories were to reduce their consumption of fuel by 37 percent, shipping by 10 to 15 percent. Automobiles were to absorb a 65 percent reduction. Fishing boats, which furnished an appreciable amount of Japan's food, were forced to revert entirely to wind-power.[67]

64. GDS43, 1–7.
65. Okada was promoted to this rank in November 1937.
66. DR1, 547. GDS43, 283–94, 295–304 reproduces these shortfall amounts in exhaustive detail.
67. Nakamura Takafusa and Hara Akira, Introduction to GDS43, lxi, and Tanaka,

These sharp steps still compelled the imposition of greater economic controls. The Planning Board argued that harsh new restrictions were necessary on the use of "strategic materials," especially metals. Somewhat more controversially, the board recommended the invocation of two clauses of the National General Mobilization Law to control wages, prices, and the allocation of laborers to industries.[68]

The cabinet gave the Planning Board all it asked for, and we can attribute the lack of resistance in large part to a political shakeup that Konoe had instigated only a month before. Finance Minister Kaya Okinori, whose growing complaints about the army's prodigality had made him unpopular in military circles, was replaced by Ikeda Seihin. Ikeda had been instrumental in securing approval in financial circles for the production expansion plan of May 1937. He now entered the cabinet, serving also as minister of commerce and industry, to oversee the general mobilization effort. In the reshuffle Sugiyama stepped down as army minister, and Itagaki Seishirō, lately a division commander in Manchuria known for acting on his own initiative, succeeded him. Former general Araki Sadao, retired from active duty, received the education portfolio. Another old army hand, Ugaki Kazunari (Kazushige), became foreign minister and minister for overseas affairs (the latter portfolio included civil jurisdiction over occupied China). Of these men, only Ikeda balked at the provisions that the Planning Board suggested. And even he assented to the rather limited versions of controls begun in mid-1938.[69]

All of these men realized that the current situation was intolerable, and one day after the Planning Board's presentation the Konoe cabinet formulated a new policy for the China Incident. This uninspired document resolved to draw Japan's belt one notch tighter; it hoped to force Chiang's capitulation by driving him out of his new capital of Hankow and amalgamating the smaller Chinese puppet regimes into rival central government.[70]

Behind this policy paper, however, some real change had occurred.

24–25. The plan actually listed 2.55 billion yen of imports, but 130 million of this total was to be "requisitioned" from north and central China, thus requiring no expenditure of yen. See *RGD2*, 213, 218, 221. A thorough review of the economies needed can be found in *GDS43*, 305–39.

68. Arthur Tiedemann, "Big Business and Politics in Prewar Japan," in *Dilemmas of Growth in Prewar Japan*, ed. James W. Morley (Princeton: Princeton University Press, 1971), 311.

69. *RGD2*, 187–88, and *DR1*, 547.

70. *DR1*, 547. For a masterly discussion of this new central China government, see Boyle, 116ff.

By mid-1938 Konoe had begun to realize that a military solution could not be attained readily. In part, the belief lay behind his choice of a new foreign minister—Ugaki had entered the cabinet only after receiving assurances that Japan would try to reach peace with China.

The initiative found strong support within the Foreign Ministry itself. Ishii Itarō, chief of its Asian Bureau, had composed a long memorandum in June to brief his new chief. He pointed out that Japan's new economic policy, relying on the exploitation of China to meet part of the revised materials plan,[71] was, in John Boyle's translation, like "an octopus eating its own tentacles." Confiscation led only to reduced Chinese purchases and in the long run to even lower Japanese exports. New campaigns after Hankow seemed futile. Ishii believed that holding the territory already taken was too draining. The current Chinese puppets were unpopular, nor was any coalition among them and the Kuomintang likely to work. The only course left was to negotiate with Chiang. Ugaki agreed. The new foreign minister drew obvious parallels between Bismarck's offering lenient terms to Austria in 1866, to ensure postwar amity and a secure southern flank for Prussia's coming war with France, and Japan's situation with China and the Soviet Union.[72]

The same thought occurred to Tada, with redoubled strength, at the commencement of skirmishes between Japanese and Russian forces in early July 1938. Indeed, Tada was willing to enlarge the Changkufeng Incident, not to satisfy any atavistic urges on the part of the Imperial Army but to pressure Tokyo to break off the fighting against China. Although the navy, Ugaki, and even the Army Ministry, represented by Vice-Minister Lieutenant General Tōjō Hideki, opposed a military solution at Changkufeng, the five ministers' conference of 19 July yielded to the General Staff and Tada. It approved operations, albeit limited ones.[73]

The stance ensured escalation. Tada's Operations Section chief, Colonel Inada Masazumi, authorized an attack for the twenty-first on Changkufeng Hill. Despite a rebuke from the emperor himself concerning the projected amount of force, and consequent orders from Inada, the attack went forward. The Soviets reinforced their positions, compelling a reluctant Tokyo to allow the Kwantung Army to dispatch additional troops of its own. Even so, Japanese losses

71. See note 67.
72. Boyle, 147–51, 155.
73. *DR1*, 553–54, and Hata Ikuhiko, "The Japanese-Soviet Confrontation," in *Deterrent Diplomacy: Japan, Germany, and the USSR, 1935–1940*, ed. James W. Morley (New York: Columbia University Press, 1976), 144–45.

mounted, and they were due in no small part to the first economic effects of waging war on the basis of Konoe's mortgage. Ordnance shortages, especially of antitank shells, were common. By mid-August even the General Staff was convinced that withdrawal was necessary. A negotiated solution was soon reached.[74]

Tada's latest gambit, one born of weakness, had failed to arrest the much more draining escalation of the war with China. A second effort, Ugaki's behind-the-scenes talks with representatives of Chiang's regime, proved equally unavailing. The foreign minister would resign in September.[75] On 22 August the Imperial Army began its campaign to seize Hankow.

The campaign proved that Tada's fears were well founded. Japan's advantage in both men and materiel had become slim by the summer of 1938, and the slow mobilization of additional divisions in Japan delayed the offensive's start. Once in action, moreover, these divisions acquitted themselves poorly. Despite this disappointing showing, the Japanese entered Hankow on 26 October.[76]

On 3 November Konoe took to the airwaves to broadcast a speech on the new order in east Asia. He opened by declaring that Chiang's was now a local government on the continent; the Nationalist leader no longer could speak for China. China's future was in Japanese hands. But Japan could show mercy as well as justice. Japan was about to begin the reconstruction of China and the creation of East Asia's new order, and the Nationalists could join in this task. They had only to repudiate past policy and remove their discredited leaders.[77]

Four days later Chiang responded. In a bitter denunciation of the Japanese offer he scoffed at Konoe's willingness to drop demands for an indemnity and his forbearance in annexing no Chinese territory— of course Japan had *no* ambition for Chinese cash or land. With sim-

---

74. Hata, 145–53, 155–57.

75. For the failure of Ugaki's negotiations, see Boyle, 156–59.

76. *DR1*, 563–64; Dorn, 205; and *DR1*, 565.

77. F. C. Jones, *Japan's New Order in East Asia: Its Rise and Fall* (London: Oxford University Press, 1954), 78–80. More specifically, Konoe proposed that China recognize Manchukuo and enter into an anti-Comintern military alliance with Tokyo, which would keep Japanese troops in north China and Inner Mongolia. These two regions would become the core of Japan's resource exploitation efforts on the mainland. Japanese advisers would supervise Chinese land and water communications and would "improve and adjust" Chinese military and police forces. North China, the lower Yangtze Valley, and certain south China islands would become special zones of collaboration. All of China's currency, tariff, and customs matters would be regeared to promote trade among Japan, Manchukuo, and China.

ilar sarcasm, the Nationalist leader proceeded to discuss Tokyo's remaining terms.[78]

Konoe had no chance for rejoinder, for by 4 January 1939 Baron Hiranuma Kiichirō had become the new premier. Konoe fell from power for three principal reasons. Within the cabinet the Foreign, Finance, and Navy ministries had banded together in the last months of 1938 to oppose the army regarding the terms of an alliance with Germany. Moreover, the political parties had perceived Konoe's efforts at "spiritual mobilization" in the second half of the year as aimed squarely at their influence, even their existence; Ugaki's departure had undermined Konoe's earlier effort to coopt political opponents. Finally, the capture of Hankow had not ended the China Incident.[79]

This last reason proved to be fundamental. Konoe had counted on the fighting to last long enough to secure Diet passage of his reform legislation, and in this he succeeded. By mid-1938 Japan had created an economic structure dedicated to the twin goals of central control in time of need and a heavy industrial base (constructed through the five-year plan) capable of supporting total war.

But Konoe had also calculated that the fighting would not last long enough to jeopardize these goals. His cabinet had committed Japan to a mighty effort, defeating Chiang long before the economic consequences of the drive, including drastic restrictions on imports, became clear. In this he failed. By mid-1938 the Planning Board was signaling that substantial, even radical sacrifices were necessary immediately to forestall economic chaos. Japan's ability to support the five-year plan was in doubt. And, as Tada's ill-starred attempts to limit the China fighting indicated, Japan seemed powerless to halt the immense and growing drain on its economic capacity. Konoe's gamble, in short, had created the key instruments for Japan's drive to autarky while subverting that very drive. As it entered the crucial year of 1939, Japan was becoming more, not less, dependent on outside powers, and especially on the United States.

78. Jones, 80–81.
79. Berger, 204, and David J. Lu, *From the Marco Polo Bridge to Pearl Harbor* (Washington: Public Affairs, 1961), 44–45.

[6]

To Defend the Open Door

From the aftermath of the Manchurian Incident to the attack on Pearl Harbor, American policy in East Asia attempted to uphold the principles of the Open Door. These principles in essence committed the United States to equality of commercial opportunity in Asian markets and territorial integrity for all Asian nations. Often it proved difficult to support one without injuring the other. Even more often it proved awkward to support either without becoming involved across the Pacific.

In late 1933 most Americans, including Stanley Hornbeck, chief of the State Department's Far Eastern Division, and Joseph Grew, America's new ambassador to Tokyo, were convinced that Japan had seized Manchuria as a matter of pride for the Imperial Army, not one of life or death in some grand scheme to achieve autarky. They concluded that, sooner or later, the army would find the development of Manchuria prohibitively expensive. Then Japan would have to disgorge its conquest, the army would be disgraced, and the moderate civilians who favored close ties with the West would return to power.[1]

This shared view did not lead to shared prescriptions for American action. Grew was certain that natural economic processes would act on an economically frail Japan to achieve the desired result without American action. Hornbeck, however, believed that Tokyo would prove stubborn. He doubted that the army would relinquish power peacefully or easily, and he feared that in time the Kwantung Army

---

1. See Chapter 2, especially pp. 58–63.

could make itself self-supporting in Manchuria even if Japan were financially ruined in the process. As a result, Hornbeck advocated active pressure, chiefly in the form of sharp increases in American tariffs on goods imported principally from Japan.[2]

American policy fell uneasily between the two positions. Although the United States was unwilling to embark upon punitive measures to protest Japan's seizure and to foil its economic assimilation of Manchuria, neither was it moved to assist Japan in that assimilation. By employing the somewhat awkward device of refusing to permit official quotation of Manchukuo's currency in the United States, Secretary of State Cordell Hull effectively denied the puppet regime direct access to American credit markets. But Hull also allowed American businesses established before the incident to continue operations in Manchuria.[3]

This curious defense of the Open Door was hardly clarified by Washington's reaction to the Amau Doctrine of April 1934. At a press conference Amau Eiji of Japan's Foreign Ministry claimed Japan's right to supervise all of China's economic development, and he asserted that this task belonged neither to the League of Nations nor to any other state or group of states. Hornbeck was convinced that symbolic protest only made the tasks of diplomacy harder; he argued that any American attempt to circumvent the Amau Doctrine would goad Japan to further aggression on the continent, forcing the empire to assume a more strident opposition to principles that America cherished. To avoid friction with Tokyo, he wanted to work through an international consortium, complete with Japanese participation, to supply credits and aid to China.

Hornbeck, in fact, was inclined to scrap the effort to defend the Open Door. In his view its principles, however praiseworthy, did not always accord with America's national interests. The United States could not allow Japan to achieve hegemony over the western Pacific. But neither should it cause needless friction by seeking to guarantee

---

2. *FRUS, 1932*, 4:143–48, 372–73; Joseph Grew to Henry Stimson, 13 August 1932 and 3 December 1932, Joseph Grew Papers, vol. 57; *FRUS, 1932*, 4:323, 344; Hornbeck memo, 12 July 1932, Stanley Hornbeck Papers, Box 453; Hornbeck memos, undated (October–November 1932), 27 September, 14 October, and 10 November 1932, Hornbeck Papers, Box 369; and Hornbeck memo, 29 November 1932, Hornbeck Papers, Box 453.

3. *FRUS, 1933*, 3:407–8, 438–39. In fact, while Hull instructed Grew not to lobby for those firms in obtaining orders from the Japanese, the ambassador was to watch carefully for evidence of discrimination against American businesses in Manchuria.

abstractions. Equal opportunity and territorial integrity in China were first and foremost China's fight.[4]

This attitude resurfaced a year later. After receiving news of the conclusion in May 1935 of the Umezu-Ho and Doihara-Ching agreements, which expelled Kuomintang influence from Hopei and Chahar provinces, Hornbeck proposed that not a single representation be made to Tokyo, a policy that the State Department followed. He agreed with Grew that Japan's industrialization was combining with overabundant population and a dearth of resources to foster growing appetites in the name of economic nationalism. Though the United States had to avoid any appearance of collaboration with Tokyo's program, Hornbeck asserted, it was equally vital to avoid confrontation.[5]

Hull did not entirely agree. A dedicated disciple of Open Door principles, he was clearly displeased as Japan's activities in north China continued through 1935. In June he bluntly informed Yoshida Shigeru, Tokyo's ambassador to Britain,[6] that many Americans believed Japan intended to dominate China and deny Chinese markets to the rest of the world. This violation of the Open Door was not in Japan's own interests. No single nation on earth, Hull argued, could supply the capital to develop China. There was room for all to invest and trade, increasing China's prosperity and buying power and, in the process, the wealth of all East Asia.

Though Hornbeck opposed public protests, he concurred with Hull's analysis. In time Japan's experiment in autarky would fail. When it did, Yankee capital and technology would return to the Asian mainland. In the meantime, however, Japan's very encroachments served to sap China's ability to develop itself and therefore prolonged Tokyo's willingness to pursue an essentially futile self-sufficiency.[7]

If the Chinese themselves could break this circle, they would revolutionize East Asian relations and American involvement in them. If

4. Dorothy Borg, *The United States and the Far Eastern Crisis of 1933–1938* (Cambridge: Harvard University Press, 1964), 75, and Hornbeck memo, 13 April 1935, Hornbeck Papers, Box 454.

5. *FRUS, 1935*, 3:95–100, 59–60, 34–36, 2–4; Grew to Hull, 6 February 1935, DF 894.00/541; Kenneth G. McCarty, "Stanley K. Hornbeck and the Far East, 1931–1941" (Ph.D. diss., Duke University, 1970), 77–78; and Cordell Hull, *The Memoirs of Cordell Hull*, 2 vols. (New York: Macmillan, 1948), 1:290–91.

6. This Yoshida is not to be confused with his namesake, the first head of Japan's Cabinet Investigative Bureau.

7. *FRUSJ*, 1:241–44, and McCarty, 83.

China joined the Open Door world, it would compel Japan's return to that world. During 1935 and 1936 Hornbeck and Hull could see few signs of such a trend, but by mid-1937 their views were changing. Chiang Kai-shek's able handling of a revolt in China's Southwest Political Council in late 1936, the indications of rising Chinese nationalism in incidents at Chengtu, Pakhoi, and Shanghai, and the Sian Incident of December all signaled an end to the weak, disorganized China of the preceding decades. The stunning Chinese victory at Pailingmiao over the Kwantung Army–sponsored Mongols under Prince Teh furnished additional proof of resurgence. It also ended Sino-Japanese negotiations in Nanking and with them, for the moment at least, any chance of an agreement on Japanese projects in north China, thwarting further encroachments there.[8] How would Japan react to these developments? Grew, ever the optimist, interpreted the appointment of Satō Naotake in March 1937 as foreign minister of the new Hayashi cabinet as an abandonment of "desperation diplomacy"—a return to the peaceful, traditional brand practiced by Baron Shidehara Kijūrō in the twenties. In Satō's first speech before the Japanese Diet the foreign minister had declared that in China Japan's policy should respect the ideals of the Open Door, to improve relations with Britain and America. Elements in the army detested Satō, Grew acknowledged, but, in a bad misreading of the forces that had brought Hayashi to power, he felt that the liberals were at last resuming control of Japanese foreign policy. Even in June, when the Hayashi cabinet fell and the incoming Konoe Fumimaro appointed Hirota Kōki foreign minister, Grew believed that the consensus on a new China policy might not necessarily rehearse old ambitions. At the least, it appeared that Tokyo had apparently abjured the use of force.[9]

Hornbeck too welcomed Satō's appointment. But he believed that America's refusal to antagonize Japan on behalf of an abstract Open Door moderated Japanese chauvinism, as increased Chinese confidence and a growing American fleet were calming relations across the Pacific. Tokyo's chauvinism was still running high, but conditions seemed much more promising than they had in the wake of the Manchurian Incident.[10]

8. Borg, 183–84, 187–89, 224–26, 231.

9. *FRUS, 1937*, 3:1–10, 29–31, 41–42; James B. Crowley, *Japan's Quest for Autonomy* (Princeton: Princeton University Press, 1966), 317–18; and *FRUS, 1937*, 3:58–62, 710–14, 801–2, 96–100, 118–21.

10. McCarty, 84–85.

This cautious hope did not survive the exchange of shots near the Marco Polo Bridge; but America's basic stance did. Excellent reports on the China Incident came from Grew, Ambassador to China Nelson Johnson and, in Peking, Willys Peck. By early August the State Department knew that Japanese forces were ejecting Sung Che-yuan's troops from Peking and Tientsin. No settlement, local or general, was likely. Would the United States now come to the defense of the Open Door and, by implication, China?[11]

Hornbeck recognized the central issue immediately. America, he wrote, finally had to choose between its own "peace with security" and its global "disapproval of aggression." Hornbeck, though sympathetic to China, nevertheless believed that American interests did not warrant alignment with Chiang's cause or China's territorial integrity. Those interests were, however, deep enough to justify a continued American presence in China, particularly at the vital port of Shanghai. Even after serious fighting had erupted there, Hornbeck was arguing that American nationals should not be withdrawn. Rather, he urged, they should be protected, by the dispatch of naval units if necessary.[12]

He thus ran directly counter to America's passage of three neutrality acts in the previous two years. These required the president to determine whether a state of war existed and if so, to ban the export of arms and munitions from the United States to any belligerent. American goods were not to be transported to belligerent ports in American bottoms. No citizen of the United States could extend credits to governments at war. Under a "cash-and-carry" provision, the president had discretionary power to end the export to warring nations of any articles he chose to designate unless the belligerents paid for them in cash and carried them in their own ships.

If these acts were invoked, they would hurt China far more than Japan. China needed credit to continue the fight; Japan did not. China had no ships to transport supplies imperative for its resistance; Japan did. Japan could manufacture its own armaments; China could

11. *FRUS, 1937,* 3:139–44, 152–53, 167–70, 178, 216–18, 261–62, 274–75, 252–53.

12. *FRUS, 1937,* 3:420–23; Hornbeck memo, 1 October 1937, Hornbeck Papers, Box 457; *FRUS, 1937,* 3:164–66, 278–80, 312–13; and Hornbeck memo, 14 September 1937, Hornbeck Papers, Box 456. Hornbeck has acquired the reputation of a virulently pro-Chinese partisan inside the State Department. My reading differs. Hornbeck was far more concerned with preserving America's status as a great power globally, and specifically in Asia, than in fighting other nations' fights. This stance ensured, among other things, hostility toward Japan and a desire for a strong American military. But Hornbeck was not the "China crusader" he is sometimes made out to be.

not. To apply the neutrality acts, therefore, would be to apply economic sanctions against the victim of aggression. To some officials in Washington, this hardly seemed neutral.

The administration's first impulse was to stall for time. On 16 July in a public statement, Hull declared his government's objection to "the use of force in pursuit of policy [and] . . . interference in the internal affairs of other nations." And he spoke at length about "effective equality of commercial opportunity" and removing barriers to international trade. But he came no closer than this to a defense of China's territorial integrity. Nor did he mention Japan by name.[13]

Hull's statement was little more than a recapitulation of American policy in East Asia since 1933. In the circumstances of the summer of 1937, however, this position seemed to many Americans no longer adequate. Some academics, journalists, intellectuals, and plain citizens sent sharp protests to the State Department, attacking Hull for his failure to use the Nine Power Treaty and the Pact of Paris to condemn Japan. Others, representatives of American isolationist sentiment such as Senator Gerald Nye and Congressman Hamilton Fish, demanded that the president invoke the neutrality acts at once.[14]

By August, Roosevelt hoped to satisfy both groups. The outbreak of fighting in Shanghai convinced Washington that the conflict would be prolonged, and it compelled the U.S. government to reassess Japan's aims.[15] It also led to a reconsideration of the neutrality acts, this time as a means of exerting pressure upon Japan. At a cabinet meeting in late August one Treasury Department official asked whether Japan was capable of absorbing China. He believed that Tokyo, unless given credit, could not afford to import materials from the United States much longer. If Japan's financial position really was so precarious, then to invoke cash-and-carry provisions might hurt Japan more than China. The U.S. government might mollify American advocates of aid to victims of aggression and proponents of invocation alike.[16]

13. United States, Department of State, *Press Releases*, 17 July 1937, 41–44.

14. J. Pierrepont Moffat, Journal entry of 31 July–1 August 1937, Moffat Papers, vol. 39.

15. In an incisive analysis Hornbeck conjectured that the Konoe government had approved an extension of hostilities to restore domestic unity as much as absorb China's great potential wealth. Hornbeck memos, 14 July and 5 August 1937, Hornbeck Papers, Box 456.

16. Robert A. Divine, *The Illusion of Neutrality* (Chicago: University of Chicago Press, 1962), 203, and Harold L. Ickes, *The Secret Diary of Harold L. Ickes*, 3 vols. (New York: Simon & Schuster, 1954), 2:199.

This was Roosevelt's hope, but did it rest on a false premise? Grew acknowledged that the large appropriations passed by a special session of the Diet provided a potent argument for peace. But he was sure that Japan counted on delivering a decisive blow against China, to end the conflict quickly and without financial strain. In the meantime Tokyo would actually welcome application of the neutrality laws, as evidence of American impartiality. Hull and Roosevelt again deferred action on those laws, contenting themselves with a ban on American government–owned ships carrying goods to China or Japan.[17]

Roosevelt's balancing act did not last. In late August, Imperial warplanes machine-gunned and badly wounded Britain's ambassador to China, Sir Hughe Knatchbull-Hugessen. On 21 September, Japan bombed Nanking. On both sides of the Atlantic, among people still unused to the idea of hostilities harming noncombatants, these acts provoked outrage. They confirmed prejudices that the Japanese were irrational beings beyond hope of control.[18]

Immediately the State Department blasted the Nanking attack as "unwarranted and contrary to the principles of law and humanity," words that Grew himself used in a stiff note to Foreign Minister Hirota. But the British were considering further steps. On 1 October the British chargé in Washington, Victor Mallet, visited the Department of State to test attitudes regarding an economic boycott against Japan designed to end the Far East conflict.[19]

The dominant sentiment inside the State Department opposed any boycott as contrary to American law. But a vocal minority within the department, led by Hornbeck, and outside State, led by Secretary of the Treasury Henry Morgenthau, argued that a boycott carried twin advantages: it demonstrated America's moral resolve, and it damaged Japan's actual capacity to carry out aggression. Hornbeck, now retitled political adviser, argued that an unofficial, private boycott could circumvent the law. Even before Japan bombed Nanking, Hornbeck had suggested to an inquiring Edgar Smith of General Motors that if private companies ended trade with aggressor nations,

17. Joseph Grew, Diary entries of 6 and 18 August 1937, Grew Papers, vol. 85; *FRUS, 1937*, 3:515–16, 437–39, 516–17; and Divine, 207–8. Private American vessels could continue such trade at their own risk.

18. Moffat, Journal entries of 30 September and 1 October 1937, Moffat Papers, vol. 39; Johnson (London) to Hull, 2 October 1937, DF 793.94/10380.

19. *FRUSJ*, 1:499–500, 504–5, 505–6, 506; Peter Lowe, *Great Britain and the Origins of the Pacific War* (Oxford: Clarendon, 1977), 21; Anthony Eden, *Facing the Dictators* (Boston: Houghton Mifflin, 1962), 606; and *FRUS, 1937*, 3:560.

their government "would be in a position to apply processes which are ordinarily envisaged under the term of 'economic sanctions.' "[20]

Morgenthau was convinced that Japan was near the end of its financial tether, able to continue fighting only by exporting ever greater amounts of its gold. If the West were to refuse to provide hard currency in exchange for Japanese gold, it might bring peace to Asia. Morgenthau could point to Department of Commerce reports indicating that Japan had imposed drastic exchange controls and had ended all imports of cotton—surely a sign that Tokyo was in difficulty. A splashy, inaccurate article by Nathaniel Peffer in the October 1937 issue of *Foreign Affairs*, arguing that Japan's economy was "at the danger point," did nothing to change Morgenthau's mind.[21]

But the State Department's economic affairs office, led by Herbert Feis, interpreted Japan's finances differently. Economic Affairs concluded that Japan, though it had indeed increased its production of gold significantly in an attempt to offset specie exports, retained substantial other exchange reserves—nearly six billion yen. Only one-third of this sum was readily convertible, but the office maintained that Japan could finance its exchange deficit for at least two years, longer if foreign loans could be secured. In an important statement, Feis himself argued that Japan had more than counterbalanced its lower level of imports since July with exceptionally high purchases from the United States early in the year. Feis did not assert openly that Tokyo had planned the Marco Polo Bridge Incident in advance, but he clearly implied that Tokyo had been preparing for something throughout the first half of 1937. If the Japanese had made advance plans, it seemed unlikely that they had miscalculated their economic situation so badly. Substantial material reserves must have been in place before July. Feis conceded that crippling Japan's ability to convert gold into exchange would make Tokyo's task of cowing or conquering China more difficult but not impossible. And even this limited step required the complete cooperation of all countries, because an independent American refusal to accept Japanese gold would have no effect.[22]

---

20. Moffat, Journal entries of 2, 3, and 4 October 1937; Hornbeck draft, 3 October 1937, Hornbeck Papers, Box 457; Hornbeck memo, 10 September 1937, Hornbeck Papers, Box 155.

21. Hornbeck to Hull, 14 September 1937, Hornbeck Papers, Box 238; Henry Morgenthau, Jr., Morgenthau Diaries, entry of 1 October 1937, Book 91, pp. 1–2, Morgenthau Papers; and Daniel Roper report, 10 September 1937, Franklin D. Roosevelt Papers, OF3, Box 3, Commerce.

22. Jones study, 22 September 1937, DF 894.5151/44; Feis to Hull, 8 October 1937, DF

Hull accepted Feis's logic and declined to pursue the proposal. Then, suddenly, came news of Roosevelt's Quarantine Speech in Chicago.[23] The president had left Washington on a trip to the west over a week before Mallet had broached the boycott idea. He had played no role in the State Department's response. Before Roosevelt departed, however, he had conferred with Hull, and Hull had asked for a speech during the trip to fend off pressure in favor of invoking the neutrality acts.

Roosevelt began his journey in a distinctly anti-Japanese frame of mind, one he maintained for the next four years. He shared an unreasonable American fear of Japanese subversion along the West Coast, to the point of asking Admiral William Leahy to check on Japanese crabbing operations lest the wily Orientals were surreptitiously looking for possible forward bases to use in the event of war with the United States. The bombing of Nanking angered the president deeply. His response was a forceful address against the "reign of terror and international lawlessness." In the most striking passage of the speech he declared:

> It would seem to be unfortunately true that the epidemic of world lawlessness is spreading.
>
> When an epidemic of physical disease starts to spread the community approves and joins in a quarantine of the patients in order to protect the community against the spread of the disease.[24]

Roosevelt did not call for any specific measures, nor did he mention Japan by name. Yet he had not ruled out pressure beyond moral suasion. At a press conference upon his return to Washington he argued that sanctions were "out of the window." But he insisted that steps were possible in "a very practical sphere," not simply a moral one, and would be consonant with neutrality legislation.[25]

These assertions puzzled reporters at the time and historians ever

---

694.11/10; and Feis memo, 5 October 1937, DF 894.515/31. It is high irony that the forced reduction of Japanese imports after July 1937 should be interpreted in the United States as evidence that Japan had preplanned the China Incident and was therefore relatively immune to American economic pressure. But even Hull agreed with this assessment; see Hull to Morgenthau, 27 November 1937, DF 694.11/14.

23. *FRUS, 1937*, 3:582–83.

24. Roosevelt to Leahy, 22 August 1937, Roosevelt Papers, PSF, DEC, Box 78, Navy; Hull, 1:544; Robert A. Divine, *Roosevelt and World War II* (Baltimore: Johns Hopkins University Press, 1969), 16; and Speech File, Roosevelt Papers.

25. Borg, 382–84, and Franklin D. Roosevelt, *The Public Papers and Addresses of Franklin D. Roosevelt*, 13 vols. (New York: Random House, 1938–50), 6:423–25.

since.[26] How could Roosevelt support practical measures while stead-fastly opposing sanctions? The answer lies in Roosevelt's understanding of "sanctions." In October 1937 there was only one international agreement that used the term: under Article 16 the Covenant of the League of Nations bound league members to apply sanctions against nations branded aggressors. Roosevelt wanted no part of this mandatory, all-or-nothing process, especially one connected to the unpopular league. He sought other vehicles for the application of pressure. One, the Saavedra Lamas Anti-War Pact, he mentioned in a paper he gave to Norman Davis two weeks before his Quarantine Speech. In that paper Roosevelt wrote of the pact as a way to coordinate a group of neutral nations that might "make their influence felt" short of the threat of force. Signatories that desired to condemn aggression were free to devise stronger measures of any sort and any degree.[27]

Just how strong would these measures be? The State Department was mystified, and Roosevelt gave only hints in his first conference with Hull, Undersecretary Sumner Welles, and Davis. He said, cryptically, that if the coming nine-power conference in Brussels failed to resolve the Sino-Japanese conflict by mediation, further steps might become necessary. But clearly he was tending toward a hard line. When Roosevelt received urgings from Admiral Harry Yarnell of the Asiatic Fleet that the United States conduct economic warfare against Japan by depriving Tokyo of raw materials, the president took up the matter with Leahy with visible enthusiasm. At a cabinet meeting soon after he listened intently as Secretary of Commerce Daniel Roper read off a long list of American-made articles that Japan no longer purchased because of its growing trade controls. Roosevelt, more interested in hurting the Japanese military than helping American exporters, wondered whether these restrictions might justify American bans on imports from Japan of equivalent value. If so, he believed, the effects on Japan would be serious.[28]

Roosevelt's forwardness had unfortunate results at the conference that convened at Brussels on 3 November. Davis, the American dele-

26. For the historical debate in summary, see Divine, *Roosevelt*, 17–18; John McVicker Haight, Jr., "Franklin D. Roosevelt and a Naval Quarantinbe of Japan," *Pacific Historical Review* 40 (May 1971); Dorothy Borg, "Notes on Roosevelt's 'Quarantine Speech,'" *Political Science Quarterly* 72 (September 1957); and Borg, *Crisis*, 381–86.
27. Borg, *Crisis*, 385, and Hull, 1:322–23.
28. Moffat, Journal entry of 5 October 1937, Moffat Papers, vol. 39; Robert Dallek, *Franklin D. Roosevelt and American Foreign Policy, 1932–1945* (New York: Oxford University Press, 1979), 150–52; William E. Kinsella, Jr., *Leadership in Isolation* (Cambridge, Mass.: Schenkman, 1978), 85–86; and Ickes, 2:223–24.

gate, had long supported the concept of collective security and especially Anglo-American cooperation. The president's Chicago address had encouraged British supporters of stronger measures, such as Anthony Eden, to propose economic pressure against Japan. The conference quickly determined that it faced a choice between adjournment without action and discussion of sterner steps; Davis suggested to Hull and Eden that their governments refuse to recognize Japanese conquests and ban credits to Tokyo.[29]

Such medicine was far too strong for State's taste. Hornbeck's successor at the Far Eastern Division, Maxwell Hamilton, counseled patience. Vigorous steps would drive Japan's warlords only to further madness. If, on the other hand, Tokyo could be offered a chance for economic security and protection against Soviet attack, Japan's drive toward imperialism might perhaps be defused. This analysis was to Grew's liking. Japan's leaders were not barbarians, Grew wrote; they sought outlets for trade, investment, even surplus population,[30] outlets denied them by the white powers. If Japan could meet these needs in parts of China, it might well return to its "natural" place within the Anglo-American sphere.[31]

To Hornbeck, this suggestion smacked of appeasement. Japan was entitled to a measure of security, he admitted, but only after it abandoned its illegal attempt to subjugate China. Any attempt to mediate such as Grew seemed to suggest would invite another Hoare-Laval sellout, with all the disgrace and loss of principle it had entailed. And real American security interests, not just the maintenance of lofty principle, demanded that Japan be halted before it achieved hegemony in Asia. Only force could halt the empire. If it could not be applied directly by the West, then the best course was to aid Chiang.[32]

Hornbeck won half of his argument when Hull ordered Davis to halt discussions with the British. But the secretary also recommended that the conference remain in session and not admit failure. Davis, thinking this a recipe for humiliation, continued to cause speculation

29. Moffat, Journal entry of 28 October 1937, Moffat Papers, vol. 39; Norman Davis memo, 20 October 1937, Norman Davis Papers, Box 4; Roosevelt memo, 19 October 1937, Roosevelt Papers, PSF: State, CT; Moffat, Journal entries of 10 and 15 November 1937, Moffat Papers, vol. 39; *FRUS, 1937*, 4:118–19, 124–25, 134–35, 157–58; and Grew Diary entry of 30 October 1937, Grew Papers, vol. 85.

30. A marvelous study remains to be written on the great myth of population pressure as a force for expansionism in Japan (or any other nation).

31. *FRUS, 1937*, 3:596–600, 612–16, and Moffat, Journal entry of 28 October 1937, Moffat Papers, vol. 39.

32. Hornbeck memos, 6, 10, 12, and 13 October 1937, Hornbeck Papers, Box 457, 13 October 1937, Box 318.

in the international press, leaving Hull no alternative but to order him home. Roosevelt seconded this step, admitting that American public opinion did not seem to support economic pressure. The conference adjourned on 24 November. It did not meet again.[33]

The Roosevelt administration had come close to considering concrete pressure on Japan after the bombing of Nanking, only to back off during the Brussels Conference. The cycle was repeated during the Panay Incident. As the powers conferred in Belgium, the Imperial Army drove for Chiang's capital city of Nanking. On 13 December 1937 its lead elements entered the city. The Chinese leader had already fled to Hankow, and all the Chinese and foreigners who could followed him upriver. Part of this exodus were three tankers of the Standard-Vacuum Oil Company escorted by the American gunboat *Panay.* Japanese planes attacked the vessels, sinking the gunboat and killing several Americans.[34]

Roosevelt was outraged. Even before details of the sinking reached Washington, he instructed Hull to convey shock and concern to Japan's ambassador, Saitō Hiroshi. One day after the attack the president spoke with Morgenthau to consider reprisals. The treasury secretary came prepared with statistics about Japan's liquid assets in the United States and its total reserves of foreign exchange. Morgenthau favored striking at both, ending Japanese trade with the United States and indeed the world. At first Roosevelt wanted to investigate only the seizure of Japanese assets to cover damage done to American ships, but he soon became attracted to a ban on transactions in foreign exchange with the government of Japan. One of Morgenthau's subordinates, Herman Oliphant, had discovered a legal basis for such action if Roosevelt declared a national emergency.[35]

For Morgenthau, however, Oliphant's proposal did not go far enough. The exchange ban covered government transactions only, not those involving Japanese subjects or companies. In a Treasury meeting on 17 December, Oliphant suggested licensing all trade with Japan and then delaying or denying licenses. Harry White pointed

33. *FRUS, 1937*, 4:180–81, 197–98, 200–201, 212–14, 215–21; Moffat, Journal entry of 18 November 1937, Moffat Papers, vol. 39; and Stimson to Roosevelt, 15 November 1937, Roosevelt to Feis, 16 November 1937, and Feis to Stimson, 22 November 1937, Henry L. Stimson Diary and Letters. Utley rightly points out that, to proceed further with any consideration of pressure, Roosevelt would have had to overrule his own secretary of state. See Jonathan G. Utley, *Going to War with Japan, 1937–1941* (Knoxville: University of Tennessee Press, 1985), 21.
34. Grew, Diary entry of 13 December 1937, Grew Papers, vol. 85.
35. Morgenthau, Diary entries of 17 December 1937, Book 101, 322–24, Book 102, 2.

out that licensing would still permit Japan to trade, in sterling through London instead of in dollars through New York. Morgenthau resolved to phone John Simon, Britain's chancellor of the exchequer, to deny that outlet to the Japanese. He then excitedly told his staff to examine possible Japanese sources for vital commodities such as oil if American supplies were cut off, and he departed for a cabinet meeting.[36]

There Roosevelt did nothing to discourage Morgenthau's enthusiasm for extreme steps. Deeply angered by reports that the *Panay*'s American markings were clearly visible from the air and that Japanese soldiers had boarded the gunboat before it sank, the president spoke of applying sanctions, to be called quarantines, against Japan. Roosevelt asserted that these "will not lead to war." He even pondered a blockade by American, British, French, and Dutch naval forces from the Aleutian Islands to Singapore. This move, he thought, could bring Japan to its knees within a year.[37]

Morgenthau returned to Treasury in a buoyant mood. He reached Simon by phone and presented Oliphant's proposal. Simon was leery, particularly of Morgenthau's desire to exclude the State Department and the Foreign Office on the dubious premise that the Oliphant plan was a financial, not a diplomatic, affair. Four days later Simon officially replied that an exchange ban was impossible without special legislation from Parliament. Moreover, economic pressure would have to be prolonged or extremely severe to be effective. Roosevelt may also have had second thoughts, for on 23 December he accepted Japan's official apology and indemnity payments. An American naval captain, Royal Ingersoll, visited London and conferred with the Admiralty, but neither navy was eager for hostilities against Tokyo. The Panay Incident was over.[38]

Although Japan's prompt redress for the *Panay* losses avoided immediate crisis, Prime Minister Konoe's *aite ni sezu* declaration indicated that further Japanese force against China and further friction with America was likely as 1938 began. It was clear that Chiang would fight on. Japan would not negotiate for peace; indeed, Tokyo intended to construct wholly new arrangements for occupied China,

36. Ibid., Book 103, 20–32, 35–58.

37. Roosevelt Papers, PSF, DC, Box 37; Morgenthau, Diary, Book 103, 59–62; and Ickes, 2:273–77.

38. Morgenthau Diaries, Book 103, 63–77, 234–35; Haight, 215–23; and Stephen Roskill, *Naval Policy Between the Wars*, vol. 2: *The Period of Reluctant Rearmament, 1930–1939* (Annapolis: Naval Institute, 1976), 367–68.

beginning with a puppet regime for the northern provinces.[39] These developments boded ill for the Open Door. How should the United States respond?

Again Hornbeck took up the cudgels. Alarmed by Grew's report of a national mobilization law in Japan, he feared that Tokyo might after all prosecute its designs in China—and, worse, fight thereafter on a much more equal basis against other industrialized nations.[40] That Japan's growing might rested largely on its increased dependence on American materials particularly distressed Hornbeck. What was the point of strengthening the U.S. Navy when American iron and steel was being exported for Japanese warship construction? Hornbeck knew that Japan's mobilization program could not be used as a pretext for ending U.S. trade with the empire. But the principles of the Open Door were of such vital interest to the United States that Japan's violations of them in China could perhaps justify economic reprisals.[41] Under Hornbeck's close guidance, the Far Eastern Division examined this possibility. Hornbeck himself wrote Grew privately, asking how Tokyo's leaders would react to an American naval demonstration or economic embargo designed to compel their empire to respect the rights of the United States.[42]

Grew replied on 12 April in a long, thoughtful letter. He too was troubled by the implications of Japan's program. If it succeeded, American treaty rights in China would vanish along with China's territorial integrity. Worse, Japanese expansionism would continue, endangering even the Philippines in time, and Japan would become economically self-sufficient and politically dominant over all East Asia. If the program failed, on the other hand, Grew foresaw Japan's own political and economic collapse. The consequences for the entire

39. Utley rightly observes Grew's attempts to counter this growing conviction in Washington—one shared even by Hamilton and his assistant, Joseph Ballantine, who were certain that Japan meant to eliminate equal treatment for foreign businesses in China, among other things—with arguments that Japanese "moderates" remained influential. He is not on firm ground in implying that Grew's analysis may have been correct; Utley, 32. For Hamilton and Ballantine's views, see *FRUS, 1938,* 3:32–33, 53, 65–67; Hamilton memo, 26 November 1937, DF 894.503193/12; Grew to Hull, 4 December 1937, DF 894.51/527; and Leahy to Roosevelt, 6 January 1938, Roosevelt Papers, PSF, DC, Box 57.

40. Again, in this important regard Hornbeck demonstrated the clearest view in Washington of the overall goals of Japanese policy.

41. Grew to Hull, 14 February 1938, DF 894.11/772, and Hornbeck memos, 14 and 17 February and 16 March, Hornbeck Papers, Box 457.

42. *FRUS, 1938,* 3:89–93, and Hornbeck memos, 16 and 31 March 1938, Hornbeck Papers, Box 457.

area would be unpredictable and probably unwelcome. Neither outcome was desirable.

But Grew doubted that Hornbeck's suggestions would have any good effect. Tokyo would regard American pressure as aimed at frustrating Japan's most basic policies; it would only redouble its efforts, causing more damage to the Open Door and more friction with the West. War would become more likely, not less. In legalistic terms Grew questioned whether a case existed for pressure. Japan did not deny the Open Door rights of the United States even if it did not permit their free exercise. Between 1914 and 1917, after all, Germany had infringed upon more and much greater American interests without provoking Washington to economic warfare.[43]

The conclusion of the Far Eastern Division's study also discouraged Hornbeck. Existing laws empowered the president to retaliate against nations that discriminated against American trade, by imposing additional duties on their imports. But Japan's exchange controls, though they certainly hampered American trade, applied equally to goods from other nations. Hence they did not discriminate, and under current American law there was no case for retaliation.[44]

This latest consideration of economic pressure languished throughout the spring of 1938, but it was abruptly revived in June by Japan's ferocious bombardment of Canton. In three days of raids more than a thousand Chinese civilians were killed or wounded. Moreover, the Japanese used equipment and some aircraft made in America. An incensed Hull condemned the attack and called a meeting of his advisers for 10 June. All agreed that sales of American bombers and related equipment to Japan were intolerable, but thereafter the consensus broke down. The more cautious diplomats in Washington, such as J. Pierrepont Moffat (Grew's son-in-law), argued that the government should publicly disapprove of such sales. Others wanted an outright embargo. Hull consulted Roosevelt, who believed that the best course was to discourage the sale of aircraft and related equipment by contacting the manufacturers directly.[45]

At first Roosevelt and Hull hoped to implement the policy unobtrusively, but the attempt was not practicable. At a press conference

43. Grew to Hornbeck, 12 April 1938, Grew Papers, vol. 91.
44. Jones memo, 16 April 1938, DF 611.9431/158. Feis, who was considerably closer to Hornbeck's views of Japan than to Grew's, was angered by Far Eastern's findings. See Utley, 35.
45. *FRUS, 1938*, 3:192–93; *FRUSJ*, 1:595–96; and Moffat, Journal entry of 10 June 1938, vol. 40.

on 11 June, Hull announced that his department would be "reluctant" to issue export licenses for the items involved. At once the companies pressed to learn whether any licenses at all would be granted. The problem was simple: if one license were issued, all of the companies denied licenses would complain bitterly, and quite rightly, of discrimination. With Hull's consent, Joseph Green, chief of State's Office of Arms and Munitions Control, clarified the "moral embargo" with a circular letter to the firms on 1 July. Sales of aircraft and aeronautical equipment to Japan virtually stopped by the end of the summer.[46]

This first step of pressure on Japan addressed the outrage about the bombing of Chinese civilians. It did nothing to obtain satisfaction for Tokyo's violations of American rights and interests in China, much less obstruct Japan's bid for Asian hegemony. Washington's wider grievance focused on three principal issues. Japan had blocked neutral navigation of the Yangtze River during the Hankow campaign and had not reopened it after that city's capture. The North China Army had established a new currency system in northern China, causing immediate reductions in all but Japanese imports into the area and forcing businesses to accept the puppet currency. And Japan's creation of the Asian Development Board (Kōa-in) strongly suggested that further Japanese monopolies would soon be appearing elsewhere in China.[47]

Hull observed these developments with growing anxiety. On 1 October he instructed Grew to present a comprehensive letter of protest to Japan. Not sure that words alone would suffice, he also asked his department chiefs to study stronger measures against Japan.[48]

This, for Hornbeck, was a happy chore. The chief difficulty was the

46. Hull to Roosevelt, 16 June 1938, DF 700.00116/355; Roosevelt to State, War, and Interior, 26 September 1935, Roosevelt Papers, Official File 20c, Box 17; Moffat, Journal entry of 20 June 1938, Moffat Papers, vol. 40; *FRUSJ*, 2:201–2; Stimson memo, 24 October 1938, Stimson Diary; and Welles to Roosevelt, 13 December 1938, Roosevelt Papers, PSF, DC, Box 59.

47. *FRUSJ*, 1:757–92; *FRUS, 1938*, 3:203–5, 278–79; *FRUS, 1938*, 4:6–7, 8–9, 30, 763; and Johnson to Hull, 19 July 1938, DF 894.515/40. Grew, again referring to the 1914–17 antecedent, protested the Yangtze closure to Foreign Minister Ugaki; he claimed that because Japan had not declared war, it was not entitled to exercise belligerent rights in blockading the river. Even if it had such rights, Grew continued, the United States had not allowed Germany or Britain to exclude its ships from war zones. If only Nye and Fish (and Hornbeck) could have heard these words!

48. *FRUS, 1938*, 4:48–53, 53–55; *FRUSJ*, 1:781–90; and Grew, Diary entry for October 1938, Grew Papers, vol. 93. Technically, Hull's request for the study was made in March, but the results were considered only in the autumn, at about the time Hull asked Grew to deliver the protest.

Treaty of Commerce and Navigation with Japan, signed in 1911. That agreement had not envisaged modern restrictions on trade, such as exchange controls and special monopolies or barter arrangements, which had arisen since the Great War. It failed to cover Japan's injuries to American commerce in non-Japanese territory. But it did prohibit U.S. reprisals against Tokyo for those injuries. The obvious step was to give the six months' notice required to terminate the treaty.[49]

Hornbeck's suggestion found little support among his colleagues, who as usual could agree only to oppose him. Hamilton, willing to consider only tariff increases on goods imported predominantly from Japan, opposed abrogation.[50] Harry Hawkins, chief of the Division of Trade Agreements, objected vehemently to Hamilton's proposal. To use the trade agreements law as a vehicle for economic retaliation was repugnant, and it would be better to revise the trade treaty with Japan.

Hamilton opposed revision, which would single out Tokyo blatantly. He proposed instead that Congress grant the president power to act against any state that violated American rights abroad. This suggestion drew fire from Feis's assistant economic adviser; Herbert Livesey pointed out that such power could be used against nations that had defaulted on bonds held by American citizens such as Mexico, or even war debts, including Britain and France.[51]

This dissension among his advisers decided Hull to wait for Japan's reply to his 1 October protest. It came a month later, in Konoe's "New Order in East Asia" address. In remarkably bald terms Konoe announced that Japan controlled the destiny of the Japan-China-Manchukuo bloc, and it would not tolerate from other powers any economic demands that cloaked political ambitions. A bitter Grew conceded that the premier had broken his earlier promise of respect for the Open Door. The new Japanese foreign minister, Arita Hachirō, was equally blunt. In a formal response to Hull's note Arita argued that the principles of the Open Door should not apply to China alone when they were not observed elsewhere in the world.

49. *FRUS, 1938*, 4:62–65, and Hornbeck to Hull, 19 July 1938, Hornbeck Papers, Box 458. Most useful to my entire discussion of the decision to abrogate the trade treaty is a memorandum by R. B. Bacon, 30 April 1940, DF 711.942/627, hereafter cited as Bacon memo.

50. Hamilton to Hull, 22 August 1938, DF 611.9431/162.

51. *FRUS, 1938*, 3:244–46; *FRUS, 1938*, 4:62–65; and Livesey to Feis, 10 October 1938, DF 611.9431/163 1/2. For Hull's opposition to various projects to aid China, see K. Marlin Friedrich, "In Search of a Far Eastern Policy: Joseph Grew, Stanley Hornbeck, and American-Japanese Relations, 1937–1941" (Ph.D. diss., Washington State University, 1974), 109–19.

The United States and Britain could demand the Open Door only because they were economically self-sufficient and militarily secure already. The Japanese Empire was not, and so it had to complete plans for "economic national defense." Western diplomats pointed out that Japanese trade with Britain and America had actually flourished during the 1930s, but Arita replied ingenuously that his nation needed access to materials "in territory from which she could not be cut off by belligerent action of third powers."[52]

These pronouncements drove the State Department to consider economic pressure again. Grew insisted that Japan simply was not vulnerable: sanctions could not shut off Tokyo's trade with the yen bloc. What was more, Japan had been preparing for war, probably against Russia, for some time, and so it had doubtless built substantial stockpiles of critical goods. Japanese leaders, if pressed, surely would attempt to find substitutes for the materials they were denied, and the Japanese people were ready for levels of sacrifice that Americans would find intolerable. Even if the West did undertake economic steps of great severity over a long period, those steps were more likely to end capitalism and political liberalism in Japan than to force Japan to leave China.[53]

Hornbeck dismissed these arguments. Economic pressure alone might accomplish little; it had to be supported by a willingness to proceed to military action. But Hornbeck doubted that any escalation would be necessary, because Japan was far more vulnerable than Grew and his allies had asserted. At the least, as China experts Willys Peck and John Carter Vincent maintained, pressure would prevent Japan from consolidating gains on the continent. And perhaps, as George Luthringer, another of Feis's assistants, held, it might thwart Japan's attempt to achieve self-sufficiency and gravely impair the empire's military efficiency. Whether Japan suffered internal revolution or not, Tokyo would have to revise its foreign policy objectives.[54]

In the past such a standoff would have resulted in no action. But by the spring of 1939 the tide was running toward sterner measures. Japan's successes led Hull to conclude that natural economic forces

---

52. *FRUS, 1938*, 3:366–68; *FRUS, 1938*, 4:87–89, 98, 93–95; and *FRUSJ*, 1:801–8.

53. Grew to Hull, 14 February 1939, DF 894.50/109, and *FRUS, 1939*, 3:516–19. Japan specialists in the Far Eastern Division such as Laurence Salisbury seconded Grew's assessment. Joseph Ballantine asserted that Tokyo was actually becoming less susceptible to economic sanctions as its productive capacity in war goods expanded and imports from the United States declined. See *FRUS, 1939*, 3:496–97, and Ballantine memo, 24 January 1939, DF 894.51/610.

54. *FRUS, 1938*, 3:483–85, 523–24; Hornbeck memo, 8 March 1939, Hornbeck Papers, Box 369; and Luthringer to Feis, 13 February 1939, DF 793.94/14671.

were not going to restrain Japan. A fundamental reordering was under way in Asia, to America's disadvantage. Trends in Europe were equally disturbing; it seemed imperative for the United States to embark upon bolder initiatives. Roosevelt agreed. "At the very least," he said in his message to Congress in January, "we can and should avoid any action, or any lack of action, which will encourage, assist or build up an aggressor." In an April press conference the president sharpened his criticism of economic "aggressor nations."[55]

The American public played an increasing role in these debates. Chief among vocal lobbying organizations was the American Committee for Non-Participation in Japanese Aggression. The group, an amalgam of pacifists and friends of China, had formed during the summer and autumn of 1938 to tell the man in the street about, in the title of its first mass pamphlet, "America's Share in Japan's War Guilt." It had good connections: Henry Stimson served as honorary chair, and Hornbeck discreetly encouraged its activities. By 1939 the campaign was bringing results: legislators and State Department officials were showered with letters protesting the shipment of American oil and scrap iron to Japan.[56]

In the wake of the moral embargo and in the midst of this new public mood, American business leaders took to consulting State before selling to Japan. This too strengthened the hardliners' position without formal steps by Washington. When Thomas Lamont, representing U.S. Steel, advised Hornbeck that Japan sought a large order for construction projects in Manchuria, Hornbeck warned that the American public might not approve. If firms did not observe voluntary restrictions on this sort of deal, he added, legal restrictions might be forthcoming. The company put the Japanese off. Hornbeck likewise discouraged a group of businessmen approached to build a steel mill in Japan by observing that his government was discouraging all credit transactions with Tokyo.[57]

Hornbeck's activities did not pass unnoticed. Hamilton suggested

---

55. Pittman memo, undated, Key Pittman Papers, Box 150, and Utley, 54.

56. Donald J. Friedman, *The Road from Isolation* (Cambridge: Harvard University Press, 1970), chap. 1; *FRUS, 1939,* 3:475–78; and Senator Arthur Capper to Hull, 27 January 1939, DF 894.24/586. See also Utley, 54–55.

57. *FRUS, 1939,* 3:482–83, 503–5. This hardening de facto embargo alarmed some businessmen. Guy Holman of New York's National City Bank confronted Hornbeck, maintaining that good business with Japan was being lost in the name of the Open Door. A California oilman echoed similar concerns, first voiced to him by Colonel Hori Mitsuya of the Japanese Planning Board. Hori feared that public pressure might halt all oil exports to his country (and endanger his crash build-up plan; see Chapter 5). See Grew to Hull, 14 February 1939, DF 894.6363/326, and *FRUS, 1939,* 3:376–78, 397–99.

that no official encourage private boycotts,[58] but Hamilton himself hardly encouraged business with Tokyo. When a Japanese industrialist inquired about a large credit with J. and W. Seligman, a New York investment house, its officers elected not to deal with him after phoning Hamilton. Other American firms did not bother to consult. Alcoa simply notified State's Controls Division that none of its products would be sold for export to Japan, cutting a major source of Tokyo's aluminum.[59]

Nor was Hornbeck's implied threat of coming legislation illusory. By springtime the Congress was considering several bills to embargo shipments of iron and steel scrap to Japan. Although Hornbeck favored these bills, most of his colleagues in State hoped to head off extreme measures by returning to the question of terminating the trade treaty, or at least its commercial clauses.[60] In early April, Hamilton composed a suitable draft. He then prepared to confer with senators Key Pittman and Hiram Johnson of the Foreign Relations Committee.[61]

Before Hamilton could act, however, Pittman introduced his own resolution, authorizing the president to restrict trade with any signatory of the Nine Power Treaty which endangered American lives or restricted American trade contrary to the treaty. Soon three more similar resolutions were placed before Congress. The State Department was flooded with letters in their support. Legislators received petitions with over 350,000 signatures in a drive organized by the Non-Participation Committee.[62]

When Hamilton learned of Pittman's move, he urged Hull to drop the treaty issue entirely. If the senator's resolution passed committee, it would have to be considered on the floor, with predictable complications for relations with Japan. It was best to soft-pedal the entire affair and stall for time. Hull needed no encouragement. Alarmed by rumors of a Japanese alliance with Germany, he ignored the urgings of Hornbeck, Hawkins, and Assistant Secretary Frank Sayre to proceed with abrogation and promptly distanced himself from Pittman.[63]

58. Grew to Hull, 14 February 1939, DF 894.6363/326; *FRUS, 1939,* 3:376–78, 397–99; and Hamilton to Hornbeck, 22 March 1939, Hornbeck Papers, Box 155.

59. *FRUS, 1939,* 3:494–95, and Yost memo, 1 February 1939, DF 894.24/600.

60. Various divisions objected to abrogating the whole treaty, which involved rights of residence, entry, property ownership, and other issues.

61. Bacon memo, and Hamilton to Sayre, 3 April 1939, DF 711.942/138.

62. Hamilton copy, 28 June 1939, DF 894.24/683. The DF 894.24 file has scores of these letters. See American Committee for Non-Participation in Japanese Aggression to Hull, undated, DF 894.24/657.

63. *FRUS, 1939,* 3:535–37, 533, 634–37, and Hornbeck memo, 12 May 1937, DF 711.942/634.

Pittman's bill soon became lost in a political labyrinth as Congress considered revising the neutrality acts to meet the new situation in Europe, and Hull might have succeeded, but the Japanese refused to accommodate him. During June incidents in which Imperial troops mistreated American citizens in China multiplied. In early July, Chungking, Chiang's latest capital, was savagely bombed. In response Roosevelt ordered Hull to demand a direct explanation from Tokyo instead of going through the diplomatic niceties of an exchange of notes.[64]

On Capitol Hill these latest outrages redirected attention to the Far East. Pittman asked, in vain, for new consideration of his bill. Instead, Republican senator Arthur Vandenberg offered his own proposal. Introduced on 18 July, it resolved that the United States give notice to abrogate the trade treaty and call for a resumption of the Brussels Conference.[65]

On the morning of 26 July the Senate Foreign Relations Committee discussed the Vandenberg resolution. The measure attracted bipartisan support, but not enough to ensure its passage without a floor fight. Hull dreaded both the debate to come and the even more embarrassing possibility of open hearings. For the entire day, top officials of the State Department met. The conclusion was foregone: the trade treaty with Japan would be denounced that evening. With it went the only legal barrier to formal economic pressure on the Japanese Empire.[66]

64. E. Roosevelt, 903–4.
65. Bacon memo.
66. Moffat, Journal entry of 26 July 1939, Moffat Papers, vol. 43.

[7]

Swastika and Red Star: The Imperial Army's Economic and Strategic Dilemmas of 1939

Konoe's failure to bring the China Incident to a quick conclusion had critical economic, and therefore political, implications. Because material allocations to the military could not rise in 1939, the interservice consensus forged in 1936 broke down. The army, the key actor for the next eighteen months, sought to end the fighting in China if possible; but in any event it looked to safeguard its existing allocations by stressing the Soviet threat and the necessity of alliance with Germany to meet that threat. The Imperial Navy attempted to preserve the huge quotas, especially of steel, necessary for its construction plans by directing national priorities toward a southward advance. In the middle of these disputes was the Cabinet Planning Board. The board would try to introduce a measure of economic realism into both services' requirements until, in the spring 1941 purge known as the Planning Board Incident, it was effectively removed from any policy role.

When Baron Hiranuma Kiichirō assumed power as prime minister in early January 1939, the army's position was unenviable. The immense Hankow campaign of the autumn of 1938 had not driven Chiang to the surrender table. For all the resources mustered, the army had little to show besides nonproductive territory. Moreover, the army was beginning to appreciate that those resources had limits and that further China campaigns were not worthwhile. One immediate result was friction with the navy, which had demanded the seizure of Hainan Island and Kwangtung Province in south China. Although a five ministers' conference had approved landings in Kwangtung in July 1938, an acute shortage of shipping had delayed the operation until October. The army had blocked the invasion of

Hainan outright in 1938, in part because of the shortage. To cut off foreign aid to the Nationalists was of course attractive, but the army would endorse no further campaigns that entailed additional commitments of material.[1]

To underline its stance, the Army General Staff again announced its decision not to expand operations in China for 1939 and, on 9 May of that year, sent its chief of staff, General Prince Kan'in Kotohito, before the emperor to present a long, formal report. This detailed exposition of the army's view of the developing global situation argued that nearly every great power was rearming. By 1942 or 1943 these programs would be completed. World war would break out soon after, catching Japan unprepared and weakened by its diversion on the continent.[2] But both the navy and the Planning Board frustrated the army's attempts to consolidate its position in China, avoid further expansion of the conflict there, and redirect its efforts to preparing for war against the Soviet Union.

The Planning Board began its struggle against the military with the support of Hiranuma, who was determined not to repeat Konoe's disastrous economic errors. During Hiranuma's premiership the Planning Board took the first steps to redirect Japan back to long-term self-sufficiency. Konoe's approach, diverting all efforts to win the war against China quickly, was abandoned for attempts to achieve true self-sufficiency.

This effort began with the materials mobilization plan for 1939. In addition to changing the plan from calendar to fiscal year (April 1939 to March 1940), to improve financial coordination, the board resolved upon three central priorities. Konoe's policy of starving all civilian industries was reversed. Japan's export industries were to be guaranteed access to necessary imported materials so that further declines in production—and further erosion of Japan's earnings of foreign exchange—could be prevented. Second, the long-deferred five-year production expansion plan, brainchild of the departed Ishiwara Kanji, was to begin. Third, materials and money were to be allotted to develop Manchuria and the occupied provinces of China, especially north China, so that these regions could contribute their share to the Japanese Empire's long-term economic capacity.[3]

1. *DR1*, 566–67, and Frank Dorn, *The Sino-Japanese War, 1937–1941* (New York: Macmillan, 1974), 146–52, 157.

2. *DR1*, 588–92, is the text of Kan'in's report. See Hata Ikuhiko, "The Japanese-Soviet Confrontation, 1935–1939," in *Deterrent Diplomacy*, ed. James W. Morley (New York: Columbia University Press, 1976), 157.

3. Tsūshō Sangyō-shō, *Shōkō seisakushi 11: Sangyō tōsei* (Tokyo: Shōkō Seisakushi Kankōkai, 1964), 206–7, which reproduces President of the Planning Board Taki Masao's presentation of the materials mobilization plan.

Each priority received its own category in the 1939 materials plan, a plan that was itself more sophisticated and detailed than its predecessors. But it was not more optimistic. Even the modest goal of the revised 1938 plan, importing 2.42 billion yen worth of goods—a reduction of 20 percent from the original—had been beyond Japan's ability. For 1939, the Planning Board estimated that barely 2.03 billion could be purchased abroad and of this total, only 1.8 billion would be furnished by foreign exchange earned from the export of Japanese goods. Gold shipments would have to account for the remainder.[4]

Even these steps demanded further stiff reductions in outlays. As before, general civilian quotas were cut sharpest—each by an average exceeding 40 percent of 1938's lean figures. But the board adhered to its own priorities elsewhere. Allocations for production expansion were reduced from 1.05 billion yen to 800 million, an economy that ensured at least steady maintenance of existing plant and still provided for the construction of additional capacity, albeit at a pace only slightly over one half of that hoped for. Materials destined for China and Manchuria fared worse, but only because—as the Planning Board itself pointed out—the Manchukuan government's own plans were far behind schedule and pacification had yet to be completed in China. Only the export industries in Japan went unscathed.

The military did not. In an unprecedented move the Planning Board, many of its own members in uniform, resolutely maintained that the military would have to suffer short-term reductions so that the longer-range target of autarky could be reached. No longer would military needs receive unquestioned or even top priority. Specifically, the 1939 plan proposed to trim imports destined for military use from 1.6 billion to 1.35 billion yen. The resulting furor led to frantic negotiations between the Planning Board and the ministries, civilian and especially military. The services got 40 million yen restored but no more, for the Planning Board warned that any increases meant either the loss of more specie abroad or further reduction in stockpiles at home. For the first time during war, the army and navy had suffered actual reductions in their ability to import badly needed materials.[5]

For the army, the impact of these reductions was most dramatic on its cherished mission of war against the Soviet Union. In keeping with Kan'in's assumption of general war in 1942, the General Staff's Operations Section had drafted two plans for an attack on the Soviet

4. *GDS43*, 358–78, 382–83, and Tanaka Shin'ichi, *Nihon sensō keizai hishi* (Tokyo: Conputa Eijisha, 1975), 27–28.

5. *GDS43*, 382–83, 388–90, 391–92, 410–15, and *RGD2*, 297–99. Those debates caused the plan's implementation to be delayed past its scheduled start in April.

Union. Plan B was the traditional plan long favored by the army. It called for large thrusts north and west from Manchuria at the outset of hostilities and subsequent defeat of the enemy in detail. The other, Plan A, stipulated only an investment of Vladivostok and the coastal areas of the Soviet Maritime Province inland to the Amur-Ussuri line. Only after investment and occupation of the coast would spearheads advance north and then turn west toward Lake Baikal.

From field commanders in the Kwantung Army to leaders of the General Staff, sentiment strongly favored Plan B. But Plan B required at least three more rail lines in Manchuria, nearly 200,000 ground vehicles, quite a few of them armored, and a similarly heavy commitment of supporting resources. The overall economic situation and the Planning Board's unwelcome position put Plan B beyond the army's means. The more modest Plan A, which did not, according to the operations planners, guarantee decisive victory, would have to be adopted instead.[6]

It was the army that took the initiative in proposing solutions to the economic constraints. Led by Minister Itagaki Seishirō, who remained at his post under Hiranuma, the army called for still tighter economic controls. An important first step was the Business Promotion for General Mobilization Ordinance, which the cabinet promulgated in late July. It gave the Army and Navy ministries direct authority to order plant owners and operators to produce goods according to the military's specific schedule. More broadly, the Planning Board drew up allocation procedures for commerce, transportation, and electric power. Additional measures, also approved in July, allowed for the comprehensive mobilization of labor and capital. In those areas not covered by the mobilization law, the Diet itself enlarged government authority. The Imperial Mining Development Company was created to oversee all mineral extraction throughout the empire. The shipping industry received special attention: after forming the Greater Japan Shipping Company, the Diet brought all private Japanese and chartered foreign shipping under unified supervision. Supplemental enabling legislation also allowed the Hiranuma cabinet to issue a plethora of ordinances for further economic control.[7]

The army's second proposal was more far-reaching. As scarcity grew, so the Imperial Army found an alliance with Nazi Germany all the more appealing. Prince Kan'in's report had revealed that over the

---

6. *DR1*, 584–85, 587.

7. International Military Tribunal for the Far East (IMTFE), Narrative Summary of the Record, 1234; *RGD2*, 278 79; and *GDS43*, 416–21, 422–27, 428–36, 437–41.

previous year the Army General Staff had become alarmed that forces on the continent were becoming increasingly less able to deal with the growing Soviet military menace. Total war officers could point to the army's sorry performance during the Changkufeng Incident—when Japan had run out of antitank shells before fighting had begun. Itagaki could not ignore the Russian buildup, but plans to divert Japanese divisions from China to Manchuria appeared less likely to succeed. One obvious way to redress the growing imbalance on the Soviet border was to seek an alliance with the Germans. The army's representatives had high hopes that such a pact would, as a bonus, also end Berlin's ambivalence regarding the Sino-Japanese conflict, ending one outside source of succor for Chiang.

The Imperial Navy was also affected by the Planning Board. In the 1939 materials mobilization plan its steel quota declined from a 1938 total of 532,000 tons to 500,000. The reduction was relatively modest, but still it came as unwelcome news to a service accustomed to the lion's share of government steel production in peacetime and embarked upon a huge third replenishment plan to maintain its position against the American fleet. Aggressive middle-echelon navy officers, such as the influential captain Oka Takazumi, chief of the Navy Ministry's First Section of the Military Affairs Bureau, emphasized Japan's future to the south; the nation needed a fleet to give substance to its great destiny. Japan had to accord the Southward Advance a role at least equal to the army's northward defenses against the Soviets. Was the advance merely a device for obtaining additional steel and other materials? As Captain Takagi Sōkichi assured Baron Harada Kumao shortly after the key five ministers' conference of 19 January, no one was to wrongly assume that "the navy, although prepared to use Britain and the United States as pretexts for a budget, actually did not want to confront them."[8]

The navy was at best lukewarm toward the alliance with Germany. Indeed, all navy factions had grounds for questioning it, especially if the alliance was directed solely against the Soviet Union. The moderate navy minister Yonai Mitsumasa, who also retained office under Hiranuma, feared that a Japanese connection with Germany would force Britain into America's arms. An Anglo-American alliance could

8. Asada Sadao, "The Role of the Japanese Navy," in *Pearl Harbor as History*, ed. Dorothy Borg and Shumpei Okamoto (New York: Columbia University Press, 1973), 246–47; and David J. Lu, *From the Marco Polo Bridge to Pearl Harbor* (Washington: Public Affairs, 1973), 47–48. Takagi is quoted in Harada Kumao, "The Saionji-Harada Memoirs," mimeo., International Legal Studies Library, Harvard Law School, entry of 25 January 1939.

apply unbearable economic pressure against Japan, forcing Tokyo either to surrender or to wage a war of desperation. In Yonai's judgment, which dated back to the days of the Washington Naval Conference of 1921–22, the fleet existed to prevent conflict with the Americans, not cause it. An alliance with Germany against any other power, therefore, was not good "deterrent diplomacy." And if the fleet was to be a successful instrument of deterrence, its construction program had to be completed. This completion, in turn, required good relations with the United States, a principal source of materials for the replenishment plan. Middle-level officers of the navy argued for their part that, if the army was to have its alliance with Germany, the alliance should at least not specify only the Soviets as its target. If it did, the Southward Advance would languish and the navy receive few materials for its replenishment program.[9]

Debate over the German alliance was resolved by compromise. The first showdown came on 19 January 1939 at the five ministers' conference. The army was prepared to bring down the cabinet over the issue of the alliance; the navy's middle-level officers were determined that no alliance should specify the Soviet Union as its sole target. Foreign Minister Arita Hachirō, as wary as Yonai was of the implications of such a pact, sought to defuse its worst consequences by proposing that Japan be obligated to provide only political and economic aid to the Nazis if Britain and France were to be designated as targets. In addition, to minimize difficulties with the Western democracies, the treaty would be announced publicly as a simple extension of the Anti-Comintern Pact negotiated in 1936. Itagaki was willing to pay Arita's and the navy hardliners' price: the conference also approved the seizure of Hainan as a first step toward the Southward Advance.[10]

These terms ensured consensus in Tokyo, but they did not satisfy Berlin and Rome. Japan's ambassadors in both capitals, Major (in March, Lieutenant) General Ōshima Hiroshi and Shiratori Toshio, refused even to transmit them to Ribbentrop and Ciano. By March, Arita was willing to leave open the issue of Japanese military intervention should Germany and Italy go to war with any power other than the Soviet Union. But he refused to go further; the emperor

9. Asada, 247.

10. Ōhata Tokushirō, "The Anti-Comintern Pact, 1935–1939," in *Deterrent Diplomacy*, ed. James W. Morley (New York: Columbia University Press, 1976), 79–80; Lu, 48; Nihon Kokusai Seiji Gakkai Taiheiyō Sensō Gen'in Kenkyūbu, ed., *Taiheiyō sensō e no michi*, 8 vols. (Tokyo: Asahi Shinbunsha, 1962–63), 6:9–10; and Stephen E. Pelz, *Race to Pearl Harbor* (Cambridge: Harvard University Press, 1974), 213.

made a rare intervention in the policy process late in the month to support him. When Ōshima agreed independently to enlarge Japan's commitment, Arita was outraged. The foreign minister sought to terminate the alliance negotiations, but Itagaki blocked the move.[11]

This deadlock continued until late April, when fast-moving events in Europe led Ribbentrop to impose a deadline on Tokyo's reply to Ōshima's unauthorized draft. The deadline passed. Soon after, the Germans submitted a fresh proposal authored by Friedrich Gaus, chief of the German Foreign Office's Treaty Bureau. Gaus wanted Tokyo at least to agree that the pact would apply in case of attack by a nation under the Comintern's influence—that is, any nation that might sign an alliance with Moscow. Yet in his draft, unlike in Ōshima's version, the contracting parties would promise to enter into consultations (*setsumei-furui*) and render military assistance (*buryoku-enjo*) by assuming the status of a belligerent, even if no belligerent acts were committed.

These efforts failed to end the impasse. Arita and Yonai were joined by Finance Minister Ishiwata Sōtarō in opposing the Gaus draft. Hiranuma appealed to the two general staffs: if the services compromised, the Foreign Ministry and Finance would have to fall into line. But this ploy did not succeed either. The Naval General Staff absolutely refused to consider joining Germany against only Britain and France. Neither Yonai nor the mid-level officers sought wars dictated by Berlin.[12]

By mid-May the Imperial Army's economic and strategic dilemmas were still unresolved. Hopes for ending, or at least reducing, involvement in China still seemed remote. The alliance with Germany had encountered strong obstacles. The Planning Board had been unyielding. Indeed, only two days after Kan'in's report to the throne all of these difficulties were exacerbated by the onset of the Nomonhan Incident.

Errant Mongolian forces had attacked Manchurian puppet troops in mid-May. Army authorities in Tokyo, aware of their material limitations, sanctioned only a swift chastisement. On 18 June, in response to this action, the Soviets counterattacked, and Itagaki's senior staffers refused the Kwantung Army's request for a division-level assault with heavy air support. They relented only after Lieutenant General Hashimoto Gun and Colonel Inada Masazumi of the General Staff's Operations Division convinced Itagaki that some re-

---

11. Ōhata, 82, 86–87, 93; Lu, 50–51; and *DR1*, 587–88.
12. *DR1*, 587–89; Lu, 52–54; and Ōhata, 98.

sponse was necessary. Even Hashimoto, however, moved to cancel action when he learned that the Kwantung Army contemplated airstrikes deep into Outer Mongolia. His orders were circumvented by Major Tsuji Masanobu, who moved the strike date forward to 27 June. As Tokyo sat helpless, the Kwantung Army drove forward until the Soviets responded with armor. The Kwantung Army brought up artillery and launched a new attack on 23 July, firing 15,000 shells every day—an expenditure hardly welcome in Tokyo. The Soviets replied with even more intense barrages, heavily reinforced their ground troops, and began their own attack a month later. The Japanese were badly mauled. The Kwantung Army, deeply disgraced, readied four divisions and every artillery piece in Manchuria for all-out war in the spring. But news of Germany's attack on Poland—with Stalin's connivance—instilled a modicum of caution. By mid-September 1939 a truce had been arranged in Moscow.[13]

By that time the Hiranuma cabinet had fallen. The chief cause, as most historians have noted, was the Nazi-Soviet nonaggression pact, which Tokyo had not anticipated and which shocked the cabinet's foreign policy to the core. Less well known but nearly as important a reason was the mounting domestic problems of the summer of 1939.

Some of these problems could not have been anticipated. The summer of 1939 saw severe flooding in north China and Taiwan while Japan and Korea were experiencing their worst drought in over a century. By early August, Japan's stores of rice had declined to 19.8 million *koku* (one *koku* equals 4.96 bushels) from the previous year's level of 22.2 million koku. In response to this alarming drop the Hiranuma cabinet had formed the Japan Rice Company, with a monopoly over the purchase and sale of rice, and raised the market price for rice. This step gave farmers more incentive to produce, perhaps, but did nothing for their scorched paddies. By year's end the Planning Board—increasingly a prophet of gloom—had completed a dismaying study that projected a food shortfall of five million koku for 1940. An emergency import program from French Indochina, Thailand, and other regions of Southeast Asia was rushed through, draining an additional and unlooked-for hundred million yen from Japan's already burdened foreign exchange reserves. Even then, additional supplies had to be found, by restricting saké production, eating substitutes such as barley, and ending the practice of polishing rice.

The weather had other effects. Production of hydroelectric power in Japan dipped, forcing factories to burn coal. Coal output had fallen

13. Hata, 162–70.

below quota in late 1938 and had not yet caught up (another legacy of Konoe's policies), and so these new demands resulted in shortages of energy. On the continent, meanwhile, overabundant rainfall had curtailed shipments of industrial salt to the home islands and halved the cotton crop.[14]

The Planning Board and other economic analysts, primarily from the economic bureaus of the South Manchurian Railway, had other concerns. In particular they feared the likely effects of America's formal intent to abrogate the Treaty of Commerce and Navigation, opening the way to economic pressure from Washington. The situation in scrap iron provoked most concern. Japanese production of steel was rising, but this growth was underwritten by increasing supplies of imported scrap. The United States furnished almost 75 percent of Japan's scrap imports during 1938, over one million tons (see Table 7.1). And as Japan produced more steel, particularly high-quality steel, the ratio of scrap to pig iron—the other main ingredient—tended to increase. If the United States now ended shipments of scrap, Japan could easily lose over 1.3 million tons of steel production, with devastating effects on civilian and military usage alike.

Copper was one product where Japan traditionally had produced enough to meet domestic needs and still export. By mid-1939 this was no longer the case. Copper's use in shell casings, electric plants, and the expanding heavy industry sector required imports in growing amounts. In 1939 Japan had produced almost 90,000 tons but imported nearly 105,000 tons, 93 percent of it from America. Here, too, an embargo would bring on near disaster. In the rarer elements vital for special steel alloys, such as vanadium and molybdenum, the United States held a similarly dominant import market share.

Japan had grown heavily dependent on America for machine tools also. In 1938 the United States supplied over 60 percent of Japan's imports of this vital product. Germany ran a poor second. Production of machine tools in Japan was growing rapidly, but because of the China war and the general rearmament effort, demand rose faster. An American embargo would cause Japan production bottlenecks in key industries.[15]

14. IMTFE, Narrative Summary, 1263, 3820; *RGD2*, 151–52; *FES*, 25 October 1939, 14 February 1940; Ishigawa Junkichi, comp., *Kokka sōdōinshi*, 6 vols. (Tokyo: Kiyomizu Insatsujo, 1975), 1:337; and *GDS43*, 461–68. The rice shortage forced the army to grant special furloughs to men to help in the harvest and planting in late autumn; see *RGD2*, 153.

15. Nakamura Takafusa and Hara Akira, Introduction to *GDS43*, x1, and Mantetsu, Tokyo shisa, chōsashitsu, *Nichi-Bei tsūshō kōkai jōyaku haki no eikyō narabini sonotaisaku* (Tokyo, 1939), n.p.

Table 7.1. Japanese imports of scrap iron by source country, 1929–38 (in metric tons)

Source	1929–32 (average)	1929–32 (percent)	1933–36 (average)	1933–36 (percent)	1937	1937 (percent)	1938	1938 (percent)
Manchuria	9,600	2.1%	13,500	1.0%	43,900	1.8%	47,200	3.5%
China	13,900	3.0	17,200	1.2	10,700	0.4	30,200	2.2
British colonies	111,800	24.4	132,800	9.5	200,100	8.3	81,700	6.0
Netherlands East Indies	25,200	5.5	40,600	2.9	97,400	4.0	66,700	4.9
United States	163,500	35.7	942,100	67.2	1,777,000	73.4	1,006,700	74.1
Australia	11,600	2.5	27,200	3.4	84,000	3.5	30,400	2.2
Others	122,400	26.7	210,200	15.0	206,700	8.5	95,000	7.1
Total	457,900	100%	1,403,800	100%	2,419,800	100%	1,357,900	100%

SOURCE: Mantetsu, Tokyo shisa, chōsashitsu, *Nichi-Bei tsūshō kōkai jōyaku haki no eikyō narabini sonotaisaku* (Tokyo, 1939), n.p.

Table 7.2. Targets and results for Japan's synthetic oil plan, 1937–44 (in thousand kiloliters)

Year	Planned Target	Actual Production
1937	87	5
1938	446	11
1939	489	21
1940	930	24
1941	1243	194
1942	1807	238
1943	2233	272
1944	6935	765

SOURCE: Bōeichō, bōei kenshūjo, senshishitsu, *Kaigun gunsembi* (Tokyo: Asagumo Shinbunsha, 1969), 710.

The situation in the most critical commodity, oil, was even worse. Overall, Japan relied on America for 80 percent of fuel needs. For special distillates, such as gasoline, the dependence ran over 90 percent. During 1938 alone Japan had imported almost four million kiloliters of crude oil from the United States. There were no available substitutes, and Japan's stockpiles were at their lowest point in years because of operations in China. Some Soviet oil could be imported, though this solution was hardly ideal (particularly in the army's eyes). Romania could furnish supplies—if the Germans permitted diversions from their own needs. The Netherlands East Indies did look promising, however, and staff preparations began in the summer of 1939 for an economic mission to the Indies.

For the alternative, synthetic oil, results had been less than spectacular. In 1938 Japan's synthetic fuel program had produced only 11,000 kiloliters of a planned target of 446,000. Results for the first part of 1939 were scarcely better (see Table 7.2). To expand output substantially, however, Japan would have to turn to America. The synfuel industry relied especially heavily on American equipment, particularly machine tools, and American firms were the only ones outside Germany to have mastered the appropriate technology. To count on German equipment seemed risky in the summer of 1939. Accordingly, the navy sent a special team of technicians to the United States to buy processes both for the synthetic production of crude oil and for better yields of distillates.[16]

16. *GDS43*, 442–60; *KGS1*, 710; Mantetsu, *Nichi-Bei . . . eikyō*; Mantetsu, Tokyo

When General Abe Nobuyuki assumed power in late August 1939, none of the pressing concerns of his Imperial Army had been addressed. China still drained it of men and material. The Soviets had become increasingly belligerent and effective. The navy continued its pressure for the Southward Advance, lest it lose materials allocations. The Planning Board continued to insist that Japan's economic position was currently bad and had the potential to become considerably worse. Such a deterioration was sure to make interservice discord sharper yet. On 1 September Germany invaded Poland, and the new premier saw the board's predictions starting to come true.

---

shisa, chōsashitsu, *Nichi-Bei tsūshō jōyaku haki no wagakuni sekiyogyō ni oyobasu eikyō to taisaku* (Tokyo, 1939), n.p.; *KG*, 699, 711; and Tōyō Keizai Shinbunsha, ed., *Shōwa sangyōshi*, 3 vols. (Tokyo, 1950), 3:60. The army strongly urged the purchase, on that mission, of synthetic oil–processing equipment in addition to plans for the processes from the Americans. The navy felt this request to be an affront to its own work in the area and refused. The Finance Ministry allied with the navy because of the high cost of the machinery. In the end the navy's own processes did not work well. By that time, however, the United States had embargoed the export of processes as well as equipment. The only tangible result was a series of suits against American oil firms for failing to deliver the processes, suits that (predictably) went nowhere in 1940 and 1941. See *RGD2*, 315.

[8]

Caretakers and the Quest for Autarky: Marking Time

In the immediate aftermath of the outbreak of war in Europe, it appeared that Japan would be compelled to become relatively autarchic whether prepared or not. Initial studies of the economic impact of European war warned that Japan's current policies—a refusal to retrench in China and the beginnings of the Southward Advance, as well as an inability to address the grave economic situation even before the German invasion of Poland—could lead to disaster. A fundamental redirection of Japan's foreign and domestic policies was in order. None took place under the caretaker cabinets of Abe Nobuyuki and Yonai Mitsumasa. The fault lay not with these two premiers, however, but with the army, unable to abandon or even reduce its commitment in China so that preparations against the Soviets could proceed; the navy, unwilling to forego the material advantages of a southward advance; and the Planning Board, stubbornly insisting that Japan, even with greater economic controls at home, could not afford both services' commitments.

Japan's initial assessments of the impact of European war were made by the Planning Board and research agencies of the South Manchurian Railway in Tokyo. Both agreed that the new hostilities would mimic those from 1914 to 1918. A quick win by Germany against the Franco-British alliance was possible; Germany was sure to defeat Poland rapidly. Berlin and Rome would probably make peace overtures to the west; these would be rejected. As Britain and France moved toward active belligerency, Italy would join the war on Germany's side. At first the Soviets would maintain benevolent neutrality toward the Nazis, and the United States would stay clear of the fighting for six months or so. The western front then would degenerate into a stalemate that even the spread of hostilities to Scandinavia and the Balkans would not relieve. The result would be a prolonged war of attrition which would see the belligerents, including the British dominions, redouble their armament efforts. So would America, which would probably commence active aid to the democracies. Washington, London, and Paris would rely on Latin America, Africa, and parts of South Asia as their "resource acquisition zones."[1]

The consequences for Japan promised to be baleful. The nation was about to encounter enormous obstacles in its attempts to obtain critical materials, and those materials most vital to the military and to the effort to expand production would be the hardest to secure. Even when they could be purchased, their price was certain to soar. If strategic materials were to be gotten at all, moreover, they would have to come from the British Empire and the United States. Before the fighting started, Japan had been obtaining two-thirds of its imports of iron and steel from British and American territories. Iron ore was mined in British Malaya and the Philippines; scrap iron came overwhelmingly from America, nearly 70 percent of Japan's requirements for steel production, with much of the balance from Australia and British India. It was possible to decrease reliance on scrap by purchasing more pig iron, but here too Japanese dependence on the United States had grown markedly (see Table 8.1). In certain essential specialty steels and finished steel products the United States held a commanding position that could only grow—Japan's other prewar suppliers, Germany, Belgium, and Britain, could hardly be expected to boost exports to Tokyo.

American preeminence in oil was still more marked. The Tokyo office study considered two contingencies. One, that the Americans would aid Britain and France while maintaining reasonably friendly relations with Japan, was bad enough; the other, that Japan's relations with Britain and America would become strained, was worse. Even projected increases in Franco-British demand would dry up much of Japan's share, which before 1939 had been first or second in American exports of most major categories of crude and its distillates.

The picture was equally bleak for other goods. The Planning Board itself concluded that vital, albeit esoteric, equipment such as mercury rectifiers, gas separators, and precision industrial machinery could henceforth come only from America, if any came at all. Chemicals in

1. Mantetsu, Tokyo shisa, chōsashitsu, *Shina jihen shori narabini Ōshū sensō boppatsu ni tomonau senji keizai taisaku* (Tokyo, 1939), n.p.

Table 8.1. Sources of Japanese imports of pig iron, 1936–37 (in metric tons)

Source	1936 Calendar Year	1937 First Half
Manchukuo	271,225	120,570
Great Britain	2,263	4,642
United States	573	148,741
British India	375,323	171,660
Others	322,585	69,548
Total	971,969	515,771

SOURCE: Mantetsu, Tokyo Shisa, chōsashitsu, *Shino jihen shori narabini Ōshū sensō boppatsu ni tomonau senji keizai taisaku* (Tokyo, 1939), n.p.

quantity, from caustic soda (used to refine alumina) to ammonium sulphate (for fertilizer) would be increasingly difficult to purchase abroad.[2]

Initial Anglo-American economic reactions to war in Europe made this dismal picture appear still gloomier, as did estimates of Japan's own efforts to supply itself with key commodities. By mid-September 1939 the governor of British Malaya had brought all ores under an export licensing system. Soon after, the American president announced his government's hope that materials important for military use would not be exported. Roosevelt also began to pressure Congress for revision of American neutrality legislation. The Tokyo office study was unsure how far revision would progress, but the effect, it asserted, would be to divert additional materials toward Britain and France and away from other potential purchasers.[3]

These projections made it a simple matter for the Planning Board to predict substantial economic setbacks, with major consequences for Japan's foreign policy, especially for the overarching materials mobilization plan for 1939, which had just entered its third quarter. The board flatly stated that shortages of foreign exchange, coupled with higher prices and freight rates (when shipping could be found at all), would reduce Japan's planned production of steel materials to a quarter-million tons below results achieved in the modest, indeed disappointing, first two quarters of the 1939 plan. Other equally essential commodities would fare no better.[4]

2. *GDS43*, 219–30.
3. Mantetsu, *Shina*.
4. *GDS43*, 442–60.

As the first agency in Japan to predict the effects of the European war, the Planning Board led the way in advocating policies to head them off. Japan could seize the opportunity created by the new war to move into Latin America, South Asia—especially the Netherlands East Indies—and other markets as European suppliers became unable to fulfill their usual functions, much as it had in the 1914–18 period. But during World War I Japan had been effectively at peace and thus easily able to exploit Europe's difficulties. As the board itself realized, the Japan of 1939 did not possess the capability to fill gaps in demand overseas. Moreover, it was also regarded with suspicion, even fear, in many of the regions it banked on to relieve its dependence on the United States and Britain. And Washington and London, neither of them friendly in 1939, were in strong positions to influence the scope and nature of Japan's trade ties around the world, as their September steps had shown.

A second possibility was to enact crash programs to import goods, as had been done to meet the rice shortage of the summer of 1939. These, however, would have to be undertaken on a vast scale, especially for those commodities most needed by the military: scrap iron, aluminum, nickel, and alloy metals. The Planning Board did not believe that Japan's increasingly modest reserves of foreign exchange· would be sufficient. Likely to result was a bankrupt empire with stockpiles of strategic materials barely able to last a year—even if Britain and America permitted such massive purchases from their territories in the first place.

Japan could rely more on Manchukuo and occupied China, raising production there as rapidly as possible (as the 1939 materials mobilization plan had initially envisioned). This, however, would require an even greater diversion of existing resources away from current priorities and toward investment of capital, materials, and manpower in these regions. Given shortages already occurring in the home islands, few members of the Planning Board believed that such a diversion was politically feasible. Doubts about the economic wisdom of banking on uncertain investments in still hostile areas, at least in China, served to render this choice less palatable as well.

One route did exist which avoided reliance on foreign nations or occupied areas, was politically possible, and was especially attractive to the Planning Board. Still harsher controls could be imposed on consumption within the Japanese Empire. If the military could be persuaded to seek no increases in its material requirements, and if the civilian sector could be squeezed further, by giving the premier such additional "mobilization leadership" powers as wage and price controls and "total labor mobilization" prerogatives, the empire might avoid the worst of the consequences of the European war.[5]

Prime Minister General Abe Nobuyuki attempted to embrace a foreign policy that would address the Planning Board's concerns. A fresh emergency import program began in October under the supervision of Colonel Atami Saburō. Atami was to secure from America high-grade machine tools and industrial machinery to produce heavier Japanese armor and artillery, so that the Imperial Army could put to good use the hard lessons of Nomonhan. To help the mission succeed, and to allow for further Japanese penetration of colonial markets, Abe awarded the foreign ministry portfolio to Admiral Nomura Kichisaburō. Nomura knew Franklin Roosevelt personally and so, it was hoped, his appointment would improve Japanese-American relations. Plans also went forward for increased exploitation of Manchukuo and north China.

None of these initiatives succeeded. Abe's own service destroyed whatever goodwill Nomura's appointment had generated by demanding in early September that the belligerent powers withdraw their garrisons from China. Only Britain and France had forces stationed there. Nomura began personal conversations with American ambassador Joseph Grew to renew the trade treaty and so head off American economic pressure on Japan. But the American's demands that Washington's neutral and treaty rights in China be respected were not satisfied by Japanese field commanders there, who were eager for further military operations certain to trample those rights. Even within the Foreign Ministry members of the American Bureau insisted that Nomura demand American recognition of Japan's New Order—overlordship of China and dominance over East Asia—before a satisfactory trade agreement could be negotiated.[6]

Washington's reaction was a stronger "moral embargo," imposed in early December. This new step blocked many of Atami's orders for tools and machinery. Some purchases were made, but in the spring the U.S. Navy diverted the ordered equipment to its own building programs, as the Planning Board had predicted.[7]

The most critical setback to the Planning Board's recommendations came from the Operations Division of the Army General Staff. The army's own economic staffers readily agreed with the board that ma-

5. Mantetsu, *Shina*, and *GDS43*, 159–60, 172–76, 161–62, 442–60.

6. Bōeichō, bōei kenshūjo, senshishitsu, *Daihon'ei rikugunbu 2* (Tokyo: Asagumo Shinbunsha, 1968), 6, and *RGD2*, 364, 332–33; David J. Lu, *From the Marco Polo Bridge to Pearl Harbor* (Washington: Public Affairs, 1961), 60, 62–66.

7. *RGD2*, 324–25.

terial needs had to be constrained, but operations officers quickly overruled their recommendation that the number of troops in China be reduced from 850,000 to 500,000 men by mid-1941. These men saw the outbreak of war in Europe in a markedly different light. Where the Planning Board became more cautious, the operations officers saw the new war as a boon to the effort against Chiang Kai-shek. Japan might suffer some additional privations, they conceded, but Chiang would go begging too. European powers would scale down their aid to the Chinese voluntarily, and where necessary they could be forced to do so. One promising avenue was to pressure France to ban shipments through Indochina to the Nationalists. Army studies had concluded that the Indochina route accounted for over 40 percent of Chiang's foreign supplies. Nearby ports in southern China represented another 40 percent. Operations officers argued not for Japanese retrenchment in China but for a large-scale attack on Nanning, a key city in southerly Kwangsi Province near the Indochinese border.

The outcome of this difference in views—it can hardly be called a debate—was never in doubt. The Planning Board urged retrenchment, even deprivation, so that Japan could prepare for a protracted, stalemated struggle against China in a hostile international environment. Army operations planners promised to knock Chiang out of the war at last, with a series of blows in southern China—exactly the area where ambitious mid-level navy officers wished to begin an advance to parts further south. On 16 October the army's supreme command ordered preparations to begin for the Nanning campaign. Once the city had been taken, Japanese forces in southern China were to be ready to occupy northern French Indochina on short notice.[8]

Far from retrenchment, Nanning was the first major Japanese operation since the desultory efforts at Nanchang in the spring of 1939 and the later failure to secure Changsha. By early December, Nanning was under siege. Japanese troops fanned out to the north and west. Then, only two weeks later, the Chinese launched a massive counteroffensive. In Kwangsi the Japanese retired to Nanning and awaited reinforcements—of more than a division in size—rushed from the

8. Donald S. Detwiler and Charles B. Burdick, eds., *War in Asia and the Pacific*, 15 vols. (New York: Garland, 1980), 8: "China Area Operations Record, July 1937–November 1941," 33–35; *DR2*, 5; *DR1*, 627, 614; and Tanaka Shin'ichi, *Nihon sensō keizai hishi* (Tokyo: Conputa Eijisha, 1975), 35–36. The remaining 20 percent of foreign supplies to China came via central Asia or the Burma Road; *DR1*, 617–18. It is worth noting that the planning for the Nanning operation occurred before the outbreak of the war in Europe.

home islands. In central China the Nationalist attack led to fierce fighting around Hankow. To the north the Imperial Army suffered heavily in the Chinese siege and attempted Japanese relief of Paotao. Only additional reinforcements that arrived on 24 December carried the day.[9]

These expanded operations failed to resolve the China Incident, but they did undermine Nomura's attempts to build goodwill with the Western powers and Atami's crash import mission. They denied resources for the exploitation of Manchukuo and occupied China. Most obviously, they ensured that military requirements for strategic materials would increase markedly.

That operations officers disregarded the economic constraints imposed by the outbreak of war in Europe did not mean that those constraints were illusory. By the end of 1939 Japan was living beyond its means. Of all the Planning Board's recommendations, however, the Abe cabinet enacted only the fourth, stricter controls on civilian consumption. On 18 October under the authority of the National Mobilization Law, all prices, wages, salaries, rents, fees, freight rates, and other fixable economic measures were frozen at their levels of one month before. Although a step toward controlling ever-mounting inflation, itself a result of increasing scarcity, this move did not go far enough for the Planning Board, which had wanted an attack on the basic problem, scarcity itself.

The controls went too far, however, for over two hundred members of the Diet, who signed a condemnation of the Abe cabinet in December. The members, in fact, had a veritable litany of complaints against Abe. Abe's son-in-law, Colonel Arisue Seizō, chief of the Army Ministry's Military Affairs Section, had irritated many Dietmen with thinly veiled attempts to use the Abe cabinet to enact fundamental political reforms that would entail, among other things, the dissolution of the legislature. Arisue hoped to establish a reformist political party as well, something that endeared neither him nor his father-in-law to the existing political leadership. Abe's new controls, meanwhile, were seen as a harbinger of worse oppressions to come. Nor was Abe blessed by nature: the winter of 1939–40 was unusually cold, contributing to greater shortages of rice, coal, and other key goods. The army informed Abe that elections were intolerable at a time of such popular discontent, and by mid-January the old general had no choice but to resign.[10]

9. Frank Dorn, *The Sino-Japanese War, 1937–1941* (New York: Macmillan, 1974), 286, 310, 316, and *DR2*, 28.

10. Lu, 59; Chalmers Johnson, *MITI and the Japanese Miracle* (Stanford: Stanford Uni-

His successor, Admiral Yonai Mitsumasa,[11] inherited an economy measurably worse than that of the previous September. The first reports on the impact of the European war on Japan were completed within a month of Yonai's accession. Prices of key commodities were rising rapidly. Scrap iron, for example, had cost 90 yen per ton before September 1939. By early 1940 it was approaching 150 yen per ton. Potassium salts, which had been shipped from Germany and France, were rising similarly in cost, a problem that prompted the Planning Board to warn that rice and other crop yields might not recover in 1940 even with better weather.[12] Shortages and inflation both promised to worsen: the prices of goods exported from Japan were not rising at a pace to equal increases in the costs of these critical materials. Although Abe's freeze had temporarily checked inflation, hoarding and black market transactions, some on a huge scale, were growing common.

These trends necessarily affected progress on the all-important materials mobilization plan for 1939 and the production expansion plan. Economic researchers predicted that output of regular steel would reach only 87 percent of the materials plan's goal, representing an absolute decline of steel production from 1938 levels even though military demands for steel had risen sharply. Part of the problem was Japan's heavy reliance on scrap iron. But shortages of machine tools and industrial machinery were obstructing attempts to construct blast furnaces and facilities to process raw iron ore. Even if these were built, supplies of coal, the other ingredient critical to steelmaking, were down and of poorer quality. The plan had hoped for production of 73 million tons, but only 69 had been obtained. In 1938, 1.7 tons of coal were required to make one ton of pig iron. A year later, 2.1 tons were needed.

Underlying these numbers were two unsettling themes. First, Ja-

---

versity Press, 1982), 144, 147–48; Gordon M. Berger, *Parties out of Power in Japan, 1931–1941* (Princeton: Princeton University Press, 1977), 218, 222–25; and Jerome B. Cohen, *Japan's Economy in War and Reconstruction* (Minneapolis: University of Minnesota Press, 1949), 330, 358. Johnson is correct to argue that the freeze order completed the divorce of commodity markets from the price mechanism. This trend had been apparent since the origins of the materials mobilization plans, which from the first had relied upon allocations in tons and kiloliters, not yen.

11. For details concerning Yonai's selection, and the relatively weak political hand of the army in that selection, see Harada Kumao, "The Saionji-Harada Memoirs," mimeo., International Legal Studies Library, Harvard Law School, entries of 10 and 20 January 1940, and Berger, 243–45.

12. Japan's increasing inability to secure adequate supplies of fertilizers also led the Ministry of Agriculture and Forestry to expand its compulsory system of fertilizer allocation.

pan was becoming ever less able to sustain the previous year's output of critical materials. Second, to the extent it could do so, it was growing sharply more reliant on imports from the United States. The Planning Board pointed out that over 91 percent of commodities and equipment destined for military use came from imports, most of them from America. In scrap iron, aluminum, nickel, and petroleum products the American dominance was so great that any economic pressure applied by Washington could not be mitigated. Even if the Americans did not act, the situation was sure to deteriorate. During 1939 Japan's reserves of foreign exchange expressed in U.S. dollars had fallen nearly 20 percent. They would fall far more in the FY1940 materials plan, the board forecast, because Japanese exports would generate only 2,370 million yen to meet import needs set at 2,500 million. The balance would have to be made up by compelling Japanese corporations, banks, and even individual subjects to liquidate their foreign holdings to pay for needed commodities and ship them homeward. Even with such measures, Japan's ability to acquire necessary commodities abroad was declining.[13]

The Yonai cabinet, unlike its predecessor, possessed the personnel that might have heeded these alarms and committed the Japanese Empire to a reorientation of its foreign policy. Yonai and his foreign minister, Arita Hachirō, favored friendlier relations with the Western maritime powers, and so they firmly opposed any alliance with Germany directed against them. The new chief cabinet secretary, Ishiwata Sōtarō, paid close attention to economic reports and was another voice for better relations with the West. Yonai's president of the Planning Board, Takeuchi Kakichi, actively disliked the drift toward a centrally planned economy and other reforms sought by the army and the reformist bureaucrats. Fujihara Ginjirō, named to head commerce and industry, opposed Abe's recent tightening of government economic controls, views emphatically shared by the four political party leaders with other cabinet portfolios.

Yonai therefore sought a balanced policy abroad and at home. Friendship with the Axis would be maintained, but Japan would draw closer to the West. The New Order for Asia was not to be

13. B. F. Johnston, *Japanese Food Management in World War II* (Stanford: Stanford University Press, 1953), 109–10, and *GDS43*, 58–132, 461–68, 469–95. Imports of potassium salt fertilizers fell from nearly 177,000 tons in 1939 to 142,000 in 1940 and 56,000 in 1941, the last year any were available; Johnston, 257. The liquidation of foreign holdings appears on the materials plan as "exchange-less imports from Japanese overseas." The 1940 plan stipulated an import capability of 2,370 million yen, only a paper increase, given inflation, over the 1939 figure of 2,228 million.

rejected (in fact, the Wang Chiang-wei regime was at last officially organized to rival Chiang's); economic interference with China, meaning Western aid to the Nationalists, would be prevented. But Japan would respect existing foreign interests and rights in China.[14]

This balanced policy was dealt a first blow on 21 January, with the Yonai cabinet barely a week old, when a vessel of the British Royal Navy stopped the Japanese steamer *Asama-maru* and removed twenty-one German passengers barely thirty-five miles off Japan's coast. Anti-Western groups, led by several hardliners (former admiral Suetsugu Nobumasa, General Matsui Iwane, and maverick Minseitō party leaders such as Adachi Kenzō, Nakano Seigō, and Nagai Ryūtarō), were quick to turn the incident to their advantage.[15]

In the midst of the furor over the *Asama-maru*, Diet member Saitō Takao delivered a long, fiery speech on 2 February blasting Japan's policy toward China. His speech provided the army with a perfect vehicle by which to recoup the political ground it had lost during Abe's tenure. The army observer at the Diet debates wasted no time in demanding successfully that the most offensive passages—nearly the entire second half of the address—be stricken from the record. He also had a commission established to investigate the propriety of Saitō's remarks, and in early March, Saitō was expelled from the Diet by overwhelming vote. On 9 March the Diet unanimously passed a declaration of support for the "holy war." Henceforth it would be difficult for the Planning Board, or any other body, to pressure the army to retrench in China.[16]

On the home front, too, the army struck at Yonai's economic allies. Unhappy that civilian industrialists were circumventing a year-old ordinance under the National General Mobilization Law designed to limit dividends so as to promote expansion of productive capacity, in April 1940 the army issued its own "Proper Profit Rates Calculations Outline." This strident document, which applied to plants producing goods for direct military consumption, attacked management as operating under "profit-first" instead of country-first priorities. Its imposition of limited dividend payments came as a terrific shock to in-

14. Hosoya Chihiro, "The Tripartite Pact, 1939–1940," in *Deterrent Diplomacy*, ed. James W. Morley (New York: Columbia University Press, 1976), 201–2; Berger, 245; Johnson, 143, 148; *DR2*, 8–10; and Japan, Gaimushō, *Nihon gaikō nenpyō narabini shuyō bunsho*, 2 vols. (Tokyo, 1955), 2:422ff.

15. Berger, 228–29, and Itō Takashi, "The Role of Right-wing Organizations in Japan," in *Pearl Harbor as History*, ed. Dorothy Borg and Shumpei Okamoto (New York: Columbia University Press, 1973), 507–8.

16. Berger, 245–46, 249, and Misawa Shigeo and Ninomiya Saburō, "The Role of the Diet and Political Parties," in Borg and Okamoto, *Pearl Harbor as History*, 331.

dustrial and financial circles and created further political difficulties for Yonai and his balanced program.[17]

The army did still more damage to Yonai in China, where it launched a great new offensive in the spring of 1940. The decision to do so was itself a sign that advocates of caution within the army, holdovers from Ishiwara's day, had lost more ground. In the aftermath of the Nanning campaign even officers in the General Staff's Operations Division had begun to question the wisdom of commitments to China, especially the south. As one officer in the division put it, "couldn't the Soviets sweep through Manchuria like the Germans through Poland?"[18]

But these operations officers were unable to resist pressure from field commanders to avenge the setbacks of the Chinese counteroffensive of December. In March 1940 Army Minister Hata Shunroku overruled the Operations Division and ordered additional reinforcements for the China Expeditionary Army. Improvements to Japanese positions in Manchuria were to be deferred yet again. The troops instead moved on Ichang in mid-April. Despite stout Chinese resistance, particularly at Tsaoyang, that cost the Japanese nearly 50,000 casualties, Ichang fell by 20 June. By that time the Imperial Army and Navy had agreed to increase their air strength in China (mainly in the central and southern regions) by 25 percent. Western powers strongly denounced the attack and the renewed violations of treaty rights which followed in its wake. Yonai's policies seemed anything but balanced.[19]

While the Ichang operation was under way, army leaders determined to pursue a still more aggressive policy. Upon learning of immense German successes in western Scandinavia, the Low Countries, and France, the Imperial Army resolved to occupy northern French Indochina as rapidly as possible and certainly before the summer was out.[20] In fact, the radically changed global situation inspired the army to think beyond Indochina. By mid-June, Colonel Okada Jūichi, leader of the General Staff's Operations Section, allowed Lieutenant Colonel Nishiura Susumu to draw up the army's first opera-

---

17. Tsūshō Sangyō-shō, *Shōkō seisakushi 11: sangyō tōsei* (Tokyo: Shōkō Seisakushi Kankōkai, 1964), 434–40, and Cohen, 18.

18. *DR2*, 28, 33, 34.

19. RGD2, 364; *DR2*, 34–35, 38–39, and Dorn, 327–31. For American protests arising from the Ichang operation, see Cordell Hull, *The Memoirs of Cordell Hull*, 2 vols. (New York: Macmillan, 1948), 1:729–30, and *FRUSJ*, 1:674–75, 690–95.

20. *DR2*, 40–41, 44–45.

tions plan for a southward advance into Indochina and the islands.[21]

More grandly, the senior army leaders—ministry and General Staff section and division chiefs—held a series of conferences from 21 June to 2 July which would lead, on the third, to the drafting of the famous "Outline for Dealing with the Changes in the World Situation" (*Sekai jōsei no suii ni tomonau jikyoku shori yōkō*). The draft was a bellwether of army opinion in early July. Opening with the question of how to resolve the southern problem, the outline acknowledged that the fighting in China had a direct bearing on the matter. The seizure of Ichang would break Chiang's morale, it was hoped, and end his resistance. But if it did not, Japan had to be ready to advance south by the end of August, when Hitler would invade Britain. At the same time economic considerations mandated that friction with Washington be avoided. The best way would be the "possession by purchase and diplomacy" of resource concessions in the Indies and, possibly, French Pacific islands such as New Caledonia. Even so, the Americans might apply pressure, perhaps go to war in time. The outline therefore recommended that Japan make itself economically independent by the greatest possible regulation of imports, new and far-reaching domestic economic reforms, and additional efforts to expand production and replenish armament. Diplomatically, an alliance with Berlin was imperative.[22]

The document was important not simply because it represented the army's first formal commitment to an aggressive southward advance but also because it was a strident call for renovation at home, renovation that the Abe cabinet had been unable and the Yonai cabinet unwilling to sponsor. This renovation—meaning ever stricter controls over the civilian economy—was all the more necessary because the army had no hope of concluding the draining China Incident even as it clung to a sixty-five division replenishment program, further reinforcements for Manchuria, a rejuvenation of the stillborn production expansion plan (see Table 8.2), and preparations for a large-scale southward advance.[23]

---

21. *DR2*, 47–48. Okada had been pressured to do so by Colonel Iwakuro Hideo, head of the Army Ministry's Military Affairs Section.

22. *DR2*, 49–51.

23. The army was aware that it could not have a blank check for all these goals, an awareness revealed, interestingly, most clearly in Nishiura's draft for a southward advance. Nishiura assumed that the advance did not necessitate war against the United States. The top target was the resource-rich Netherlands East Indies. Nishiura hoped

Table 8.2. Goals and results of Japan's production expansion plan for 1939 (as tabulated July 1940)

Items/Units	Goal 1939	Results 1939
Regular steel/tons	5,719,400	4,856,560
Special steel/tons	377,718	439,426
Pig iron/tons	3,962,310	3,512,663
Iron ore/tons	2,385,000	1,948,504
Coal/tons	66,649,000	64,521,487
Aluminum/tons	33,448	30,835
Crude oil/kiloliters (kl)	466,004	383,221
Aviation gasoline/kl	75,000	76,571
Natural regular gasoline/kl	644,307	605,242
Synthetic regular gasoline/kl	21,296	3,817
Natural fuel oil/kl	456,081	477,476
Synthetic fuel oil/kl	46,978	23,583
Machine tools/thousand yen	118,500	149,244
Shipping/tons	406,211	335,274

SOURCE: *Gendaishi shiryō 43: Kokka sōdōin 1* (Tokyo: Misuzu Shobo, 1970), 240–42.

The first agency to object to the army's bold plans for the summer of 1940 was the Cabinet Planning Board. When Army Minister Hata Shunroku met board president Takeuchi on 6 June to discuss the army's material requirements, Takeuchi offered a plan covering only 80 percent of the army's requests. Overall, he warned, the 1940 materials plan confronted a 14 percent reduction compared to the 1939 plan's production goals and, of course, a 20 percent cut compared to the amounts agencies had requested overall.

Opposition to what was dubbed the "80 percent compromise plan" was especially intense among operations officers of the Army General Staff. These men held, quite rightly, that the compromise plan jeopardized every major army goal. Sixty-five divisions or the strengthening of units in Manchuria would be impossible, much less a southward advance. Although there were some voices for economic sanity, notably Colonel Okada Kikusaburō, chief of the War Preparations Section and one of the few remaining disciples of the old pursuit of autarky,

---

that the Netherlands could be isolated from Britain, allowing a direct thrust into Sumatra, Java, and south Borneo from bases acquired in French Indochina and Thailand. He recognized that operations against Singapore were probably unavoidable. Even then, his draft assumed that war against Britain need not involve the United States. Only reconnaissance units were to visit the Philippines. See *DR2*, 48–49.

they were drowned out by operations officers and the ever-head-strong Iwakuro. In the end Hata agreed to the compromise plan with slight changes that gave the army 82.5 percent of its original requests, but the concession was accompanied by a list of demands. Civilian allocations were to be reduced further. A firm commitment to achieving self-sufficiency from Britain and America, by an advance to the south and further economic reforms at home—especially in tight controls over materials mobilization—was essential.[24]

Hata's consent cleared the way for formal approval of the FY1940 materials mobilization plan.[25] But the army had resolved to remove Yonai, who had supported Takeuchi throughout the materials deliberations and who, as historians have known for some time, opposed the German alliance, a forward foreign policy, and the far-reaching domestic reforms that the army had demanded. The army's chief political officer, Major General Mutō Akira,[26] indicated that Prince Konoe Fumimaro was again available for the premiership, and the Army General Staff called for Yonai's ouster. Hata resigned on 16 July and brought the cabinet down. But though Yonai was gone, the Planning Board still had to be reckoned with. So did the Imperial Navy.[27]

---

24. *DR2*, 369–70, 373. The FY1940 materials plan presented by Takeuchi included an estimate of import capability of 2,629 million yen, an increase in this category over 1939's amount. But because of price inflation in imported goods, the "exchange-less" transactions from abroad (both noted in the text), and the inclusion in this figure of imports from the yen bloc, Takeuchi's overall assessments of the material plan's implications for the military were accurate.

25. The materials plan was destined to be delayed further. During the evening of 20 June 1940 a lightning bolt struck the Planning Board's offices, immediately setting them afire. Staffers, who often worked into the night, were stunned but unhurt. Many documents burned, however, especially those of the older Resources Bureau. Many of those which survived are published in *GDS43*, Ishigawa, Tanaka, and Tsūshō Sangyōshō. See also Inaba Hidezō, *Gekidō sanjūnen no Nihon keizai* (Tokyo: Jitysugyō no Nihonsha, 1965), 54–55.

26. Mutō was head of the Army Ministry's Military Affairs Bureau.

27. Berger, 254–61.

[9]

The Navy's Price: Japan
Commences the Southward Advance

In early July 1940 spirits in the Imperial Army were high. Abroad, the resource-rich lands of French Indochina and the Netherlands East Indies were vulnerable to diplomatic intimidation or, if necessary, armed force. At home, Konoe's return to power put a charismatic leader and powerful supporter of army programs for expansion to the south and reform inside the nation in a key position. Japan at last seemed set firmly on the path to autarky. There remained to determine only the precise course of that path.

This proved difficult. Although Yonai was gone, although the rising mid-level officers indeed favored a southward advance, the navy had its own strategic conceptions, its own diplomatic requirements, and its own economic demands. In short, the navy would exact a price for agreeing to the army's favored policies.

The fundamental difference between the two services arose over the military consequences of any advance to the south. The army initially hoped that military operations, if they proved necessary, could be confined to Dutch or, at worst, Anglo-Dutch targets. The United States was not to be involved, the Philippines not to be attacked.[1] But this stance ran counter to naval orthodoxy and the navy's strategic requirements. Because the Anglo-Dutch naval presence was only token, the navy saw no role for itself in any advance limited to those countries' possessions. The fleet then would not be positioned to demand the materials allocations necessary for the com-

---

1. See *DR2*, 48–49, for the army draft by Nishiura.

pletion of current building plans, much less the initiation of new ones.

It was not merely economic factors, of course, which prompted the navy's belief that the Americans could not be ignored. In the course of preparing for a possible lightning strike to the south, the Naval General Staff held map maneuvers to determine the likely long-range outcome of a seizure of the Indies. The exercises demonstrated that, staging from the Palaus (to which the Fourth Fleet had been ordered on 11 May), Japanese units could occupy the oilfields of Netherlands Borneo, the nickel mines of Celebes, and other "resource zones" under Dutch control. But Britain and the United States would then intervene, from Malaya and Hawaii. At that time the fleet would have to change from "emergency" to "wartime" organization, a move that would radically increase its fuel and material requirements. Surveying the results, Navy Minister Yoshida Zengo observed that Japan would have to make substantial military preparations and stockpile materials in advance. A rush to the Indies was sure to bring an American embargo that would deprive Japan of critical commodities already in short supply.[2]

Any southward advance, then, would have to involve the United States and would require lengthy preparations. On 4 July, Captain Usui Shigemitsu, chief of the Naval General Staff's Eighth Section, conveyed the navy's views to his counterpart, Colonel Okada Jūichi of the Army Staff's Operations Section. Usui first challenged the idea that Britain and America were divisible. He pointed out that talks between naval leaders of the Western powers had commenced months before. The United States was already sending a steady stream of naval aid to Britain, even warships, and both nations would likely join with the remnants of Royal Dutch forces in Asia to defend the Malay Barrier and frustrate any attempt to occupy the Netherlands East Indies. They were sure to have the ability to do so after completion of the U.S. Navy's vast second Vinson program, which would produce an American fleet four times the size of the Imperial Navy even after the Third Replenishment Plan was finished.

Usui therefore advocated caution. To prepare for the Southward Advance, he wanted the fighting in China ended. To ensure that materials would not be diverted northward, he wanted a nonaggression pact negotiated with the Soviets. To assist a swifter build-up of stockpiles, he wanted a stronger domestic system. In the meantime

2. DR2, 42–43.

the advance itself would have to proceed at a deliberate pace, one designed not to provoke Britain and the United States.[3]

These interservice differences were papered over only thinly in the "Outline for Dealing with the Changes in the World Situation." The China Incident was to be brought to a rapid close, as the navy wanted, but there were no assurances given to this end. Japan would open peaceful, nonprovocative negotiations to acquire by concession the resources necessary for the execution of the Southward Advance. But the immediate occupation of northern French Indochina was agreed to. If hostilities resulted, they were to be limited to Britain. The outline accepted that Japan had to prepare for war with the United States if necessary.[4]

The first step of the Southward Advance, into northern Indochina, confirmed navy fears that the army did not want to avoid provocation. Major General Tominaga Kyōji, chief of the General Staff's Operations Division, impetuously rushed air units from the Kwantung Army to southern China and secured the temporary removal of Japan's South China Army from the authority of the China Expeditionary Army, so that it could "respond to quick changes in the international situation." In Tokyo, Foreign Minister Matsuoka Yōsuke and French ambassador Gaston Henry-Haye soon reached a general agreement. But the agreement omitted details concerning the number of troops Japan would be permitted and the precise airfields that the Japanese could use, prompting Tominaga to order the South China Army to prepare for hostile action as Japanese aircraft, and in one case a battalion of troops, crossed the Indochinese border.[5]

Tominaga next obtained approval to enter into negotiations with the French personally and impose a deadline of 22 September for the occupation to commence. In his discussions with the French commander, General Maurice-Pierre Martin, Tominaga demanded far more than the original Japanese terms[6] and imposed a deadline of 20 September. When the date passed without Vichy's submission, Tominaga urged invasion. In Tokyo the General Staff instructed re-

---

3. DR2, 51–53.

4. DR2, 58–59, and Japan, Gaimushō, *Nihon gaikō nenpyō narabini shuyō bunsho*, 2 vols. (Tokyo, 1955), 2:437–38.

5. Hata Ikuhiko, "The Army's Move into Northern Indochina," in *The Fateful Choice*, ed. James W. Morley (New York: Columbia University Press, 1980), 162, 182–83; DR2, 71–73, 76, 84, 87, 89; and David J. Lu, *From the Marco Polo Bridge to Pearl Harbor* (Washington: Public Affairs, 1961), 143.

6. Tominaga demanded the use of five airfields, up from three, and that 25,000 troops, not the earlier 5,000, be employed as occupation forces.

straint. As a result some units on the border moved to invade, others did not. As the operations officers of the South China Army started to receive reports of skirmishes, they elected to recall all troops. The actual, peaceful move into Indochina took place only on the twenty-ninth.[7]

The blustering occupation of northern Indochina confirmed the navy's fears that its rival service intended to provoke hostilities and ensure that the army's version of the Southward Advance would be adopted. The navy's senior officers had never been keen on demanding rights of troop passage. They had insisted on two months' notice before any fighting could occur, and then only after the navy had given its consent. Tominaga's insistence on a large-scale occupation astounded navy leaders, and his handling of the actual occupation enraged them. An accidental bombing of Haiphong after the occupation had commenced only underscored naval beliefs that the army was headstrong and unreliable. Even Tominaga's removal did not appease the admirals.[8]

The outline endorsed, as a second element of the Southward Advance, negotiations to secure resources from the Netherlands East Indies. Four weeks after the approval of talks by an imperial conference on 27 July, the Planning Board completed a policy outline that envisioned substantial concessions for Japanese businessmen, public and private, in Indonesian oilfields, rubber plantations, and mineral mines. The board even listed promising locations for the exploitation of each required resource.[9]

Konoe and Matsuoka first chose to lead the Japanese negotiating team General Koiso Kuniaki, who had been governor-general of Korea, but Koiso wanted to travel to Batavia in a warship with a landing team standing by. This stance drew strong opposition from Navy Minister Yoshida. The more moderate Kobayashi Ichizō, minister of commerce and industry, was selected instead. Kobayashi was instructed to obtain, if possible, the far-flung concessions outlined in the Planning Board's report. He was in any case to ensure that such vital materials as oil, tin, and rubber, which Tokyo expected to be embargoed imminently by the Americans, would be shipped to Japan

7. *DR2*, 90, 93–96, 104.
8. See, for example, Hata, "Indochina," 162, 178–79, 198, 204, and Hosoya Chihiro, "The Japanese-Soviet Neutrality Pact," in Morley, *Fateful Choice*, 49–50. During the abortive skirmishing the navy's landing detachment, scheduled to move into the port of Haiphong, was held offshore, Tominaga's successor was Tanaka Shin'ichi.
9. *RGD2*, 402, and *GDS43*, 179–82.

Table 9.1. Japanese requests to the Netherlands East Indies and oil firms offers, autumn 1940 (in long tons of 2,240 pounds)

Product	Request	Offer
Aviation-grade crude oil	1,100,000	120,000
Other crude oils	1,150,000	640,000
Aviation gasoline (87 octane and over)	400,000	33,000[a]
Gasoline (under 71 octane)	nil	250,000
Other products	500,000	312,500
Subtotal	3,150,000	1,355,500
Prior import agreements	n.a.	494,000
Total	3,150,000	1,849,500

SOURCE: Irvine H. Anderson, Jr., *The Standard-Vacuum Oil Company and United States East Asian Policy, 1933–1941* (Princeton: Princeton University Press, 1975), 154.

[a]Amount already contracted for with Shell but undelivered as of early October.

from the Netherlands East Indies. In keeping with the navy's wishes, he was not to indulge in provocations or ultimatums.[10]

Kobayashi reached Batavia on 12 September. Authorities there quickly dismissed any possibility of further oil (or other) concessions in their colony, leaving Kobayashi little choice but to turn to purchases. His oil expert, Mukai Tadaharu, chairman of Mitsui Trading, asked for 3.15 million long tons of crude and distillates.[11] High on Mukai's list were aviation gasoline and crude oil refinable to aviation grade, a direct result of the American cutoff of July (see Table 9.1). The Dutch responded that some of the amounts desired would require increased production or cancellation of prior contracts. Western oil firms were reluctant to sell any grade of crude, preferring to use their refineries on the islands and deal in distillates. As a result Batavia's reply of 8 October offered less than 1.5 million tons of crude and distillates. Mukai, after consulting with Tokyo, astounded the Dutch by accepting the proposal. Kobayashi returned to Japan by month's end.[12]

10. *GDS10*, 466–70, and Nakamura Takafusa and Hara Akira, Introduction to *GDS43*, l-li.

11. These long tons were marginally larger than metric tons.

12. Testimony of Ishizawa Yutaka, consul general at Batavia during the negotiations, in International Military Tribunal for the Far East, Narrative Summary, 3839–43; Irvine H. Anderson, Jr., *The Standard-Vacuum Oil Company and United States East Asian Policy, 1933–1941* (Princeton: Princeton University Press, 1975), 151–54; Hubertus J. van Mook, *The Netherlands Indies and Japan: Battle on Paper, 1940–41* (New York: Norton, 1944), 50–52, 58–60; and *RGD2*, 401. The amounts requested for aviation gasoline

Kobayashi's restraint reassured navy leaders, but another foreign policy initiative, a renewed drive for alliance with Germany, threatened their desire for a measured, cautious southward advance. Wariness within the navy was widespread. Minister Yoshida Zengo and Vice Admiral Yamamoto Isoroku, commander of the Combined Fleet, continued to believe that war against the Western powers was ill-advised under any circumstances. Further ties with Germany would worsen relations with America, leading to economic pressures beyond what Washington had already imposed. Naval hardliners believed that current embargoes made an advance to the south all the more urgent. But even these officers, including impetuous section chiefs such as commanders Shiba Katsuo and Kami Shigenori, agreed that an alliance with Germany was not to be permitted if it became the instrument of a Russo-Japanese conflict. Such a war, all agreed, would increase the army's prestige, power, and quotas of materials.[13]

Despite this apparent unity within the navy, Yoshida's position was precarious. Mid-level officers had reservations about the alliance, but they were prepared to consent to it if they could obtain their other objectives, particularly a primary role for the navy in any advance to the south. Outside the navy Yoshida came under great pressure from Matsuoka and Major General Mutō Akira, chief of the Army Ministry's Military Affairs Bureau. Both argued that a German alliance would restrain the Soviets and permit an unmolested southward advance. Both maintained that an alliance would not lead to further American economic pressure. Washington had already halted shipments of aviation fuel and some scrap iron—Japan should acting to render itself less vulnerable to future embargoes begun at Washington's whim.[14]

Under such pressure Yoshida collapsed, entering hospital on 3 September. Adm. Oikawa Koshirō became the navy minister two days later. On the nineteenth an imperial conference formally considered the alliance with Germany.

The navy still objected. Its chief of staff, Prince Fushimi, led the questioning at the Imperial Conference. Would the alliance improve

---

represent a rough measure of what the Japanese thought might be the impact of the American cutoff. See also Nagaoka Shinjirō, "The Drive into Southern Indochina and Thailand," in Morley, *Fateful Choice*.

13. *DR2*, 71; Asada Sadao, "The Japanese Navy and the United States," in *Pearl Harbor as History*, ed. Dorothy Borg and Shumpei Okamoto (New York: Columbia University Press, 1973), 251; and Hosoya Chihiro, "The Tripartite Pact, 1939–1940," in *Deterrent Diplomacy*, ed. James W. Morley (New York: Columbia University Press, 1976), 220.

14. Hosoya, "Tripartite," 229; Asada, 251; and *DR2*, 109.

Japan's relations with the Soviets? Matsuoka was soothing, but Fushimi predicted that the alliance would increase difficulties in obtaining goods from the West at a time when the China Incident had depleted Japan's resources. Konoe agreed that hardship was unavoidable but argued that it could be confined largely to the civilian sector. Planning Board president Hoshino Naoki provided the numbers. The partial American embargo on scrap had done some damage already; if the ban became total, steel production would drop from 5.4 million tons per year to 4 million tons. But because the army and navy used only 1.4 million tons, the civilian allotment of 4 million could be slashed to make up the difference. With similar logic Hoshino surveyed other crucial materials.[15]

Fushimi was not entirely convinced. The navy, he said, did not have enough oil in its own stockpiles to wage a protracted war.[16] Hoshino replied that the Netherlands East Indies and northern Sakhalin could provide oil, and synthetic oil production was rising too. A dissatisfied Fushimi retorted, "may I interpret this to mean that there is, in general, no assurance that more oil can be obtained?" Matsuoka insisted that Germany could compel the Dutch to provide oil from the Indies. Fushimi was unimpressed: "Since the Dutch Government has fled to Britain, can Germany freely dispose of the Indies' oil?" After further consideration, however, Fushimi indicated navy approval of the alliance provided the Southward Advance was as peaceful as possible and war with America avoided. Germany's agreement to the right of independent entry for Japan would clear the last diplomatic block to the Tripartite Pact.[17]

The navy, it may seem, sold its consent to the German alliance rather cheaply. But this was not the case. Instead, the navy was beginning a practice that was to continue through November 1941. Its agreement to more vigorous foreign policies was exchanged for higher materials allocations.

Five days before the Imperial Conference, Oikawa had broached the navy's demands. He asked that "the Cabinet and particularly the army authorities would give special consideration to naval

---

15. Ike Nobutaka, ed. and trans., *Japan's Decision for War: Records of the 1941 Policy Conferences* (Stanford: Stanford University Press, 1967), 5. All quotations from Ike are his translations.

16. This was quite true. In fact the Imperial Navy's stocks, the largest in Japan by a considerable margin, actually declined from 1940 to 1941. See Nenryō konwakai, *Nihon kaigun nenryōshi*, 2 vols. (Tokyo: Hara Shobō, 1972), 1:623, 657.

17. Ike, 7–13, and Hosoya, "Tripartite," 251, 253–54.

[168]

preparedness."[18] Specifically, the navy demanded a fundamental re-vision in its favor of the 1940 materials mobilization plan. In steel materials alone the navy requested an increased allocation of 150,000 tons in each of the two quarters remaining, more than doubling its initial quota of 137,000 tons per quarter. An increase this large—over 10 percent of Japan's entire production of steel for the period—could not come entirely from the civilian sector.[19] A portion had to be diverted from the army's allocation, giving the navy, for the first time since the China war began, a share higher than its rival's. Similar changes followed in the distribution of nickel, aluminum, lead (deemed especially vital by the navy), and other materials. Through-out August captains Nakazawa Tasoku and Hashimoto Shōzō, chiefs of the Operations and Mobilization sections, met with Colonel Okada Kikusaburō of the Army Ministry's War Preparations Section. Okada raised protest. But the cabinet resolved to pay the navy's price for its consent to the alliance with Germany on 26 September, two days after the Imperial Conference.[20]

These revisions made a mockery of the 1940 plan. The original materials mobilization plan, to run from April 1940 to March 1941, had placed Japan's import capability at 2,629 million yen. Worsening terms of trade, further weakening of Japan's foreign exchange re-serves, and outright shortages in world markets actually diminished Japan's overall ability to meet its growing, particularly military, needs compared to 1939.[21] Open American pressure exacerbated an already deteriorating situation. To address this pressure, the 1940 materials plan commenced a series of "cover" or special import programs in June. These were openly intended to stockpile vital materials, prepar-ing Japan for the further embargoes sure to result from the advance to

---

18. Hosoya, "Tripartite," 234, 236–39; Oikawa is quoted from p. 239 (trans. James W. Morley). Stephen E. Pelz, *Race to Pearl Harbor* (Cambridge: Harvard University Press, 1974), 218.

19. In other words the navy knew in advance that Hoshino's assurances at the Imperial Conference were not entirely correct.

20. Nihon Kokusai Seiji Gakkai Taiheiyō Sensō Gen'in Kenkyūbu, ed., *Taiheiyō sensō e no michi*, 8 vols. (Tokyo: Asahi Shinbunsha, 1962–63), 7:47, 50; *GDS10*, 497–503; Tanaka Shin'ichi, *Nihon sensō keizai hishi* (Tokyo: Conputa Eijisha, 1975), 95; *GDS43*, 596–98; and *TSM*, 8:353–54. Planned production of steel for FY1940 was set at 5.2 million tons (somewhat lower than the figure given by Hoshino), but actual production turned out to be just under 4.6 million tons. The revised allocations were formally incorporated into the materials plan in mid-December.

21. Tsūshō Sangyō-shō, *Shōkō seisakushi 11: Sangyō tōsei* (Tokyo: Shōkō Seisakushi Kankōkai, 1964), 361–63.

the south.[22] The main items were scrap iron, as ever, followed by special-alloy steels, optical glass, quartz, and petroleum. The prime source was again to be the United States. Although the cover programs achieved most of their goals,[23] their cost (over 500 million yen) caused a further, severe drain on Japan's subsequent ability to import a wide range of necessary commodities.

One result of growing stringency in Japan was subversion of the ancillary economic controls, especially on commodity allocations and sales of finished goods, that had been established to make the materials plans work. By the summer of 1940 sugar, gasoline, rubber, leather, copper, cotton, and some forms of electricity use were being rationed. The first steps toward a control system for rice had been taken, and all luxury goods had been banned from the market place. One inexorable consequence was a growing black market. Nor were businesses shy about directly circumventing the mobilization plan's allocations. Diversion of goods, even steel from military quotas, grew, and contractors began to "pad" required amounts of materials. Primitive statistics made enforcement virtually impossible, as most members of the Planning Board admitted after the war.[24]

These growing problems, and particularly the revisions obtained by the navy, compelled an overhaul of the entire 1940 materials mobilization plan. In mid-December the Planning Board formally sanctioned a new plan that acknowledged the reduction of Japan's ability to import goods from 2,629 to 2,146 million yen, a drop of nearly 20 percent. These decreases were to be entirely absorbed over the plan's second half (October 1940 to March 1941). Steel production would be hit especially hard just as the navy had won a large increase in its allocation.[25]

Throughout the summer and early autumn of 1940 the Planning Board became a voice for extreme caution in Japan's foreign policy. This guaranteed collision with the army. Eager to see the Southward Advance under way as rapidly as possible, army leaders directed Colonel Okada's War Preparations Section to ask the Planning Board

22. The existence of the cover programs, and their start in June, strongly implies that Japan—or at least the drafters of the materials plan—anticipated American economic pressure rather than reacted to it.

23. *RGD2*, 397. Obtaining scrap iron from America became impossible after September 1940 (some shipments went out through early November due to earlier purchases). Other items, except oil, were made unavailable later.

24. Jerome B. Cohen, *Japan's Economy in War and Reconstruction* (Minneapolis: University of Minnesota Press, 1949), 362, and Watanabe Yoshimori, "Senjika no shihon-chikuseki to 'Busshi dōin keikaku,'" *Keizaigaku zasshi* 75 (August 1976), 76–77.

25. *TSM*, 8:353–54; Tsūshō, 361–63, 369; and Tanaka, 61–63.

for an emergency materials mobilization plan. That plan was to assume complete reliance on the yen bloc for all imports, increased economic requirements for the military, and an absolute priority for meeting those requirements.

The board's response, delivered by Lieutenant Colonel Mishima Yoshisada, head of its Materials Mobilization Group,[26] was a condemnation of any attempt to become self-reliant. If that was what the Southward Advance required, it would be impossible to attempt. Mishima warned that if supplies from the West ended, military needs could be met, if at all, only with unprecedented sacrifices. Allocations to other public agencies would have to be slashed over 60 percent, barely permitting upkeep of such existing facilities as national rail lines. Investment in the yen bloc would virtually disappear, precluding further development in and exploitation of its areas. The struggling effort to expand production would be halted. The general civilian sector would see its materials quotas nearly halved. Only essential industries could be maintained at close to past production levels, and for any but the shortest period the overall consequence would be ruinous economic dislocation. Japan could not survive without imports from the West.

These grim estimates surprised the army's operations planners, who had expected smoother going once Yonai had gone and the navy had approved a limited version of the Southward Advance. One officer, pronouncing the Planning Board's work "slovenly," asked if the economic experts advised Japan to run when cornered. The immediate result was the cashiering of Mishima, who was sent off to Germany. A naval commander, Mayama Kanji, took his place.[27]

There were further changes in store for the Planning Board. One solution to Japan's increasing difficulties, it seemed to the army, an increasingly steel-hungry navy, and Konoe and his political allies, was to strengthen Japan's economic controls further and recast them into a new economic order. To assist in creating that order (and to encourage the board to adopt a more accommodating stance toward the military), the Planning Board received an infusion of new staffers. Representative were Colonel Akinaga Tsukizō, who had close ties to renovationist bureaucrats, and renovationists themselves, including Sakomizu Hisatsune of the Finance Ministry, Minobe Yōji, recently

26. Mishima, a veteran of the old Resources Bureau before joining the Planning Board, was a true "economic officer."

27. Tanaka, 65–70, 73–76, 78; Tsūshō Sangyō-shō, *Shōkō seisakushi 11: Sangyō tōsei* (Tokyo: Shōkō Seisakushi Kankōkai, 1964), 361; GDS43, 532–78; and Inaba Hidezō, *Gekidō sanjūnen no Nihon keizai* (Tokyo: Jitsugyō no Nihonsha, 1965), 61–66.

returned from Manchuria, and Okumura Kiwao, the Communication Ministry's author of electric power legislation. These individuals were convinced that the time had come to achieve self-sufficiency by creating a new, noncapitalist society for Japan.

Despite the economic regulations in force by the summer of 1940, Japan's economy was by no means government-controlled. Cartel-like "control associations" had existed since 1930 under the aegis of the Major Industries Control Law. But in most cases it was industry representatives who operated the associations, the only exceptions being in sectors such as iron and steel in which the bulk of production was publicly owned. The China Incident had brought stricter supervision, to be sure. Bound first by government licensing of all transactions involving foreign exchange, then by a direct permit system for imports and exports, the associations had cooperated grudgingly with the Planning Board's materials mobilization plans and other programs. Wartime Diets had given the cabinet additional powers, from the ability to channel capital investment into military-related enterprises to price and wage controls. Still, as Konoe came to power in July 1940, the Planning Board had no formal representatives at association meetings. Those bodies still decided which companies received the shares, whether of resource allocations or of markets, that the myriad regulations allowed, nor were they above an increasing involvement in the black market. Moreover, banks still enjoyed relative freedom in a wide range of financial activities.[28]

The new activists in the Planning Board were determined to change all this. They fired their opening shot in mid-September, with "Plan for Establishing the New Economic Structure," written by Akinaga, Minobe, and Sakomizu. In this and subsequent proposals produced throughout the autumn, the board advocated replacing the control associations with economic control organs on an industry and regional basis, including banks. Government officials as well as the usual company or bank directors would serve on these organs. In addition, organ decisions would have the force of law over members; punishment would attend violation. Each organ was to have task groups devoted to imports, production, domestic allocation of products, and exports. Above all, such organs would be a supreme economic body, a possible successor to the Planning Board, to oversee economic policy in comprehensive detail for the whole Japanese Empire. Management

28. Nakamura Takafusa and Hara Akira, "Keizai shintaisei," in *Konoe shintaisei no kenkyū*, ed. Nihon Seiji Gakkai (Tokyo: Iwanami Shoten, 1972), 88, and Inaba, 53.

of all enterprises would pass to the state or, as the Planning Board's members put it, "capital will be divorced from management."[29]

Japan's capitalist managers stiffly resisted. They had voiced their complaints in March, in a report by the Japan Economic Federation. "Deficiencies in Present Production Controls and Views for Reform" called, as might be expected, for a greater role for the industry-led control associations—without changes in their constitution—in setting economic policy. It bitingly criticized Planning Board and other economic bureaucrats (an indirect swipe at the military) who, it charged, notoriously were unable to coordinate conflicting regulations. Price controls made it impossible to meet production expansion goals. The government's handling of the rice and coal shortages had been at best short-sighted and expensive. Since the first materials mobilization plan in 1938, not a single plan had survived without substantial revision. It was impossible for managers to anticipate business conditions three months in advance, much less the year or more required for sound economic planning.[30]

The federation continued the assault until Commerce and Industry Minister Kobayashi returned from his diversion in the Netherlands East Indies.[31] Then, in a series of economic bureaucrats' roundtable conferences (*Keizai kanryō kondankai*), which included various government and business representatives, Kobayashi led accusations that the Planning Board could not champion the public interest and that its record inspired no confidence. In even stronger terms he attacked

29. Chalmers Johnson, *MITI and the Japanese Miracle* (Stanford: Stanford University Press, 1982), 150, and Nakamura and Hara, "Keizai," 88–89, 91, 94, 96, whence the quotation. Although the Planning Board's new members led the fight for the New Economic Order, they had impressive allies. Colonel Akinaga symbolized the army's commitment to fundamental economic reform. Obata Tadayoshi, also recently assigned to the board, served as liaison to Konoe's new political organ, the Imperial Rule Assistance Association and also maintained connections with the Sumitomo *zaibatsu*. Minobe had long service and some allies in the Ministry of Commerce and Industry. The Manchurian connection was especially strong. Besides Minobe, Kishi Nobusuke was an important ally. Kishi, vice-minister of commerce and industry, had been Hoshino's second when the Planning Board president himself had led the General Affairs Agency (Sōmuchō) of Manchukuo and had been a major figure in drafting the 1936 production expansion plan for Manchukuo and its industrial organization along the lines of "one industry, one company." See William M. Fletcher III, *The Search for a New Order* (Chapel Hill: University of North Carolina Press, 1982), 148–49; Nakamura and Hara, "Keizai," 99–100; and Johnson, 129–32.

30. Tsūshō, 431–34, and Nakamura and Hara, "Keizai," 92–93.

31. It seems appropriate to call Kobayashi's presence at the Indies' negotiations a diversion: Konoe ordered all ministries to draw up plans for implementing the New Economic Order after Kobayashi left Japan. See Johnson, 151.

the renovationists' plans as "red," solemnly warning that production was sure to decline if the Planning Board's program were approved.

It was a well-crafted attack. The navy, which had secured sharp increases in its allocations of materials, especially steel, immediately expressed its concern through Minister Oikawa at a cabinet meeting on 29 November. Oikawa conceded that it was necessary to prepare for rigorous, long-term hostilities, but not at the immediate cost of further declines in productive power and rising public unease. In early December the cabinet endorsed a new order decidedly less centralized than what the renovationists had desired. There would be no supreme control organ, although the control associations for major industries would be strengthened marginally. Industries were not to be nationalized. Businessmen, not Planning Board staff, would head the cartels. Profits would be permitted. The army and the Imperial Rule Assistance Association (IRAA), clearly unhappy with the outcome, pushed for a reconsideration, but Konoe, accurately sensing the political winds, blocked any fight on the Diet floor and, on 6 December, brought Hiranuma Kiichirō, a foe of IRAA-Planning Board ideas, into his cabinet. By year's end Kobayashi and the business community were assuming the offensive. The New Economic Order had been stillborn.[32]

As Japan entered 1941, there were a number of fundamental questions unanswered, important details unsettled, concerning its foreign policy. Of these, perhaps the most important was the nature and timing of the Southward Advance, where deep interservice differences prevailed. The Imperial Army wanted to move rapidly and forcefully to secure only the French and Dutch colonies. It might have to meet Britain in battle, but to include the Americans would be to demand too great a drain from the efforts to finish off China and develop a credible defense (and possibly an offensive capability) against the Soviet Union. The Southward Advance was to be a rapid strike, promising great rewards but carried out on shoestring allocations.

The navy was obliged to favor the Southward Advance. Without it, and without an advance that committed Japan to possible war with America, the navy would not be able to justify increased material allocations in its struggles with the army and the Planning Board. But

---

32. Fletcher, 151–52; Inaba, 53; Nakamura and Hara, "Keizai," 97, 99–104; and Gordon M. Berger, *Parties out of Power in Japan, 1931–1941* (Princeton: Princeton University Press, 1977), 332. See Berger, Chap. 6, for a detailed analysis of the IRAA and its role in Japanese politics in 1940 and 1941. Hiranuma was made home minister on 21 December, a step Konoe had been contemplating since late November. See Berger, 328.

the navy's sort of advance demanded lengthy and massive preparations. These in turn required temporary tranquillity with the West, so that critical materials could be imported and so that more huge allocations of materials could permit the navy to attempt to keep pace with the Americans' mammoth naval construction programs. The navy approved an advance only after this price had been met.

The Planning Board argued against antagonizing the West, lest severe economic dislocation result, and against the navy's demands for more steel and other materials. It found itself reorganized, with more aggressive renovationists taking positions within it. These renovationists sought to address Japan's economic difficulties through fundamental reforms to be embodied in the New Economic Order, but these reforms were not enacted, leaving a second unanswered question: Could Japan endure on its own resources long enough to ensure an advance to the south would be possible? As the Planning Board's negative answer of the summer of 1940 indicated, a reconciliation between Japan's strategic ends and economic means still had to be found.

The key factor in any reconciliation promised to be the United States. It was within America's power radically to affect the course of the debates over policy in Tokyo. Rather than seize the initiative, however, Washington sought to rearm itself for battle even as it appeased Japan in the market place. It was unaware that the two courses clashed.

[10]

To Arm and Appease

By the end of January 1940 the trade treaty between America and Japan had expired, opening the way to formal economic pressure against the empire. Throughout the year that followed, American leaders debated the wisdom of applying such pressure even as the United States commenced its own rearmament program. The effort to arm America while, in essence, appeasing Japan led to a confused, ill-considered stance that pleased few in Washington and sent unhelpful signals to Tokyo

The debate was opened forcefully by Henry Stimson in a letter to the *New York Times* two weeks before the treaty lapsed. America's might, both economic and moral, had not been active on the side of right in Asia, Stimson wrote. Its people's conscience and its national interest demanded sanctions against Tokyo. This stand, the former secretary of state argued, would not lead to hostilities. Japan was anxious to avoid war with the United States because its leaders knew they could not win such a struggle.[1]

American ambassador Joseph Grew vigorously dissented from Tokyo. He admitted that Tokyo saw Japan's drive to self-sufficiency, first made explicit under Konoe's cabinet in late 1938, as necessary for the empire's security. But Grew argued that this drive actually provided Washington with an opportunity to improve relations. Japan's dependency on the United States, growing because of the outbreak of war in Europe; Grew's own harsh warning of a severe deterioration in trans-Pacific relations to an incredulous Tokyo audience three months after the trade treaty had been abrogated; and the failure to end the

---

1. William L. Langer and S. Everett Gleason, *The Challenge to Isolation, 1937–1940* (New York: Harper, 1952), 578.

fighting in China—all had convinced many Japanese that a greater moderation was in order. There were some encouraging signs already, among them indications that parts of the Yangtze River might be opened to neutral commerce. It was true that Japan had determined to seek alternative sources of supply, from Latin America to the Netherlands East Indies. But if the United States could devise and support "a sound postwar economic plan"[2] that struck a proper balance between have and have-not nations, it could persuade Tokyo to return to pro-Western ways.

For these reasons, Grew continued, the United States should not impose economic sanctions. These would only force Japan to retaliate, certainly by attempting autarky no matter what the cost or how small the chance of success, perhaps by going to war. The vicious cycle of Japan's pursuit of self-sufficiency, further American economic sanctions, and further pursuit of self-sufficiency had to come to an end. Throughout the spring, particularly while his conversations with Japanese foreign minister Arita Hachirō were taking place, Grew emphasized the real chance that Japanese "moderates" might be resurgent. It was not a time for American intransigence, which would help the radicals in Tokyo put down this latest attempt for rapprochement with the West.[3]

Stanley Hornbeck, senior adviser for East Asian affairs in the State Department, took issue with some of Grew's facts and all of his assessments. Japan, like Germany, was a nation of "Iron and Blood," dedicated to a quest for domination. Its leaders were quasi-fanatics who could not be trusted to respect agreements.[4] Their aims had to be defeated or accepted. They would move in the Far East, perhaps against the Netherlands East Indies, as a result of military and diplomatic developments in Europe—and a belief that the United States would acquiesce in such a move by taking no action, either to deter or

2. Grew to Hornbeck, 11 February 1940, vol. 98, Grew Papers.

3. Grew to Hull, 11 March 1940, DF 794.00/171, National Archives; Grew to Hornbeck, 31 January 1940, vol. 98, Grew Papers; *FRUS, 1940*, 4:282–84, 495–96; Grew to Hull, 12 April 1940, DF 611.9431/200; Grew to Hull, 28 March 1940, DF 611.9431/198; and Grew diary entries, March 1940, and 10 April 1940, vol. 100, Grew Papers. For a good exposition of Grew's continuing (and, I would argue, near-quixotic) hopefulness, see Jonathan Utley, *Going to War with Japan, 1937–1941* (Knoxville: University of Tennessee Press, 1985), 89–91.

4. In Hornbeck's mind was Ambassador to China Nelson Johnson's report that the Japanese offer to open the Yangtze was worthless because the Imperial Army was in complete control of its valley and had utterly destroyed its commercial usefulness. In addition Grew himself had written that Foreign Minister Arita had not changed his views on the desirability of self-sufficiency. See *FRUS, 1940*, 4:490–92, 514–16.

to punish. The worst course for the United States, therefore, was to approach Japan with the olive branch. Such a move would be seen as a "go signal" for exactly the actions that America sought to prevent. Washington should continue to give more aid to China, withhold assistance from Japan, and keep the fleet at Hawaii.[5]

Hornbeck believed that economic pressure would have great effect at little risk. Unlike Grew, he considered the Japanese economy weak and vulnerable. Japan's dependence on America was higher in the spring of 1940, as the ambassador himself admitted, than ever before. Tokyo might in time locate alternative sources, but this was simply an argument for applying pressure at once, when it would be most effective. In heavy machinery, machine tools, and iron and steel the United States had a virtual stranglehold on Japan, as the Japanese themselves well realized. America had either to accept the New Order, which meant writing off China and the principles of the Open Door, or to bring Japan's program to a halt through systematic economic pressure backed, to be sure, by the determination to use military force if it became necessary.[6]

Whatever else may be said of Hornbeck's advice, his warnings about the drawbacks of having no systematic program were on the mark. From the outbreak of the European war until the end of 1940 American policy toward Japan was a series of ad hoc actions seldom based on the critical questions that Grew and Hornbeck had raised.

The first of these actions was the administration's reaction to the Soviet Union's attack on Finland. The bombings of Finnish civilians in Helsinki on 29 November 1939 stirred an even greater public outcry in America than had earlier Japanese attacks on China. On 30 November Hull summoned his principal advisers to his office to consider the proper response. Undersecretary of State Sumner Welles favored breaking diplomatic relations with Moscow to deter the Soviets from more atrocities. The step might sober extremists in Tokyo, too, Welles added. Most of the others present, however, agreed with J. Pierrepont Moffat of the European Division that a full break with Russia

---

5. *FRUS, 1940*, 4:334–36; Hornbeck to Hull, 24 May 1940, Box 246, Hornbeck Papers; Hornbeck to Welles, 14 May 1940, Box 311, Hornbeck Papers; and Hornbeck memo, 10 April 1940, Box 155, Hornbeck Papers.
6. Hornbeck memo, 1 April 1940, Box 414, Hornbeck Papers; Naval attaché report, 14 February 1940, Box 198, PSF, SF, Roosevelt Papers; Hornbeck memo, 30 April 1940, Box 236, Hornbeck Papers; Lt. Norman Towson to assistant chief of staff, War Department, 16 April 1940, DF 894.50/119 1/2; and Hornbeck to Hamilton, 19 December 1939, Box 369, Hornbeck Papers.

would create strong pressure for identical actions against Germany and Japan.[7]

Allusions to Japan suggested an alternative: a moral embargo, this time on selected exports to the Soviet Union. Roosevelt readily agreed to express his government's hopes that American makers and shippers of "airplanes, aeronautical equipment, and materials essential to airplane manufacture" would not export them to nations that bombed civilians.[8]

But which materials were essential to the making of aircraft? A cabinet meeting on 4 December agreed that aluminum clearly qualified. Secretary of the Treasury Henry Morgenthau, seizing the initiative, called as well for an embargo on molybdenum—a metal alloy important for airframe construction and, by coincidence, machine tools. With Roosevelt's concurrence, Morgenthau met with the heads of the mining companies, Climax and Kennecott, chiefly responsible for American (and global) production of the metal. Both firms felt that if Russia were to be stigmatized, then Japan should be as well. On cue Morgenthau called the president, who agreed that such a ban would be in keeping with Hull's earlier moral embargo against Tokyo.[9] The number of materials on moral embargo snowballed. As the molybdenum companies pointed out, other materials, such as nickel, could be substituted for their product. In the interests of fairness and effectiveness this metal had to be included. Because Canada was the world's leading producer of nickel, Morgenthau first visited Arthur Purvis, British head of the Allied Purchasing Mission in the United States. Purvis agreed to ask the Canadians to end nickel exports to Russia and Japan and soon obtained results. His conversations with International Nickel, in turn, directed attention to two other substitutes for molybdenum, tungsten and vanadium. The latter, mined chiefly in Peru, was controllable. Morgenthau and Purvis cooperated to purchase as much of that nation's output as possible.[10]

These developments were unwelcome to Secretary of State Cordell

7. J. Pierrepont Moffat journal entry of 30 November 1939, vol. 43, Moffat Papers.

8. *FRUSJ*, 2:202.

9. John M. Blum, *From the Morgenthau Diaries*, 3 vols. (Boston: Houghton Mifflin, 1959–67), 2:126–27; Morgenthau Papers, Presidential Diaries, 2:386; and Morgenthau Papers, Diaries, 227:78, 153.

10. Morgenthau Papers, Diaries, 229:80, 123–26; Roosevelt to Hull, 14 December 1939, Official File 176, Roosevelt Papers; *FRUSJ*, 2:202–3; Yost memo, 19 December 1939, Box 155, Hornbeck Papers; Moffat journal entry of 19 December 1939, vol. 43, Moffat Papers; Green memo, 20 December 1939, DF 700.00116 M.E./201; and Allen to Green, 24 January 1940, DF 811.24 Raw Materials/570.

Hull. He knew that the Japanese would be following such moves in Washington, particularly since the trade treaty was due to expire, and so he had reservations about extending the moral embargo against Tokyo. But he did not object when, on 15 December, Roosevelt ordered him to call publicly for an end to shipments of aluminum and molybdenum to nations bombing civilians and, four days later, to include nickel and tungsten on the restricted list. In part, Hull's reluctance to press his opposition stemmed from the agreement of Maxwell Hamilton, head of the Far Eastern Division in State, and Hornbeck that U.S. policy ought to embargo exports to Russia and to Japan evenhandedly. In part, it came from the discovery of Joseph Green's Controls Division—alert for ways to increase pressure on Japan and extend its own purview in the process—that in October, Roosevelt had authorized the Army-Navy Munitions Board to ask for an end to the export of materials that could be replaced only by such imports as nickel, tungsten, tin, and antimony. Green, Hull, and Herbert Feis, State's economic adviser, had been unaware of this development. On consideration, however, they decided to discourage the export of these new materials too.[11]

In none of these metals had American shipments to Japan been substantial. For all of them, therefore, advocates of caution in the Department of State saw little reason to block an export ban, particularly since that ban was necessary to the American defense effort as well as morally correct. But these issues were more serious when applied to another commodity that the United States did export to Japan in bulk and that was vital to America's rearmament effort: high-quality aviation gasoline. Even after conflict had erupted in Europe, the U.S. War Department was willing to allow some of this valuable fuel to reach Japan. But it strongly opposed the sale of patents and processes used to refine aviation gasoline from crude petroleum. State disagreed, and its differences with the War Department came to a head in late November as two American firms—Phillips and Badger—prepared to sign contracts with Japan which included manufacturing rights to aviation gasoline processes. Frank Howard of Standard-Vacuum Oil Company alerted the War Department and strongly urged that Japan not be allowed to obtain such important information. With navy support, the War Department appealed to

11. Morgenthau Papers, Diaries, 229:80, 123–26; Roosevelt to Hull, 14 December 1939, Official File 176, Roosevelt Papers; *FRUSJ*, 2:202–3; Yost memo, 19 December 1939, Box 155, Hornbeck Papers; Moffat journal entry of 19 December 1939, vol. 43, Moffat Papers; Green memo, 20 December 1939, DF 700.00116 M.E./201; and Allen to Green, 24 January 1940, DF 811.24 Raw Materials/570.

State to issue the necessary instructions. Welles, Hornbeck, and Green agreed, believing that quick action was called for.[12]

Indeed it was. A Japanese negotiating mission was en route to Oklahoma to formalize the contract with Phillips, and it would arrive shortly before Christmas. Badger's talks with Japan had progressed even further. Its president strongly opposed ending them, terming this latest moral embargo—with some justice—a trick by Standard-Vacuum to hurt competitors. In any event, Badger claimed, the process to be sold required continual supplies of a catalyst that only American firms could furnish.[13]

Matters were made no simpler by Hamilton's discovery on 14 December that Universal Oil had already signed a lucrative long-term contract with Japan. A good deal of information about aviation gasoline processes had been transferred to Mitsubishi, the Japanese contractor, and Universal engineers were supervising the construction of a half-completed plant to produce catalytic agents.[14]

The State Department's dilemma was clear. If it did not end the export of processes for manufacturing aviation gasoline, probably Badger and certainly Universal would proceed with their contracts. If they did, the War and Navy departments were sure to be displeased, and the moral embargo would appear a mockery just as sentiment in Congress was rising to inflict further economic punishment on aggressors. In addition, other American firms might enter into equally objectionable agreements with the Japanese. If State did include aviation gasoline processes under the moral embargo, on the other hand, Japan would be angered, and Universal would be forced to withdraw from its obligations.

To Hull and his advisers, the latter seemed the lesser evil. On 19 December Green issued new guidelines to the oilmen. It was against the national interest, as determined by the War and Navy departments, to export "plans, plants, manufacturing rights, or technical information required for the production of high quality aviation gasoline." Sales of catalysts and blending agents could continue, but the companies were to report them to the State Department regularly. Universal cancelled its contract and recalled its personnel from Japan. When Japanese diplomats visited the company's head office to pro-

---

12. Green to Berle, 15 November 1939, DF 894.24/742.
13. Ibid.
14. E. A. Badger to Green, 6 December 1939, DF 894.24/748; Green memo, 7 December 1939, DF 894.24/749; Green memo, 14 December 1939, Box 155, Hornbeck Papers; and Green memo, 14 December 1939, DF 894.24/759.

test, Universal's representative, H. J. Halle, interpreted Green's memorandum as a governmental order. The Japanese noted that the guidelines had no legal power; Halle asked if Japan had the legal power to violate American interests in China. Ambassador Horinouchi Kensuke next protested to Hull, using language uncommon for a diplomat: if Universal had reneged on its contract without explicit orders from Washington, it was liable to legal action. An unmoved Hull dismissed the ambassador with the rejoinder that, "in the language of the Japanese Government relating to the Nine Power Treaty, the gasoline understanding has become 'obsolete.'"[15]

This resolution was not final. Charles Yost, assistant chief of the Controls Division, pointed out that Japan could still purchase manufacturing rights for all other kinds of petroleum products, some of which could be made to fit aviation gasoline standards. The only way to stop Japanese production would be to ban the sale of all such rights. This was the only fair way too, a point vigorously seconded by Universal. It had lost its contract, but other firms were free to sell all sorts of other technical information to Japan.[16]

By early spring of 1940 the State Department's senior officers were engaged in a full reassessment of the moral embargo. If the embargo aimed to stop or at least reduce the bombing of Chinese civilians, it had failed badly. If it meant to disengage the United States from the immorality of those bombings, here too it had stumbled. As one departmental study bluntly stated, "it is a foregone conclusion that practically everything which Japan buys in this country are [*sic*], strictly speaking, munitions of war destined to further Japan's military activities in China." The only real solution, the study continued, was to end the incomplete and (to some companies and industries) unfair moral embargo and ban all military trade with Japan.[17]

Hamilton and Hornbeck agreed with these findings. But they diverged on what to do. Hornbeck argued that it was time to scrap the hodgepodge moral embargo and begin a calculated, comprehensive program of official economic pressure on the Japanese Empire. Hamilton was more cautious. American pressure could drive Japan close to the Nazis.[18]

His was a caution that Hull only partly shared. The Germans seized

15. *FRUSJ*, 2:203–4; *FRUS, 1939*, 3:549–50; Green memo, 21 December 1939, DF 894.24/764; and Hull memo, 31 January 1940, DF 711.94/1407. Japan did sue Universal, but the action had not yet reached a decision by Pearl Harbor.

16. Moffat to division chiefs and political advisers, 21 March 1940, DF 700.00116 M.E./253.

17. Anonymous memo, undated (early April 1940), DF 894.24/915.

18. Hornbeck memo, 10 April 1940, Box 460, Hornbeck Papers.

Denmark and Norway in mid-April. The secretary feared that Holland would be next, casting the status of the Netherlands East Indies into doubt. Perhaps Germany would declare those oil-rich islands a gift to Japan. Hull was worried enough to consider sending the American fleet to the islands or to Singapore. Assistant Secretary of State Breckinridge Long dissuaded his chief from so drastic a step, but on 17 April Hull did issue a strong warning to Tokyo about using force.[19]

A month later, after consulting with Hornbeck and Hamilton, he reinforced the message. Hornbeck had argued forcefully that the United States could do little to wean Japan away from a Germany now triumphant over Holland, Belgium, and France. Japan would attack in the East Indies if the United States failed to indicate its willingness to resist. Hull agreed, instructing Grew to impress upon Japan's leaders that America would not compromise with aggressors. So did Roosevelt; he decided to retain the fleet in Hawaiian waters following routine spring maneuvers there.[20]

After Germany's victories in Europe, however, the most important influence on American-Japanese relations was less direct. The Nazi invasion of Flanders moved Roosevelt to bring two Republicans, Henry Stimson and Frank Knox, into his cabinet as secretary of war and secretary of the navy. Both favored a hard line against Japan. The president established the Council of National Defense to oversee America's rearmament needs, order strategic goods, and purchase strategic materials. The opportunity to end strategic exports to Japan was not lost upon the American Committee for Non-Participation in Japanese Aggression, which had conducted a vigorous public campaign for harsh measures against Tokyo since 1938. With urgings from the committee, sympathetic political leaders such as Senator Key Pittman, an anxious army, and inside supporters like Hornbeck, Hull directed Assistant Secretary of State Adolph Berle to draft a bill appropriate for the defense council. On 2 July the National Defense Act became law, with provisions that permitted the president to ban exports of commodities he designated to countries he chose.[21]

19. Fred L. Israel, ed., *The War Diary of Breckinridge Long* (Lincoln: University of Nebraska Press, 1966), 81–82; Moffat journal entry of 17 April 1940, vol. 44, Moffat Papers; and *FRUS*, 2:281–82.

20. Cordell Hull, *The Memoirs of Cordell Hull*, 2 vols. (New York: Macmillan, 1948), 1:895; *FRUS, 1940*, 4:334–36; Hornbeck to Welles, 14 May 1940, Box 311, Hornbeck Papers; Hornbeck to Hull, 24 May 1940, Box 246, Hornbeck Papers; Hornbeck memos, 17 and 18 May 1940, Box 461, Hornbeck Papers; *FRUS, 1940*, 4:336–38, 345–46; and Robert J. Quinlan, "The United States Fleet: Diplomacy, Strategy and the Allocation of Ships (1940–1941)," in *American Civil-Military Decisions*, ed. Harold Stein (Birmingham: University of Alabama Press, 1963), 158.

21. Israel, 111; Harold L. Ickes, *The Secret Diary of Harold L. Ickes*, 3 vols. (New York:

Who would control the licensing system to regulate exports? Hornbeck and Green felt that Green's Division of Controls in the State Department could handle the duty, much as it had under the neutrality legislation and successive moral embargoes. Berle disagreed. If any part of State administered the controls, he persuaded Hull, the department would become entangled in complex issues of domestic politics as supplies grew scarcer. In addition, restrictions for the purpose of conservation would be perceived abroad as intentional foreign policy whether meant as such or not. Berle prefered an export control unit under the Council of National Defense which would operate tacitly under the Controls Division.[22]

Hornbeck and Green were amenable to this arrangement, but Morgenthau was not. Throughout June he worked diligently to secure licensing authority for his department, railing against the creation of yet another bureaucracy (particularly one not under his control). Hull stood his ground, however, sure that Morgenthau would employ any tool to impose drastic reductions on American exports to Japan. Hull won. Roosevelt appointed Lieutenant Colonel Russell Maxwell administrator of export control. Maxwell's office was to set guidelines for export controls, but the Division of Controls in State would actually issue the licenses. Maxwell could call for restrictions on a given commodity because of defense needs, but Green could refuse to implement them if important issues of foreign policy were involved.[23]

Invariably such issues were involved. Although Berle's proposal was adopted in substance, none of his arguments was really addressed. Indeed, in the months to come the Department of State would find itself attacked from the outside, by Japanese diplomats for thinly veiled attempts to impose sanctions by the back door, even as it was assaulted from within the administration by advocates of more rapid rearmament for America and those who wanted greater pressure against Japan.

Green's staffers first confronted the nettlesome question of how— or whether—to incorporate moral embargo on items from aircraft to aviation gasoline processes into a system of legal export restrictions.

Simon & Schuster, 1954), 3:232; Jonathan G. Utley, "Diplomacy in a Democracy: The United States and Japan, 1937–1941," *World Afairs* 193 (1976), 133–34; Utley, *Going,* 93–95; Herbert Feis, *The Road to Pearl Harbor* (1950; New York: Atheneum, 1967), 72; and Donald J. Friedman, *The Road from Isolation* (Cambridge: Harvard University Press, 1970), 33–34.

22. Berle memo, 8 June 1940, Adolf A. Berle Papers.

23. Feis, *Road,* 73–74; Morgenthau Papers, Diaries, 276:59–62; and Irvine H. Anderson, Jr., *The Standard-Vacuum Oil Company and United States East Asian Policy, 1933–1941* (Princeton: Princeton University Press, 1975), 129–30.

Most assumed that the new controls would cover all items under the older, voluntary embargoes automatically. Berle, conscious of the growing threat in Europe and wanting to avoid further provocation of Japan, was not so sure. In his view, the National Defense Act superseded the moral embargoes. Previous embargoes had been based on moral disapprobation of certain forms of international conduct. The defense act called for restrictions arising only from national security needs. If those needs did not exist, the embargo would have to be lifted.[24]

Berle's argument was logically irrefutable and virtually ignored. Roosevelt's call for a sharply increased defense establishment, including an immense air force, ensured that a large number of materials on the moral embargo list would be deemed necessary for national defense. But Maxwell's office counseled banning the export of some commodities, such as molybdenum, to harm Japan, not to protect scarce holdings in the United States, under the ostensible authority of the National Defense Act. That act was five minutes old when the president put under license the export of such arms and implements of war as aircraft, aluminum, antimony, manganese, molybdenum, tungsten, and vanadium—thus making it possible to end further shipments to Japan. A host of chemicals and other products were listed, too, plus one vital to Japan: machine tools.[25]

This last inclusion illustrates how the line had blurred between protecting American supplies for defense and embargoing shipments to Japan as pressure. Six months earlier, in January 1940, Purvis had warned Morgenthau that U.S. supplies of machine tools were low, perhaps insufficient for adequate production of warplanes and other arms. Morgenthau learned that only four nations—Britain, France, Russia, and Japan—received exports of American machine tools in significant amounts. The treasury secretary then met with the Na-

24. Harold Moseley memo, 12 June 1940, DF 894.24/963; Berle to Hornbeck, Green, and Moore, 13 July 1940, DF 700.00116 M.E./302; and *FRUS, 1940,* 4:582–83.

25. William Emerson, "Franklin Roosevelt as Commander-in-Chief in World War II," *Military Affairs* 22 (Winter 1958), 185–86; Civilian Production Administration, *Industrial Mobilization for War: Program and Administration* (Washington: GPO, 1947), 71–73; Robert Dallek, *Franklin D. Roosevelt and American Foreign Policy, 1932–1945* (New York: Oxford University Press, 1979), 221; World Peace Foundation, *Documents on American Foreign Policy,* vol. 3: *July 1940–June 1941* (Boston, 1941), 473; *FRUSJ,* 2:211–13; and Green to Hull, 17 July 1940, DF 700.00116 M.E./303. This last reported that all products under the moral embargoes were now legally licensed under the defense act except plans, processes, and technical information regarding the production of aviation gasoline. No evidence suggests that any of this information reached Japan after July 1940, however.

tional Machine Tools Builders Association and asked them to assign lowest priority to Soviet and Japanese orders, ensuring substantial delays. The fruits of this step became apparent in mid-May, when Roosevelt instructed the navy to requisition outright all the machine tools under contract to foreign governments, in preparation for the immense program to create a two-ocean fleet. The navy's zeal in executing the presidential directive quickly brought protest from the Japanese Embassy in Washington; State Department officials were asked why shipments of machine tools on New York wharves could not be loaded onto waiting Japanese freighters. These officials, notably Green, were in a delicate position. The navy wanted export permits for the machine tools denied. But the National Defense Act was not quite yet law, so no authority existed to issue or deny such permits. After several skirmishes with Treasury, which argued for delay until the bill passed Congress, Green freed nearly half of the held-up shipments. Once the act did come into effect, however, shipments virtually ended.[26]

Nevertheless, nothing the United States had yet undertaken could be construed as a direct challenge to Japan. Shutoffs of molybdenum and other rare alloy exports could not be justified on grounds of national defense, but neither did they impair the Japanese economy. Shutoffs of machine tools did impair the Imperial economy, but they clearly were for legitimate American defense purposes, as Japanese diplomats themselves conceded tacitly with the ending of protests. But what was Washington's policy to be for a commodity of some importance to the rearmament effort and of great importance to the Japanese economy? What policy, in other words, for scrap iron?

State had been receiving a stream of reports from Grew and naval intelligence which stressed Japan's increasing dependence on American scrap and, as a result, increasing sensitivity to the possibility of a scrap embargo. Hamilton worried openly that a cutoff might affect

26. Morgenthau Papers, Diaries, 238:295–302 and 240:70–75, and Franklin D. Roosevelt, *Complete Presidential Press Conferences of Franklin D. Roosevelt*, 25 vols. (New York: Da Capo, 1972), 16:41–42. Utley, whose research on the rather involved story of machine tools is in many respects deeper than mine, notes that export licenses were being granted for certain categories of machine tools through the autumn of 1940. The licenses certainly were being granted, but it seems that they had little meaning given legitimate domestic needs (which Utley's work also reveals) and Morgenthau's influence with the producing companies, influence that he had applied earlier in the case of the moral embargo on the rare metals. This, plus Green's initiative of moving against licensing machine tools used in aircraft construction, again illustrates how advocates of harsher action used the moral embargo as a lever to their ends, despite the above-mentioned objections of Berle. See Utley, *Going*, 120–21.

Japanese policy. Seeking to prevent a total ban once the National Defense Act became law, he suggested that, if scrap were licensed, exports to Japan be permitted in an amount equal to a "normal" year's shipments.[27]

Hamilton had cause for concern. By mid-July the National Defense Act had stimulated great pressure for an embargo on scrap exports. The spring campaign of the American Committee for Non-Participation in Japanese Aggression, which featured a missionary doctor's tale of removing made-in-America scrap iron from Chinese civilians' bodies, was yielding results in the form of protests from both houses of Congress. Within the executive branch Morgenthau and Secretary of the Interior Harold Ickes complained about Hull's inaction on scrap. Leon Henderson, head of the Price Stabilization Division in the National Defense Advisory Commission (NDAC), a new body to oversee the rearmament effort, favored export restrictions. And Lauchlin Currie, the president's administrative assistant, pointed to increased Japanese purchases to support his recommendation for an embargo.[28]

These were precisely the sorts of arguments that State did not want to use to justify restrictions on the export of scrap iron and steel. Roosevelt himself had publicly proclaimed that there was no shortage of scrap in the United States. Asked whether China would not favor an American scrap embargo, the president had replied that Japan had no shortage itself, so a cutoff would do no practical good. To make matters even clearer, the Army-Navy Munitions Board informed the State Department that scrap was relatively unimportant for the defense effort; any decision should be made from the perspective of America's foreign relations.[29]

So State acted to head off diplomatic repercussions. On 22 July,

27. James Jones memo, 12 April 1940, DF 894.24/921; Grew to Hull, 20 June 1940, DF 894.24/984; Office of Naval Intelligence, Reports, 19 June 1940, File O-1-k, 12073-d, Record Group 38, Records of the Office of Naval Intelligence, National Archives; and *FRUS, 1940,* 4:577–78. The figures Hamilton saw noted that Japan had imported an annual average of 365,200 tons of scrap between 1926 and 1935, but 1,886,722 tons in 1937 and 1,378,216 tons in 1938.

28. *FRUS, 1940,* 4:577–78; Friedman, 37; protests from legislators are contained in DF 894.24/994–1000; Ickes, 3:232; Feis, *Road,* 88; Donald Nelson, *Arsenal of Democracy: The Story of American War Production* (New York: Harcourt, Brace, 1946), 98; and Currie to Roosevelt, 19 July 1940, Official File 342, Roosevelt Papers.

29. Roosevelt, *Press,* 15:552; *FRUS, 1940,* 4:587–88; Hornbeck to Welles, 20 July 1940, Box 155, Hornbeck Papers; Veatch to Hull, July 1940, Box 372, Hornbeck Papers; and Veatch memo, 19 July 1940, DF 811.20(D)REGULATIONS/150. Roosevelt was absolutely wrong about Japan's scrap supplies. See for example Hoshino's figures, Chapter 9, p. 168.

Joseph Ballantine and Harold Moseley (of Control) reassured the Japanese that any decision to embargo scrap would be based solely on defense considerations. Even as they spoke, Morgenthau was at Hyde Park warning Roosevelt that valuable strategic materials, including scrap, were being shipped abroad every day. A day later he telephoned Edward Stettinius, head of the National Defense Advisory Commission's Industrial Materials Division. Morgenthau boldly asked how long Stettinius would need to draft a justification for an embargo on scrap iron or steel if he or the president requested one. Stettinius was doubtful, because American supplies of low-grade scrap were substantial. Justification for high-grade scrap might be possible, however, because American industry needed number-one heavy melting scrap. Warned not to tell the State Department, Stettinius agreed to provide Morgenthau with a draft order within forty-eight hours, and he had an official report before Morgenthau on 25 July. Holding that the American steel industry could operate at only 60 percent of capacity if no scrap supplies were available, and observing that exports had been large during the past four years, the report recommended regulating scrap exports. That same day Morgenthau forwarded the necessary orders to Hyde Park for Roosevelt's signature.[30]

Nor did the treasury secretary stop there; the orders on Roosevelt's desk also included restrictions on the export of aviation gasoline and other oil products. In early June alarming reports had reached the State, Navy, and Treasury departments of immense Japanese orders for aviation gasoline. Hornbeck at once conferred with Hamilton, Green, and Admiral Harold Stark, chief of naval operations, to enlist their support for stalling the Japanese until the National Defense Act passed Congress. All agreed that a temporary ban should be imposed at once. A more permanent policy could be devised after reviewing the country's total supplies of aviation gasoline.[31]

But Morgenthau's draft to Roosevelt included petroleum products beyond aviation gasoline, in part because of a dinner held at the British Embassy on 18 July for Morgenthau, Stimson, and Knox. There Morgenthau and Stimson hit upon denying all oil supplies to Tokyo—and the European Axis—as the best way to prevent a Japanese strike southward. The British would do their part by destroying oil wells in the East Indies and by bombing German synthetic fuel

30. Morgenthau Papers, Diaries, 285:1, 124–26, 185, 366–67, and 286:190–96.
31. Hornbeck memos, 7 June and 18 July 1940, Box 155, Hornbeck Papers; Morgenthau Papers, Diaries, 279:248; and *FRUS, 1940*, 4:586–87.

plants in Europe, effectively snapping an indispensable sinew of war.[32]

The next morning Morgenthau presented the plan to Roosevelt, adding that Ickes would forestall State's objections by agreeing that the United States needed the oil itself. The proposal, brought forward at a cabinet meeting that afternoon, opened a deep and sometimes bitter debate over the wisdom of applying significant economic pressure on the Japanese. Welles, standing in for Hull, did not strongly oppose ending American shipments to Germany via Spanish and other European ports. But he voiced Hamilton's view that cutting off oil to Japan would bring about an attack on the Dutch East Indies. Morgenthau and Stimson disagreed vigorously. The State Department had claimed that Japan would go on the rampage after the first American loan to China, two years before. It had not. Hull's associates had opposed extending the moral embargoes to metal alloys, but Japan had done nothing in retaliation.[33]

In the days after this meeting Morgenthau lobbied powerfully. He had Ickes write the president that an oil shortage was possible along the Atlantic coast. Ickes observed that, along with Britain and Canada, Japan was the largest purchaser of American petroleum. Stimson warned that if recently placed Japanese contracts were honored, there would not be enough aviation gasoline in the country for minimum defense needs. At the same time the Council of National Defense certified aviation gasoline as a highest-priority "critical" material for national defense and steel and scrap iron as "essential."[34]

Roosevelt had no objection to restricting all shipments of oil products to European ports accessible to Germany. Nor was the president

32. *FRUS 1940*, 4:365–66, 367; Sir Llewellyn Woodward, *British Foreign Policy in the Second World War*, 5 vols. (London: HMSO, 1970–76), 2:95, 100; Henry L. Stimson diary entry of 18 July 1940, Henry L. Stimson Papers; Blum, 2:349; and Morgenthau Papers, Diaries, 284:201–6.

33. Hornbeck memo, 7 June 1940, Box 155, Hornbeck Papers; Morgenthau to Roosevelt, 19 July 1940, PSF, Departmental Correspondence, Box 97, Roosevelt Papers; Morgenthau Papers, Diaries, 284:212–16, 217–20; and Stimson diary entry of 19 July 1940, Stimson Papers.

34. Ickes to Roosevelt, 23 July 1940, Box 219, Harold L. Ickes Papers; Morgenthau Papers, Diaries, 286:86–88; Stimson diary entry of 24 July 1940, Stimson Papers; and Council of National Defense report, 24 July 1940, PSF, Departmental Correspondence, Box 142, Roosevelt Papers. Morgenthau did not press the scrap issue as vigorously as he did aviation gasoline and oil, even admitting that the State Department could demonstrate that conservation of most grades of scrap was not necessary for national defense. See Morgenthau Papers, Diaries, 284:212–16 (of 19 July 1940). Hornbeck, for his part, was concerned that the large Japanese purchases themselves signified an impending attack.

likely to permit the export of goods certified as critical—and therefore to be conserved—such as aviation gasoline and number-one heavy melting scrap. He asked Welles to prepare the necessary papers. But when he received Morgenthau's draft, which included all types of scrap and oil, Roosevelt assumed that it had received State's approval, signed it, and forwarded the documents to Welles to be formalized.[35]

The acting secretary of state needed only one glance to discern the wider cast of the amended order. Hastily putting aside other business, he called his colleagues into his office to consider their next step. As they arrived, Welles learned that the White House had already made the order public. In the discussion that followed, Green was agitated, knowing that demands for administrative details would soon deluge his division. He quickly deduced that Treasury was responsible. Hamilton and other Far Eastern advisers likewise dreaded the order's consequences for relations with Japan. Welles phoned Roosevelt, securing a presidential announcement that a clarifying order would be issued.[36]

Now it was Morgenthau's turn to be angry. During the morning of 26 July he called Ickes to have the Interior Department rule for the conservation of all oil products. The conversation, not surprisingly, saw frequent use of unregulated language directed at Green in particular and State in general. Morgenthau next urged Stimson to rally the Army-Navy Munitions Board to the cause. He then contacted Henry Grady at the State Department to demand an explanation. Grady was defensive, arguing that the order (as Morgenthau had amended it) could not be administered properly. Morgenthau rejoined that if the question were simply administrative and the Controls Division was not up to the task, his Treasury Department could take over the licensing system.[37]

Grady's response gave Morgenthau the opening he thought he needed at a cabinet meeting that afternoon. He sparred with Welles over the question of administration but was unable to deflect State from its position on that issue or on the substantive one of the scope of the new restrictions. The clarification order, issued that day, specified only aviation gasoline and lubricating oil, tetraethyl lead (a blending agent), and number-one heavy melting scrap iron and steel.

35. Anderson, 133–34, and Morgenthau Papers, Diaries, 285:185.

36. Herbert Feis, *The Spanish Story* (New York: Knopf, 1948), 43–46, and Feis, *Road,* 92.

37. Morgenthau Papers, Diaries, 287:151–52, 154–57, 158–61.

By 6 August the ban on aviation fuel had been clarified further as including gasoline of 87 octane or higher.[38]

The result was a triumph for consistency. As far as Hull, Welles, Hamilton, and the other advocates of caution were concerned, the United States could maintain that it was acting simply to promote its own defense efforts. No step singling Japan out for punishment, no overt pressure, had been applied. At the same time Washington had achieved the laudable goal of indicating disapproval of Tokyo's course of action. American rearmament had been assisted. And, to some extent, the public pressure to do more had been assuaged.

But a consistent policy is not always a sound one. The debates of late July 1940 focused ultimately on whether a commodity was or was not so necessary to American rearmament that its export should be prohibited. But the likely impact of export bans on Japanese foreign policy was hardly discussed. What little discussion did take place focused solely on the petroleum issue. Hamilton, Grew, and, in consequence, Hull maintained that a wide-ranging oil embargo would drive Japan to attack the East Indies. Hornbeck, Morgenthau, and Stimson believed that the military situation in Europe (and for Hornbeck the military disposition of the United States) would determine Japan's acts. No one on either side of this debate produced evidence, much less convincing evidence, for his assessments.

Nor did anyone except Hornbeck consider the impact on Japan of the other major item covered by the July orders: scrap iron. For the balance of the summer Hornbeck observed American scrap exports to Japan increasing rapidly in the medium- and lower-quality grades. If these grades were also banned, Hornbeck believed, the Japanese economy would be hurt because there were no alternative sources. In the oil situation, by contrast, Japan was importing more gasoline just under 87 octane and boosting it with additives. More significantly, other sources, most conspicuously in the East Indies, were available to circumvent any American embargo. To Hornbeck the conclusion seemed clear: if the United States did wish to give pause to Japan's leaders without resorting to the threat of military force (or needlessly endangering the Indies), a full scrap embargo was in order.[39]

---

38. Anderson, 134–37; Utley, *Going,* 97–99; Stimson diary entry of 26 July 1940, Stimson Papers; and *FRUSJ,* 2:217–18.

39. Hornbeck to Hull, 13 and 19 September 1940, Box 461, Hornbeck Papers. Hornbeck also urged increased American aid to China and, somewhat oddly, higher tariff duties on imported Japanese silk. Hornbeck did not comprehend Japan's foreign exchange situation, which, while hardly encouraging, was becoming overshadowed by

Hornbeck's urgings for such a ban came as gloom was deepening in Washington over Japan's intentions. From Tokyo, Grew provided news of Konoe's resumption of power and his 1 August announcement that Japan would strive to become totally self-reliant by creating a new economic order. By early September it was clear that Japan would demand the right to station troops in and march them through the northern half of French Indochina. Prominent Japanese figures, such as General Koiso Kuniaki, had proclaimed a renewed Japanese interest in closer connections, ostensibly economic, with the Netherlands East Indies. Just as ominous was the fact that the Nazis had sent a special representative, Heinrich Stahmer, to Tokyo to negotiate Japan's formal association with Germany and Italy.[40]

These developments prompted Grew to send a "green light" message to Washington on 12 September. In it he wrote that the time to offer a new trade treaty or other concessions had passed. Konoe's new cabinet would interpret American conciliation as a sign that the United States would not resist its bold programs. But Grew did have some warnings also.

The Japanese leaders had been intoxicated by Germany's spring victories. They might attack Britain in the Far East, particularly if the United States ended shipments of oil or other commodities that America possessed in abundance and therefore did not need for defense purposes. It was even conceivable that offices in the Japanese Army or Navy would act, if goaded, without the cabinet's knowledge or assent, as they had nine years before. If the United States could refrain from extreme economic measures and maintain the status quo in the Pacific until Britain triumphed in Europe, Japan would eventually return to sobriety.[41]

Grew's message accurately reflected the thinking of most of the State Department's senior officials. Firmness had to be shown, but measures directed against Japan rather than for American defense could trigger war in the Pacific. Roosevelt agreed too. Despite complaints by Morgenthau and Stimson that Japan was subverting the intent of the July restrictions by boosting purchased gasoline above 87 octane with

---

late 1940 by a simple dearth of materials available from overseas at any price. His assessment of Japan's vulnerability to a scrap embargo, however, was accurate—in contrast to Roosevelt's breezy assertions of July.

40. Grew diary entries, July and August 1940, Grew Papers; *FRUS, 1940,* 4:92–93, 95, 103–4, 398–400; and Grew to Hull, 5 August 1940, DF 756D.94/44.

41. *FRUS, 1940,* 4:598–603; Grew to Moffat, 1 September 1940, vol. 99, Grew Papers; and Grew diary entry, September 1940, vol. 101, Grew Papers.

additives, the president refused to extend the licensing system (and hence a virtual embargo) to any other petroleum products.

Roosevelt was reluctant to antagonize Japan on the eve of Tokyo's negotiations with the authorities in Batavia. But this reluctance did not stop Morgenthau and Hornbeck from lobbying the American oil companies involved in those negotiations. Morgenthau tried to get them to refuse outright to discuss shipment of most petroleum products from the Indies to Japan. Hornbeck argued that providing Japan with gasoline which could be upgraded to aviation quality from the Indies would undermine the American government's action of July and amount to appeasement.[42] The oilmen agreed with Hornbeck and, in ensuing talks with the Japanese negotiators, provided no such gasoline. But they were not prepared to refuse other products, and they rejected Morgenthau's angry sallies by dismissing his estimates of Japanese oil stocks (at 70 million barrels) as too fantastic to be taken seriously.[43] Japan could not have such massive supplies, whether it was preparing for a major war or not, and so there could be no harm in selling gasoline and some other oil products. The contract was signed on 8 October.[44]

By that time the U.S. government had acted to end the export of all steel and iron scrap except to Britain and nations of the Western Hemisphere. Once again Morgenthau led the fight, but this time he had a crucial ally in Henderson. Since July, Henderson had been warning that the American rearmament effort would have to proceed at a pace faster and on a scale more massive than most other NDAC members, particularly those from industry, believed advisable. He strongly opposed selling any scrap to Japan and by early September was recommending to Roosevelt, with the commission's approval, an embargo on scrap exports. Within days Morgenthau's staff had drafted an amendment to the July measure to include all grades of scrap.

Hull was in a difficult position. He had just received Grew's "green light" message and had resigned himself to continued Japanese ag-

42. That the United States permitted exports of this type of "upgradable" fuel from its own shores should not go unnoticed.

43. Actual Japanese reserves were slightly under 30 million barrels. See United States Strategic Bombing Survey, *The Effects of Strategic Bombing on Japan's War Economy* (Washington: GPO, 1946), 134.

44. Ickes, 3:297–98; *FRUS, 1940*, 4:75–79, 597–98; Blum, 2:354–55; Morgenthau Papers, Diaries, 290:53–81; and Anderson, 147–48. Royal Dutch Shell, not an American company, did provide some aviation gasoline. See Anderson, 148–49.

gression in Southeast Asia. But Hull did not want to provoke that aggression, particularly not before he knew the outcomes of the Battle of Britain, then fiercely raging, and Japan's negotiations with the Vichy authorities in Indochina. He knew that he could not oppose Henderson, the NDAC, and advocates of harsher measures against Japan for very long, but he was determined to stall for time. Moreover, his own economic adviser, Herbert Feis, conceded that there were no real alternatives to a complete scrap embargo against Tokyo. The licensing of scrap without an embargo would drive up exports as Tokyo anticipated an embargo's imposition. Annual limits on shipments would be hard to enforce. Besides Roosevelt, although public disclaimers about impending scrap shortages continued, had indicated that he wanted to halt shipments to Japan if they could be stopped without interrupting Britain's supplies. So Hull, after obtaining Morgenthau's promise to defer action, had Green prepare the necessary orders. A week passed. Over Britain the Royal Air Force not only survived but began to blunt the offensives of the Luftwaffe. In Japanese councils, decisions were made formally to join the Axis and to present the authorities of French Indochina with an ultimatum. When the American cabinet met again in Washington on 19 September, Hull was ready to act. Although he preferred positive assistance to China rather than additional pressure on Japan, Hull offered only token resistance to an embargo on scrap exports. The cabinet authorized both assistance and pressure. One week later, after the NDAC had worked out the details, Roosevelt made the new restriction public. Henderson proudly noted that hardly a pound of scrap iron would reach the Japanese Empire. The next day, 27 September, that empire joined the Axis.[45]

The development of the scrap embargo illustrated the awkward position that the State Department found itself in. Its senior officials had initially welcomed the National Defense Act as a way to avoid singling out Japan as a target for American export cutoffs. But their welcome also made it difficult for State to object to cutoffs that could

45. *FRUSJ*, 2:220–21; Nelson, 98; Morgenthau to Hull, 11 September 1940, DF 811.20(D)REGULATIONS/566; Morgenthau Papers, Diaries, 302:147–48, 305:120, 308:42; Roosevelt to Stettinius, 5 September 1940, Official File 342, Roosevelt Papers; Morgenthau Papers, Presidential Diaries, 3:647–48; Berle conversation with Roosevelt, 7 September 1940, DF 859B.01/291; Morgenthau to Roosevelt, 11 September 1940, PSF, Departmental Correspondence, Box 97, Roosevelt Papers: Green memo, 13 September 1940, Box 155, Hornbeck Papers; *FRUS, 1940*, 4:131; and Feis memo, 6 September 1940, DF 811.20(D)REGULATIONS/556. For a fine and fuller discussion of the road to the complete scrap embargo, see Utley, *Going*, 105–7.

be justified as necessary for rearmament. Advocates of sanctions against Japan sought just such a justification, of course, whether it was strictly appropriate or not.

Nor were advocates of sanctions confined to the American government. In early October, Canada asked why the United States had not followed its example in licensing the export of nickel, copper, and other metals. The British were more direct: the effectiveness of export controls imposed by the United States, Canada, and Britain had been reduced because application had been uncoordinated and less than comprehensive. The United States should combine with Britain to impose embargoes on cobalt, copper, carbon black, and other materials.[46]

In Washington, Hornbeck vigorously supported these proposals, arguing that any further buildup of Japanese war resources had to be prevented. Green agreed—but for different reasons. He was under pressure from the NDAC and the military to restrict exports of gasoline, nickel, iron, steel, and other strategic materials. Colonel Maxwell favored more bans too, pointing out that the Japanese, once denied scrap, would increase their orders for pig iron and related products, causing further shortages in America. Henderson continued to prod Roosevelt for embargoes on iron and steel, pressure that the president made Hull aware of.[47]

By the end of November, Hull was ready to yield. At Roosevelt's request he drew up a proclamation adding iron and steel (including iron ore, pig iron, and ferroalloys) to the licensing system. Exports would continue to Britain and the Western Hemisphere as before, and the materials would also be offered for sale to other countries, as far as possible in amounts consistent with prewar supplies. But this concession, in truth, was largely rhetorical. Maxwell, the NDAC, and the fast-expanding American rearmament effort combined to ensure that "as far as possible" was not very far at all. The same forces

46. *FRUS, 1940*, 4:605–7, 613–14.

47. Hornbeck memo, 22 November 1940, Box 461, Hornbeck Papers; Hornbeck memo, 2 January 1941, Box 462, Hornbeck Papers; Morgenthau Papers, Diaries, 308: 49–51; Henderson to Roosevelt, 19 October 1940, Official File 176, Roosevelt Papers; *FRUS, 1940*, 4:624–25; and Green to Hull, 31 December 1940, OF20c, Office A. and Munitions Control, State, Box 17, Roosevelt Papers. Feis was unhappy with the British list, arguing that it was blatantly unfair to American interests. British Malaya would supply Japan with raw rubber, but America was not to provide the carbon black necessary to manufacture tires. It was all right to ship Malayan iron ore to Tokyo, so long as no American cobalt allowed the ore to be turned into high-grade steel. See *FRUS, 1940*, 4:615–16.

compelled Hull to add nickel, copper, zinc, and other strategic goods to the restricted list by the end of 1940.[48]

Hull did not always yield. As 1941 arrived, he knew that his chief task in the Pacific was to delay Japan's commencement of a forceful advance to the south. He was convinced, as was Roosevelt, that an oil embargo would provoke Tokyo to attack the Dutch East Indies. Nor, except for aviation gasoline, could any case be made that the United States needed to conserve oil for its own defense effort. As a result Hull had been able to block Morgenthau's attempt of early October to prevent the sailing of a ship carrying drums of gasoline to Japan on the grounds that the ship was to be scrapped after reaching its destination. And he thwarted Harold Ickes's efforts to embargo oil exports when, in late December, the secretary of the interior argued again that shortages along the Atlantic coast would soon compel rationing.[49]

Nevertheless, the link between economic pressure on Japan and the needs of the U.S. arms program badly obscured some key questions in American policy for the western Pacific. The debate between Grew and Hornbeck over the nature and vulnerability of the Japanese government had been stillborn. There emerged no sort of consensus, much less a clear one, at any time in 1940 concerning the nature and inclination of the regime in Tokyo. Nor were convincing assessments ever produced, or even educated guesses, concerning the likely impact on Japan's economy of export cutoffs and how such cutoffs would affect Japanese foreign policy. There was a belief, without underpinnings, that an end to shipments of petroleum (except aviation gasoline) would cause the Japanese military to run wild. And there was an implied belief that to end shipments of nearly everything else—all forms of iron, steel, and other critical materials—would not.

The actual result of arming and appeasing was almost serendipitous. The American pressures of 1940 hurt the Japanese economy, the scrap embargo gravely. One can argue persuasively that those pressures were largely responsible for the inability of the Imperial economy to function effectively in the later years of the Pacific War, when the failures of earlier efforts to expand production and inadequacies in maintaining existing capital plant and transportation

48. Hull to Roosevelt, 30 November 1940, Official File 342, Roosevelt Papers; *FRUSJ*, 2:233–235; and Stettinius to McReynolds, 17 December 1940, Box 8, Papers of the National Defense Advisory Commission, Roosevelt Library.

49. Blum, 2:323–24, 362; Ickes, 3:339, 387–88; Stimson diary entry of 4 October 1940; and Ickes to Roosevelt, 20 December 1940, Box 219, Ickes Papers.

(especially seaborne) would become glaring.[50] But wherever the United States did act in 1940, the Japanese Planning Board was able to provide the military services with the materials they required to continue preparations for the Southward Advance. In the navy's case, in fact, great increases in steel were being provided just as the United States was imposing virtual embargoes on the export of materials essential to the production of steel in Japan. At the same time American pressure provided advocates of the Southward Advance with a potent argument: a complete economic rupture was imminent, and hence the advance had to be commenced. In only one major category of commodities could deficiencies not have been made up, could the Japanese civilian sector not have been further deprived: oil. And when, in July 1941, the Roosevelt administration did finally end petroleum shipments to Japan, its timing of the step ensured that earlier American predictions about the impact on Japan's military would be realized.

50. See, for example, the second five-year production expansion plan, approved by the Japanese cabinet on 8 May 1942, which gave highest priority to just those materials cut off by the United States in 1940: steel, aluminum, aviation gasoline, and machine tools. Tsūshō Sangyō-shō, *Shōkō seisaku shi 11: Sangyō tōsei* (Tokyo: Shōkō seisaku Shi Kankō Kai, 1964), 501.

[11]

Unsettled Details: The Debate over the Southward Advance

At the start of 1941, three fundamental questions concerning the Japanese Empire's foreign and economic policies awaited answers. What was to be the nature and timing of the strike to the south? Could the economy sustain such a strike? Would the economy be reformed along the lines of the New Economic Order?

The first question drew the most attention, in large part because the Imperial Army and Navy still held widely divergent views. The generals were increasingly frustrated about their inability to halt the draining conflict in China, either by backdoor negotiations or by limited campaigns in the south to cut Chiang's supplies. They were also under growing pressure from field commanders to attempt a full-scale expedition against Kunming as the southern wing of a giant two-pronged assault on the Nationalists' latest capital, Chungking. Central headquarters, keenly aware of the materials situation, had refused to consider any such operation. But the same awareness led army leaders to insist that the advance southward be confined to the possessions of the British and the Dutch. A simultaneous effort against the Americans was unnecessary. As in 1940, the army placed its hope in Germany. In 1941 the British home islands would be invaded, paralyzing Britain in Asia. The United States would perforce direct its attention to more pressing concerns in the Atlantic. The Southward Advance, as Major General Tanaka Shin'ichi, chief of the Operations Division, averred in a formal conference on 16 January to set long-range army policy, would take place against minimal opposition. Only five months would be required to complete it. Afterward the divisions could be transferred back to the north, before the Soviets could react.

The navy refused to agree. As map maneuvers at the Naval War College from 26 to 28 November[1] had demonstrated, the advance meant war against Britain and the United States. The navy had to prepare for operations against those powers and the Dutch from the outset. To this end, it had requisitioned 600,000 tons of shipping in August and September—placing a further strain on an already overtaxed capacity for transportation.[2] And Minister Oikawa Koshirō had ordered the fleet to wartime organization on 15 November.[3]

The navy's insistence on Anglo-American indivisibility contributed, ironically, to resolving some elements of the interservice impasse, because it compelled the army to undertake a fundamental reassessment of Japan's defense posture. By mid-March no less a figure than the army chief of staff, Sugiyama Gen, was conceding at a conference of division chiefs that the interservice accord embodied in the principles of July was moribund. The army was duty-bound to carry out the southern operation, Sugiyama admitted, but the China Expeditionary Army had received approval for a punitive operation into southern Shansi Province to wear down Chinese forces there, and nothing had diminished army fears that the Soviets might strike while the southern assault was under way. Should Japan wait for a few years to replenish its national power after incorporating Indochina and Thailand? Or should Japan throw caution to the winds and advance southward come what may?[4]

Sugiyama's questions were examined under the auspices of Colonel Okada Kikusaburō, chief of the Army Ministry's War Preparations Section.[5] The document, completed by 26 March, opened with a blunt and unwelcome refutation of one of the army's cherished

1. Presided over by Chief of the Combined Fleet Yamamoto Isoroku.

2. In mid-November 1940 this difficulty was brought to the navy's attention. Japan possessed only 5.4 million tons of shipping. The army had 700,000 tons for its use. The navy had already procured nearly that amount itself and would require 2.4 million tons to complete its wartime mobilization. This left 2.3 million tons for executing the materials mobilization plan, nearly 25 percent under the absolute minimum judged necessary to keep the economy going. See Tsunoda Jun, "The Navy's Role in the Southern Strategy," in *The Fateful Choice*, ed. James W. Morley (New York: Columbia University Press, 1980), 280.

3. DR2, 139–43, 146–48, 201, 207–8; and Tanaka Shin'ichi, *Nihon sensō keizai hishi* (Tokyo: Conputa Eijisha, 1975), 95.

4. DR2, 211, 215.

5. The designation of Okada for this critical assignment again reveals the centrality of economic factors to Japanese decision making, even in the post-1937 Imperial Army.

hopes. The Southward Advance did mean war against the United States as well as Britain. Japan could wage war against America for two years, but thereafter supplies, especially of fuel, would become critical. The two years might be extended, however, if the East Indies could be seized rapidly and the sea lanes to Japan kept open.

In equally stark terms Okada maintained that the Southward Advance made war with the Soviet Union absolutely impossible. Only if the advance were delayed, and Britain and America were persuaded to provide resources to nurture Japan's economic power, could Tokyo hope to deal with the Soviets.[6]

Okada's conclusions were only one of a series of disappointments for the army's operations planners in the early spring. A second came from the Planning Board as it prepared the materials mobilization plan for FY1941 (April 1941 to March 1942). Production of nearly every commodity had either fallen or was rising much more slowly than the burgeoning needs of the military. Steel, unfortunately, was in the former category. Its 1940 production had amounted to 4.6 million tons but, the board believed, 1941's output would drop to 4.02 million. Actual military consumption of steel, in large part because of the increases negotiated in late 1940, had reached 1.44 million tons. But even with civilian usage trimmed to the "minimum bearable standard," according to the Planning Board, and trimmed another 400,000 tons below that standard, only 1.125 million tons were left for the army and navy to share.[7]

These findings produced immediate furor and what became known as the Planning Board Incident. Early on 17 April board members were arrested on charges of communist activity. In part they were victims of the last offensive of the business community, led by the Japan Economic Federation and the minister of commerce and industry, Kobayashi Ichizō, against the remnants of the New Economic Order. Kobayashi's dislike of Hoshino Naoki, president of the Planning Board, was particularly intense. But the Planning Board was mainly done in by deepening dissatisfaction within the military with the allocations that it proposed in the materials mobilization plans. Hoshino himself was spared arrest, but his resignation, and Kobayashi's (for balance), came quickly. Major General Suzuki Teiichi left active duty to become the Planning Board's new chief. To preserve interservice balance and assure complete military control over Japan's economic planning in the future—and no steel shortages for either

6. *DR2*, 214–16.
7. *GDS43*, 620–42; and *RGD2*, 443.

service in the present—Admiral Toyoda Teijirō assumed the commerce and industry portfolio soon after.[8]

The first task for Suzuki and the remaining Planning Board staffers was to adjust the military's allocations in the 1941 materials plan. A quick arrangement boosted each service's quota of steel to over 165,000 tons for the first quarter of the plan—an increase of 15 percent over the board's original figures (before the arrests). It won quick approval, so implementation could be begun immediately. The Planning Board warned, however, that the bulk of the increases was contingent upon increasing production (by stripping China and part of Manchuria of scrap iron, for example), and that Japan's overall economic situation in the spring of 1941 gave no cause for optimism.

These warnings had substance. Shortages of labor, especially skilled labor, were worsening. The European war and the American armament program had caused further harm. Even without them, moreover, Japan's foreign exchange holdings did not permit increased purchases from overseas to feed the military's widening maw. Those holdings had fallen so low that Japan could no longer draw on them to support its balance-of-payments deficit with the United States. American exports to Japan were dropping sharply well in advance of Washington's economic sanctions of late July.[9]

The military paid little heed to these admonitions. As the deadline for implementing the second quarter of the materials plan approached in late June, both branches were preoccupied with gaining further additions to their quotas, especially in steel. The army was particularly wary. Its chief economic staffer, Okada, understood that the American embargo on scrap iron had tellingly affected Japan's ability to produce steel. Growing difficulties in transporting coal—a consequence of the military's huge shipping requisitions—added to the problem. But Okada's job was to secure as much steel as possible

8. Robert M. Spaulding, Jr., "Japan's 'New Bureaucrats,' 1932–1945," in *Crisis Politics in Prewar Japan*, ed. George M. Wilson (Tokyo: Sophia University Press, 1970), 65; statement of Obata Tadayoshi, Exhibit 3216-A, Records of the International Military Tribunal for the Far East; Inaba Hidezō, *Gekidō sanjūnen no Nihon keizai* (Tokyo: Jitsugyō no Nihonsha, 1965), 73–75; Andō Yoshio, ed. and comp., *Shōwa seiji-keizaishi e no shōgen*, 3 vols. (Tokyo: Mainichi Shinbunsha, 1966), 2:253; and Nakamura Takafusa and Hara Akira, "Keizai Shintaisei," in *Konoe shintaisei no kenkyū*, ed. Nihon Seiji Gakkai Nenpyō (Tokyo: Iwanami Shoten, 1972), 107, 110–15.

9. Ishigawa Junkichi, comp., *Kokka sōdōin-shi*, 6 vols. (Tokyo: Kiyomizu Insatsujo, 1975), 1:616–17; GDS43, 592–615, 616–19; and *FES*, 30 June 1941. Dowd uses even stronger phrasing on the point of foreign exchange shortages. See Laurence P. Dowd, "Japanese Foreign Exchange Policy, 1930–1940" (Ph.D. diss., University of Michigan, 1953), 400.

for his service, and he saw as his chief antagonist not the American scrap embargo but the Imperial Navy.[10]

When even the purged Planning Board dug in its heels, insisting that further reductions in the civilian steel allotment were unthinkable, it set the stage for an interservice clash every inch as bitter as the one over the nature of the Southward Advance. In a three-day conference in mid-June, Okada dueled with his counterpart, Captain Minato Keijō of the navy's War Preparations Bureau. Okada recalled the diversion of 20,000 tons of "army steel" to the navy in the 1940 materials plan. What had been the result? For the army, tank manufacturing capacity was reduced by a third and field guns by 20 percent. Operations in China had been scaled back as a result. Unless the army could secure a total allocation of 1.2 million tons of steel in the course of the 1941 plan, it could not guarantee its national defense responsibilities.

Minato was not to be outbid. The navy had responsibilities too—and war preparations—which required 1.5 million tons of steel. Okada rejoined that the navy would invariably seek to pilfer steel from the army's quota in the name of war preparations. Last time the navy had expressed confidence that it could proceed with its duties—without further adjustments. Now it was playing the same game. Minato maintained that any naval preparations required large quantities of steel, but Okada sat unmoved.

As the hours wore on without resolution, representatives of the Planning Board grew restless. Unless army and navy reached accord on all allocations to the military, not just on steel, implementation of the materials plan would be impossible. As the first encounters had made it clear that neither branch would yield, it fell to Commander Mayama Kanji, chief of the materials mobilization group on the board, to suggest further reductions in the civilian sector. Civilian planners were privately outraged, predicting (among themselves) deep dislocations and additional disruptions throughout the economy as a result of Mayama's submission. But after the Planning Board Incident they were hardly of a mind to voice their objections, much less champion them. The army, it was agreed, would receive 736,000 tons of steel for the balance of the 1941 materials plan, the navy 787,000 tons. Both were dramatic increases over the already boosted allocations of the first quarter (see Table 11.1). Similar adjustments in other commodities soon followed.[11]

10. *RGD2*, 445–47.
11. Tanaka, 137–42; and Ishigawa, 1:626–762. These numbers assumed production

Table 11.1. Steel allocations in the 1941 Materials Mobilization Plan (in thousands of tons)

Quarter:	1	2	3–4 (combined)
Army	165	320	416
Navy	165	341	446
Civilian	759	511	1593

SOURCES: Ishigawa Junkichi, comp., *Kokka sōdōin-shi.* 6 vols. (Tokyo: Kiyamizu Insatsujo, 1975), 1:626–762; Tanaka Shin'ichi, *Nihon sensō keizai hishi* (Tokyo: Conputa Eijisha, 1975), 141–42.

A similar compromise, over the Southward Advance, was more easily reached but of less certain resolution. The "Outline of Policy toward the South" of 17 April declared that the objective southward was to establish imperial self-sufficiency and rapidly replenish the country's economic power by establishing close economic, political, and military relations with Thailand and Indochina and economic ties with the East Indies by diplomatic, not military, methods. If an Anglo-American embargo or Western military pressure threatened the empire's existence, however, force would be used.

In the basic respects—methods and targets—the navy seemed to have won. War would be considered only in extremis, not at the "favorable opportunity" urged by the army since the spring of 1940. The United States was explicitly mentioned in both contingencies that would require the use of force, an implicit acknowledgment of Anglo-American indivisibility. Yet a broader reading of the outline permits other conclusions. The army, and many of the navy's section chiefs, could believe that the advance had been endorsed despite the risk of war with the United States, and with good reason. The navy accepted a supplement to the outline stating that the Southward Advance would continue even if the China Incident were not settled; the advance, it seemed, would take place whatever the circumstances. The navy was insisting on sharp increases in its materials allocations, hardly a position consistent with a refusal to consider hostilities that might arise out of the advance. But fundamentally, in mid-April 1941 the naval hardliners and the army believed that the Southward Advance need not mean war with America, that a small-scale and per-

---

of 4.72 million tons of steel, in keeping with the Planning Board's earlier admonition that such an increase over its estimates of production would be necessary. Actual supplies for 1941 fell short, as the board warned: 4.7 million tons, with only 4.3 million produced and an additional 400,000 tons coming from Manchuria, stockpiles, and "reclamation." See *RGD2,* 445.

haps bloodless operation might achieve a self-sufficiency sphere. For proof, they could point to the electrifying Draft Understanding from the United States.[12]

Ambassador Nomura Kichisaburō's report of that understanding (which failed to point out that it was not an American proposal and that American secretary of state Cordell Hull had not accepted its basic tenets) reached Tokyo during the evening of 17 April.[13] It provoked emotions ranging from elation to shock. The terms seemed almost unbelievably favorable to Japan. The draft explicitly allowed Japan to observe its obligations under the Tripartite Pact. Each nation was to refrain from deploying naval and air forces to menace the other—a provision affecting only the stationing of the American fleet at Pearl Harbor. Each would "mutually supply" commodities required by the other. Negotiations would begin for a new commerce treaty, and a modus vivendi along the lines of actual trade conditions under the expired treaty was to be implemented at once. In the southwestern Pacific, "American cooperation and support shall be given in the production and procurement of natural resources (such as oil, rubber, tin, nickel) which Japan needs." Most important, the American president would request Chiang Kai-shek to negotiate a peace with Japan based on merger of the Chiang and Wang regimes and the recognition of Manchukuo. It is little wonder that the Japanese foreign vice-minister, Ōhashi Chūichi, excitedly told Konoe that the draft "could change the course of history."[14]

The army's mood was more one of confidence than exuberance. Major General Isoda Saburō, military attaché to the United States, reported to Tōjō on the eighteenth. Most Americans, he observed, were certain that their nation would become a belligerent, either because of the German U-boat war or because of Japan's Southward Advance. They were therefore anxious to avoid a two-front war, at least until American rearmament was completed in the autumn of 1942. Isoda concluded that the Draft Understanding was designed to delay Japan's advance for a year or two. In Tokyo, Major General

12. *DR2*, 217–19. For a text in English, see Morley, *Fateful*, 303–4.

13. For a discussion of these negotiations, see, inter alia: David J. Lu, *From the Marco Polo Bridge to Pearl Harbor* (Washington: Public Affairs, 1961), 156–57, 159–62; Nihon Kokusai Seiji Gakkai Taiheiyō Sensō Gen'in Kenkyūbu, ed., *Taiheiyō sensō e no michi*, 8 vols. (Tokyo: Asahi Shinbunsha, 1962–63), 7:147–49; Robert J. C. Butow, *The John Doe Associates* (Stanford: Stanford University Press, 1974), 24; Tsunoda, "Navy's Role," 247, 289; Hosoya Chihiro, "The Tripartite Pact, 1939–1940," in *Deterrent Diplomacy*, ed. James W. Morley (New York: Columbia University Press, 1976), 151; *TSM*, 7:153–54; and for initial Japanese reactions, Nobutaka Ike, ed. and trans., *Japan's Decision for War: Records of the 1941 Policy Conferences* (Stanford: Stanford University Press, 1967), 17.

14. *FRUSJ*, 2:398–402; and Lu, 163.

Wakamatsu Tadakazu, chief of the General Staff's Intelligence Division, seconded these views, which to a large extent reflected in a conference of army division chiefs which met on the twentieth. Although suspicious that acceptance of the Draft Understanding would end the alliance with Germany, they endorsed an agreement that could end hostilities with China on favorable terms while not betraying the Tripartite Pact. No one considered the notion that the Draft Understanding might not be a genuine American position.[15]

The navy likewise believed the draft authentic but was warier than the army. Taken unawares by Nomura's telegram, naval officers found it difficult to change their estimates of the probability of war with America. Section and division heads in the Naval General Staff in particular believed the Draft Understanding to be a colossal American trick: the crafty Yankees sought to delay a clash with Japan until the naval balance favored them. Both staff and ministry leaders, including Oikawa, concluded that Japan had to avoid signing a narrow and temporary modus vivendi. Fundamental questions had to be answered, if not by diplomacy then by force, regarding the future of the western Pacific and East Asia. The draft was only a start in this direction.[16]

On the afternoon of 21 April army and navy leaders met at the Suikosha club to formulate the military's position. Foremost among those in attendance were Mutō Akira, chief of the Army Ministry's Military Affairs Bureau; Rear Admiral Oka Takazumi, his naval counterpart; the Army General Staff's Operations Division chief, Major General Tanaka Shin'ichi; and his opposite number, Fukudome Shigeru. These men agreed that the Draft Understanding was an American artifice designed to stop the Southward Advance and to enable the Americans to send increased aid to Britain while allowing Roosevelt to build up his nation's military and bid for global hegemony. At the same time, however, an open diplomatic—and economic—rupture had to be avoided. The service chiefs therefore approved continuing negotiations on several conditions. The army demanded that no agreement, even of a preliminary sort, was to run counter to the spirit of the Tripartite Pact. Negotiations and any accord arising from them had to contribute to resolving the China Incident and to replenishing Japan's material strength. The navy insisted that the talks and accord lay the foundation for a long-term, worldwide peace.[17]

15. *DR2*, 253–54, 257–58; and Tsunoda, "Navy's role," 290.
16. *TSM*, 7:169–70.
17. *DR2*, 259. For a text of the interservice agreement, see *TSM*, 8:408–9.

At the top, a series of liaison conferences between the cabinet and the Supreme Command began on the evening of 22 April; they determined that America should not be unduly alienated. Army Minister Tōjō Hideki was adamant that Japan should seize any opportunity to settle the China Incident. In the meantime Tokyo could improve its position in Thailand and southern French Indochina. Navy Minister Oikawa agreed, stressing that negotiations with Washington should continue at least until America became involved in a naval war with Germany. Then the Imperial Navy would have greater freedom to act.[18]

Foreign Minister Matsuoka Yōsuke preferred more drastic measures. Just returned from a trip to Berlin and Moscow, he advocated an immediate strike against Singapore, as the Germans had urged. Overruled by Tōjō, Oikawa, and Konoe, he resorted to delaying tactics, hoping to scotch the negotiations through foot-dragging.[19]

It was precisely because both army and navy took the Draft Understanding seriously that they objected to Matsuoka's posturings. Through early May, Isoda's reports from Washington were indicating that Roosevelt was about to initiate American convoys across the Atlantic, a step that meant a virtual naval war with Germany. Should not Japan use this development, Mutō's bureau asked, to end American aid to Chiang, conclude the China Incident, and proceed with Japan's security program? Oikawa openly wondered whether the Draft Understanding might not be a serious American attempt to come to terms with the altered global situation. Could Japan afford to ignore the opportunity?[20]

Both questions were answered by American actions in mid-May. Roosevelt postponed an address to the American people (in which Isoda believed he was to have announced convoying) and declared a state of full national emergency. He and Hull gave forceful speeches pledging strong American aid to Britain. And the secretary of state presented Nomura with a preliminary response to the Japanese reply (which Matsuoka had delayed) to the Draft Understanding. That response proposed that Japan's obligations under the Tripartite Pact should obtain only if Germany were attacked aggressively—that is, if American forces fired the first shot—not by defensive measures such as convoying. Negotiations to end the fighting in China were possible, but peace would be based on the withdrawal of Japanese troops

---

18. Ike, 20–24, and *DR2*, 262, 264–65.
19. Ike, 24–31; *FRUSJ*, 2:411–15, 418–19; and *DR2*, 267–68.
20. Ike, 28–34, and *DR2*, 269, 282–83.

from Chinese territory. Equal access to the resources of the south-western Pacific was acceptable provided Japanese activity in this regard was peaceful.[21]

America's stance toward Britain and China now seemed clear enough, but Washington's attitude regarding the Southward Advance was not altogether plain. Perhaps the Americans were not unafraid of a two-front conflict? This uncertainty became all the more disturbing in Tokyo as, by the end of May, it was clear that diplomatic methods to promote the advance were not going well.

The most important effort was a new attempt to negotiate with the Netherlands East Indies. The first mission, under Kobayashi, had enjoyed little success. But Tokyo, despite Dutch wishes to the contrary, had sent a second delegation, this time with diplomat Yoshizawa Kenkichi at its head. He landed at Batavia on 28 December 1940. The first formal Japanese proposal, presented on 16 January, asked for amalgamation of the East Indies into Japan's coprosperity sphere. The draft called not only for the direct purchase of colonial commodities but also for free entry for Japanese prospecting teams and an increase in the quotas allowed for the import of Japanese goods.[22]

The Dutch reply of 3 February opened with a declaration that the East Indies would belong to no nation's economic sphere. There would be no free entry for prospectors. The Dutch were willing to consider more Japanese imports, but only if Japan lifted import restrictions on their sugar, coffee, and other tropical products and ended its stern exchange controls on the yen balances accruing to Dutch nationals or firms operating in Japan. The Dutch authorities warned that no agreement would survive if Japan occupied southern Indochina. To underscore their points, they began an export licensing system on 8 February, restricting all exports, including those to Japan, to normal amounts needed for "home" consumption. To this end, Batavia offered modest quantities of goods, including petroleum products, as a basis for discussion.

In the uncertainties of late winter both services concluded that this Dutch offer—meager and defiantly insulting as it was—had to be accepted. The immediate acquisition of strategic commodities was far more vital, at least for the moment, than creating a coprosperity sphere. On 17 March, after Matsuoka left for his trip to Europe, Konoe, as acting foreign minister, ordered Yoshizawa to obtain con-

21. *FRUSJ*, 2:432–36, and Ike, 44.
22. These imports of Japanese goods in all likelihood would have been on a barter basis.

tracts for whatever amounts he could get. In a related decision Tokyo asked the Anglo-American oil companies in Japan to renew for six more months oil contracts at previously negotiated amounts. Yoshizawa's second proposal to the Dutch, presented in mid-May, asked for no amounts greater than those already specified in contracts signed in June 1940.[23]

At the liaison conference of 22 May the recently returned Matsuoka, anticipating further Dutch intransigence, asserted that economic war with the United States and Britain was inevitable. The Southward Advance would have to proceed, as a result, and use force if necessary. This was not what the services wanted to hear, but the foreign minister's gloomy assessment was vindicated by the Dutch reply to Yoshizawa of 6 June. Batavia insisted on Japanese guarantees for imports of sugar and other tropical items, the last things on which Tokyo's economic planners were willing to squander scant foreign exchange and shipping space. Five days later the liaison conference decided to recall Yoshizawa.

The question of a southward advance using force now had to be addressed. The military hoped that the initial stages would be bloodless, even with America's new, apparently sterner stance. Sugiyama asked Matsuoka to begin conversations to allow the stationing of troops in the southern half of French Indochina with that colony's government. The foreign minister asked whether this step might not compel the British to send troops into Thailand, in which case it was preferable to commence outright hostilities immediately; naval chief of staff Nagano Osami vigorously insisted that Sugiyama was right. Bases in Indochina and Thailand were imperative—but, Nagano added, Japan had to be ready to make war against anyone in the way.[24]

The navy leadership had been reluctant to embrace an armed southward advance a year earlier, and it had taken a cautious stance during the occupation of northern Indochina. Nagano's statement now was striking. In essence, it had three sources.

First were changes from September through April in key naval personnel. Unlike his predecessor, Navy Minister Oikawa saw no reason to oppose more bellicose subordinates. His vice-minister, Sawamoto Yorio, was like-minded. Sawamoto, moreover, had been

23. Hubertus J. van Mook, *The Netherlands Indies and Japan: Battle on Paper, 1940–1941* (New York: Norton, 1944), 84–94, 104–6; *FES*, 26 February 1941; *TSM*, 6:94–95; Nakamura Takafusa and Hara Akira, Introduction to *GDS43*, lii; Irvine H. Anderson, Jr., *The Standard-Vacuum Oil Company and United States East Asian Policy, 1933–1941* (Princeton: Princeton University Press, 1975), 167; and *DR2*, 275–77.
24. Ike, 37–39, 47–51, and van Mook, 104–6.

appointed despite the urgings of Yamamoto that the firmly anti-Axis Inoue Shigemi receive the post. As a result, the navy's policy-making power was seized by bureau and section chiefs determined to see the Southward Advance through, even if (and perhaps because) the consequence might be a Pacific war. This new alignment within the navy made advocates of caution, such as Yamamoto, few and weak.[25]

A second reason for Nagano's forwardness in mid-June 1941 stemmed from his service's improved preparedness. In the previous autumn the navy had already received substantial additions to its allocations of vital commodities, especially steel, and it was on the verge of nailing down still further boosts. These increases made it difficult for Yamamoto, or any navy man, to argue that the fleet could not be successful. They also made it difficult for the navy to use demands for material preparations as a device to delay the Southward Advance.[26]

More recent, and more immediate, was a third reason: growing reports of a possible German attack on the Soviet Union. These, coming mainly from Ambassador Ōshima Hiroshi in Berlin, began to arrive in mid-April. Fearful that the army would favor war against the Russians, with a consequent renegotiation of levels of preparedness (in basic terms, commodity allocations), the navy resolved to adopt circumspection toward the north, insisting on no increases in force readiness there. The Southward Advance had to proceed.[27]

The navy's suspicions had substance. There was strong support within the army for scrapping the advance and initiating hostilities against Moscow. Tanaka and the field officers of the Kwantung Army particularly favored this switch.[28] But the Kwantung Army was no better prepared to confront the Russians in June 1941 than it had been during the near-disaster of the Nomonhan Incident two years earlier. Tanaka, who had just returned from a tour of Manchuria, was appalled by its materials situation. Sugiyama agreed. At a crucial conference of the General Staff's division chiefs on 10 June he reproached those eager to head north at once. Japan's power did not permit it to wage a long war at present. Where could limited resources be put to best use? The chiefs agreed with Sugiyama that the best answer was a

---

25. *TSM*, 7:202–3; and Asada Sadao, "The Japanese Navy and the United States," in *Pearl Harbor as History*, ed. Dorothy Borg and Shumpei Okamoto (New York: Columbia University Press, 1973), 252.

26. Minato's debate with Okada, noted earlier in this chapter, is a good case in point.

27. Hosoya Chihiro, "The Japanese-Soviet Neutrality Pact," in *The Fateful Choice*, ed. James W. Morley (New York: Columbia University Press, 1980), 93–94.

28. Ibid., 92, 93, 103.

quick resolution of the southern question—bloodlessly, with luck, perhaps of restricted scope—and then a concentration to the north. To prepare for the latter, Tanaka proposed Kwantung Army Special Maneuvers, or *Kan-toku-en,* which would lead to the formation of a sixteen-division core force. A northern advance, if later sanctioned, would build upon that core.

Kan-toku-en did not mean an end to the Southward Advance, only a limit. The army continued to support the occupation of southern Indochina, to construct air bases and prepare for possible further steps. Its leaders insisted that troops accompany base construction crews. At the liaison conference of 16 June, Sugiyama insisted that the occupation, whether through diplomacy or force, be commenced by the end of July. Three months were needed to construct airfields for heavy bombers, and if Japan and its army were to have meaningful options for the summer and autumn, it was necessary to proceed into Indochina. Army leaders planned to go no further for the time being, however, for Hitler might begin his assault eastward on the morrow.[29]

This position ignited navy doubts about the army's intent and led to a fresh round of interservice bickering. The admirals knew about Kan-toku-en and sentiment within the army for a strike north. But their firm resolution to continue the Southward Advance, they had believed, would prevent an outbreak of hostilities with the Soviets and a diversion of resources to the army. Indeed, the navy counted on that resolution. On 22 June, Nagano explained to Sugiyama the navy's newest program of fleet expansion. The Fifth Replenishment Plan, incorporating the yet-unbuilt portions of the third and fourth plans, was to be immense, spanning fully ten years and including three superbattleships mounting twenty-inch guns as well as many other warships of improved design.

But the possibility that the Southward Advance might trigger an Anglo-Soviet combination, and hence a two-front conflict, threatened the navy's stratagem. Already Sugiyama was dubious about the fifth plan: What effect would it have on the army's ability to carry out a northward advance? The army's Okada Kikusaburō was bitterly resisting the navy's requests for short-term increases in steel and other commodities. And Tanaka was, if anything, less accommodating toward the navy: the Southward Advance "is nothing more than a means to secure naval force replenishment and acquire funds and

29. *DR2,* 290, 301–4, and Ike, 51–53.

materials," the army operations chief said. If the navy was so gutless, Japan should strike north at any good opportunity.[30]

Nevertheless, the actual opening of Germany's Operation Barbarossa against the Soviet Union forced an interservice compromise over materials allocation and Japan's military strategy. The compromise on strategy did not come easily, in the main because of the navy's awkward position. Its leaders were daunted by immense American warship building plans, but they could hardly admit that there was no prospect for meeting the U.S. Navy successfully—especially after they had insisted on Anglo-American indivisibility as a premise of the Southward Advance. As a result, during late June the navy constantly bewildered army chiefs with its shifting stand on the advance. On 21 June, for example, Rear Admiral Oka Takazumi assured Tanaka that the navy had no objection to operations against the Soviets—if the right opportunity arose. And if Britain fell, Oka's service supported a quick strike at Singapore. Dumbfounded, Tanaka asked if the navy was prepared to accept war with the United States at once, before additional preparations (and materials allocations) could be made. Oka stated the navy's continued reluctance; but, he went on, if the alternatives were war and surrender, the choice was obvious.[31]

At the liaison conference on the twenty-fifth, Oikawa echoed these ambiguities. The navy minister argued that simultaneous advances north and south were dangerous. But he stood by an interservice agreement that favored a cautious advance south and additional preparations against the Soviets. The navy was confident about a war with the Anglo-Americans, Oikawa said, but not if the Soviet Union were also involved.[32]

Matsuoka was quick to take advantage. The foreign minister, who (after Barbarossa) favored an attack against Russia, asked whether that interservice agreement gave priority to the north or the south. Sugiyama declared that both had equal importance. Nagano confessed that he was not sure what the agreement meant, but after consulting with Vice Admiral Kondō Nobutake, vice-chief of staff, he indicated that the south came first. Kondō's army counterpart, Lieu-

---

30. *DR2*, 306–7, and Stephen E. Pelz, *Race to Pearl Harbor* (Cambridge: Harvard University Press, 1974), 217.

31. *DR2*, 305–6.

32. Ike, 56–60. There would be problems, of course, because the army could be expected to demand materials for Kan-toku-en and more, thus endangering the navy's Fifth Replenishment Plan.

tenant General Tsukada Osamu, then explained that Japan would not advance in both directions at once. It would, however, observe developments and act according to the situation. Over the next several days, Matsuoka attempted to wean the army to his latest scheme, an immediate attack on the Soviets. But Sugiyama and his subordinates (except Mutō, who wavered briefly) refused to budge. The army would continue preparations in the north. It would use force if the German-Soviet war developed to "extreme advantage." It was pledged to secure bases in Indochina to permit possible future steps to the south, but it would make no other commitments.[33]

The foreign minister had no more success with the vacillating navy. There his argument that a thrust south could lead to a combination of Britain, America, and the Soviet Union against Japan found attentive ears. Conflict with the Soviets under any circumstances would provide the army with a powerful opportunity to demand materials, demands that would ruin the navy's construction plans. When, at the liaison conference of 30 June, Matsuoka proposed delaying the occupation of south Indochina by six months, Oikawa and Kondō inclined to agree. When Home Minister Hiranuma Kiichirō proposed a northward attack, however, the navy counseled delay again, arguing that fifty days would be necessary to switch preparations.

The army found this waffling intolerable. Its rival service appeared reluctant to take the first step of the Southward Advance—that imperative first step which would permit others to be taken if the situation warranted. Yet the admirals, though securing ever greater steel allocations at the army's expense, also seemed cool to the idea of any northern operations. At the conference Tsukada insisted that the occupation of southern Indochina was already a matter of policy and that troops were already gathering. Mutō stressed that the move would ensure continued supplies of rubber and tin.[34]

The Imperial Conference of 2 July ratified the army's policies for both south and north. The rest of Indochina was to be occupied regardless of the risk of war with Britain and the United States. Preparations against the Soviets would continue—indeed *had* to continue. As Sugiyama virtually admitted under questioning, the Kwantung Army was unready for combat even if the army desired an immediate assault into the Soviet Union.[35]

The emperor's authority thus bestowed, Tōjō commenced the rein-

33. *DR2*, 312, and Ike, 60–67.
34. Ike, 70–75, 71n. Mutō might have added that Indochinese rice was becoming increasingly important to Japan's food supply.
35. Ike, 77–90.

forcement of the Kwantung Army on the fifth. The sixteen-division core force called for by Kan-toku-en was approved. A first new division was mobilized and dispatched to Manchuria, and the army moved to mobilize 850,000 men and an unprecedented 800,000 tons of shipping by 25 July. In addition the army created a self-defense general headquarters directly under the emperor which, for the first time, organized fighter squadrons solely to safeguard Japanese airspace against the threat posed by Soviet bombers.[36]

These steps confirmed the navy's fears that the army laid primary emphasis on a northern campaign. Two days after Tōjō had acted to implement Kan-toku-en, Captain Tomioka Sadatoshi, head of the Naval General Staff's Operations Section, visited his counterpart, Lieutenant Colonel Hattori Takushirō. Tomioka was blunt. The navy would approve any move to provide essential defense in the north, but anything diminishing the army's contribution to southern operations was out of the question. Hattori promised that his service would do its part, even if the troops had to come from Manchuria. Tomioka, driving the point home, declared that the navy's airpower was not available for use against the Soviets, and he cast barely veiled aspersions on the adequacy of the army's civil defense measures. At a conference of army and navy bureau and division chiefs held on 8 July, naval representatives voiced similar reservations. And Kondō's warnings to Tsukada four days later—that under no circumstances would the army be permitted to use naval factories, workers, or materials for Kan-toku-en—hardly eased tension between the services. By mid-July many in the army, especially Hattori and his superior, Tanaka, believed that northern operations risked an irreparable breach with the navy.[37]

But the advance into southern Indochina was another matter. There the army had a firm accord with the navy to begin the occupation by diplomacy or, if necessary, by force. Negotiations with the Vichy authorities had been delayed by French-Thai skirmishing in January and Matsuoka's trip to Europe in March and April, but the foreign minister finally began them in mid-July, just before his forced resignation on the sixteenth over divergent approaches to the American negotiations. The French accepted Tokyo's terms three days later, and the Japanese Supreme Command ordered the peaceful occupation of southern Indochina to commence on the twenty-fourth. On that day the liaison conference met to consider the implications.[38]

36. DR2, 325–29, 340, and Hosoya, "Neutrality," 104.
37. DR2, 329–30, 348.
38. DR2, 180–83.

Many details of Japan's foreign policy were still unsettled. The army had commenced preparations for war against the Soviets, but it had determined neither what an "extremely favorable opportunity" to attack would be nor when it might arise. It had won the navy's approval to occupy all of Indochina but had left the navy guessing whether the generals would endorse any further steps in the Southward Advance. The navy, for its part, had not sorted out its position on the scope and timing of the advance. The admirals wished the advance to proceed to the extent that it could prevent the outbreak of hostilities against the Soviet Union. The navy feared a northern war for two reasons: either the army would fight the Russians alone, in which case the allocations of the Fifth Replenishment Plan were doomed; or the Soviets would ally themselves with the British, in which case the replenishment program would be insufficient for operations to both north and south.

Yet the navy did not embrace the Southward Advance too warmly. The longer the advance could be delayed, the more warships could be constructed for the imperial fleet and the more steel could be requisitioned to build those warships. Too much delay, however, would be disastrous, because it would give the Americans time to accomplish their own colossal naval expansion programs.[39]

Matters were no clearer on the diplomatic front. Japan still had to determine its views on the continuing (if sputtering) negotiations with the United States. Were these to be a serious effort to obtain objectives without resort to war? Or should they be a ruse, allowing war preparations against the West to continue?

Finally, no one was quite sure about Japan's economic standing. Earlier American cutoffs, especially of scrap iron and steel, had strongly affected critical areas of Japanese production. The German-Soviet war effectively foreclosed the remaining sources of supply in Europe. Would Japan have the wherewithal to fight either in the south or in the north, or both? As the liaison conference gathered on 24 July, none of these questions was answered. Within ten days the American freeze of Japanese assets would answer all of them, and the doors to any peaceful settlement of Pacific differences would be all but shut tight.

39. This is one of many important points raised in Pelz, *Race to Pearl Harbor*.

[12]

Soft Words and Big Sticks

By early 1941 the United States had in place an imposing number of embargoes on the shipment of materials to Japan. Nearly all of these had been justified, and most of them correctly justified, as measures necessary for the American rearmament effort. But for this very reason they had a substantial impact on Japan's own war economy. Tokyo's only source of materials crucial for war—scrap iron, steel, machine tools, ferroalloys, aluminum—was, excepting a trickle of supplies from Germany that came over the trans-Siberian railroad, the United States.

U.S. measures had been enacted on the initiative of officials involved in the rearmament effort, men who gave little thought to the effect of the embargoes on relations with Japan. The efforts of advocates of harsher sanctions against Tokyo were also important, but these policy makers had little knowledge of the likely impact on the Japanese Empire. Enacted measures had harmed the Japanese economy, to be sure, but thus far had done little to hinder Japan's military efforts. The only cutoff that would have hindered (and perhaps crippled) those efforts—an embargo on oil—had been avoided. Grew and other American diplomatic personnel in Japan had argued that Japan was a desperate nation led by desperate men. Any oil embargo would lead to an attack southward despite the hopelessness of the subsequent conflict. Hardliners such as Hornbeck continued to insist that Japan was not an insane nation but a drained one, terribly weakened by the conflict in China. Tokyo might consider an attack to the south, to be sure, and to this end it might accumulate huge stockpiles of necessary materials, especially oil. Further restrictions on oil exports were all the more necessary, therefore, to restrain the Japanese. Until July 1941, Roosevelt and Hull adhered to Grew's position, but the basic assumptions of that position virtually insured a misreading, through the code-breaking successes of MAGIC, of the Japanese decisions of early July. The misreading would lead, indirectly and nearly unconsciously, to a total embargo on oil exports to Tokyo. The embargo would have momentous consequences across the Pacific. Until July, however, exports to Japan of petroleum products (except for gasoline over 87 octane) continued in unrestricted amounts.

The man most frustrated by these developments was Stanley Hornbeck. For months he had been urging a calculated, comprehensive program of economic pressure against Japan, a program backed by willingness to use force and matching appropriate pressure to Japanese provocation. Like many top policy makers, Hornbeck believed that the Japanese would not risk war with the United States. Too many of his associates, he had written in November 1940, overestimated Japan's war-making capacity, which had been drained by the long conflict against China. America's way was clear. The United States had to aid the Chinese, and now the Dutch, and keep the Pacific Fleet strong—to deter Japan by strengthening the forces arrayed against it. And it was essential that the United States prevent the build-up of Japanese war reserves—to deter Japan by weakening the forces it could muster.[1]

The logical way to accomplish the second of these objectives was sharply to reduce oil shipments to Japan. As early as June 1940 Hornbeck had warned that something was afoot. Japan had dramatically increased orders of oil and in October and November of 1940 alone had bought tanks for storing over one million barrels of oil.[2] During the entire year of 1939, by contrast, it had purchased only enough tankage for 40,000 barrels.[3]

Hornbeck realized that Hull's opposition made direct cutoffs of oil infeasible. But he did believe that the export of metal drums and storage tanks could be prohibited. It would be an effective and rela-

1. Hornbeck memo, 29 November 1940, Box 461, and Hornbeck memo, 2 January 1941, Box 462, Hornbeck Papers.

2. A fair share of this activity was due to the 1940 "cover" import programs adopted by Japan's Cabinet Planning Board. See Chapter 9 and Jonathan G. Utley, *Going to War with Japan, 1937–1941* (Knoxville: University of Tennessee Press, 1985), 126, which notes from American sources that Japanese purchases of gasoline alone rose from 1.2 million barrels in 1939 to 3.4 million barrels in the last six months of 1940.

3. Hornbeck memo, 7 June 1940, DF 894.24/961, Record Group 59, General Records of the Department of State, National Archives; Hornbeck memo, 8 January 1941, and Butler to Hornbeck, 17 January 1941, Box 338, Hornbeck Papers.

tively unprovocative way to inhibit Japan's build-up of oil reserves. In addition, the oil companies might be asked to divert tankers from the Pacific trade.[4]

In this effort Hornbeck had some assistance. The United States had already banned the export of iron and steel products. Drums and tanks could be interpreted as falling into this category, one that Charles Yost of the Controls Division thought could include well-drilling machinery too. The U.S. Navy had a special interest in keeping storage tanks at home, an interest that Colonel Maxwell of Export Control was ready to serve. At a meeting with representatives of the oil industry on 14 January, moreover, Hull learned that Japan had obtained contracts in America for seven million barrels of gasoline, an amount considered equivalent to three years' normal supply.[5]

The revelation clinched Hornbeck's argument that the Japanese were actively stockpiling oil for future (and probably aggressive) use. It opened the way to further restrictions. But the debates inside the State Department in January revealed great uncertainty over how far the administration should proceed. Those closest to China, such as Willys Peck, lately counselor to the American Embassy in China, argued for the strongest steps, of course, including a graduated escalation to total economic nonintercourse. Peck was certain that Japan, weakened by the protracted struggle with the Chinese, would not go to war against the United States. From the Controls Division, Yost pushed hard for dropping the octane limit from 87 to 80 or lower, to prevent further large Japanese purchases of gasoline. In this way, he maintained, additional build-ups of reserves could be hindered. Maxwell Hamilton, head of the Far East Division, was doubtful. A second Japanese negotiating mission to Batavia under Yoshizawa Kenkichi had just resumed talks with the Dutch, and any American cutoff of oil exports might invite an attack on the Indies. A build-up of Japanese reserves might be unwelcome, but Pacific war would be worse. From Tokyo, Grew's commercial attaché, Frank Williams, argued that an attack on the Netherlands East Indies was a distinct possibility. Japan, he conceded, had been making the same "economic mistakes" that the Germans had committed in World War I and was under great

4. In July 1940 the U.S. Maritime Commission withdrew most American-flag tanker traffic from trade with Japan. Hornbeck wished to include American-owned tankers sailing under foreign flags. See Irvine H. Anderson, Jr., *The Standard-Vacuum Oil Company and United States East Asian Policy, 1933–1941* (Princeton: Princeton University Press, 1975), 159–60.

5. Hornbeck to Hull, 15 January 1941, Box 338, Hornbeck Papers; *FRUS, 1941*, 4:776–79; and Yost memo, 16 January 1941, Box 338, Hornbeck Papers.

economic strain. But these mistakes simply made Tokyo's stake in the negotiations with the Dutch all the more vital and, perhaps, worth the risk of war. And the tin and rubber of the East Indies, Williams reminded Hull, were themselves vital to the American defense effort.

In the end Hornbeck largely had his way. Arguing that the time was not ripe for lowering the octane limit, for precisely the reasons given by Hamilton, Hornbeck secured the endorsements of the Far Eastern, Economic Adviser, and Controls divisions to a ban on drums, tanks, and other instruments of storage. Maxwell discreetly included them in orders issued on 4 February.[6]

Still, Hornbeck considered this only an interim step. So did the British, who were alarmed by a war scare in early February. On the seventh the London government informed Washington that there was clear evidence of Japanese movements to the south, perhaps in preparation for an attack on Singapore which would be coordinated with a German assault on the British home islands. In Washington the British ambassador, Lord Halifax,[7] told Hull and Roosevelt that Japan would push forward unless some move to deter Tokyo were soon devised. The British echoed Hornbeck's idea that oil tankers be diverted from serving Japanese ports.[8]

At issue was how best to achieve deterrence. Further economic pressure seemed out of the question as long as the Japanese-Dutch talks were in progress. There was the option of doing nothing—Grew had suggested as much in an earlier letter to Roosevelt. For the United States to become engaged in war with Japan would divert aid from Britain, Grew wrote. Roosevelt was determined to stand firm, however, insisting that the conflict was global: to allow British possessions to fall in Asia would hurt the British cause in Europe. The administration elected to employ the devices of both diplomacy and military force. A few days before the president met with the new Japanese ambassador, Nomura Kichisaburō, he conferred with Hull, Stimson, Knox, Harold Stark (chief of naval operations) and Stark's

6. Peck memo, 18 January 1941, Box 155, Hornbeck Papers; Yost memo, 16 January 1941, DF 894.24/1200 4/5; Hornbeck memo, 21 January 1941, Box 155, Hornbeck Papers; *FRUSJ*, 2:241–48; Hornbeck memo, 11 January 1941, DF 894.6363/378; *FRUS, 1941,* 4:779–81; Utley, *Going,* 132; and Williams to Hull, 25 January 1941, DF 894.50/155.

7. The previous British ambassador to Washington, Lord Lothian, had died in mid-December.

8. United States Congress, Joint Committee on the Investigation of the Pearl Harbor Attack, *Pearl Harbor Attack,* 39 parts (Washington, 1946), 19: Exhibit 158, 3444; British aide-memoire to United States, 7 February 1941, *FRUS, 1941,* 5:61–64; and Sir Llewellyn Woodward, *British Foreign Policy in the Second World War,* 5 vols. (London: HMSO, 1970–76), 2:120–21. For the tanker proposal, see Utley, *Going,* 128.

army counterpart, George Marshall. The group agreed that Stark's Plan Dog of November, which gave clear priority to the Atlantic theater, had to be upheld. But the meeting also sanctioned the evacuation of American women and children from the Far East, military and naval staff conversations with the British, and a formal warning to Nomura. To prepare for that warning, Hull wrote Roosevelt:

> It may be advisable—in the light of indications from the Far East—to "speak softly" (carefully avoiding any word that might to a wishful thinker imply that we would consider offers of "compromise"), while simultaneously giving by our acts in the Pacific new glimpses of diplomatic, economic, and naval "big sticks."[9]

The conversation between Nomura and Roosevelt was amicable, as it should have been considering that the two were long acquainted. The president, true to the wishes of his advisers and the British, conveyed his opposition to any further Japanese moves southward and warned that American-Japanese relations were poor and still deteriorating. Nomura offered no rebuttal and, to Hull, seemed to be agreeing with Roosevelt's observations. Equally reassuring were reports soon after the meeting which indicated that Japan would embark upon no new aggression, at least for some time. But Roosevelt and his diplomats were not overly relieved. MAGIC, a top secret operation that had broken the Japanese diplomatic code the previous autumn, had deciphered Nomura's instructions from Japanese foreign minister Matsuoka Yōsuke. Roosevelt read these instructions as confirming his view that Japan aimed for hegemony throughout the western Pacific. Roosevelt termed Matsuoka's document "the product of a mind which is deeply disturbed."[10]

Throughout the administration spread a deepening belief that the Japanese were incorrigible and respected only strong stands. The belief led to surprise and consternation two weeks later, when Postmaster General Frank Walker informed Roosevelt that a Japanese

---

9. *FRUS, 1941*, 4:6–8, 21–22; Henry L. Stimson diary entry of 10 February 1941, Stimson Papers; Fred L. Israel, ed., *The War Diary of Breckinridge Long* (Lincoln: University of Nebraska Press, 1966), 177; Waldo H. Heinrichs, Jr., "The Role of the U.S. Navy," in *Pearl Harbor as History*, ed. Dorothy Borg and Shumpei Okamoto (New York: Columbia University Press, 1973), 221–22; and Hull to Roosevelt, 12 February 1941, Personal Secretary's File, Diplomatic Corespondence, Box 59, Roosevelt Papers.

10. *FRUSJ*, 2:387–89; Elliott Roosevelt, ed., *F.D.R., His Personal Letters*, 4 vols. (New York: Duell, Sloan, & Pearce, 1947–50), 2:1126; and United States, Department of Defense, *The "Magic" Background of Pearl Harbor*, 5 vols. and appendixes (Washington: GPO, 1977), 1:A3–A4.

plenipotentiary had arrived in the United States to negotiate all out-standing problems with the United States. Walker was acting as inter-mediary for two American Catholics, Father James Drought and Bishop James Walsh, who sought peace between America and Japan. In late January, Walsh had written Roosevelt, and the president had steered the inquiry to Hull, who shunted it aside to work through Nomura. But now, according to Walker, the Japanese representative had arrived to propose that Roosevelt personally mediate the Sino-Japanese conflict, that Japan annul the Tripartite Pact, and that both powers pledge nonaggression, economic cooperation, and a freeze on the status quo in the Pacific through mutual recognition of autono-mous "political units."[11]

Hornbeck led a chorus of doubters. Who was the mystery envoy? Did Nomura consent to, or even know of, this mission? And anyway, what issue between China and Japan was Roosevelt to mediate? The only issue, for Hornbeck, was whether Tokyo or Chungking was to control China's destiny. If Japan were sincere about negotiations, it had to demonstrate good faith, perhaps by nullifying its Axis alliance, before negotiations could begin. Tokyo would also have to pledge to engage in no further aggression while negotiations continued.[12]

Hornbeck and Hamilton closely followed reports from Grew, who paid close attention to Matsuoka's trip to Moscow and Berlin, that Japan and the Soviet Union were drawing closer; perhaps each would recognize the sphere of influence vital to the other. News that Japan had forced the authorities of French Indochina to accede to Japanese mediation of the Franco-Thai border dispute seemed ominous. Both men believed it best to put Father Drought's initiative aside, open discussions with Nomura, and discern Japan's intentions (if indeed any change was in the wind) while keeping its leaders guessing about future American moves.

Hull concurred. He met with the Japanese ambassador on 8 March, stating that he would confer only with Nomura and no one else on all official matters unless Nomura requested otherwise. The ambassador replied with a series of cryptic bows, though he later indicated that Colonel Iwakuro Hideo, soon to reach Washington, would serve as his adviser on military matters.[13]

Even as Hull awaited the next Japanese move in the diplomatic

11. *FRUS, 1941*, 4:14–16, 17–18, 17n, 54.
12. *FRUS, 1941*, 57–58, 54.
13. *FRUS, 1941*, 5:99–101, 4:58–60, 62–63, and *FRUSJ*, 2:389–96.

arena, his government was considering its military and economic options. American-British naval conversations had been begun in late January and were completed on 27 March in the form of the ABC-1 Agreement. Neither power got all it wanted. Britain wanted American warships to aid in Singapore's defense. The Americans were determined to keep their fleet no further westward than Pearl Harbor. Indeed the U.S. Navy and its chief, Stark, were eager to transfer additional ships to the Atlantic, despite a pledge in ABC-1 to employ the Pacific Fleet offensively "in the manner best calculated to weaken Japanese economic power."[14]

The fleet, however, was used first to strengthen Hull's diplomatic hand. Shortly after ABC-1, Roosevelt conferred with Stark and agreed to send nearly a quarter of the Pacific Fleet, including three battleships and an aircraft carrier, to the Atlantic. Hull's conversations with Nomura were reaching a crucial stage; the secretary was also somewhat alarmed by Japanese foreign minister Matsuoka's tour through Germany and the Soviet Union. Hull asserted that it was no time to weaken the forces at Pearl Harbor; Roosevelt agreed, and on 18 April the president authorized the transfer of only one carrier and one destroyer squadron.[15]

Hull was not willing to act on the economic front. In early March, British ambassador Halifax told Hull of recent large Japanese purchases of strategic materials, especially oil, far beyond the empire's normal requirements. Halifax believed that Tokyo might well be preparing a spring offensive.[16] London was not proposing a total cutoff of oil to Japan, but it did wish to prevent additional stockpiling. It suggested Washington limit exports by establishing a central, interdepartmental unit to regulate shipments.

This had long been Hornbeck's line, and he immediately favored the British recommendations. Dissatisfied with Hull's inaction through March, Hornbeck even penned a long memorandum on 1 April: "Observations on the Relation between Restrictions on Japanese Trade and Japan's Southward Advance." This connection, Hornbeck argued,

---

14. Robert J. Quinlan, "The United States Fleet: Diplomacy, Strategy and the Allocation of Ships (1940–1941)," in *American Civil-Military Decisions*, ed. Harold Stein (Birmingham: University of Alabama Press, 1963), 164–65; Heinrichs, 222–223 and U.S. Congress, *Pearl Harbor Attack*, 15:1490–92.

15. Quinlan, 181.

16. Again, although Halifax was reading the numbers correctly, the large Japanese purchases were due to the "cover" import programs, not any foregone military decision to advance rapidly to the south.

was wrongly accepted as axiomatic. Economic concessions would not satisfy Japanese ambitions, nor could Tokyo's fears of sanctions be removed. It was on Japan's perception of its overall military situation, not the application or nonapplication of economic pressure by the United States, that Tokyo would base its decision whether to advance to the south. The firmness that adopting the British proposals would display was overdue.

Hamilton saw things differently. He sympathized with Hornbeck's desire to prevent Japanese stockpiling; indeed he was prepared to restrict oil shipments to "normal," prewar quantities. But he could not support an interdepartmental unit to regulate quantities. In such a unit State could be outvoted by Morgenthau's Treasury and Ickes's Interior and the amounts set arbitrarily (and provocatively) low. Nor did Hamilton believe the timing right for any further economic restrictions. Perhaps in a year, when both Britain and America would be stronger militarily, additional economic steps could be considered. As his position implies, Hamilton was certain that a connection did exist between American pressure and Japanese bellicosity.

Hull agreed. Although he wished to keep the Pacific Fleet strong and to avoid a massive Japanese build-up of oil stockpiles, he refused to endorse any economic steps that Tokyo might regard as hostile. In late March he had Assistant Secretary of State Breckinridge Long ask all American owners of oil tankers to divert them from Pacific routes, as Hornbeck wished. But Hull would not cooperate with Britain to apply additional economic restraints against Japan. He elected to await the arrival of Nomura's military adviser.[17]

Negotiations led to the proposal of a draft understanding to the American secretary of state on 9 April.[18] The document produced immediate misgivings within the State Department. It had no provisions for directly including the British or Chinese in the U.S.-Japan peace process. It did not commit Japan to leaving the Axis alliance. The Sino-Japanese peace was to be "just," as long as it allowed for close economic cooperation and joint defense against communism. Hull ascertained from Nomura that the Japanese ambassador had

17. *FRUS, 1941*, 4:150–52, 789–91, 793–94, 797–98, 800; Hornbeck memo, 1 April 1941, Box 249, Hornbeck Papers; Hornbeck memo, 5 March 1941, DF 894.24/1339 2/5; Lynn Edminster to Hornbeck, 10 April 1941, Box 414, Hornbeck Papers; Hamilton memo, 9 April 1941, DF 694.119/361; and Quinlan, 177–79.

18. The military representative, Colonel Iwakuro, himself cooperated with the Drought initiative and with Ikawa Tadao, a Japanese financial bureaucrat and banker. See Robert J. C. Butow, *The John Doe Associates* (Stanford: Stanford University Press, 1974), 39–40, 157.

helped draw up the draft; the draft represented the opening of pre-liminary negotiations between governments and not a proposal of private citizens. Hull pondered his reply.[19]

Hornbeck was concerned that any reply, any negotiations, might embolden Japan, so he suggested a number of Japanese concessions before talks began. Japan was to exempt itself from the obligations of the Tripartite Pact if the United States, out of self-defense, found itself engaged in hostilities against Germany. Japan was to withdraw its troops from Chinese territory and respect the Open Door there. America would permit exports of goods to Japan—except for those needed for its own defense—up to prewar amounts. Neither power would tolerate changes to the map of the southwestern Pacific made under force or duress.

Hull certainly did not wish to give the Japanese encouragement, but he did not seek to provoke them either. He informed Nomura on 16 April that while the United States could agree to much in the Draft Understanding, Japan would have to renounce its reliance on military conquest and subscribe to four key principles: respect for the ter-ritorial integrity of all nations, noninterference in the domestic affairs of other countries, equality of commercial opportunity, and no change in the status quo throughout the Pacific except by peaceful means. Nomura noted that the principle of equal opportunity might be subject to negotiation, because Japan claimed something similar to the Monroe Doctrine in its relationship with China. Hull was not pleased by the analogy, but he allowed Nomura to forward the draft to Tokyo as an informal and unofficial basis for further discussions.[20]

At this point, as historians—notably Robert Butow—have ob-served, Nomura committed a huge error. No word of Hull's princi-ples reached Tokyo.[21] Nomura instead gave the impression that the Draft Understanding was an American proposal to Japan and that he had indicated areas in which his government might seek further con-cessions. He wrote as well that the "American proposal" clearly im-plied that Manchuria was not Chinese territory and that Chinese recognition of Manchukuo could be assumed as part of the American position.[22] The effect in Tokyo was nearly the opposite of what Hull

19. See ibid., and *FRUS, 1941,* 4:130–31, 135–39, 142–46, 148–49.
20. *FRUS, 1941,* 4:143–48, and *FRUSJ,* 2:406–10.
21. Utley (in *Going,* 144) writes that Nomura did report Hull's four points to Tokyo. This is technically correct. But the way Nomura embedded them in his report, it would have required a magician to detect them as the cornerstone of a firm, relatively inflexi-ble American negotiating position. See *"Magic,"* 1:A35–A39. Japanese records indicate that no such detection occurred.
22. Butow, 164–65; *"Magic,"* 1:A35–A40; and Utley, *Going,* 146.

intended. The Japanese concluded that the United States greatly wanted to avoid any clash in the Pacific and was disposed to yield on some important issues as a result. Hull's strategy was to encourage the reemergence of moderate sentiment within Japan by disgracing the militarists (by compelling them to yield up all of China proper and subscribe generally to his principles).[23] The reaction in Tokyo, however, was a greater determination to proceed with the Southward Advance.

Only gradually and incompletely did Washington realize that something was amiss. Grew's reports from Tokyo and MAGIC reports in particular indicated some of the confusion that Nomura had created. Some policy makers, such as Stimson, saw further evidence of Japanese deviousness. Others, including Hornbeck, saw Tokyo's bewilderment over the draft as proof that Nomura and the unofficial diplomats had not secured the commitment of Japan even to the draft's terms, much less to any modifications of those terms which the Americans might suggest.[24]

The tumult makes it hardly surprising that the Hull-Nomura conversations achieved little progress. On 7 May, Hull brusquely dismissed Matsuoka's proposal for a simple nonaggression pact. A more comprehensive Japanese proposal asserted that Tokyo would fulfill its military obligation to Germany if the United States entered the European war, hardly a promising stance. Japan and China were to work out their destinies through direct talks, without American assistance or interference. Nor would Japan pledge not to use force in the southwestern Pacific.[25]

By the end of May, Hull realized that Japanese-Dutch negotiations were about to break down, and he had scarcely better hopes for his own talks with Nomura.[26] A working committee drawn from Nomura's embassy, Hull's department, and interested private citizens gathered to produce a compromise. In the meantime Hull doggedly stuck to his middle course, neither encouraging nor provoking further Japanese moves. He kept the negotiations alive but declared his intent to wait for a clearer sign that Japan would pursue the ways of peace. He moved to keep the Pacific Fleet strong but refused to countenance any restrictions in the supply of oil to Japan.[27]

---

23. As Utley argues throughout *Going*, chap. 8, on the whole persuasively.
24. Stimson diary entry of 22 April 1941, Stimson Papers, and *FRUS, 1941*, 4:179.
25. *FRUSJ*, 2:411–15, 420–25.
26. Hull estimated his chances of success at barely one in ten. Another source of worry was the dispatch of units of the American fleet from the Pacific to the Atlantic in early May.
27. *FRUS, 1941*, 4:164–67, 189, 190–94, 200, 260–67; *FRUSJ*, 2:428–34, 434–37, 454–

This last ingredient became progressively more difficult to maintain. The chief reason was the secretary of the interior. Harold Ickes had long been a proponent of using American economic muscle against foreign aggressors (one of his ideas had been to cut off helium exports to Germany to cripple the Nazi balloon fleet). He was particularly galled by the continued shipment of American oil to Japan. Ickes was named petroleum coordinator for national defense on 2 June, just as his department discovered that the coming summer promised the American east coast shortages of oil and gasoline worse than those of the previous year.[28]

This prospect had obvious political ramifications that Roosevelt could not ignore, especially not with Ickes's boisterous lobbying. At a cabinet meeting on 6 June the interior secretary displayed articles and editorials from eastern newspapers complaining about exports to Tokyo while Americans went begging. The same message was heard in the halls of Congress, where four bills and resolutions to limit exports of petroleum products were pending. To make matters worse, Ickes's allegations were true: Yost's Controls Division in the Department of State had licensed over nine million barrels of gasoline for export to Japan, and licenses for another two million barrels were pending. Current licenses alone represented over twice Japan's normal, prewar imports from all sources and triple those from the United States in 1940—a most abnormal year and hardly "prewar."[29]

The cabinet reached no immediate decision, and Ickes decided to act on his own. First he wrote to Maxwell for information on all approved oil exports to Japan, also asking Hull to refrain from granting further export permits through Maxwell's office. On 17 June, Ickes learned that a Japanese freighter was to transport over 200,000 gallons of lubricating oil from Philadelphia; he ordered its loading stopped and wrote Roosevelt to ask for a presidential appeal, if not an order, to all oil producers not to ship their products from the east coast.[30]

Roosevelt, though temperamentally more inclined than Hull to

55, 473–92; and Hosoya Chihiro, "The Role of Japan's Foreign Ministry and Its Embassy in Washington, 1940–1941," in *Pearl Harbor as History*, ed. Dorothy Borg and Shumpei Okamoto (New York: Columbia University Press, 1973), 155.

28. Anderson, 165.

29. Hornbeck memo, 23 May 1941, Box 462, Hornbeck Papers; *FRUS, 1941*, 4:805–8, 817; and Harold L. Ickes, *The Secret Diary of Harold L. Ickes*, 3 vols. (New York: Simon & Schuster, 1954), 3:537. The press clippings Ickes showed the cabinet can be found in Box 219, Ickes Papers. Colonel Maxwell of Export Control had suspended consideration of further applications for licenses on 6 March but unless new regulations were imposed, the additional two million barrels would have to be approved eventually.

30. *FRUS, 1941*, 4:818–19, and Ickes to Early, 17 June 1941, Box 219, Ickes Papers.

take a strong stand against Japan, and more than ever sure that the fleet's presence at Pearl Harbor had to remain imposing, agreed with his secretary of state that to deprive Japan of oil might precipitate an attack on the Indies. Ickes's draft of a press release to ban oil exports was returned from the White House with orders that it not be issued. Roosevelt further instructed Ickes not to regulate the export of oil from the United States. Ickes retorted that the oil shortage was real, not of his making; if State continued to permit exports, perhaps the diplomats ought to answer the rising tide of public protest.[31]

Roosevelt was sensitive to that protest. On 20 June he ordered that oil not be exported from the east coast except to ports in the British Empire, Egypt, and the Western Hemisphere.[32]

But the president would go no further. When Ickes pressed for a total oil embargo against Japan, Roosevelt balked. Hull had just delivered the first actual American negotiating proposals to Japan, on 21 June, and one day later Germany had invaded the Soviet Union. Roosevelt realized that Japan might attack the Soviets instead of advancing southward and pointedly asked Ickes if he still favored an embargo. Ickes would not relent; he offered his resignation as petroleum coordinator, but Roosevelt refused to accept it. He firmly refused to consider additional pressure on Tokyo, however, at least until the Japanese decided which way they would go.[33]

Roosevelt's reply reveals many of the basic American assumptions concerning Japan. Nearly all of the president's advisers believed that Japan would strike somewhere; that Tokyo would act in a restrained manner was beyond their imaginings.[34] This perception played them wrong when MAGIC revealed the results of the Imperial Conference of 2 July. The American decryptment of the text itself was highly accurate. Japan, it read, had decided to seize naval and air bases in (southern) French Indochina, to take advantage of any opportunity to expand southward, and to adopt a wait-and-see attitude toward the Soviet Union. When Japan presented Vichy France with an ultimatum for the total occupation of its Asian colony, it seemed to confirm MAGIC once again.[35]

31. Quinlan, 185, and Roosevelt to Ickes, 18 June 1941, Box 219, Ickes Papers.

32. Morgenthau Papers, Diaries, 411:73.

33. Roosevelt to Ickes, 23 June 1941, Ickes to Roosevelt, 25 and 30 June 1941, Box 219, Ickes Papers; Roosevelt, *Personal*, 2:1173–74.

34. For more information on American preconceptions about the Japanese by this time, particularly inside the U.S. Navy, see Michael Vlahos, *The Blue Sword: The Naval War College and the American Mission, 1919–1941* (Newport: Naval War College Press, 1980), chap. 9.

35. U.S. Congress, *Pearl Harbor Attack*, 12:1–2; FRUS, 1941, 4:298–99, 311–14; and *FRUS, 1941*, 5:210.

Yet even MAGIC could be deceiving. Washington knew nothing of the deep rift between the Japanese army and navy which the Imperial Conference had thinly covered over. Hull, Hornbeck, Hamilton, no one could reliably discern how deep the feelings of Sugiyama, Tanaka, or Tōjō ran for special maneuvers in Manchuria which would prepare for a northward attack. Nor could the Americans suspect that the army had agreed to the occupation of southern Indochina to keep peace with the navy and that additional steps in any southward advance would have caused intense debate in Tokyo—had the United States not frozen Japanese assets in late July.

Instead, Washington assumed that the Southward Advance was inexorable. Its previous warnings to Japan against altering the status quo of the Pacific by force now called for a strong reply on grounds of policy and principle. But there was disagreement over how strong the reply should be. Only Hamilton, who was not privy to MAGIC, believed (correctly) that Japan still might turn on the Soviet Union. He opposed further economic pressure. Hornbeck agreed that a strike north was conceivable but preferred to deflect Japan from further southern advances by retaliating after the occupation of Indochina. Although Indochina could not be saved, economic sanctions on oil and America's resolve to defend the area, demonstrated by aggressively reinforcing the Philippines and sending a cruiser squadron to tour the western Pacific, could deter further advances. No sane government would embark upon so hopeless a conflict.

Roosevelt and his senior advisers were not so certain that the hopelessness was apparent. MAGIC and the Japanese ultimatum to Vichy convinced Hull (an exhausted man who was resting in White Sulphur Springs, West Virginia), Welles, acting secretary in Hull's absence, and Roosevelt that the Japanese threat to the East Indies and Malaya was real and imminent. Hull in particular dreaded the possibility that Japan would strike south simultaneously with a German drive on Gibraltar through Spain, dealing a severe, perhaps a mortal, blow to the British Empire. He was willing to wait a few days to determine if the latest Konoe cabinet—without Matsuoka—intended actually to occupy Indochina. If it did, however, Hull was ready to approve a wide-ranging program to block further Japanese expansion, a program including economic and financial restrictions carried out in consultation with the army and navy.[36]

The U.S. Cabinet met to study these questions on 18 July. Roosevelt at once ruled out a complete embargo on oil, for he believed it

---

36. Hornbeck memo, 16 July 1941, Box 246, Hornbeck Papers, and *FRUS, 1941,* 4:325–26, 331.

would drive Japan to attack the Indies. Welles suggested freezing Japanese assets as an alternative; Roosevelt was amenable. Ickes complained about gasoline rationing on the east coast: Could Japanese purchases at least be limited to normal amounts? Roosevelt asked Welles (whose State Department had long been considering just such a yardstick as a way to limit Japan without undue provocation) to investigate the idea. Morgenthau wished to drop the octane level of permitted exports from 87 to 67, ensuring that nothing transformable to aviation-grade gasoline could reach Tokyo. Roosevelt hesitated, but when Welles signaled State's assent, he went along.[37]

This meeting arrived at three vital decisions. Exports of high-grade gasoline to Japan would be banned altogether. Shipments of other types of petroleum products would be restricted to "normal" amounts. And all Japanese assets in the United States were to be frozen.

The decision to freeze Japanese assets had two roots. One was purely domestic. Roosevelt, Morgenthau, and Hull alike were concerned about possible "fifth column" activity by Axis agents inside the United States. One effective way to hinder such activity seemed to be depriving the spies of readily available funds. On 14 June a foreign funds control committee was ordered to freeze German and Italian assets. But State had blocked a similar step for Japanese holdings, which were only registered. There was concern, mainly in Morgenthau's Treasury, that Japanese funds could find their way to German and Italian operatives.[38]

The second root was Japanese. Ever tighter exchange controls in Japan were threatening by late March to drive American banks and businesses out entirely. The future seemed especially gloomy after Japan's Finance Ministry asked the National City Bank to invest all its local deposits in national bonds. No funds were to leave Japan.[39]

This Japanese policy led to calls for American retaliation, in this case to freeze Japanese assets in the United States. Before the Japanese decision to occupy southern Indochina, the State Department had forestalled any freeze. As Hamilton had warned prophetically in March:

37. Morgenthau Papers, Presidential Diaries, 4:946–48; Ickes, 3:583–84; and *FRUS, 1941*, 4:832–33.
38. Roosevelt to Hull and Morgenthau, 26 February 1941, Personal Secretary's File, Departmental Correspondence, Box 90, Roosevelt Papers, and Morgenthau Papers, Diaries, 418:157–58. When Japanese assets were frozen in July, one effect indeed was to hinder Japanese intelligence efforts in the United States. See, for example, *"Magic,"* 3A:219–20.
39. Grew to Hull, 24 March 1941, DF 894.5151/235, and White to Treasury, 3 April 1941, Box 68, Record Group 56, General Records of the Department of the Treasury.

Experience indicates that, if Japanese funds were frozen on an announced basis of preventing the flight of funds but of permitting Japan to continue to have normal trade with the United States, the tendency of control machinery would be to tighten so that, within a very short period, the character of the control would be completely changed, the yardstick of normal trade forgotten and very drastic pressure applied against Japan's purchases in this country. In order to avoid such development a very clear-cut specific and written directive from the President would be needed stipulating that no change should be made in the formula except upon the initiative and with the full concurrence of the Secretary of State. It is believed that the action suggested in this memorandum should not be attempted without such precaution.[40]

In July, however, when Roosevelt approved the freeze order, he did not include a clear-cut, written presidential directive giving Hull ultimate administrative power. Instead, Welles simply asked Assistant Secretary of State Dean Acheson, the department's representative to the Foreign Funds Control Committee, to draw up the papers necessary to implement the cabinet's three decisions. Acheson's draft proposed that the export and exchange control system allow the export of American oil, cotton, and other products provided that exports were paid for by equivalent Japanese goods such as silk. Even then, Japan was not to obtain higher grades of gasoline and other materials already banned completely, and it could purchase other goods only up to normal, prewar amounts. In addition, arranging for the barter to provide for payment was to be Japan's responsibility.[41]

This arrangement satisfied Welles, who assured Roosevelt that General Marshall did not object to its reduction of American access to silk (used to make parachutes). The cabinet gathered on the afternoon of 24 July to consider implementing the freeze order. There was general agreement that Acheson's draft was suitable, but how would the Japanese perceive the measure? At first glance, the order might appear to close off any chance of their obtaining supplies in America. Only when the Japanese asked for licenses and provided a way to pay

---

40. Far Eastern Division memo, 21 March 1941, DF 840.51 Frozen Credits/1403 1/2. The division proposed that, if assets were frozen, Japan be permitted to sell gold and securities freely in the United States and use these to buy needed products up to normal, prewar amounts.

41. *FRUS, 1941*, 4:832–33, and Morgenthau Papers, Diaries, 423:194–96. As Jonathan Utley notes, Acheson wanted a total blockage of trade with Japan until the controls system could be set up. But Welles acted only to provide the controls system with operational guidelines and so activate it (thereby allowing limited trade with Japan) as rapidly as possible. See Jonathan Utley, "Upstairs, Downstairs at Foggy Bottom: Oil Exports and Japan, 1940–1941," *Prologue* 8 (Spring 1976), 23.

for the licensed goods would they discover that trade was still possible. Neither Roosevelt nor Welles was concerned. They preferred to implement the orders as written and license shipments of oil to Japan as applications were presented to the Treasury. Later this policy might change, and the government could refuse any and all licenses regardless of their nature. Generally, however, by forcing the Japanese to seek licenses rather than providing them with regulations that indicated which applications would be accepted or rejected, the United States retained much greater flexibility for the future. The freeze was formally announced on 25 July.[42]

Acheson's draft stipulated the general procedure for continued trade with Japan. This machinery, a two-step affair, now had to be put into operation. Prospective Japanese purchasers first had to secure an export license from the State Department's Division of Controls. They then needed an exchange license to provide funds for the goods for export. Treasury would issue these exchange licenses upon approval by the interdepartmental Foreign Funds Control Committee. Until both the Controls Division and the committee received instructions, neither would issue any licenses. This short delay would enable the officials involved to determine how much of each product Japan could receive under the "normal, prewar" guidelines. It would also permit coordination with similarly administered policies of friendly foreign governments.[43]

Welles forwarded his guidelines to Roosevelt on 31 July. His recommendations on export licenses were clear: oil exports to Japan were to be restricted but not denied, and guidelines for issuing exchange licenses were left vague—intentionally. Welles instructed Acheson to give the Japanese no general, advisory opinions concerning what sort of purchases would be allowed. Each request was to be considered independently, according to proposed method of payment, size of order, and probable use for the goods to be bought.[44]

This procedure left effective control of exchange licenses, and hence exports, to the Treasury Department and the Foreign Funds Control Committee. The committee was willing enough to grant ex-

42. *FRUS, 1941*, 4:834, and Morgenthau Papers, Diaries, 424:145–47. My reading here follows Anderson, *Standard-Vacuum Company*, to whom all students of this episode are in debt, and differs somewhat from Utley's in *Going*. Utley sees Roosevelt as believing that licenses would be granted on *American* initiative and that this initiative might later end. Anderson emphasizes that *Japan* had to come up with a method of payment and had to shoot in the dark to find one acceptable to the Americans. See Anderson, 178.

43. Utley, 24, and *FRUS, 1941*, 4:844–46.

44. Dean Acheson, *Present at the Creation* (New York: Norton, 1969), 26.

change licenses for export-licensed petroleum products, but it had one significant reservation. Treasury was determined not to allow Tokyo to make payments from blocked Japanese accounts in the United States if Japan had unfrozen funds elsewhere convertible into American dollars. Morgenthau's associates had been monitoring the transfer of Japanese funds from the United States to various Latin American countries since January. These transfers had accelerated in early May when Washington had begun considering a freeze on Axis assets. Treasury officials were convinced that Japan had intended to use these transferred dollars as a reserve to finance exports from the United States after an official American freeze. They were determined that Japan should exhaust this reserve before using any funds blocked within the United States.[45]

Acheson wholly sympathized with Treasury's hardline position. When commercial staff of the Japanese Embassy protested to him that the Imperial Navy, not the private Japanese companies that wanted to purchase oil, had control of the funds in Latin America, Acheson replied that the navy ought to be persuaded to release those funds. Surely the shipment of any oil to Japan was in the fleet's interest. The Japanese suggested several other methods of payment, none of which relied on unfrozen funds outside the United States, but Acheson turned them all down.[46]

Acheson reported his actions to Welles in August and September, pointing out that Japan had at least six million U.S. dollars in Latin America and perhaps half that amount still freely circulating in the United States. All of this money was supposedly under the control of the Japanese Navy. Japanese purchasers had filed applications for two million dollars' worth of materials since the freeze had been imposed, but by Welles's "normal, prewar" guidelines, they should be allowed only $600,000 per month. This amount, Acheson recommended, should be met in currency or from balances in Latin American banks, not from frozen accounts. Welles did not object, and by September the two-tiered licensing system had hardened into a full-scale embargo on all trade with Japan. The Japanese Embassy made

45. Morgenthau Papers, Diaries, 395:67–69, 424:268–69, and Clarence Dillon to Roosevelt, 6 May 1941, Personal Secretary's File, Departmental Correspondence, Box 90, Roosevelt Papers.

46. *FRUS, 1941*, 4:857–58. Utley maintains that Acheson and the Foreign Funds Control Committee intended all along to deny the Japanese exchange permits of any type and gave the Japanese "the run-around." This is certainly a plausible position, though my somewhat more lenient reading is also possible and certainly does not exclude the chance that Utley is correct. See Utley, *Going*, 153ff.

one last try to transfer funds from Latin America to pay for oil for two tankers in San Francisco, but Japan's spiraling mobilization for the Southward Advance compelled the withdrawal of all Japanese shipping from the Americas, including the tankers.[47]

Hull refused to alter these arrangements after his return from White Sulphur Springs on 4 August, and Roosevelt never attempted to change them after his return from Argentia.[48] There remained only the resolution of the two nations' differences: Would it be by diplomacy or by force? On both fronts the Americans were active. Marshall declared that the United States would defend the Philippines—reversing military dogma that had stood virtually since those islands had been acquired—and on 26 July Douglas MacArthur was named commander of the Filipino-American forces on the scene. Modern fighters and new long-range bombers, B-17s, were sent to the Philippines. Hull, for his part, resolved to meet again with Nomura.[49]

Their talks did not resume on an encouraging note. Japan's latest proposal, which Nomura handed to Hull on 6 August, offered no withdrawal of Japanese forces from Indochina until the China Incident was settled. Even then, the United States would have to recognize that Indochina had a special status for the Japanese Empire. Tokyo was prepared to guarantee the neutrality of the Philippines. That guarantee required that no Japanese businesses there be subject to discrimination and that the United States suspend its military buildup in the southwestern Pacific, restore trade with Japan, and persuade the British and Dutch to do the same.[50]

A pessimistic Hull pocketed the proposal without comment. The American reply, delivered two days later, blandly stated that Japan

47. Ibid., 858–60, 868–69, 876–78, and Acheson, 27. Evidence of Japan's acute shipping shortage was already apparent in the autumn of 1940. See Chapter 11, note 1, and Chapter 13. This is one answer to Utley's question about why Japan never pressed hard for purchases of petroleum after the freeze.

48. Anderson ventures a guess that Hull and Roosevelt left the freeze-cum-total embargo in place because a modification could be seen as appeasement. It is also possible that Hull and Roosevelt, like Welles, agreed with Acheson's arguments that balances in Latin America ought to be exhausted first. Less charitably, it may be that Roosevelt was preoccupied with preparation for the meeting with Churchill at Argentia and that Hull, still a thoroughly tired man and increasingly pessimistic about chances for peace, simply accepted the freeze as implemented for what it was. The Japanese, for their part, did attempt to buy oil using Latin American balances until late September. But by then additional complications, involving the financial obligations of Japanese banks in the United States, had arisen. See *"Magic,"* 3A:231–32, and Acheson, 27.

49. Daniel F. Harrington, "A Careless Hope: American Air Power and Japan, 1941," *Pacific Historical Review* 48 (1979), 221–24.

50. *FRUSJ*, 2:546–50.

had not responded to Roosevelt's neutralization proposal. Nomura thereupon announced that Prime Minister Konoe wanted a summit conference with Roosevelt, perhaps at Honolulu.[51]

Roosevelt, upon returning from his meeting with Churchill, was interested in resuming informal negotiations (which America had considered suspended by Japan's occupation of southern Indochina). But few of his advisers were enthusiastic. Hull was increasingly certain that Japan soon would invade Thailand, forcing Britain to intervene. Stimson was sure, from reading the MAGIC intercepts, that the cunning Orientals intended the summit as a cover for further menacing steps. Hornbeck and Ballantine stoutly opposed a summit. Tokyo first had to show evidence of its good faith, such as allowing an American passenger ship to evacuate U.S. citizens from Japan and ending the bombings of Chinese cities.[52]

Hornbeck and Ballantine based their demand on the assumption that the Japanese "moderates," meaning civilians, would not be able to control the military. By the summer of 1941 this proposition appeared to be beyond challenge. For nearly a decade, Americans believed, the Japanese military had been taking effective control of Japanese foreign policy, an indication by American lights that something was fundamentally wrong, and dangerous, with the policy. The idea that any Japanese in uniform could have been a voice for restraint seemed preposterous in view of the Manchurian Incident, the encroachments in north China, the apparent conspiracy to begin fighting around the Marco Polo Bridge, and the intimidation of the Vichy authorities in Indochina.

Konoe dined with Grew on the evening of 6 September; he lauded Hull's principles and indicated that, if a summit could be arranged quickly, he could commit the leaders of the army and navy to a settlement based on those principles. Hull's preconceptions about Japan made him openly dubious. As a more complete picture of Japan's latest terms formed in late September,[53] hopes for a diplomatic settlement diminished further. Japan still refused to withdraw troops from China even after a settlement. Chiang was to recognize Manchukuo as an independent country. Japan would interpret its obliga-

---

51. *FRUSJ*, 2:550–53.

52. *FRUSJ*, 2:554–55; Israel, 211; Stimson diary entry of 9 August 1941, Stimson Papers; and *FRUS, 1941*, 4:387–88, 403–5, 384–87, 412–16. The request for a ship to evacuate Americans from Japan was itself hardly an expression of Washington's faith in the negotiations.

53. On 22 September, Grew received a text of Japan's terms for China. Nomura gave those terms to Hull a day later.

tions under the Tripartite Pact independently if the United States went to war with Germany but offered no assurance that its forces would refrain from attacking American forces in such an event. Hornbeck repeated the key question: Could Konoe really bind the military to his promises?[54]

Hull concurred with these objections. On 2 October, with Roosevelt's approval, he met with Nomura to reply formally to the latest Japanese proposal and the summit question. In a long oral statement Hull observed that Konoe had subscribed fully to his four principles on the same day that Washington had received details concerning Japanese designs on China and the southwestern Pacific—details that hardly squared with the principles. The contradiction between words and deeds made Hull doubt that a summit was possible.[55]

Writing shortly after the end of the Pacific war, Herbert Feis argued that Hull's statement of 2 October ended actual negotiation between Japan and the United States. Thirty years and the availability of Japanese records make Feis's conclusion still seem unimpeachable. For the first time, each government had a clear and full idea of the other's terms for peace. They could agree on virtually nothing. On Japan's obligations under the Tripartite Pact, its desire to station troops in parts of China even after a Sino-Japanese settlement and its insistence that none be withdrawn from Indochina until that time, its wish for a special economic position in China and perhaps the French colony as well—on all of these questions Tokyo and Washington found themselves at odds. The Japanese Empire was determined to retain the rights and privileges it considered necessary for its economic and political security. The United States thought these rights and privileges contrary to its own deeply held principles and to the survival of what were now in effect its allies in the struggle against global aggression.

Behind the scenes in Tokyo, Konoe cast about frantically for any concession that would allow the negotiations to continue. Grew earnestly appealed to Washington to find some common ground. Neither succeeded. Konoe, rather than reap the harvest he had done so much to sow in the summers of 1937 and 1940, resigned.[56] His successor, General Tōjō Hideki, obeying an instruction from the em-

---

54. Grew to Hull, 6 September 1941, DF 711.94/2262; Grew diary entry of 6 September 1941, 1941 box, Grew Papers; *FRUS, 1941*, 4:432–34, 449–50, 493–94; *FRUSJ*, 2:633–37; and Ballantine memo, 25 September 1941, DF 793.94/17017 1/2.
55. *FRUSJ*, 2:656–61.
56. Ever the optimist, Grew believed that Tōjō's appointment would keep the radicals in line behind any peace accord that might be negotiated!

peror, asked his cabinet to formulate a set of minimum demands upon the United States. Two offerings resulted. Proposal A, given to Hull on 7 November, did not differ significantly from Japan's earlier position. Hull rejected it eight days later. On the twentieth, Nomura presented Proposal B. An interim measure only, it offered an evacuation of Japanese troops from southern Indochina in exchange for the restoration of American-Japanese trade relations prior to the asset freeze. The United States would also supply Japan with oil and help Tokyo procure "necessary materials" from the East Indies. In addition Washington was not to hinder peace efforts between Japan and China. Hull knew that this last provision meant an end to American aid to Chiang. Approaching the matter obliquely, he asked Nomura to predict the American public's reaction if Roosevelt were to announce the immediate end of all aid to Britain.[57]

Despite this thinly veiled rejection, Hull was under pressure from the American military and Roosevelt to buy time that would enable the American build-up in the western Pacific to continue. Accordingly, the State Department composed a draft for a modus vivendi. For three months, it offered to relax America's economic pressure and to allow trade on a limited, barter basis. Japan would receive petroleum products but only enough for civilian needs. Japan would withdraw all forces from south Indochina and reduce its total forces in the French colony to 25,000 troops. Any Sino-Japanese peace would have to be in accordance with "the fundamental principles of peace, law, order, and justice."[58]

The modus vivendi, even as worded, however, could not surmount the first critical hurdle: approval by America's allies. In part the difficulty was one of time: MAGIC informed the Americans—but not the British or the Chinese—that Japan's deadline for diplomacy was 29 November. But the chief stumbling block was terms. Churchill was alarmed that the modus vivendi would have unfortunate, perhaps ruinous, effects on China's will to keep fighting. Any doubts on this score were erased by a bitter message from Chiang, which came close to accusing the United States of a sellout. The formal British reply and reactions from representatives of the British dominions, Holland, and China all indicated that an agreeable consensus on terms with Japan would be exceptionally difficult to achieve. Hull had no time to find an agreement and saw no choice but to drop the

57. Feis, *Road*, 277; Stimson diary entry of 16 October 1941, Stimson Papers; *FRUS, 1941*, 4:523–24; Woodward, 2:155–56; and *FRUSJ*, 2:706–9, 731–37, 753–56.
58. *FRUS, 1941*, 4:642–44.

modus vivendi. Roosevelt agreed, his decision helped by an army intelligence report that five Japanese divisions had already sailed southward from central Chinese ports. Hull saw Nomura on 26 November to present America's formal reply to Proposal B. It was a modus vivendi of sorts, one based firmly on past American terms and Hull's four principles. Japan was to withdraw fully from Indochina and China. Chiang alone was to be recognized as China's legitimate ruler. Japan was not to allow the Tripartite Pact to lead to conflict in the Pacific, regardless of developments elsewhere.

Japan's leaders viewed Hull's last offer as both an ultimatum and an insult. Hull was under no delusions himself. On 27 November he informed Stimson, "I have washed my hands of it, and it is now in the hands of you and Knox—the army and the navy." Exactly four months earlier his counterpart in Japan might have uttered the same words.[59]

59. *FRUS, 1941,* 4:654–61; Morgenthau Papers, Diaries, 465:313; U.S. Congress, *Pearl Harbor Attack,* 11:5411–12; Stimson diary entry of 26 November 1941, Stimson Papers; *FRUSJ,* 2:764–70; *FRUS, 1941,* 4:655–61; Francis L Loewenheim, Harold D. Langley, and Manfred Jonas, eds., *Roosevelt and Churchill: Their Secret Wartime Correspondence* (New York: Saturday Review, 1975), 166–67; "*Magic,*" 4A:89; and Stimson diary entry of 27 November 1941, Stimson Papers. A good description of the British predicament and position is David Reynolds, *The Creation of the Anglo-American Alliance, 1937–1941* (Chapel Hill: University of North Carolina Press, 1981), 242–45.

[13]

A Final Wager:
Japan Consummates the
Southward Advance

The second liaison conference of the third Konoe cabinet met on 24 July in a mood of optimism and relief. The troublesome Matsuoka was gone. Vichy authorities had now signed the necessary local agreements permitting an unconfused occupation of the remainder of Indochinese territory. That occupation would commence within days. And harmony between the army and navy, however temporary, was intact.

Only Matsuoka's successor as foreign minister, Toyoda Teijirō, a former navy vice-minister and most recently minister of commerce and industry, was troubled. With uncanny foresight, Toyoda warned that the United States would react to the Indochina occupation by freezing Japanese funds in America and imposing a partial embargo on the exports of oil. The freeze, Toyoda continued, would create a serious shortage of funds for purchasing whatever petroleum products Washington still permitted, with obvious consequences for the Japanese Empire. The foreign minister urged conferees to allow Nomura to explain the occupation to Roosevelt. His colleagues listened attentively but were not inclined to upset, or even to rearrange, an imperial policy that had been so difficult to arrive at.[1]

Japanese policy ensured a rude shock when the United States did impose a freeze on assets, one that rapidly evolved into a complete

---

1. Nobutaka Ike, ed. and trans., *Japan's Decision for War: Records of the 1941 Policy Conferences* (Stanford: Stanford University Press, 1967), 108–10, and *DR2*, 361–62.

cutoff of oil. Since mid-January the army had been persuading itself that America would not trouble itself over the initial stages of the Southward Advance. Army Ministry and General Staff had predicted strong economic measures to follow the occupation of the Netherlands East Indies, but they had not expected so sharp a riposte to the Indochina operation. As late as 21 July the navy's chief of staff, Nagano Osami, was reiterating his belief that the Americans had offered to negotiate in order to stall Japan until their rearmament was completed. The freeze now compelled Tokyo to undertake a fundamental reassessment of U.S. intentions.[2]

It also forced renewed consideration of Japan's economic position. Even before Washington's latest step, that position was unenviable. Resolution of the bitter interservice wrangling over steel allocations had been achieved only on 20 June, and two days later the German invasion of Russia destroyed the calculations on which the resolution was based. Japan's last link with Germany, the trans-Siberian railroad, was severed. In no case was the amount involved great, but the importance of the materials—from humble necessities such as potash and mercury to highly sophisticated items, including machine tools and heavy machinery used for mineral smelting, oil refining, and optical glassmaking; from 1,375 tons of specialty steels to thirteen kilograms of pilocarpine—was undeniable. As the Planning Board realized, the ripple effect would be enormous, especially for plans to develop advanced steel-manufacturing facilities in Manchuria and to satisfy the navy's needs for refined specialty alloys and equipment.[3]

Germany's attack had other, wider ramifications. The army diverted labor and materials that the 1941 materials mobilization plan had earmarked for production expansion to immediate preparations for possible war against the Soviets and, on 1 July, ordered an end to all expansion of production facilities under its supervision. Because the army operated a substantial number of steel mills, including Japan's largest, at Yawata, the impact on steel production promised to be great. On 9 July, accordingly, the cabinet ordered the Planning Board to redraft the second quarter of the FY1941 materials plan, assessing the effect of the army's diversion on provisions for a plan emphasiz-

2. *DR2*, 207–8.
3. Inaba Hidezō, *Gekidō sanjūnen no Nihon keizai* (Tokyo: Jitsugyō no Nihonsha, 1965), 98–99, and Tanaka Shin'ichi, *Nihon sensō keizai hishi* (Tokyo: Conputa Eijisha, 1975), 146–51. Commander Mayama Kanji was outraged by the German attack and lobbied incessantly in the Foreign Ministry to get as many of the navy's shipments out of Europe as possible. The German attack also ended Japan's imports of specialty steels from Sweden.

ing increased iron and steel production to make up for shortfalls expected in the future. To this gloomy task the cabinet added a fantastic order: until the new materials plan was ready, monthly allocations would be increased by 50 percent over those in the old materials plan. It was a paper move, of course, and shortages began appearing within days. Nevertheless the Planning Board labored through July to produce a revised materials mobilization plan that allowed for the end of all supplies from central Europe and possible Japanese operations against the Soviet Union. Working in conjunction with the General Staff's operational planners and the Army Ministry's Equipment Bureau—which had to estimate the material requirements of the planned operations—the board was nearly ready with the belated plan for the second quarter of FY1941 by the last week of the month. Then came the American freeze.[4]

The immediate consequence of the freeze was what Washington had hoped to avoid: a firm decision in Tokyo to proceed with the Southward Advance. The critical element in this decision was the army, where even the most vigorous advocates of an attack on the Soviet Union now agreed that the south demanded first attention. Led by Major General Tanaka Shin'ichi, head of the General Staff's Operations Division, these officers had agreed in July to hold off mobilization orders until 10 August while special preparations in Manchuria, known as *Kan-toku-en*, progressed. Then the collapse of Stalin's regime or the fall of Moscow would have made an attack both attractive and feasible. With the news of the American freeze, however, the army conceded that first consideration had to be given to the United States, not the Soviet Union. By 2 August, Tanaka was speaking of a purely defensive effort in the north; the resources necessary for Japan's survival lay southward. Within the Army Ministry, too, sentiment turned sharply against any northern attack.[5]

During the remainder of the first week of August two sources confirmed the army leaders' decision to end planning for Russian operations in 1941. One was the General Staff's Intelligence Division, which predicted that the Soviets would not surrender in 1941 (certainly not by October, which the Japanese needed to start operations in eastern Siberia before deep winter set in). Nor was Intelligence optimistic that the Soviets would capitulate in 1942. A second report, from the Army Ministry's Equipment Bureau, warned that the Ameri-

---

4. *RGD2*, 461–62, 464, and Ishigawa Junkichi, comp., *Kokka sōdōin-shi*, 6 vols. (Tokyo: Kiyomizu Insatsujo, 1975), 1:763–66.

5. *DR2*, 367, 373–74, 376.

can freeze rendered Japan able to wage war for at best two years. Unless Tokyo secured the oilfields of the South Seas and brought them into production, it could not fight a major war against the Soviets with any confidence about the outcome.[6]

These conclusions were enough for General Sugiyama Gen, chief of the General Staff. At the liaison conference of 4 August he approved Toyoda's proposal to inform the Soviet Union that Japan would respect the Tokyo-Moscow Neutrality Pact. Sugiyama stipulated only that the Russians were not to transfer any Pacific territory to a third power—they were not to allow the construction of American airbases, that is, on Soviet territory.[7]

Five days later Sugiyama acted formally to realign the army's defense policy. Operations planning for an invasion of the Soviet Union in 1941 was suspended. The Kwantung Army was ordered, with Army Minister Tōjō Hideki's full concurrence and personal support, to discipline or transfer officers who could not obey the new priorities. Army central headquarters also ordered two divisions from Manchuria into north China for pacification operations, although the sixteen-division core force in the north was to be maintained. A new basic army directive was issued: prepare for an attack on Britain and the United States by the end of November.[8]

The army was not alone in counseling war against America. The Planning Board, which in 1940 and early 1941 had issued reports clearly warning of the economic disaster that would ensue from war with the West, now advised resolute and hasty action. One study, dated 29 July, argued that Japan's economic position was deteriorating alarmingly. The "cover" import plans of the 1940–41 winter had failed to achieve anything resembling true self-sufficiency. Even to maintain 1940s output in crucial materials would require massive imports from abroad at a time when foreign exchange to pay for them and shipping to transport them were diminishing. Japan's stockpiles of critical materials were low as well.

This report, drawn up before the American freeze was imposed, sounded themes familiar long before the summer of 1941. But Washington's move made it read quite differently. Now it was *because* the economic situation was bleak and deteriorating that the Planning Board—restaffed heavily with loyal army officers after the Planning Board Incident—advised a quick decision for or against hostilities. The navy agreed. Its own studies of early August, under Rear Admi-

6. *DR2*, 377–78.
7. Ike, 112–14, 114–15.
8. *DR2*, 378–80.

ral Oka Takazumi, chief of the Naval Affairs Bureau, concluded that Japan's oil stocks would decrease by 400,000 kiloliters per month if no hostilities were undertaken. This figure gave Japan at best two years of reserves, provided there were no major naval operations. If war was inevitable, Oka's study suggested, it ought to be begun as rapidly as possible.[9]

Debate now turned on the question of inevitability. The American freeze and service planning for an attack on the United States alarmed Prime Minister Konoe Fumimaro. He visited Tōjō and Navy Minister Oikawa Koshirō on 4 August to suggest that he hold a summit meeting with Roosevelt. Oikawa had no particular objections.[10] Tōjō rightly suspected that his subordinates did, and he excused himself to consult with them. Tanaka was, as usual, most vocal in his opposition, but he did speak for the General Staff. As long as a summit conference continued, he reasoned, there was no possibility of resolving upon war with America. The delay would be paralyzing and could be disastrous. For the same reason, it would be impossible to accept any limited, short-term agreement with which Konoe might return. Sugiyama thereupon asked Tōjō to inform Konoe that the General Staff would accept no accord lasting less than ten years. Tōjō endorsed this demand and added his own: the premier should not consent to any terms contrary to those sanctioned by the liaison conference of 4 August, and, if he failed, he should not resign but lead Japan into war. With the army's agreement, however qualified, Konoe was able to secure the approval of the liaison conference to a summit on the seventh. Nomura, in Washington, was informed of Konoe's proposal that same day.[11]

9. Donald S. Detwiler and Charles B. Burdick, eds., *War in Asia and the Pacific, 1937–1949*, 15 vols. (New York: Garland, 1980), 2: "Political Strategy Prior to Outbreak of War, Part IV," 71–75; Tsūshō Sangyō-shō, *Shōkō seisakushi 11: Sangyō tōsei* (Tokyo: Shōko Seisakushi Kankō Kai, 1964), 477 79; and Nomura Minoru, "Japan's Plans for World War II," *Revue internationale d'histoire militaire* no. 38 (1978), 210–11.

10. There is evidence that Oikawa, throughout the summer and well into the autumn, favored proceeding with negotiations, summit or otherwise. Naval Chief of Staff Nagano was lukewarm to this prospect, preferring a clear-cut decision for war more quickly. See Shinmyō Takeo, ed., *Kaigun sensō kentō kaigi kiroku* (Tokyo: Mainichi Shinbunsha, 1976), 135–36.

11. DR2, 376–77; David J. Lu, *From the Marco Polo Bridge to Pearl Harbor* (Washington: Public Affairs, 1961), 192–93; Robert J. C. Butow, *Tojo and the Coming of the War* (Stanford: Stanford University Press, 1961), 243; United States Congress, Joint Committee on the Investigation of the Pearl Harbor Attack, *Pearl Harbor Attack, Hearings*, 79th Cong., 1st–2d sess., 39 parts (Washington, 1946), 12:14–16; and Oka Yoshitake, *Konoe Fumimaro: A Political Biography*, trans. Shumpei Okamoto and Patricia Murray (Tokyo: University of Tokyo Press, 1983), 139.

The requirement that Konoe adhere to the terms of the 4 August liaison conference virtually ensured that a summit, had one been held, would have failed. On the sixth Nomura had transmitted terms to Hull. Japan promised to station no troops in the southwestern Pacific except in Indochina. Troops there would be withdrawn once the China Incident was settled, although the United States would recognize that Indochina had a special status for Japan. Japan would guarantee the neutrality of the Philippines and cooperate in the production and procurement of the resources America needed in the Pacific. The United States, in addition to giving identical cooperation, especially in the Netherlands East Indies, would end its military preparations in the southwestern Pacific and restore normal commerce with Japan. America was also to use its good offices to begin talks between Japan and Chiang's regime.[12]

The Americans did not reject outright the idea of a summit. The liaison conference met again on 26 August to consider Konoe's next message. Four days earlier the army's leaders had determined their service's position on the matter. The recent Anglo-American declaration of the Atlantic Charter confirmed that both Western powers had dropped their earlier "scarecrow" warnings to Japan and were now preparing for actual hostilities against Japan.[13] There was, in Tanaka's words, no turning back; Sugiyama and the vice-chief of staff, Lieutenant General Tsukada Osamu, nodded approval. No one expected Nomura's negotiations to bear fruit. The army officers ended their meeting of the twenty-second reaffirming that any settlement had to last at least ten years. At the liaison conference Toyoda succeeded in omitting mention of the Tripartite Pact and the coprosperity sphere from the reply to Washington, but he won no substantial change in Japan's stand. Tokyo maintained that the occupation of Indochina had been executed only to settle the China Incident and that troops there would be withdrawn only when that incident ended. The statement closed with a declaration that Japan would never use force against any neighboring nation without provocation.[14]

Even as Nomura was presenting the summit proposal to Hull and Roosevelt, both services renewed operational planning for a forceful

12. *FRUSJ*, 2:546–50. The terms themselves, as this citation makes clear, have been known for decades. It is worthwhile, however, to stress that the army was on record that it would not consent to any summit agreement that ran contrary to these terms.

13. Again, the perception within Japanese ruling circles of the Atlantic Charter, coming hard on the heels of the asset freeze, has been left largely unexamined by historians.

14. DR2, 413; Ike, 124–26; and *FRUSJ*, 2:571–79.

southward advance. Details remained to be settled. The navy's flexibility and speed in mobilization permitted it to give Konoe's diplomacy much more time than the army—hampered by fairly (and necessarily) rigid troop deployment schedules—could tolerate. And it still feared the army's eagerness to strike north. After interservice map maneuvers in mid-August the navy's staffers informed their army counterparts that they would be ready for action against Britain and America by 15 October. This news astounded the army officers until they realized that the navy needed no formal war decision to prepare for war. The army, in contrast, required Imperial consent to move troops across a national border, consent needed long before troops actually moved. Throughout late August, Tanaka complained loudly about the navy's inability to see this vital distinction, and the difference plagued interservice relations well into the autumn.[15]

Tanaka was also disturbed about the still evident difference over primary targets for southern operations. The navy had argued at the maneuvers that the presence of the American fleet demanded an invasion of the Philippines first, lest bases there be used as staging areas for a counterattack. The admirals were concerned too about the size of the army's commitment to the southern strike, a mere six divisions. For its part, the army insisted that to allow the British time to protect Singapore and Burma by occupying key Thai territory was equally intolerable. The Malayan theater demanded immediate attention, especially because large commitments in China and Manchuria required that the southern force be relatively small.[16]

The army's position was the weaker. The army badly needed the navy's consent to press for a war decision, so it was Sugiyama who, in a revised army draft of 23 August, bowed to the Naval General Staff's reasoning and agreed to simultaneous invasion of Malaya and the Philippines, with a rapid follow-up into the East Indies. Sugiyama

---

15. *DR2*, 414.
16. *DR2*, 416. There was some irony in the Naval General Staff's stance. Yamamoto had submitted a bold plan for an attack on the American fleet in Pearl Harbor. A protracted debate over its merits commenced. One reason to oppose it was that, if the plan were approved and its execution resulted in the elimination of the American Pacific Fleet at the outset of hostilities, then the navy would have no case to block the army's Malaya-first plan for southern operations: no enemy fleet could menace from the unattended Philippines. See my "Planning the Pearl Harbor Attack," *Aerospace Historian* 29 (December 1982). It is possible to speculate, cynically, that the navy wished to keep the Americans "in play" for as long as possible to discourage the army's striking north and thus attempting to reverse the allocation of materials so favorable to the navy in late 1940 and 1941, although I have found no hard evidence for this speculation.

increased his service's southern commitment to ten divisions. Three days later Tanaka obtained the consent of Major General Mutō Akira, and thus the Army Ministry,[17] to the new draft, making it an official army position.[18]

The next step was to confer with the navy at an interservice conference of bureau and division chiefs, begun on 27 August. The army offered its revised draft; the navy had one of its own. The navy wanted to defer any decision regarding southern operations because of the possibility of a summit. Tanaka, who had anticipated the proposal, leaped to the attack. The time for procrastination was long passed. Japan had to decide definitively on war (*sensō ketsui*) at once and on exactly when to commence hostilities (*kaisen ketsui*). Oka obstinately opposed either move, and the conference deadlocked.[19]

It reconvened the next day. Tanaka, stressing the lead time the army would require, proposed that the navy endorse at least a decision for war. Oka refused. Even if diplomacy failed, he asserted, war against America would not be automatic; the European situation would have to be considered. When pressed, Oka conceded that if war were necessary, early November would be the best time to start it. Tanaka then pointed out that his service needed a month to concentrate shipping in the South China Sea, establish combat-ready air groups in Indochina, and organize troop units. Hence a decision to commence hostilities had to be made by early October. Oka did not budge; the navy could not support a decision for war. The reply provoked Tanaka to rage about the navy's sincerity. There was reason to surmise, he charged, that the navy was preparing to retreat from a decision to go to war at the last minute. Tanaka then cut to the quick: Was the navy up to its old game, using war preparations to secure additional allocations of funds and materials?

Oka and his colleagues understood the implications of Tanaka's question. If the navy had no confidence about facing the Americans in battle, there had been little point in maintaining warships for the preceding decade, much less in supplying extra steel for additional construction (to which the army had agreed twice in the past year). If the fleet existed only to deter other powers from encroaching upon Japan's vital interests, its mission had failed with Oka's refusal to sanction a decision for war; surrender was the only choice left. The navy's representatives avoided the logical dilemma by declaring that

---

17. Mutō was chief of the ministry's Military Affairs Bureau.
18. *DR2*, 417–19.
19. *DR2*, 420.

the actual decision for peace or war was one for the whole government, not just the military. They then conceded that a decision, while it should not be made yet, could be made in early October as the army desired. In the meantime preparations for war would proceed.[20]

By the end of August, therefore, the military had at last agreed on the scope and timing of the Southward Advance. The army would devote ten, not six, divisions, in an effort against Malaya and the Philippines simultaneously, not just Malaya. The navy had not approved a formal decision for war, but it had agreed that the decision would be made by early October. The stage was set for the marathon, seven-hour liaison conference of 3 September.

Naval chief Nagano began the deliberations. Clearly relying on Oka's study of early August, Nagano stressed that time was working against Japan. The chances of victory were good but diminished daily. Diplomacy might succeed, but Japan had to prepare for war. Any conflict, Nagano continued, would be prolonged, but if "the fruits of victory"—meaning the East Indies—could be employed and the enemy lured into a decisive naval engagement, victory was quite likely. Sugiyama stressed the need to settle the diplomatic question by early October, and Navy Minister Oikawa proposed changing a formal draft of national policy to read that Japan would take "final measures for survival and self-defense" if diplomacy could not succeed by early October. The army objected, substituting "war decision" for "final measures." The revision was carried, but it still allowed some leeway if there was a chance for a diplomatic breakthrough. With this agreement, there remained only to obtain Imperial approval.[21]

The Imperial Conference of 6 September sanctioned the policy statement, "Essentials for Carrying out the Empire's Policies," though not without some discussion. The key phrase read,

> In the event that there is no prospect of our demands being met by the first ten days of October through diplomatic negotiations mentioned above, we will immediately decide to commence hostilities against the United States, Britain, and the Netherlands.

An attached document then listed terms for those negotiations. Tokyo's position, except for a pledge that Japan would not automati-

20. *DR2*, 420–21.
21. Ike, 130–33.

cally enter hostilities in the event of war between the United States and Germany, had changed little since August.

Although Konoe had previously assured the emperor that diplomacy would receive priority over war preparations, the statements of both chiefs of staff and the explanatory appendix to the "Essentials" gave evidence otherwise. Nagano swore that Japan should never fight a war that could be avoided, but he warned against a peace that bought a little time at the price of eventual doom—a peace of the sort of the "Winter Battle at Osaka Castle." Sugiyama concurred.[22] He explained the necessity of readiness to begin hostilities by the end of October and, consequently, the need for a war decision by that month's start.

Foreign Minister Toyoda then recounted the course of negotiations with Washington since April. When Hull had appeared to reject Japan's explanation of the occupation of southern Indochina as well as the Japanese proposals of 6 August, the prime minister had felt the need for a summit with Roosevelt. But Washington wanted preliminary agreement on the main issues before any meeting took place. Accordingly, Japan had reexamined its position and presented basic conditions to American ambassador Grew on 4 September.

Suzuki Teiichi, president of the Planning Board, surveyed Japan's economic capabilities. The outbreak of the European war and in July 1940 the onset of tangible American restrictions had already pointed to an inevitable Japanese need for self-reliance. Suzuki's tone was reassuring as he noted that special import programs from late 1940 to February 1941 had secured materials worth 660 million yen. Japan was relying on supplies from Manchuria, occupied China, Indochina, and Thailand—the "first resource acquisition sphere."[23] But this was not enough. Suzuki recommended that the necessary economic base be established quickly, by force if necessary. Suzuki repeated, with some refinements, his estimates of August: if the East Indies and Malaya were seized within three or four months—by early December 1941 or January 1942—the first shipments of oil and other products could reach Honshū piers by March. By the second year of hostilities the South Seas could be providing Japan with the materials necessary to wage a war of endurance.

22. The army already had determined on no short-term solutions; see my earlier discussion of the ten-year provision.

23. Details concerning funds committed in July and August to purchase rice and other goods from that sphere can be found in Ishigawa, 1:626–762. They make clear that without these supplies—particularly rice—Japan's situation would have been most precarious by the late autumn of 1941.

Suzuki's was the last of the formal statements by ministers in attendance. The president of the Privy Council, Hara Yoshimichi, then began his questions on behalf of the emperor, and those questions made evident his desire that Japan exhaust every diplomatic avenue before resorting to force. Hara even ventured to say that Konoe, "when" he visited the United States, would be able to solve things peaceably. After Hara was finished, the emperor himself intervened; in a rare gesture he read from a poem by his grandfather chastising men who wage war needlessly.[24]

Nevertheless, two days after the Imperial Conference ended, Sugiyama appealed for the throne's approval for the first steps toward mobilization of army units for the Southward Advance. Some troops had to be drawn from China, others from Japan, and new headquarters had to be organized and staffed. Not least, a stupendous amount of shipping—2.1 million tons—had to be chartered to supplement the bottoms already serving military needs. All of these steps would take much time. The emperor registered anxiety that they would undermine talks with Washington; Sugiyama appeared before him on the ninth to reassure the emperor that the preparations would be disguised by leaking reports of imminent operations against Kunming. Hirohito gave his consent. The first mobilization orders went out on the tenth and continued, for secrecy's sake, through 8 October. All units went to emergency, though not to full wartime, organization. Two new divisions, to be used in the south, were created, and key men were attached to the new army and corps headquarters units.[25]

The army next turned to economic preparations. Operations Division chief Tanaka was concerned particularly that the necessities of military life—food, fuel, and ordnance—were all unavailable in the quantities he wanted. Stocks for the China front were especially low, estimated to last at best until March. Once southern operations began, the army would be consuming all types of ammunition at 50 percent faster than they could be replaced. Tanaka also realized that, until the South Seas were secured, fuel stocks would do even worse.[26]

The Army Ministry's Equipment Bureau shared these estimates. The bureau's plan for mobilizing materials for military use covered the second half of FY1941, from October 1941 through the end of March 1942. To meet operational requirements, the plan nearly dou-

24. Ike, 134–57.
25. *DR2*, 447–55.
26. *DR2*, 455–56.

bled amounts for acquisition—under the overall materials mobilization plan—and allocation within the army. Despite a clear need for
this increase, the chief of the Equipment Bureau, Major General
Yamada Seiichi, warned that execution would not be easy. The labor
pool was nearly dry. All available engineers had been mustered already, by a series of orders in August under the National General
Mobilization Law. No more could be found. All production expansion efforts had been suspended in the wake of the Kan-toku-en
preparations; no more material could be diverted from this category.
Machinery was being worked constantly, to the detriment of necessary maintenance. Supplies of oil in the army were down 11 percent
from June for military units in the field, which should not have to
conserve at all. In other areas the service was consuming, under
forced shortages, fully a third less than it had during the spring.
Civilian usage of materials was down 45 percent from already depressed levels, and for the military this also had unavoidable effects
on the transportation of goods and hence on overall production. In
short Japan was going to war against Britain and the United States on
a shoestring—and a ragged one at that.[27]

Konoe and Toyoda still hoped that war could be averted. The prime
minister had dined with Ambassador Grew after the Imperial Conference, lauded Hull's four principles, and led Grew to believe that
these could serve as the basis for substantive negotiations. But Konoe
had spoken without his government's support; all he could do was
hope that a summit could somehow resolve the differences between
the two nations.[28]

These differences were still large, and the American response of 10
September to Toyoda gave Konoe little room for maneuver. The
United States was willing to mediate between Japan and China, but
only if Japan's terms were consistent with Hull's principles; nor was
America willing to end its assistance to Chiang. It was time, Washington said, for a new, basic Japanese peace proposal. A liaison conference met on 13 September to formulate one containing the concrete
details the Americans called for. Little resulted. Japan's latest position
allowed for the merger of the Chiang and Wang governments in
China and no reparations on either side, but it also called for Chinese
recognition of Manchukuo. And one crucial point—Japanese troops
would be required in both Inner Mongolia and parts of north China
areas until communism was suppressed—was not forwarded to

27. *RGD2*, 473–75.
28. Butow, *Tojo*, 259–60.

Nomura in Washington. Nomura presented the "new" Japanese proposal to Hull on the twenty-third.[29]

By that time both services had run out of patience. At a liaison conference on the eighteenth Sugiyama—who had just assigned officers to units designated for southern operations and chartered over 1.25 million tons of additional shipping[30]—joined Nagano in accusing America of delaying tactics. It was time to settle all differences with Washington, either by diplomacy or by war. Forty-eight hours later another conference met to consider an army draft of positions. The army was willing to meet naval requests for some flexibility; its demand to station Japanese troops in Inner Mongolia and north China became "in certain areas for a necessary period." This comprehensive Japanese draft, which was more detailed and hence much harsher than Japan's earlier ones, went to Grew on 25 September.[31]

By then the army had imposed a deadline for the talks with America, a deadline stemming from economic necessity. The mustering of units and gathering of shipping for southern operations caused a drain on Japan's economy which was felt immediately. Tanaka and the Army Ministry's planners alike had to have a quick decision for war, for every day of preparations reduced Japan's ability to sustain protracted operations.[32] Tanaka himself felt that the limits of tolerance would be reached by mid-November. Because the final preparations required one month, the final decision to begin hostilities had to be made by 15 October—only three weeks away. Sugiyama and Nagano accepted this reasoning and pressed successfully at the liaison conference of the twenty-fifth for a deadline.[33]

On 5 October a conference of army bureau, division, and section

29. *FRUSJ*, 2:608–9, 610–13, and Ike, 169–72.

30. *DR2*, 465. The importance of these charters cannot be stressed enough. Such great withdrawals—over 10 percent of all Japan's merchant tonnage in this charter alone—played immediate havoc with the overall economy and could not be permitted to last long, come war or peace. Here again, Japan's material shortages compelled a timetable far less leisurely than the United States would have had to adopt in any analogous situation.

31. Ike, 173–76.

32. Butow, *Tojo*, 263, writes that this pressure stemmed from a "narrow military viewpoint." It surely was military, but it seems unfair to call that point narrow. If Japan had had shipping to spare, the need for haste would not have been urgent. The economic planners realized that the economic drain caused by the diversion of shipping to immediate military needs (the southern operations) alone was more quickly detrimental to Japan than the coming oil shortage. Given their duties, these planners acted properly. The shipping shortage, incidentally, also helps explain why Japan did not linger long in attempting to discover chinks in the American asset freeze.

33. *DR2*, 475.

chiefs met in an eight-hour session to consider Hull's latest reply. They concluded that there was no chance for successful negotiations, especially because neither side was willing to yield on the evacuation of Japanese troops from China and Indochina. An imperial conference to resolve upon hostilities was essential at the earliest possible moment.[34]

That evening Tōjō visited Konoe.[35] The premier, according to most accounts, bluntly told the army minister that he would continue negotiating to the end. But there was more to Konoe's position, as Tōjō reported to Oikawa two days later. Konoe, to be sure, wanted the talks with America to succeed—Tōjō declared that he did, too—but three issues (the Tripartite Pact, Hull's four principles, and the troop occupation question) presented difficult obstacles. Konoe, sharing Nomura's optimism, replied that only the matter of the occupation was crucial. Japan could not survive without resources, but would the Americans accept Japanese troops in China in the name of resource acquisition? Tōjō was openly dubious, and Konoe retreated more. Could not the United States and Britain be divided, and only the British and Dutch attacked if negotiations did fail? Tōjō's response was final and accurate: "The navy's plans allow for no division."[36]

But those plans did permit procrastination. Nagano informed Sugiyama the next day that his General Staff and the Navy Ministry were not in accord about the 15 October deadline. Nagano, wanting interservice unity, inclined to that date, but Oikawa was of another mind. Yet another conference of bureau and division chiefs was necessary. It convened that afternoon, and the same deadlock reemerged at once. The army declared that there was no prospect of a diplomatic settlement. The navy allowed that there was little chance. The army argued that this judgment made a decision to commence hostilities unavoidable. The navy disagreed. In a tense atmosphere the officers left for dinner.[37]

After the meal Tōjō and Sugiyama met to resolve upon the official army position. Hull's four principles could not be accepted; no ground could be given on the troop occupation question; negotiations with Washington could be continued only until the fifteenth, nine

---

34. *FRUSJ*, 2:654–61; PHA, 12:51–53; Ike, 178–79, 179n; and *DR2*, 505.

35. My sequence of events differs somewhat from Butow's (*Tojo*, 264), which places the army conference on 6 October.

36. *DR2*, 505–6.

37. *DR2*, 506. For more information on the Nagano-Oikawa split, see Shinmyō, 135–36.

days away. Further, Tōjō was to put a series of questions to the navy finally to pin it down on the war question.[38]

Tōjō met Oikawa during the morning of 7 October, mincing no words. Oikawa was evasive: Why not wait until the fifteenth before giving up on diplomacy? Tōjō thought diplomacy hopeless: Did Oikawa want the Imperial Conference decision reconsidered? Oikawa did not; a decision would have to be made on the fifteenth. Tōjō then asked whether the navy had confidence in victory if the decision were for war, but Oikawa evaded the question, expressing confidence over the short term. For the long term, he fell back to the navy's position that the question was better put not to just the Supreme Command but to the government as a whole. Tōjō pointed out that command and government had made the decisions at the Imperial Conference together, but he left for a late-morning cabinet meeting without satisfaction.[39]

That meeting produced little to rejoice over, either. Finance Minister Kawada Isao reported that Japan's domestic economy was nearly in extremis. The Communications Ministry observed that even without additional diversions to the military, the shipping tonnage available for civilian usage was well below the minimum necessary to satisfy basic transportation needs. Other ministers, too, indicated disquiet over the trend in Japan's foreign policy.[40] Konoe was in the van.

That evening Tōjō again conferred with the premier. The army minister repeated his opposition to any concessions on occupying Chinese territory and his insistence on 15 October as the deadline for negotiations. Konoe reiterated his belief that only the occupation issue prevented a diplomatic breakthrough; was no compromise or face-saving device possible? Tōjō denied Konoe's premise. The United States meant to end Japan's special relationship with China, he argued, and the occupation question was only a sign of this desire. In any case a compromise would take too much time. Konoe, deeply worried, proposed reexamining the decisions of the Imperial Conference. But an exasperated Tōjō questioned the purpose of a new study. Come what may, he declared, the decision for war would be made on the fifteenth.[41]

The prime minister's admission that he lacked confidence about the outcome of an American war and was willing to reconsider the Impe-

38. *DR2*, 507.
39. *DR2*, 510–11.
40. *DR2*, 511–12.
41. *DR2*, 512–13.

rial Conference's decision was the last straw for the two chiefs of staff, who met to exchange views on the eighth. Nagano asked about a five-day extension for the decision, to the twentieth, but the army chief replied that the requirements for an attack on Malaya made this impossible. Nagano confided that he himself felt that war against America would be long, its results uncertain. If the country cannot make a decision now, Sugiyama retorted, it is doomed anyway. Nagano and Sugiyama agreed that the inability of Konoe to make up his mind was intolerable.[42]

At the liaison conference on the ninth Sugiyama pushed hard for the deadline six days away. In the face of the navy's reluctance to support the army, the meeting adjourned without result. Nagano was increasingly concerned that in a short time the fleet too would need a firm decision, if preparations for conflict were to proceed smoothly. But Oikawa, who favored allowing negotiations to continue, denied him a chance to speak.[43]

Konoe tried again to break this impasse. On 12 October, at his private residence, the premier met with Tōjō, Oikawa, Toyoda, and Suzuki. Oikawa and Konoe held the keys. For the navy minister to admit that his service could not face the United States would mean total disgrace: the fleet would be exposed as worthless. Yet Oikawa did not have enough confidence in a long war to dismiss completely the prospects for diplomatic settlement. He had avoided his dilemma by insisting the decision was the government's—meaning Konoe's. The premier shared the navy's qualms, but he was in the same quandary: if he could bring no diplomatic success, he would be responsible for Japan's surrender without a shot being fired. Oikawa had shirked his responsibility, but Konoe had no one to make his decision for him.

The prime minister asked the service ministers for their views. Oikawa thought the negotiations and war preparations could continue simultaneously. "The problem isn't that simple," Tōjō snorted. The army had troops in motion already on the basis of the Imperial Conference decision and with Imperial approval. If negotiations continued after the deadline, these war preparations would have to be halted. Konoe again voiced concern for three or four years hence, but Tōjō had a devastating reply: Why had the premier not considered this in July when the Southward Advance had been approved? Konoe

42. *DR2*, 514–15, 490–91.
43. Ike, 182–84. Here again, I believe this was Nagano's position throughout the autumn. No local, short-term peace was acceptable to him any more than to Sugiyama. He had only a little more time available than his army counterpart did.

had no answer. Nevertheless, Tōjō tentatively agreed to suspend operational preparations for a time.[44]

It turned out to be an empty concession. The Army General Staff objected strongly, arguing—rightly—that a suspension would not only upset operations planning but also cause an increased economic drain upon ever scarcer materials and shipping. Tōjō took both points to heart, and to the crucial cabinet meeting of 14 October. There he launched into a long, vigorous speech. He recalled the decision of the liaison conference of early September and the Imperial Conference of the sixth. That decision required troops to be mobilized and ready for action by late October, by which time shipping requisitions were to have reached two million tons. And by early October the war decision should have been made. Now it was the fourteenth, but still there was no decision. If the decision were delayed any longer, the army would have to stop, not suspend, war preparations; the chance to use force to greatest advantage would be lost irrevocably. Did the other ministers understand?

Apparently they did not. Toyoda asked if Japanese troops could be withdrawn from Indochina as a token of good faith. Tōjō declared it impossible. Earlier the army had spread rumors of a coming campaign against Kunming so as not to handicap negotiations with Washington. Now the time had come for real preparations to attack southward. These would be observable preparations, undoubtedly hindering negotiations, and so the time for the war decision had arrived. The cabinet had to wager all upon diplomacy or resolutely determine upon war. Oikawa asked if the negotiations could not be continued anyway, and Tōjō turned livid: Konoe might be right that only the troop occupation issue remained unresolved, but once those troops left China, every sacrifice of blood and treasure there would have been in vain. Manchukuo's existence would be imperiled, and even the empire's hold on Korea would be jeopardized.[45]

By the end of that tumultuous meeting the ministers understood that Tōjō was in earnest. The army had turned the navy's maneuver inside out. If the navy and the civilians refused to decide upon war at once, the army would stop its mobilization and assume no responsibility should diplomatic efforts end in failure.

Konoe grasped the point perfectly and realized that the time for his resignation had arrived. This possibility had been in the wind for

44. *DR2*, 516–18, and Butow, *Tojo*, 276. For an account in English of Konoe's efforts, including an abortive attempt to enlist the navy's support against Tōjō, see Oka, 153–55.

45. *DR2*, 519–20.

some time; Konoe had been pleased by Tōjō's suggestion that Prince Higashikuni become the next premier. The idea of a royal figure being placed in such a position in October 1941, however, did not sit well with Kido Kōichi, lord keeper of the privy seal.[46]

Under the Meiji Constitution the emperor had the power to appoint prime ministers. As a rule he accepted the recommendation of the political elites, but his courtiers, represented by the Lord Keeper, could and sometimes did have him veto a nominee. In this case Kido feared war with America and feared having any measure of the Imperial family associated with a government leading Japan into such a war. The emperor too had misgivings, and when Konoe resigned on 16 October, his successor had not been decided. The choice soon narrowed to Oikawa or Tōjō. Anticipating army revolt if Oikawa were tapped and then refused to make a firm decision for war, Kido favored Tōjō's appointment. After some discussion in the council of senior statesmen, the successor body to the *genrō* of the past, the army minister was designated the new premier.[47]

His appointment was conditional. Speaking for the emperor, Kido ordered Tōjō to study, without regard for all previous decisions,[48] the situation of the empire and thoroughly reconsider its policy. Tōjō issued the necessary orders to the ministries on 18 October, the day he assumed power. His instructions included eleven questions to be addressed in the reconsideration. Several asked for estimates of the European war and Anglo-American preparations in the Pacific for the coming year. One asked whether Japan could limit hostilities to Britain or the Netherlands. Others directed attention to the crucial issue of materials mobilization, especially the situation in shipping. Last, Tōjō requested a list of minimum demands to the United States over both long and short terms.[49]

The answers to all of these questions, matters of spirited and often bitter debate over the next two weeks, depended critically on Japan's economic position. Rapidly declining stockpiles of war materials pushed Nagano toward insisting on a rapid decision, a stance that Sugiyama warmly welcomed. The army chief of staff was much less pleased with the navy's insistence that negotiations with Washington

46. It is possible to speculate that Tōjō favored Higashikuni precisely because he was royal and could bring the navy to support a prompt decision for war.

47. Butow, *Tojo*, 286–87, 293.

48. This was a clear reference to those decisions made at the 6 September Imperial Conference, and which Tōjō had used with good effect against Oikawa and Konoe in mid-October.

49. Butow, *Tojo*, 301, and *DR2*, 523–24, 526.

be continued. From the twenty-first to the end of the month Sugi-yama lobbied first Nagano, then Tōjō; he wanted a firm commitment to an inflexible timetable that demanded a decision on the success or failure of negotiations by 13 November and a national resolution to commence hostilities to be adopted two days later. War would start on 8 December.[50]

The navy engaged in its own lobbying. It wanted not a decision and timetable for war but the materials that it held were necessary to secure its consent for war. This latest bid began at the liaison conferences of 24–25 October. In order to wage war successfully, the navy's representatives insisted, it was essential to construct warships and merchantmen even in excess of those already planned. This construction would require large amounts of steel: for the merchantmen alone, an average of 360,000 tons per year over three years of warfare. Such requirements meant that the navy had to receive top claim on materials, repair efforts, labor, and transportation facilities. They also made necessary a reduction of the army's steel quota to 900,000 tons for the first year of hostilities. On the thirty-first Navy Minister Shimada Shigetarō (who had replaced Oikawa when Tōjō became premier) made the navy's request formal.[51]

Japan's dire shortages of steel played every bit as critical a role as the better-understood situation in oil in the final debates of October. Japan did not have enough steel to build more warships and maintain its economy's operation, even at levels slightly below those of the past twelve months; nor could Tokyo establish a synthetic oil capacity to supply the needs of the economy and the navy without American concessions. The empire possessed few options, diplomatic or otherwise, as Lieutenant General Suzuki Teiichi, president of the Planning Board, made clear during the liaison conference of 28 and 30 October. The general economy, outside the military's needs, required a minimum of three million tons of shipping to maintain 1940 levels of

---

50. Ike, 186–87; *DR2*, 524–25, 558–61. Sugiyama's timetable ran:
   X-25 (13 November): decide on success or failure of negotiations; resolve upon war
   X-23 (15 November): resolve to commence hostilities
   X-21 (17 November): operational duty orders issued
   X-7 (1 December): operational orders, with X-day specified, issued; point of no return
51. Ike, 188–90, and *RGD2*, 484, 517–18. The navy was concerned that any losses in shipping or other such deficiencies would have to be made good from the navy's steel quota. It wanted to shed this burden and ensure that it would get the steel necessary for its mammoth Fifth Replenishment Plan under any circumstances. For a discussion of the navy's material situation in late 1941, see Shinmyō, chap. 4, especially 174ff.

production. Supplies from the South Seas would be sufficient to meet the economy's material needs, although just barely and only if the army reduced its requisitions of ship tonnage by half (from 1.8 to 0.9 million tons) after seven months of war. Suzuki's figures showed the grim results that could be expected if shipping losses were higher than anticipated.[52] The use of 2.5 million tons of shipping for the economy would permit only steel and rice to be produced at the 1940 level of output. Production of coal, salt, fertilizers, cotton, and a few other critical materials would fall to 80 percent of that level. All other goods would decline by over half. If available shipping decreased further, the impact would grow geometrically—and more steel would have to be diverted to construct merchant ships.[53] The implications were obvious: Japan had to have a fundamental diplomatic settlement that included rapid resupply in American oil, or Japan had to resolve almost immediately upon war against the West, or Japan had to muddle along with its own program for synthetic oil. Because the miserable situation in steel precluded any hope for a synthetic program,[54] the choice was stark and urgent. Either negotiations with Washington had to succeed, and had to succeed in overthrowing the existing economic and commercial status quo, or war had to be embraced.

Japan's steel situation also made it clear that only the army could pay the navy's price for support for a decision for war. That price was made explicit at the critical liaison conference of 1 November. The meeting began at 9 A.M. At once Navy Minister Shimada pressed for a revision in the allocations for critical materials, including ferroalloys and aluminum but principally steel. His demands were not small. The Planning Board's draft for FY1942 had given the navy 850,000 tons of steel from a total annual production of 4.3 million. The navy asked for an unprecedented 1.45 million tons. The ensuing argument, a harbinger of things to come, raged among three figures: Tōjō, now in his capacity of army minister, Shimada, and Suzuki.

---

52. The figures explain the navy's keen desire not to have its own material allocations literally held accountable for any such losses in shipping.

53. Detwiler, 2:18, and *GDS43*, 144–46. Tanaka, 160–61, gives a sense of the desperation in the Planning Board in late October.

54. Suzuki drove this point home on the twenty-eighth. Even with a million tons of steel (of a total expected production of 4.5 million tons for the coming year), 25 million tons of coal, and over two billion yen, a project to produce 4 million tons of synthetic petroleum would require three years. Indeed, Suzuki's Planning Board judged even 4 million tons as inadequate for true self-sufficiency. Its reports called for synfuel plants producing 5.2 million tons of oil. This effort would require 2.25 million tons of steel, 30 million tons of coal, 3.8 billion yen, 1,000 tons of cobalt, 380,000 additional coal laborers—and still three years. See Tanaka, 180.

Table 13.1. Revision of steel allocations in Japan's FY1942 Materials Mobilization Plan, as approved at 1 November 1941 Liaison Conference (in thousand metric tons)

Recipient	FY1941 Plan	Planning Board's FY1942 Plan	FY1942 Plan as Revised
Army	900	810	790
Navy	950	850	1,100
Civilian	2,910	2,640	2,610
Total	4,760	4,300	4,500

SOURCE: Bōeicho bōei kenshūjo, senshishitsu, *Daihon'ei rikugunbu* 2 (Tokyo: Asagumo Shinbunsha, 1968), 562.

If total production exceeded 4.5 million tons for FY1942, the army was to receive all of the surplus until it had 900,000 tons.

Tōjō's position was not easy. He was under intense pressure from his subordinates in the Equipment Bureau, particularly its War Preparations Section chief Okada Kikusaburō. These officers objected that the army's 900,000 tons of steel (through the four quarters of the 1941 materials plan, including the special import plans) had already been reduced to 810,000 tons in the FY1942 plan. If the navy's demands were met, the army's share would be trimmed further, and the army would have to redraft all operations plans for 1942. Sugiyama had affirmed, as recently as 28 October, that preparations against the Soviet Union had to continue. Those preparations demanded greater, not less, army access to Japan's stocks of strategic materials.[55]

Tōjō probably sympathized with these arguments, but he could not tolerate the navy's threatened veto of any decision about war. If the army did pay the price, on the other hand, the navy could hardly object further to a decision. Tōjō was determined to mollify the admirals even if the army's quota fell below the Planning Board's original figure.[56] In the event, the navy did not receive all it desired, but its share, 1.1 million tons, still was a large increase when the army and civilians had to make do with reduced allocations (see Table 13.1). To make certain that Shimada understood what was expected in return, the revised plan carried an explicit proviso: new allocations would apply "in case southern operations commence."[57]

This crucial concession virtually ensured failure for the remaining

55. Ike, 192, and *DR2*, 530–36.

56. Tōjō did secure an understanding that if steel production somehow exceeded the Planning Board's revised estimates, the army would receive all the surplus until it had acquired 900,000 tons.

57. Butow, *Tojo*, 320; *DR2*, 562; *RGD2*, 517–18; and Detwiler, 4:46.

advocates of diplomatic solution to American-Japanese differences. When Finance Minister Kaya Okinori pointed to Nagano's earlier reservations about victory in a prolonged war, the navy chief of staff cut him off: "Now! The time for war will not come later!" Suzuki agreed. "In 1943, the materials situation will be much better if we go to war.[58]

But should Japan decide upon war outright, or decide for war and prepare for it while conducting earnest diplomacy? The distinction was substantial. The former permitted negotiations to continue in Washington, but only as a ruse to gain military advantage. No proposal could be permitted to alter the timetable for hostilities. The latter demanded no such rigid schedule for war, which a diplomatic solution could prevent.

The Army General Staff naturally supported outright war. Lieutenant General Tsukada Osamu, vice-chief of staff, insisted that his service could wait for talks to succeed only until 13 November, twelve days away. Vice Admiral Itō Seiichi, his naval counterpart, put his service's deadline one week later. Foreign Minister Tōgō Shigenori exclaimed that the thirteenth was outrageous and demanded the navy's later date, but Tsukada held firm and played the army's trump. If Japan waited longer, the army would be compelled to halt its preparations, losing any chance to commence hostilities at a favorable moment and rending the political fabric of the empire itself. The ensuing discussion became so intense that a brief recess was needed to allow tempers to cool. During this time, Lieutenant General Tanaka Shin'ichi, head of the Operations Division, was called in to confer with Sugiyama and Tsukada. They all agreed that 30 November was acceptable but not an instant later, because the "point of no return" order had to be issued on 1 December according to plan.[59] When the conferees sat down again, they set midnight of the thirtieth.[60]

58. Ike, 201–2, 220, and *RGD2*, 486–90. One factor in this changed stance was the Planning Board Incident. Inaba and his cohorts had resisted the huge increases in allocations demanded by both services during the autumn and winter of 1940. At the time President Hoshino Naoki had backed them up. After his resignation and their arrest, the board had been staffed with men—generally from the army—who were unwilling to forecast economic ruin if Japan engaged in prolonged war with the United States. It is possible, however, to argue that this mattered little. As Suzuki Teiichi, who was the board's president in the autumn of 1941, commented long after the war, when an interviewer asked about the board's "war or persevere under hardship" study, the real choice "was to begin war or surrender. To persevere under hardship was impossible. It would have been utterly impossible to subsist [*meshi o kuu*]; production too would have been impossible. We'd have ended up in a sorry state." See Andō Yoshio, ed., *Shōwa seiji-keizaishi e no shōgen*, 3 vols. (Tokyo: Mainichi Shinbunsha, 1966), 2:249.

59. See Sugiyama's timetable in note 50 above.

60. Ike, 202–4.

Having determined that talks with Washington would continue, the conference took up the terms to offer the Americans. Tōgō presented two possibilities. Proposal A had been considered in the preceding meetings. Proposal B was an interim measure, limited to the south, not including China. Japan would remain in north Indochina but advance by force nowhere else in Southeast Asia and the southwestern Pacific. Japan would pull its troops out of southern Indochina. Japanese-American mutual procurement of materials from the Netherlands East Indies was retained, as were the provisions on equality of commercial opportunity. The United States was to promise Japan one million tons of aviation gasoline per year.[61]

Despite the obvious sops to the military (most obviously the aviation gasoline, which could hardly have been justified as for civilian use), Sugiyama and Tsukada objected to proposal B at once. They opposed any term agreement that did not offer the chance of a general, long-term settlement, fearing that a modus vivendi would amount to eventual surrender—the "Winter Battle at Osaka Castle" that Nagano had earlier referred to. Nor, for much the same reason, could they support the withdrawal of troops from southern Indochina.

Tōgō, however, was sure that the broader proposal A stood no chance of American acceptance. He favored proceeding immediately with proposal B, noting that it would require the United States to end its freeze on Japanese assets. Tsukada retorted that rescinding the freeze would not restore pre-July commerce with America. Tōgō then agreed to incorporate into proposal B a provision restoring that commerce, with explicit assurances that the United States would resume oil shipments to Japan. The army now assented but refused to consider removing its forces from southern Indochina. Even Tōgō's willingness to include a paragraph that pledged the United States not to obstruct settlement of the China Incident failed to move Tsukada and Sugiyama. A shouting match followed, compelling another recess. In that time the army's leaders agreed that Tōgō's resignation—and hence the cabinet's fall—would be intolerable and elected to approve his revised proposal B. With this concession, the conference at last broke up, at 1:30 A.M. on 2 November, seventeen hours after it had begun.[62]

An imperial conference met on 5 November to give formal sanction to these decisions. After hearing reports that echoed the conclusions of the liaison conference, President of the Privy Council Hara exam-

---

61. Ike, 204, and Butow, *Tojo*, 322.
62. Ike, 205. It is possible that the army feared the new premier could be an admiral. Then the navy's delaying game would have to be played again.

ined the details of proposals A and B. His chief concern centered on proposal B, which seemed too weak. For example, its third clause asked America only to restore commercial relations to their state immediately before the asset freeze, not to lift any earlier sanctions. Tōgō replied that proposal B was only a first step, in case the United States could agree on nothing else. As such, the foreign minister preferred to arrange for the quick purchase of larger amounts of oil than had been possible immediately before the freeze. Even so, Tōgō did not believe that Washington would accept proposal B, much less A. Hara dutifully turned to consider the plans for war. After admonishing the government to ensure that the conflict would not be a racial one—that Germany did not sign a separate peace and allow the white powers to isolate and defeat Japan—he ended his interrogation and the Imperial Conference. The only hope for peace lay in the final four weeks of negotiations with Washington.[63]

In Tokyo this hope did not seem great. At the liaison conference of 15 November Tōgō's summary of talks was followed by approval of a draft, "What to Call the War in the South." Nomura, eight days earlier, had presented proposal A to Hull. On the fifteenth the American secretary of state made it clear that the terms were no more acceptable to his government in November than they had been earlier, although Hull did give Nomura a statement proposing a reduction in trade barriers—restoring Japanese-American trade to "a normal basis"—if Japan could demonstrate its devotion to equal commercial opportunity without stipulating that the principle be applied to the entire world. There was another qualification: during the "present international emergency" each nation could restrict exports to the other of materials necessary for security and self-defense.[64]

Nomura, who felt that anything was preferable to failure, seized upon this offer. Without authorization, he proposed that his country's troops should leave southern Indochina in return for the lifting of the freeze order. Hull was dubious; where would these forces be sent next? But his doubts did not matter, for Tōgō refused to hear of any deviations from instructions, reprimanded Nomura, and ordered him to present proposal B. Even that offer, however, was made futile when Tōgō clarified nonobstruction of efforts to solve the China Incident as meaning an end to American aid to Chiang.[65]

Nomura presented proposal B to Hull on 20 November. The secre-

---

63. Ike, 231–32.
64. Ike, 245, and *FRUSJ*, 2:706–10, 731–37.
65. *FRUSJ*, 2:744–50, and Ike, 250–51.

tary, through MAGIC, already knew of Tōgō's clarification, which seemed to him only the latest in a series of Japanese tricks, even duplicities. Had Hull been able to read other Japanese codes, his impression would have been strengthened. On 6 November the order of battle of the corps to participate in the Southward Advance was established and corps commanders formally appointed. Four days later these commanders met, to be briefed by Sugiyama and Tanaka. By 16 November army and navy commanders had reached an accord on the details of the operations. One day earlier the army had issued its invasion orders. The navy did so on the twenty-first, one day after it had wanted the war decision to be made. On the nineteenth, one day before Nomura offered proposal B to Washington, Sugiyama notified the Southern Army commander that he would receive orders

Table 13.2. Estimates of Japan's oil supplies for waging war by Navy Ministry Military Affairs Bureau, 1 August 1941, and Planning Board, 22 October 1941 (in thousand kiloliters)

Year	Navy	Planning Board
One:		
Reserves at start	9,400	6,900
Natural domestic production	200	250
Synthetic production	300	300
Imports from the south	300	300
Total supply	10,200	7,750
Consumption	5,400	5,200
Remainder	4,800	2,550
Two:		
Reserves at start	4,800	2,550
Natural domestic production	200	200
Synthetic production	700	400
Imports from the south	2,400	2,000
Total supply	8,100	5,150
Consumption	5,400	5,000
Remainder	2,700	150
Three:		
Reserves at start	2,700	150
Natural domestic production	400	300
Synthetic production	1,500	500
Imports from the south	4,770	4,500
Total supply	9,370	5,450
Consumption	5,400	4,750
Remainder	3,970	700

SOURCES: Bōeichō, bōei kenshūjo, senshishitsu, *Rikugun gunju dōin* 2 (Tokyo: Asagumo Shinbunsha, 1970), 487–91; Nomura Minoru, "Japan's Plans for World War II," *Revue internationale d'histoire militaire*, no. 38 (1978), 210–11.

to act on his invasion commands on 1 December. Only a miracle could have stopped this course of events.[66]

No miracles were found. Hull's brusque reply to proposal B shocked even those Japanese ministers who had expected rejection. Nothing had been accomplished in all the past months, and there only remained to prepare for an imperial conference to give formal sanction to war. The conference was held on 1 December. During the conference the ministers in charge of economic affairs did not question whether Japan could survive a prolonged war, they explained how Japan would survive. (For the anticipated oil situation, see Table 13.2.) The conference adjourned with the decision to commence hostilities. At 2 P.M. on 2 December 1941 both general staffs notified all commands that war would begin at midnight on 8 December. One diarist in central headquarters wrote, "at last the arrow leaves the bowstring."[67]

66. *DR2*, 629, 632, 635, 655.
67. *DR2*, 675.

[14]

The Pacific War

The immediate "cause" of the Pacific War was the failure of the Hull-Nomura negotiations. But could they ever have succeeded, or were they, to use Jonathan Utley's phrase, "reaching for the moon"?

Events inside both capitals provide the clear answer that the negotiations had no chance. The Japanese, particularly after July 1941, would not have accepted and probably could not have accepted anything less than a comprehensive agreement governing the future of the entire western Pacific and eastern Asia. The reason was that, after the asset freeze, Japan could not accept any interim solution that left it dependent on American largesse. No modus vivendi could promise anything more than continued reliance on the whims of Washington. The possibility that the Americans might supply Japan with just enough oil, steel, and other materials to maintain a starveling existence was intolerable to any Japanese statesman. Without a fundamental resolution, then, war was the only course open.

Hull, therefore, was not in error when he attempted to seek a broad, comprehensive settlement with Japan. America's objectives in East Asia in the summer and autumn of 1941 may well have been limited; they may not have justified war with Japan, as Paul Schroeder and, more cautiously, Jonathan Utley have argued. But in the absence of a settlement Japan's objectives did justify war with the United States.

All this, one might maintain, arose from the ill-timed and ill-conceived American cutoff of oil shipments to Japan in the summer of 1941. If only Roosevelt or Hull had properly controlled the lower-level bureaucrats, if only limited trade in oil had continued into the autumn, the showdown at Pearl Harbor might have been avoided, or at least deferred, again to the advantage of America's global interests. But this position overlooks a number of factors. The basic one is that the decision to freeze Japanese assets was taken in conjunction with other steps designed rigorously to limit Japan's ability to stockpile materials for a forceful advance to the south. These steps were taken in the firm belief that Japan was commencing such an advance and that nothing the United States did or failed to do would shake Tokyo's resolve. The timing, pace, and ultimate severity of the advance, however, might be controlled through a judicious use of the freeze.[1] Although historians differ somewhat about how the freeze was applied, all allow that the overall goal remained intact. To permit Japan to use frozen funds while allowing it to dispose freely of sizable assets in Latin America, assets recently removed from the United States, would hardly have accorded with the cabinet decisions of late July.

In addition, it must be remembered that Washington did not believe it had anything to lose by maintaining the freeze, even after Hull and Roosevelt realized that the freeze had hardened into a de facto total embargo. To be sure, as Irvine Anderson, Jr., has pointed out, to ease up on the freeze and permit resumed trade was seen in Washington as indicating American appeasement and was therefore unacceptable. Well before that freeze was invoked, moreover, Washington was certain that it could expect no quid pro quo from Japan if the freeze were selectively lifted; indeed, all the talk in Washington was of progressively tightening, not loosening, the freeze—which brings one back Hull's quest for a comprehensive rather than a limited settlement.

In this belief, MAGIC played a vital and tragic role. Everyone in Washington believed that it provided incontrovertible evidence of the Imperial Conference decisions of 2 July. So Grew's cries for flexibility, to permit Japanese moderates to resume power, were ignored. And yet there were "moderates," in the form of Japanese naval officers who were willing to give diplomacy more time and who were equally willing to string the Imperial Army along for increased allocations of strategic materials while the diplomats talked. If the U.S. government had comprehended the depth of interservice differences in Japan throughout 1941, it might have been able to devise a strategy—such as the carefully administered and selective asset freeze originally

---

1. Utley makes this point eloquently in *Going to War with Japan, 1937–1941* (Knoxville: University of Tennessee Press, 1985), 153ff.

intended—that would have aggravated those interservice differences and led to paralysis within the Japanese government. But the idea that this paralysis would have led automatically to a modus vivendi or a limited period of peace between Japan and the United States is speculative at best. An army coup d'état was just as likely, followed by the issuance through the emperor of orders that the Imperial Navy execute the Southward Advance at once. Such projections involve much speculation, of course, but it is difficult to exaggerate the terrific tension within the Japanese cabinets through mid and late 1941. Washington missed all of this. MAGIC combined with old but still-vital preconceptions of the Japanese as beelike, incapable of internal differences, and Grew's constantly discredited predictions that civilian moderates would replace the military to assure Washington that tinkering with the asset freeze made little sense.

The asset freeze, soon a complete embargo, decided the leaders of the Imperial Army that war against the Soviet Union was not feasible in 1941 and that the navy's version of the Southward Advance— which included an attack on the United States—had to be endorsed. Once the services had achieved this consensus, they made a Pacific war virtually inevitable. To be sure, the navy could allow the diplomats more time. It could and did employ its sincere fear of an immense American fleet practically to blackmail the army into giving it greater allocations of resources. But once Washington's embargo had brought the two services together, no civilian could have pried them apart. This interservice consensus also operated with real foreign exchange difficulties to ensure that Japan would not expend much effort or time in unlocking the American freeze, if it were indeed selective. In this respect the original freeze was too clever for its own purposes.

There is, in short, a twin irony here. The first lies in the American government's reason for imposing a freeze on Japanese assets, a freeze that quickly metamorphosed into embargo. Top officials in Washington had misread the results of Japan's Imperial Conference of 2 July. They believed that the occupation of southern French Indochina was only the first step in a planned, deliberate program of Japanese aggression in Asia against at least Britain and Holland, posing a danger to the cause of the West worldwide. They failed to understand that the debate over the Southward Advance was not settled, that the occupation was sanctioned primarily to maintain some degree of interservice harmony, and that—had the embargo not been imposed—equally bitter interservice rancor might have surfaced when a next step was considered.

[265]

The second was that Japan began the Southward Advance to achieve autarky knowing that the price was war against Britain and the United States. This was nothing less than a perversion of the self-sufficiency originally envisioned by Ishiwara, Nagata, and Ugaki. All such officers acknowledged that Japan depended on the West for economic survival. All advocated policies designed to minimize friction with the West while reforms at home and expansion abroad were reducing that dependence. The Imperial Navy's insistence on the indivisibility of Britain and America, made to ensure that the fleet would receive adequate supplies of materials, ensured an equally perverse result: Japan would not be able to place the Roosevelt administration in the delicate position of declarating war against Japan when only British and Dutch possessions had been attacked.

If the 2 July decision to resume the Southward Advance by entering southern Indochina was instrumental in bringing on the American asset freeze, why then did Japan enter south Indochina? Japanese leaders must have known that the United States was not willing to go to war with them over China alone. Why take the risk?

The answer to this question again lies in interservice rivalries within Japan. As, most recently, Akira Iriye has written, Japan's fate was not in Japanese hands. Besides its obvious economic dependence on America, Japan was buffeted by the course of the war in Europe. This was especially true for the 2 July decisions. In the aftermath of the German assault on Russia the Imperial Navy feared that the army would scotch the Southward Advance altogether and attack the Soviets. The army was willing to defer such an attack but wished for a short, limited southern operation so that its forces might be ready within months to turn against the Soviets. These circumstances meant that the navy needed a commitment to some sort of step southward, the army to future flexibility. Within this context the 2 July decisions were rational and, for that matter, the only ones politically possible within the Japanese government.[2]

These same political reasons make it difficult to see how a Japanese-American settlement might have been negotiated between the fall of France and the imposition of the asset freeze. Konoe resumed the premiership on 22 July 1940 in a mood that can only be called ebullient. In the spring and summer of 1940 China was to be isolated and dealt a final blow. The Asian colonies of the defeated European

2. The navy's dilemma is discussed fully and forcibly in Shinmyō Takeo, ed., *Kaigun sensō kentō kaigi kiroku* (Tokyo: Mainichi Shinbunsha, 1976), 133–34, cited in Akira Iriye, *Power and Culture: The Japanese-American War, 1941–1945* (Cambridge: Harvard University Press, 1981), 273.

powers were to be brought into the coprosperity sphere. The United States was to be cowed through the Tripartite Pact. A truly self-sufficient Japanese Empire, immune from outside pressures, at last seemed in sight. Only the American imposition of economic sanctions shattered this rosy picture and brought Tokyo even to consider negotiations.[3] And the imposition of sanctions would have brought Japan and the United States to positions not fundamentally different from those they occupied after July 1941. To be sure, Japan might have avoided sanctions by forsaking the Southward Advance. But to have done so would have required a navy willing to see its steel allocations held constant, or even reduced, while the United States was building an incomparably larger fleet. The odds never favored such an outcome.

Japan, then, followed a series of policies that virtually guaranteed war with the United States. Some factors were beyond Tokyo's control, among them the outbreak of war in Europe and the German attack on the Soviet Union. Some were the result of internal politics, such as the navy's intransigent and, at times, contradictory position on the Southward Advance. But the essential element that led to war was Japan's terrible economic vulnerability and its decision, in light of the lessons of World War I, to do something about it.

For Japan, there were, in essence, only two alternatives to war with the United States. On the one hand, Japan might have given up all attempts to achieve self-sufficiency. The nation might have reconciled itself to being a have-not nation in 1918 or 1929 or even 1937. Japan, as Grew put it, might have resumed its place within the Anglo-American orbit. But all the factors discussed in this book made this outcome extremely unlikely. On the other hand, Japan might have actually achieved self-sufficiency with a greater Asian empire and defied the West to overthrow it. How likely was this outcome?

From the very beginning of the pursuit for autarky, the original total war officers had stressed the importance of not antagonizing the West until self-sufficiency was achieved. They failed spectacularly, and their failure was not due to any Western actions. Nagata's effort to rein in the most radical proponents of reforms in Japan, an effort that had commenced with his opposition to Araki's crash mobilization plans for war abroad, ended in his assassination. Ishiwara and Ugaki were finally forced out of positions of influence after they were

3. Why that picture survived for so long is one subject covered in my "Japanese Intelligence before the Second World War: 'Best Case' Analysis," in *Knowing One's Enemies: Intelligence Assessment before the Two World Wars*, ed. Ernest R. May (Princeton: Princeton University Press, 1984).

unable to limit or end intrigues, in 1935 and 1936, and hostilities, in 1937 and 1938, against China.

This last was the critical turning point. As Ishiwara had predicted, the China war dramatically increased Japan's dependence on the West, particularly the United States, even as it heightened friction that in time would lead America to adopt measures of economic pressure and crippled attempts, such as the production expansion plan, that might have led to greater self-reliance. Events in the wider international arena worsened a dynamic that was dangerous enough in itself. The outbreak of war in Europe shut off alternative sources of materials for Japan as the United States was becoming slowly more willing to use its economic dominance. The fall of France led to American rearmament and so created additional, if at times unwitting, allies in Washington for measures that served to increase American pressure. The German attack on Russia effectively ended the last hopes for materials from non-American sources and helped lead to the ill-fated decisions of 2 July.

The total war officers were long gone, unable to block any of this. Nagata, Ishiwara, even Ugaki, back in power briefly as foreign minister in 1938, were all cashiered (or killed) for counseling policies designed to decrease tensions with the West (and so with China as well). But might other forces within Japan not have changed national policy? Some might have done so. Members of the Planning Board—itself a product of the China Incident, along with a spate of measures that under other circumstances the total war officers had favored—realized most clearly that the Japanese economy was feeding on itself as military demands escalated for ever greater allocations of goods. The board succeeded in damping down the most aggressive policies in 1939 and 1940. But the broader implications of its dire diagnoses were ignored or attacked. When board members fought to arrest the military's growing share again, in 1941, they were themselves arrested in the Planning Board Incident.

Nor could leadership be found among other civilian ministers. Konoe did not look to end the China conflict; on the contrary, he used it to secure Diet passage of an impressive array of reform legislation. Japanese business and financial circles—which still need to be examined thoroughly—seem to have been content to wage successful holding actions against those reforms which threatened their particular interests, such as the electric power bill or the implementation of clauses of the National Mobilization Law. What they could not oppose openly they subverted; hoarding and black markets became increasingly common after 1939. But open opposition to the military was out of the question; most did not seriously consider it. For many businessmen, outright collaboration with the military was attractive. As Japan went to war against America, indeed, the two top economic posts, president of the Planning Board and minister of commerce and industry, were in the hands of the military.

Opposition to Japan's perverse drive to autarky could have come from within either service. But in the army it stemmed after Ishiwara's departure only from narrow, operational concerns. Operations officers, from Tada to Tanaka, were concerned about the immense material drain of the conflict in China, but they worried more about a coming conflict with the Soviet Union than about autarky. So great was that worry, so thinly was the army stretched by the summer of 1941, that its representatives at interservice meetings consistently opposed a southward advance against the United States. They did so, alas, not because a war against America was hopeless in the long term but because they wished in the short term to conserve troops.

The navy's conduct was more pusillanimous than shortsighted. The admirals were ever fearful that the generals would deprive them of the resources and finances necessary to build a respectable and respected fleet, and they were deeply stung by their defeat in the London Treaty controversy. So the navy advocated versions of a forward policy to the south, from the Pakhoi Incident and the August 1936 policy guidelines to the final Southward Advance, which guaranteed roles and missions that entitled it to men and materials. The result was an orthodoxy that stressed the possibility of conflict with the United States as much for internal budgetary and resource reasons as for any truly military ones. This orthodoxy, in turn, boxed the navy into its awkward positions of 1940 and 1941, refusing to sanction a formal decision for war against America as it demanded sharply increased allocations, particularly of steel, to give its officers confidence to wage such a war. The fleet, in short, could not be exposed as an expensive but worthless toy. The navy, which ought most seriously to have considered the long-term prospects of a Pacific war (and which produced, in Yonai and Yamamoto, men who did consider these but who met fates similar to those of Ugaki and Ishiwara), was instrumental in ensuring that the United States would be involved in that war.[4]

If the obstacles within Japan to the drive for autarky were small, why were the domestic forces behind it great? The conversion or eclipse of

4. Again, see Shinmyō, *Kaigun sensō,* for details.

elites that believed in economic internationalism has already been told.[5] Certainly the onset of the Great Depression played a vital role in this regard. But it was also pivotal in allowing to emerge mid-level policy makers who had harbored alternative ideas throughout the 1920s and who believed they had the means to redeem the Japan of the 1930s. Depression was a catalyst in the merging of the drives for autarky and reform, but those drives existed well before the collapse of the American Stock Market. Both drives focused on the lessons of World War I. Both drew from foreign examples.

Still, the drive to autarky was dominant. The real engine of change in interwar Japan was the military. The rise of the Soviet system, with its stress on central planning, played a part in convincing reformist bureaucrats that planning was the way of the future, but the defeat of the German Army in 1918 was a shock felt throughout the military. The total war officers drew their conclusions. Narrow military professionalism, the desire to avoid politics in the army at the cost of keeping the army out of politics—these notions were obsolete. Ugaki, Nagata, Ishiwara—even Suzuki Tei'ichi, their conceptual godson, though he was much more a bureaucrat than an advocate—all actively entered the political arena while in uniform. Their vision, and the political skills it demanded, made the drive to autarky a dominant force in interwar Japan. These officers were instrumental in propelling Japan on a quest for autarky that would, after the China debacle, lead to collision with the United States.

Interwar America had no similar leaders. Its vision of what the world ought to be called for none. Living in a nation that enjoyed near immunity from economic or military pressures from abroad and political upheavals at home, few Americans could conceive of reasonable motives for a nation to engage in territorial expansion or fundamental domestic reordering. To engage in either was a sign of atavistic irrationality or, at the least, an immaturity that endangered liberal, commercial civilization and hence the cause of worldwide peace. In East Asia this stance encouraged odd readings of Chinese nationalism. But even more tragically, it led to a misestimation of Japan. The ideological foundations of American foreign policy never permitted the United States to reconcile itself to the sort of East Asia that Japan wanted for its security; yet the practical interests of the United States never demanded open consideration of war against

5. Akira Iriye, "The Failure of Economic Expansionism: 1918–1931," in *Japan in Crisis*, ed. Bernard S. Silberman and H. D. Harootunian (Princeton: Princeton University Press, 1974), and Iriye, *Power*, chap. 1.

Japan. This dilemma was apparent from the first, in Stimson's response to the Manchurian Incident, a policy of nonrecognition. In the aftermath of the incident attentive Americans, and even Grew and Hornbeck, believed that the incident was an aberration that would vanish under the weight of "natural economic forces," whether these were speeded by American pressures or left alone. Japan would be educated, whether by forces or by pressures, and helped back to the natural order of international relations. Later American policy toward Japan was more disciplinary than deterrent. The idea that exhaustion by the war against China would force Japan to see the error of its ways died slowly. For three years after the Marco Polo Bridge Incident, the United States confined itself to moral embargoes on aircraft and air munitions. Steel, aluminum, technology, even aviation gasoline were exported unhindered until the fall of France permitted hardliners such as Morgenthau to recruit American rearmament bureaucrats for measures that, for the first time, seriously impeded Japan's ability to make war.

Only then did America really "turn against Japan,"[6] and even thereafter policy was halting and often ill-timed. It never was clear what progressive economic pressure and retention of the Pacific Fleet at Pearl Harbor were supposed to do. Roosevelt did not intend these as measures preparatory for actual war; he did want them to restrain Tokyo. But if the United States meant to deter Japan from taking steps regarded as threatening, it ought to have been issuing far clearer warnings, as the amazement of Tokyo at the asset freeze attests. If Washington hoped to hinder Japan's ability to make war, whether as a hedge in case conflict came or to block the conquest of the southwestern Pacific and capitulation of Chiang's regime, gradual pressure was a poor road to take.[7] If a limited, tacit form of appeasement was in order, to delay any wider conflagration, the asset freeze should not have been allowed to become an oil embargo. Still, it was only by

6. The phrase is from Waldo Heinrichs, "The Middle Years, 1900–1945, and the Question of a Large U.S. Policy for East Asia," in *New Frontiers in American-East Asian Relations*, ed. Warren I. Cohen (New York: Columbia University Press, 1983), 99.

7. It is interesting to observe the differing perceptions in Washington of Japan's strength after the fall of France. Before that time the general image was of a nation exhausting itself economically in the Chinese wilderness and incapable of pursuing further aggressive policies, especially toward Western possessions in the south. After May 1940 hardliners such as Morgenthau grossly exaggerated Japan's economic capacity in order to argue against permitting Tokyo to stockpile additional materials. (Hornbeck, in fairness, read the Japanese economic situation more accurately, which ironically accounts in part for his oft-cited prediction a week before Pearl Harbor that the Japanese would not be engaging in war soon.)

September 1940 that American action, to whatever purpose, directly affected Japan's war and mobilization efforts. By July 1941 the two nations were staring at the real possibility of war.

The Pacific War was, in essence, a conflict between two visions for East Asia. Each vision had a strong economic element. Japan's fundamental war aim was to establish the Greater East Asian Coprosperity Sphere as a self-sufficient and powerful unit with the Japanese Empire at its core. The United States sought, first, to thwart Japan's attempt and, second, to "restore" the principles of "international cooperation" and the Open Door. In the early 1930s the conflict between these two visions was muted, if present at all. But certainly by the time of the Hull-Nomura negotiations it was quite clear.[8]

The war was fought overwhelmingly by economic means. Only hours after the Japanese attack on Pearl Harbor, American military chiefs issued the order to "execute unrestricted air and submarine warfare against Japan." By the spring of 1945 the results of this order had brought Japan to ruin at least as much as had the more spectacular clashes of the opposing navies, and well before the awful birth of the Atomic Age and the Soviet Union's last-minute entry ended the conflict formally.[9]

The Pacific war had its lessons, too. But the Japanese, as ever with losers, perhaps, learned those lessons better. In the 1980s America persists in its opulence and its blindness to the reasons that forces for change exist in the world. Japan has assumed an intense commitment to expand its international commerce by peaceful competition in the market place. Commerce and competition formed the basis for dramatic postwar recovery.

Still much of the past lingers. Japanese agriculture persists in relying on arguments for self-sufficiency for much of its political punch.[10] The Planning Board lives on in the Ministry of International Trade

8. Utley's *Going* contains references throughout on exactly this point on the American side from Hull (if any proof further than a casual reading of Hull's memoirs is needed) and Roosevelt; see for example 54, 69, 85–87. A good discussion of the underpinnings of American foreign policy can also be found in Iriye, *Power*, 15ff.

9. The "unrestricted" order is quoted in Clay Blair, Jr., *Silent Victory* (Philadelphia: Lippincott, 1975), 84.

10. John W. Longworth, *Beef in Japan: Politics, Production, Marketing, and Trade* (St. Lucia: University of Queensland Press, 1983). This inclination to self-sufficiency is not confined to agriculture. A good contemporary example can be found in Japan's refusal to open construction on a new $8 billion international airport near Osaka to foreign bidders. Explained a member of the Ministry of Transport, "Japan is self-sufficient in airport technology." See *Economist* 296 (13 July 1985), 73.

and Industry, which has enjoyed immense peacetime success.[11] Even the engines of war have played their part. One Japanese diplomat, reminiscing long after the war about an American fleet bombardment of the naval steel town of Muroran—the town that had the 10,000 ton hydraulic forging press over which Okada and Yagi had negotiated in early 1937, the press that had helped produce the mighty battleship *Yamato*—mused,

> The *Yamato* and the Zeros—forerunners of the postwar Japanese technology—are still very much alive, so it is said among us Japanese, in mammoth tankers, excellent automotive engines, etc., which Japan turns out by the thousands and millions. Thus, they have served our nation in a manner never foreseen in their heyday.[12]

11. Chalmers Johnson, *MITI and the Japanese Miracle* (Stanford: Stanford University Press, 1982).

12. Kawamura Yoya, comment on "Bombarding Japan," *U.S. Naval Institute Proceedings* 105 (September 1979), 84–86. For the Okada-Yagi negotiation, see Chapter 1, note 78.

Bibliography

PRIMARY SOURCES

Ballantine, Joseph W. Papers. Hoover Institution on War, Revolution, and Peace, Stanford, Calif.

Berle, Adolf A. Papers. Franklin D. Roosevelt Presidential Library, Hyde Park, N.Y.

Butler, Rohan; Douglas Dakin; and M. E. Lambert, eds. *Documents on British Foreign Policy*, 2d ser., vol. 8. London: HMSO, 1960.

Davis, Norman. Papers. Library of Congress, Washington, D.C.

Feis, Herbert. Papers. Library of Congress, Washington, D.C.

Gendaishi shiryō 7: Manshū jihen 1. Tokyo: Misuzu Shobō, 1964.

Gendaishi shiryō 8: Nitchū sensō 1. Tokyo: Misuzu Shobō, 1964.

Gendaishi shiryō 10: Nitchū sensō 3. Tokyo: Misuzu Shobō, 1965.

Gendaishi shiryō 12: Nitchū sensō 4. Tokyo: Misuzu Shobō, 1966.

Gendaishi shiryō 43: Kokka sōdōin 1. Tokyo: Misuzu Shobō, 1970.

Grew, Joseph C. Papers. Houghton Library, Harvard University, Cambridge, Mass.

Hornbeck, Stanley K. Papers. Hoover Institution on War, Revolution, and Peace, Stanford, Calif.

Ickes, Harold L. Papers. Library of Congress, Washington, D.C.

Ike Nobutaka, ed. and trans. *Japan's Decision for War: Records of the 1941 Policy Conferences.* Stanford: Stanford University Press, 1967.

International Military Tribunal for the Far East, Records: Narrative Summary and Exhibits. Mimeo. International Legal Studies Library, Harvard Law School, Cambridge, Mass.

Ishigawa Junkichi, comp. *Kokka sōdōin-shi.* 6 vols. Tokyo: Kiyomizu Insatsujo, 1975.

Israel, Fred L., ed. *The War Diary of Breckinridge Long.* Lincoln: University of Nebraska Press, 1966.

Japan, Gaimushō. *Nihon gaikō nenpyō narabini shuyō bunsho.* 2 vols. Tokyo: Gaimushō, 1955.

Koo, T. K. "Some Economic Documents Relating to the Japanese-Sponsored Regime in North China." *Far Eastern Quarterly* 6 (November 1946).

Magruder, Captain C. W. "The Potential Economic Strength and Weakness of Japan for War [24 April 1939]." Faculty and Staff Presentations. Carton for 1939. Record Group 14. Naval War College Archives, Newport, R.I.

Mantetsu, chōsabu. *Kita Shina tsūka kin'yu hōsaku.* Dairen: Mantetsu, 1937.

_____. *Kita Shina zaisei hōsaku.* Dairen: Mantetsu, 1937.

Mantetsu, Shanhai jimusho. *Chūshi ni okeru sekitan jijō.* Shanghai: Mantetsu, 1941.

Mantetsu, Shanhai jimusho, chōsashitsu. *Chūshi ni okeru kikairui jukyū.* Shanghai: Mantetsu, 1941.

_____. *Naka Shina ni okeru sekitan no jikyūryō to jikyū jisoku o tatemae to suru baai no fusokuryō.* Shanghai: Mantetsu, 1941.

Mantetsu, sōmubu, chōsaka. *Man-Mō yori nani o subekika.* Dairen: Mantetsu, 1924.

Mantetsu, sōmubu, shiryōka. *Hokushi jichi undō gaikan.* Dairen: Mantetsu, 1936.

Mantetsu, Tokyo shisa, chōsashitsu. *Nichi-Bei tsūshō kōkai jōyaku haki no eikyō narabini sono taisaku.* Tokyo: Mantetsu, 1939.

_____. *Nichi-Bei tsūshō kōkai jōyaku haki no wagakuni sekiyugyō ni oyobasu eikyō to taisaku.* Tokyo: Mantetsu, 1939.

_____. *Shina jihen shori narabini Ōshū sensō boppatsu ni tomonau senji keizai taisaku.* Tokyo: Mantetsu, 1939.

Moffat, J. Pierrepont. Papers. Houghton Library, Harvard University, Cambridge, Mass.

Morgenthau, Henry H., Jr. Papers. Franklin D. Roosevelt Presidential Library, Hyde Park, N.Y.

National Defense Advisory Commission. Papers. Franklin D. Roosevelt Presidential Library, Hyde Park, N.Y.

Pittman, Key. Papers. Library of Congress, Washington, D.C.

Roosevelt, Elliot, ed. *F.D.R.: His Personal Letters.* 4 vols. New York: Duell, Sloan, & Pearce, 1947–50.

Roosevelt, Franklin D. *Complete Presidential Press Conferences of Franklin D. Roosevelt.* 25 vols. New York: Da Capo, 1972.

Roosevelt, Franklin D. Papers. Franklin D. Roosevelt Presidential Library, Hyde Park, N.Y.

Rosenman, Samuel I., comp. *The Public Papers and Addresses of Franklin D. Roosevelt.* 7 vols. New York: Russell & Russell, 1941.

"The Saionji-Harada Memoirs." Mimeo. International Legal Studies Library, Harvard Law School, Cambridge, Mass.

Stimson, Henry L. Papers. Sterling Memorial Library, Yale University, New Haven, Conn.

Tsunoda Jun, ed. *Ishiwara Kanji shiryō 2, Kokubō ronsaku.* Tokyo: Hara Shobō, 1967.

Ugaki Kazunari. *Nikki.* 3 vols. Tokyo: Misuzu Shobō, 1968.

United States. Congress, Joint Committee on the Investigation of the Pearl Harbor Attack. *Pearl Harbor Attack, Hearings.* 79th Cong., 1st sess., and 79th Cong., 2d sess. 39 parts. Washington, 1946.

United States. Department of Defense. *The 'Magic' Background of Pearl Harbor.* 5 vols. and appendixes. Washington, 1977.

United States. Department of State. *Foreign Relations of the United States, 1931,* vol. 3; *1932,* vol. 3; *1932,* vol. 4; *1933,* vol. 1; *1933,* vol. 3; *1934,* vol. 3; *1935,* vol. 3; *1936,* vol. 4; *1937,* vol. 3; *1937,* vol. 4; *1938,* vol. 3; *1939,* vol. 3; *1940,* vol. 4; *1941,* vol. 4; *1941,* vol. 5. Washington, 1946–56.

_____. *Foreign Relations of the United States: Japan, 1931–1941.* 2 vols. Washington, 1943.

United States. National Archives. General Records of the Department of State. Record Group 59. State Department Decimal File.

Bibliography

_____. General Records of the Department of the Treasury. Record Group 56.
_____. Records of the Office of the Administrator of Export Control. Record Group 169.
_____. Records of the Office of Naval Intelligence. Record Group 38.
World Peace Foundation. *Documents on American Foreign Relations 3, July 1940–June 1941.* Boston, 1941.
Yoda Yoshiee, comp. *Nitchū sensōshi shiryō 4: Senryō shihai 1.* Tokyo: Kawada Shobō, 1975.

SECONDARY SOURCES AND MEMOIRS

Acheson, Dean. *Present at the Creation.* New York: Norton, 1969.
Allen, George C. *A Short Economic History of Modern Japan, 1867–1937.* London: Allen & Unwin, 1972.
Anderson, Irvine H., Jr. *The Standard-Vacuum Oil Company and United States East Asian Policy, 1933–1941.* Princeton: Princeton University Press, 1975.
Ando Yoshio, ed. and comp. *Shōwa seiji-keizai-shi e no shōgen.* 3 vols. Tokyo: Mainichi Shinbunsha, 1966.
Aritake Shūji. *Yoshino Shinji.* Tokyo: Komiyama Insatsu, 1974.
Asada Sadao, "The Japanese Navy and the United States." In *Pearl Harbor as History,* ed. Dorothy Borg and Shumpei Okamoto. New York: Columbia University Press, 1973.
Ashizawa, Noriyuki. *Aru sakusen sanbō no hideki.* Tokyo: Fuyō Shobō, 1974.
Baba Tsunego. "Hirota's 'Renovation' Plans." *Contemporary Japan,* September 1936.
Bamba Nobuya. *Japanese Diplomacy in a Dilemma.* Vancouver: University of British Columbia Press, 1972.
Barnhart, Michael A. "Japanese Intelligence before the Second World War: 'Best Case' Analysis." In *Knowing One's Enemies: Intelligence Assessment before the Two World Wars,* ed. Ernest R. May. Princeton: Princeton University Press, 1984.
Bassett, Reginald. *Democracy and Foreign Policy.* London: Longmans, Green, 1952.
Berger, Gordon M. *Parties out of Power in Japan, 1931–1941.* Princeton: Princeton University Press, 1977.
Blum, John M. *From the Morgenthau Dairies.* 3 vols. Boston: Houghton Mifflin, 1959–67.
Bōeichō, bōei kenshūjo, senshishitsu. *Daihon'ei rikugunbu.* 2 vols. Tokyo: Asagumo Shinbunsha, 1967–68.
_____. *Hokushi no chiansen 1.* Tokyo: Asagumo Shinbunsha, 1968.
_____. *Kaigun gunsembi.* Tokyo: Asagumo Shinbunsha, 1969.
_____. *Rikugun gunju dōin 1: Keikaku-hen.* Tokyo: Asagumo Shinbunsha, 1967.
_____. *Rikugun gunju dōin 2: Jisshi-hen.* Tokyo: Asagumo Shinbunsha, 1970.
_____. *Shina jihen rikugunbu sakusen 1: Shōwa 13-nen 1-gatsu made.* Tokyo: Asagumo Shinbunsha, 1975.
Borg, Dorothy. "Notes on Roosevelt's 'Quarantine Speech.'" *Political Science Quarterly* 72 (September 1957).
_____. *The United States and the Far Eastern Crisis of 1933–1938.* Cambridge: Harvard University Press, 1964.
Boyle, John H. *China and Japan at War, 1937–1945: The Politics of Collaboration.* Stanford: Stanford University Press, 1972.
Brune, Lester H. "Considerations of Force in Cordell Hull's Diplomacy, July 26 to November 26, 1941." *Diplomatic History* 2 (Autumn 1978).
Bunker, Gerald E. *The Peace Conspiracy.* Cambridge: Harvard University Press, 1972.

Butow, Robert J. C. *The John Doe Associates*. Stanford: Stanford University Press, 1974.
_____. *Tojo and the Coming of the War*. Stanford: Stanford University Press, 1961.
Chō Yukio. "An Inquiry into the Problem of Importing American Capital into Manchuria: A Note on Japanese-American Relations, 1931–1941." In *Pearl Harbor as History*, ed. Dorothy Borg and Shumpei Okamoto. New York: Columbia University Press, 1973.
Cohen, Jerome B. *Japan's Economy in War and Reconstruction*. Minneapolis: University of Minnesota Press, 1949.
Connery, Robert H. *The Navy and Industrial Mobilization in World War II*. Princeton: Princeton University Press, 1951.
Crowley, James B. *Japan's Quest for Autonomy*. Princeton: Princeton University Press, 1966.
Crowley, James B. "A Reconsideration of the Marco Polo Bridge Incident." *Journal of Asiatic Studies* 22 (May 1963).
Dallek, Robert. *Franklin D. Roosevelt and American Foreign Policy, 1932–1945*. New York: Oxford University Press, 1979.
Detwiler, Donald S., and Burdick, Charles B. *War in Asia and the Pacific*. 15 vols. New York: Garland, 1980.
Dingman, Roger. *Power in the Pacific*. Chicago: University of Chicago Press, 1976.
Divine, Robert A. *The Illusion of Neutrality*. Chicago: University of Chicago Press, 1962.
_____. *Roosevelt and World War II*. Baltimore: Johns Hopkins University Press, 1969.
Dorn, Frank. *The Sino-Japanese War, 1937–1941*. New York: Macmillan, 1974.
Dowd, Laurence P. "Japanese Foreign Exchange Policy, 1930–1940." Ph.D. diss., University of Michigan, 1953.
Eden, Anthony. *Facing the Dictators*. Boston: Houghton Mifflin, 1962.
Emerson, William. "Franklin Roosevelt as Commander-in-Chief in World War II." *Military Affairs* 22 (Winter 1958).
Endicott, Stephen L. *Diplomacy and Enterprise: British China Policy, 1933–1937*. Vancouver: University of British Columbia Press, 1975.
Feis, Herbert. *The Road to Pearl Harbor*. Princeton: Princeton University Press, 1950.
_____. *The Spanish Story*. New York: Knopf, 1948.
_____. *Three International Episodes Seen from E. A.* New York: Norton, 1966.
Fletcher, William M., III. *The Search for a New Order*. Chapel Hill: University of North Carolina Press, 1982.
Freidel, Frank B. *FDR, Launching the New Deal*. Boston: Little, Brown, 1973.
Friedman, Donald J. *The Road from Isolation*. Cambridge: Harvard University Press, 1970.
Haight, John McV., Jr. "Franklin D. Roosevelt and a Naval Quarantine of Japan." *Pacific Historical Review* 40 (May 1971).
Harrington, Daniel F. "A Careless Hope: American Air Power and Japan, 1941." *Pacific Historical Review* 48 (1979).
Hashikawa Bunzō. "Kakushin kanryō." In *Kenryoku no shisō*, ed. Kamishima Jirō. Tokyo: Chikuma Shobō, 1965.
Hata Ikuhiko. "The Army's Move into Northern Indochina." In *The Fateful Choice*, ed. James W. Morley. New York: Columbia University Press, 1980.
_____. "The Japanese-Soviet Confrontation, 1935–1939." In *Deterrent Diplomacy*, ed. James W. Morley. New York: Columbia University Press, 1976.
_____. "The Marco Polo Bridge Incident, 1937." In *The China Quagmire*, ed. James W. Morley. New York: Columbia University Press, 1983.
Heinrichs, Waldo H., Jr. *American Ambassador*. Boston: Little, Brown, 1966.

Bibliography

_____. "The Role of the U. S. Navy." In *Pearl Harbor as History*, ed. Dorothy Borg and Shumpei Okamoto. New York: Columbia University Press, 1973.

Herzberg, James R. "American Economic Policies toward Japan, 1931–1941." Ph.D. diss., University of Texas at Austin, 1977.

Hosoya Chihiro. "The Japanese-Soviet Neutrality Pact." In *The Fateful Choice*, ed. James W. Morley. New York: Columbia University Press, 1980.

_____. "The Role of Japan's Foreign Ministry and Its Embassy in Washington, 1940–1941." In *Pearl Harbor as History*, ed. Dorothy Borg and Shumpei Okamoto. New York: Columbia University Press, 1973.

_____. "The Tripartite Pact, 1939–1940." In *Deterrent Diplomacy*, ed. James W. Morley. New York: Columbia University Press, 1976.

_____. "Washington taisei no tokushitsu to hen-yō." In *Washinton taisei to Nichi-Bei kankei*, ed. Hosoya Chihiro and Saitō Makoto. Tokyo: Tokyo Daigaku Shuppansha, 1978.

Hull, Cordell. *The Memoirs of Cordell Hull.* 2 vols. New York: Macmillan, 1948.

Humphreys, Leonard A. "The Imperial Japanese Army, 1918–1929." Ph.D. diss., Stanford University, 1974.

Ickes, Harold L. *The Secret Diary of Harold L. Ickes.* 3 vols. New York: Simon & Schuster, 1954.

Inaba Hidezō. *Gekidō sanjūnen no Nihon keizai.* Tokyo: Jitsugyō no Nihonsha, 1965.

Inoue Shinzō. "The North China Incident through the Lens of the Bureaucratic Politics Model." Pts. 1, 2. *Shakai kagaku janeru,* nos. 13–14 (October 1975, January 1976).

Iriye, Akira. *After Imperialism.* Cambridge: Harvard University Press, 1965.

_____. *Power and Culture: The Japanese-American War, 1941–1945.* Cambridge: Harvard University Press, 1981.

Ishiwata Sōtarō Denki Hensankai, ed. *Ishiwata Sōtarō.* Tokyo, 1954.

Itō Mitsuharu. "Munitions Unlimited—The Controlled Economy." *Japan Interpreter* 7 (Summer–Autumn 1972).

Itō Takashi. "The Role of Right-wing Organizations in Japan." In *Pearl Harbor as History*, ed. Dorothy Borg and Shumpei Okamoto. New York: Columbia University Press, 1973.

Johnson, Chalmers. *MITI and the Japanese Miracle.* Stanford: Stanford University Press, 1982.

Johnston, B. F. *Japanese Food Management in World War II.* Stanford: Stanford University Press, 1953.

Jones, F. C. *Manchuria since 1931.* New York: Oxford University Press, 1949.

Kazami Akira. *Konoe Naikaku.* Tokyo: Nihon Shuppan Kyōdō Kabushiki Kaisha, 1951.

Kennedy, Malcolm D. *The Estrangement of Great Britain and Japan, 1917–1935.* Berkeley: University of California Press, 1969.

Kinsella, William E., Jr. *Leadership in Isolation.* Cambridge, Mass.: Schenkman, 1978.

Koistinen, Paul A. C. *The Hammer and the Sword.* New York: Arno, 1979.

Langer, William L., and Gleason, S. Everett. *The Challenge to Isolation, 1937–1940.* New York: Harper, 1952.

_____. *The Undeclared War, 1940–1941.* New York: Harper, 1953.

Longworth, John W. *Beef in Japan: Politics, Production, Marketing and Trade.* St. Lucia: University of Queensland Press, 1983.

Lowe, Peter. *Great Britain and the Origins of the Pacific War.* Oxford: Clarendon, 1977.

Lu, David J. *From the Marco Polo Bridge to Pearl Harbor.* Washington, D.C.: Public Affairs, 1961.

McCarty, Kenneth G. "Stanley K. Hornbeck and the Far East, 1931–1941." Ph.D. diss., Duke University, 1970.

Miller, David H. *The Drafting of the Covenant*. 3 vols. New York: Putnam, 1928.
Misawa Shigeo and Ninomiya Saburō. "The Role of the Diet and Political Parties." In *Pearl Harbor as History*, ed. Dorothy Borg and Shumpei Okamoto. New York: Columbia University Press, 1973.
Morison, Elting E. *Turmoil and Tradition: A Study of the Life and Times of Henry L. Stimson*. New York: Atheneum, 1966.
Morley, James W. *The Japanese Thrust into Siberia, 1918*. New York: Columbia University Press, 1957.
Nagaoka Shinjirō. "The Drive into Southern Indochina and Thailand." In *The Fateful Choice*, ed. James W. Morley. New York: Columbia University Press, 1980.
————. "Economic Demands on the Dutch East Indies." In *The Fateful Choice*, ed. James W. Morley. New York: Columbia University Press, 1980.
Naiseishi Kenkyūkai, comp. *Tanaka Shin'ichi danwa sokkiroku*. Tokyo, 1976.
Nakamura Takafusa. *Senzen-ki Nihon keizai seichō no bunseki*. Tokyo: Iwanami Shoten, 1971.
Nakamura Takafusa and Hara Akira. "Introduction." *Gendaishi shiryō 43, Kokka sōdōin 1*. Tokyo: Misuzu Shobō, 1970.
————. "Keizai shintaisei." In *Nihon seiji gakkai nenpyō: Konoe shintaisei no kenkyū*, ed. Nihon Seiji Gakkai. Tokyo: Iwanami Shoten, 1972.
Nenryō Konwakai. *Nihon kaigun nenryōshi*. 2 vols. Tokyo: Hara Shobō, 1972.
Nihon Kindai Shiryō Kenkyūkai, ed. *Nihon riku-kaigun no seido, soshiki, jinji*. Tokyo: Tokyo Daigaku Shuppankai, 1971.
Nihon Kindai Shiryō Kenkyūkai, comp. *Suzuki Teiichi danwa sokkiroku*. 2 vols. Tokyo, 1971.
Nihon Kokusai Seiji Gakkai Taiheiyō Sensō Gen'in Kenkyūbu, ed. *Taiheiyō sensō e no michi*. 8 vols. Tokyo: Asahi Shinbunsha, 1962–63.
Nomura Minoru. "Japan's Plans for World War II." *Revue internationale d'histoire militaire*, no. 38 (1978).
Ogata, Sadako N. *Defiance in Manchuria*. Berkeley: University of California Press, 1964.
Ōhata Tokushirō. "The Anti-Comintern Pact, 1935–1939." In *Deterrent Diplomacy*, ed. James W. Morley. New York: Columbia University Press, 1976.
Peattie, Mark R. *Ishiwara Kanji and Japan's Confrontation with the West*. Princeton: Princeton University Press, 1975.
Pelz, Stephen E. *Race to Pearl Harbor: The Failure of the Second London Conference and the Onset of World War II*. Cambridge: Harvard University Press, 1974.
Quinlan, Robert J. "The United States Fleet: Diplomacy, Strategy, and the Allocation of Ships (1940–1941)." In *American Civil-Military Decisions*, ed. Harold Stein. Birmingham: University of Alabama Press, 1963.
Reagan, Michael D. "The Far Eastern Crisis of 1931–1932: Stimson, Hoover, and the Armed Services." In *American Civil-Military Decisions*, ed. Harold Stein. Birmingham: University of Alabama Press, 1963.
Reynolds, David. *The Creation of the Anglo-American Alliance, 1937–1941*. Chapel Hill: University of North Carolina Press, 1981.
Sangyō Seisakushi Kenkyūjo. *Shōkō gyōseishi dankai sokkiroku*. 3 vols. Tokyo: Daiwa Insatsu, 1975.
Schumpeter, Elizabeth B., ed. *The Industrialization of Japan and Manchukuo, 1930–1940*. New York: Macmillan, 1940.
Shimada Toshihiko. "Designs on North China, 1933–1937." In *The China Quagmire*, ed. James W. Morley. New York: Columbia University Press, 1983.
————. "Introduction." *Gendaishi shiryō 8, Nitchū sensō 1*. Tokyo: Misuzu Shobō, 1964.

Bibliography

Shinmyō Takeo, ed. *Kaigun sensō kentō kaigi kiroku*. Tokyo: Mainichi Shinbunsha, 1976.
Smethurst, Richard J. *A Social Basis for Prewar Japanese Militarism*. Berkeley: University of California Press, 1974.
Spaulding, Robert M., Jr. "Japan's 'New Bureaucrats,' 1932–1945." In *Crisis Politics in Prewar Japan*, ed. George M. Wilson. Tokyo: Sophia University Press, 1970.
Sun, Kungtu C. *The Economic Development of Manchuria in the First Half of the Twentieth Century*. Cambridge: Harvard University Press, 1969.
Takahashi Kamekichi. "The Fiscal Policy of Finance Minister, Dr. Baba." *Contemporary Japan*, June 1936.
Tanaka Shin'ichi. *Nihon sensō keizai hishi*. Tokyo: Conputa Eijisha, 1975.
Tanin, O., and Yohan, E. *When Japan Goes to War*. New York: Vanguard, 1936.
Thorne, Christopher. *The Limits of Foreign Policy: The West, the League and the Far Eastern Crisis of 1931–1933*. New York: Putnam, 1973.
Tōyō Keizai Shinbunsha, ed. *Shōwa sangyōshi*. 3 vols. Tokyo, 1950.
Trotter, Ann. *Britain and East Asia, 1933–1937*. Cambridge: Cambridge University Press, 1975.
Tsunoda Jun. "The Navy's Role in the Southern Strategy." In *The Fateful Choice*, ed. James W. Morley. New York: Columbia University Press, 1980.
Tsūshō Sangyō-shō. *Shōkō seisakushi 11: Sangyō tōsei*. Tokyo: Shōkō Seisakushi Kankōkai, 1964.
Tupper, Eleanor, and McReynolds, George E. *Japan in American Public Opinion*. New York: Macmillan, 1937.
United States. Civilian Production Administration. *Industrial Mobilization for War: Program and Administration*. Washington, 1947.
United States. Strategic Bombing Survey. *The Effects of Strategic Bombing on Japan's War Economy*. Washington, 1946.
———. *Japan's Struggle to End the War*. Washington, 1946.
Ushisaburo Kobayashi. *Military Industries of Japan*. New York: Oxford University Press, 1922.
Usui Katsumi. "The Politics of War, 1937–1941." In *The China Quagmire*, ed. James W. Morley. New York: Columbia University Press, 1983.
Utley, Jonathan G. "Diplomacy in a Democracy: The United States and Japan, 1937–41." *World Affairs* 193 (1976).
———. *Going to War with Japan, 1937 1941*. Knoxville: University of Tennessee Press, 1985.
———. "Upstairs, Downstairs at Foggy Bottom: Oil Exports and Japan, 1940–1941." *Prologue* 8 (Spring 1976).
van Mook, Hubertus J. *The Netherlands East Indies and Japan: Battle on Paper, 1940–1941*. New York: Norton, 1944.
Vlahos, Michael. *The Blue Sword: The Naval War College and the American Mission, 1919–1941*. Newport: Naval War College Press, 1980.
Walters, F. P. *A History of the League of Nations*. London: Oxford University Press, 1960.
Ward, Robert E. "The Inside Story of the Pearl Harbor Plan." *U.S. Naval Institute Proceedings* 77 (December 1951).
Watanabe Yoshimori. "Senjika no shihonchikuseki to 'Busshi Doin Keikaku.'" *Keizaigaku zasshi* 75 (August 1976).
Watson, Mark S. *Chief of Staff: Prewar Plans and Preparations*. Washington, D.C.: Government Printing Office, 1950.
Willmott, H. P. *Empires in the Balance*. Annapolis: Naval Institute Press, 1982.
Wilson, Florence. *The Origins of the League Covenant*. London: Hogarth, 1928.

Woodward, Sir Llewellyn. *British Foreign Policy in the Second World War.* 5 vols. London, HMSO, 1970–76.

Wu, Tien-wei. *The Sian Incident.* Ann Arbor: University of Michigan, Center for Chinese Studies, 1976.

Yabe, Teiji. *Konoe Fumimaro.* 2 vols., 1951–52. One-vol. reprint. Tokyo: Yomiuri Shinbunsha, 1976.

Yamada Gōichi. *Mantetsu chōsabu.* Tokyo: Nihon Keizai Shinbunsha, 1977.

Yamamoto, Captain. "Shōwa 4-nendo sōdōin enshū ni tsuite." *Kaikosha kiji* no. 661 (October 1929).

Yomiuri Shinbunsha, comp. *Shōwashi no tennō.* 30 vols. Tokyo: Yomiuri Shinbunsha, 1967–76.

Yoshino Shinji. *Shōkō gyōsei no omoide.* Tokyo: Shōkō seisakushi Kankōsha, 1962.

Index

Cornell Studies in Security Affairs

edited by Robert J. Art, Robert Jervis, *and* Stephen M. Walt

Political Institutions and Military Change: Lessons from Peripheral Wars, by Deborah D. Avant

Strategic Nuclear Targeting, edited by Desmond Ball and Jeffrey Richelson

Japan Prepares for Total War: The Search for Economic Security, 1919–1941, by Michael A. Barnhart

The German Nuclear Dilemma, by Jeffrey Boutwell

Flying Blind: The Politics of the U.S. Strategic Bomber Program, by Michael L. Brown

Citizens and Soldiers: The Dilemmas of Military Service, by Eliot A. Cohen

Great Power Politics and the Struggle over Austria, 1945–1955, by Audrey Kurth Cronin

Military Organizations, Complex Machines: Modernization in the U.S. Armed Services, by Chris C. Demchak

Nuclear Arguments: Understanding the Strategic Nuclear Arms and Arms Control Debate, edited by Lynn Eden and Steven E. Miller

Public Opinion and National Security in Western Europe, by Richard C. Eichenberg

Innovation and the Arms Race: How the United States and the Soviet Union Develop New Military Technologies, by Matthew Evangelista

Israel's Nuclear Dilemma, by Yair Evron

Guarding the Guardians: Civilian Control of Nuclear Weapons in the United States, by Peter Douglas Feaver

Men, Money, and Diplomacy: The Evolution of British Strategic Foreign Policy, 1919–1926, by John Robert Ferris

A Substitute for Victory: The Politics of Peacekeeping at the Korean Armistice Talks, by Rosemary Foot

The Wrong War: American Policy and the Dimensions of the Korean Conflict, 1950–1953, by Rosemary Foot

The Best Defense: Policy Alternatives for U.S. Nuclear Security from the 1950s to the 1990s, by David Goldfischer

House of Cards: Why Arms Control Must Fail, by Colin S. Gray

The Soviet Union and the Politics of Nuclear Weapons in Europe, 1969–1987, by Jonathan Haslam

The Soviet Union and the Failure of Collective Security, 1934–1938, by Jiri Hochman

The Warsaw Pact: Alliance in Transition? edited by David Holloway and Jane M. O. Sharp

The Illogic of American Nuclear Strategy, by Robert Jervis

The Meaning of the Nuclear Revolution, by Robert Jervis

The Vulnerability of Empire, by Charles A. Kupchan

Nuclear Crisis Management: A Dangerous Illusion, by Richard Ned Lebow
Cooperation under Fire: Anglo-German Restraint during World War II, by Jeffrey W. Legro
The Search for Security in Space, edited by Kenneth N. Luongo and W. Thomas Wander
The Nuclear Future, by Michael Mandelbaum
Conventional Deterrence, by John J. Mearsheimer
Liddell Hart and the Weight of History, by John J. Mearsheimer
Reputation and International Politics, by Jonathan Mercer
The Sacred Cause: Civil-Military Conflict over Soviet National Security, 1917–1992, by Thomas M. Nichols
Bombing to Win: Air Power and Coercion in War, by Robert A. Pape
Inadvertent Escalation: Conventional War and Nuclear Risks, by Barry R. Posen
The Sources of Military Doctrine: France, Britain, and Germany between the World Wars, by Barry R. Posen
Dilemmas of Appeasement: British Deterrence and Defense, 1934–1937, by Gaines Post, Jr.
Crucible of Beliefs: Learning, Alliances, and World Wars, by Dan Reiter
Eisenhower and the Missile Gap, by Peter J. Roman
The Domestic Bases of Grand Strategy, edited by Richard Rosecrance and Arthur A. Stein
Winning the Next War: Innovation and the Modern Military, by Stephen Peter Rosen
Israel and Conventional Deterrence: Border Warfare from 1953 to 1970, by Jonathan Shimshoni
Fighting to a Finish: The Politics of War Termination in the United States and Japan, 1945, by Leon V. Sigal
The Ideology of the Offensive: Military Decision Making and the Disasters of 1914, by Jack Snyder
Myths of Empire: Domestic Politics and International Ambition, by Jack Snyder
The Militarization of Space: U.S. Policy, 1945–1984, by Paul B. Stares
The Nixon Administration and the Making of U.S. Nuclear Strategy, by Terry Terriff
Making the Alliance Work: The United States and Western Europe, by Gregory F. Treverton
The Origins of Alliances, by Stephen M. Walt
Revolution and War, by Stephen M. Walt
The Ultimate Enemy: British Intelligence and Nazi Germany, 1933–1939, by Wesley K. Wark
The Tet Offensive: Intelligence Failure in War, by James J. Wirtz
The Elusive Balance: Power and Perceptions during the Cold War, by William Curti Wohlforth
Deterrence and Strategic Culture: Chinese-American Confrontations, 1949-1958, by Shu Guang Zhang